Cathedrals of Consumption

The History of Retailing and Consumption

General Editor: Gareth Shaw, Department of Geography,
University of Exeter

Titles in the series include:

Trading Places: A Geography of Multiple Retailing, 1870–1950
Andrew Alexander

Nineteenth-Century Markets
Martin Phillips

Cathedrals of Consumption

The European Department Store, 1850–1939

edited by

GEOFFREY CROSSICK and
SERGE JAUMAIN

ASHGATE

Published by
Ashgate Publishing Limited
Gower House
Croft Road
Aldershot
Hampshire GU11 3HR
England

Ashgate Publishing Company
131 Main Street
Burlington, VT 05401-5600 USA

Ashgate website: http://www.ashgate.com

The authors have asserted their moral right under the Copyright, Designs and Patents Act, 1988, to be identified as the authors of this work.

British Library Cataloguing in Publication Data

Cathedrals of Consumption: The European Department Store,
  1850-1939.
  (The History of Retailing and Consumption)
  1. Department stores —Europe—History—19th century.
  2. Department stores—Europe—History—20th century.
  I. Crossick,Geoffrey. II. Jaumain, Serge.
  381.1'41'094

Library of Congress Cataloging-in-Publication Data

Cathedrals of Consumption: The European department store, 1850-1939/
  edited by Geoffrey Crossick and Serge Jaumain.
        (The History of Retailing and Consumption)
    Revised versions of papers first discussed at a colloquium at the
  Free University of Brussels
    ISBN 1-84014-236-7 (alk.paper)
      1. Department stores—Europe, Western—History—18th century.
    2. Department stores—Europe, Western—History—19th century.
    I. Crossick, Geoffrey. II. Jaumain, Serge. III. Series.
    HF5465.E82C38 1998
    381'.141'094—dc21
                                                            98-19489
    ISBN 1 84014 236 7   CIP

Reprinted 2002

Typeset in Sabon by Manton Typesetters, 5-7 Eastfield Road, Louth, Lincs, LN11 7AJ
Printed in Great Britain by Biddles Limited, Guildford and King's Lynn

Contents

The History of Retailing and Consumption
General Editor's Preface

It is increasingly recognised that retail systems and changes in the patterns of consumption play crucial roles in the development and societal structure of economies. Such recognition has led to renewed interest in the changing nature of retail distribution and the rise of consumer society from a wide range of academic disciplines. The aim of this multidisciplinary series is to provide a forum of publications that explore the history of retailing and consumption.

Gareth Shaw

University of Exeter

List of tables

List of figures and plates

Figures

Plates

Notes on contributors

Laurence Badel is Maître de Conférences in Contemporary History at the University of Paris-1 Panthéon-Sorbonne, and works in the field of international relationships. In addition to articles on the links between the worlds of large-scale retailing and politics, and on the birth of European integration, her thesis 'Un milieu libéral et européen: le grand commerce français (1925–1948)' was published in autumn 1998.

Marie-Emmanuelle Chessel is a Researcher at the CNRS attached to the Centre Pierre Léon, Maison Rhône-Alpes des Sciences de l'Homme (Lyon). She obtained her doctorate in 1996 from the European University Institute in Florence for a thesis on the history of French advertising, and this was published in 1998 under the title *La Publicité: naissance d'une profession (1900–1940)*. She is currently working on the history of management education, and on the history of consumers.

Tim Coles is Lecturer in Human Geography at Bath Spa University College. His early research focused on the evolution, availability and probity of town directories as European historical data sources. He has published widely on sources and is co-author (with Gareth Shaw) of *A Guide to European Town Directories* (vol. 1, 1997; vol. 2, 1999). His work has more recently concentrated on the historical and contemporary geographies of retailing and consumption in Germany. He has written articles on retail restructuring in the Wilhelmine era and in the five new *Länder* following Unification in 1990. He is currently writing a monograph on the historical geography of urban retail systems in Imperial Germany.

Catherine Coley is a Researcher in the History of Art in the Laboratoire d'Histoire de l'Architecture Contemporaine of the Ecole d'Architecture de Nancy. She has been director of the Archives Modernes de l'Architecture Lorraine since its establishment in 1987. She has worked principally on art nouveau, especially in relation to the School of Nancy, and on architecture between 1930 and 1950 with special reference to Jean Prouvé. Amongst her publications are *Nancy 1900. Naissance et rayonnement de l'Art Nouveau* (1989), *Jean Prouvé en Lorraine* (1990), and *Jean Prouvé* (1993). She has recently organised exhibitions and publications on the work of the architects André Lurçat and G.-H. Pingusson.

Geoffrey Crossick is Professor of History and Pro-Vice-Chancellor (Academic) at the University of Essex. After his initial research on

English working-class history, he has published widely on European social and urban history, most notably on the petite bourgeoisie and on comparative history. In addition to many articles in journals and edited collections, his books include *The Lower Middle Class in Britain 1870–1914* (editor, 1977), *An Artisan Elite in Victorian Society: Kentish London 1840–1880* (1978), *Shopkeepers and Master Artisans in Nineteenth-Century Europe* (editor with Heinz-Gerhard Haupt, 1984), *The Petite Bourgeoisie in Europe 1780–1914: Enterprise, Family and Independence* (with Heinz-Gerhard Haupt, 1995) , and most recently *The Artisan and the European Town, 1500–1900* (editor, 1997).

Gábor Gyáni is Senior Research fellow at the Institute of History of the Hungarian Academy of Sciences, and Professor at the Sociological Institute of the Lóránd Eötvös University, Budapest. He is a social historian with a special interest in the urban world. His books include *Család, háztartás és a városi cselédség* (Family, Household and Urban Domestic Life) (1989); *Women as Domestic Sevants: the Case of Budapest, 1890–1940* (1989); *Bérkaszárnya és nyomortelep. A budapesti munkáslakás múltja* (Rent-barrack and Slum. The History of Workers' Housing in Budapest) (1992); *'Változás és folytonosság'. Tanulmányok Európa XIX. Századi társadalmáról* ('Continuity and Change'. Studies in Nineteenth-century European Society) (editor, 1992); *A szociálpolitika múltja Magyarországon* (The History of Social Policy in Hungary) (1994); *Hétköznapi Budapest. Nagyvárosi élet a századfordulón* (Everyday Budapest. Metropolitan Life at the Turn of the Century) (1995); *Magyarország társadalomtörténete II. 1920–1944. Szöveggyüjtemény* (A Social History of Hungary II. 1920–1944. Essays) (editor, 1995); *A Modern város történeti dilemmái* (Historical Dilemmas of the Modern City) (editor, 1995).

Christopher P. Hosgood is Associate Professor and Chair of the Department of History at the University of Lethbridge, Canada. His published work includes studies of the Victorian petite bourgeoisie, including articles on shop life, shopkeepers and commercial travellers. He is currently working on a study of shopping and shop life in *fin-de-siècle* London.

Kathleen James is Assistant Professor of Architecture at the University of California, Berkeley. A historian of twentieth-century architecture, she has written on Louis Kahn and a number of German topics. In addition to her contributions to several exhibition catalogues, she has written *Eric Mendelsohn and the Architecture of German Modernism* (1997).

Serge Jaumain is Professor of Contemporary History at the Free University of Brussels, where he is currently Chairman of the Department of History and Director of the Centre for Canadian Studies. His research is concerned principally with the history of retailing and of employers, and with Belgian–Canadian relations. In addition to a number of articles, he has published *Aux frontières des classes moyennes. La petite bourgeoisie belge avant 1914* (editor with G. Kurgan-van Hentenryk, 1992); *The Guises of Canadian Diversity. New European Perspectives* (editor with M. Maufort, 1995); *Les petits commerçants belges face à la modernité (1880–1914)* (1995); *Dictionnaire des patrons en Belgique. Les hommes, les entreprises, les réseaux* (editor with G. Kurgan-van Hentenryk and V. Montens, 1996); *La Réforme de l'Etat ... et après? L'impact des débats institutionnels en Belgique et au Canada* (editor, 1997); and *Industrialisation et sociétés (1830–1970). La Belgique* (1998).

Erika D. Rappaport is Assistant Professor of History at the University of California at Santa Barbara. She has published articles on gender and consumption in Victorian and Edwardian London, including '"The Halls of Temptation": Gender, politics and the construction of the department store in late-Victorian London' (*Journal of British Studies*, 35, 1996) and '"A new era of shopping": the promotion of women's pleasure in London's West End, 1909–1914' in L. Charney and V. Schwartz, eds, *Cinema and the Invention of Modern Life* (1995). Her book *Shopping for Pleasure: Gender and Public Life in London's West End, 1860–1914* will be published by Princeton University Press in 1999.

Uwe Spiekermann is Lecturer at the Dr Rainer Wild Foundation in Heidelberg, having previously worked at the Universities of Münster and Exeter. He has published articles and books extensively on the social and economic history of nutrition, advertising and retailing in the nineteenth and twentieth centuries. These include *Warenhaussteuer in Deutschland* (1994) and *Basis der Konsumgesellschaft. Geschichte des modernen Kleinhandels in Deutschland 1850–1914* (1998).

Lisa Tiersten is Assistant Professor at Barnard College, Columbia University. She specialises in modern French cultural history, and has published articles on the history of the French bourgeoisie in the nineteenth century. She has just completed a book on consumer culture in *fin-de-siècle* France.

Claire Walsh is working on a doctoral thesis in the Department of History and Civilisation at the European University Institute in Florence. Her research is concerned with the culture of shopping in London and Paris, 1660–1800.

Donald Weber is a researcher at the Archief en Museum van de Socialistische Arbeidersbeweging in Ghent, having previously been a member of the Contemporary History Unit at the University of Ghent. Earlier shorter publications covered diverse areas such as discourse on penal questions in the Belgian parliament, the colonial lottery, the history of mobility, and automobile advertising, and his first book was *Homo Criminalis. Belgische parlementsleden over misdaad en straf, 1830–1940* (1997). He is currently working on his doctoral thesis on consumer culture and the automobile in Belgium between 1890 and 1950.

Preface

Recent years have seen the history of the department store move into the limelight. After many decades in which it was almost exclusively historians of retailing and company biographers who were interested in the phenomenon, the department store has now come to attract the attention of historians of culture, consumption, gender, urban life and much more. It is therefore an opportune moment to bring together a collection of articles which embrace some of the breadth of these new approaches to department store history.

These articles are all substantially revised versions of papers first discussed at a small colloquium hosted by the Free University of Brussels. We are particularly grateful to our friend and colleague Ginette Kurgan, who directs the Groupe d'Histoire du Patronat at that university, for the support which she gave to this project. We also received encouragement and support from M. Diego du Monceau, Administrator of the Groupe GIB, M. le Baron André Jaumotte, and above all M. Jacques Dopchie, former Vice-President of the Groupe GIB, and we are grateful to them all. Financial support for the colloquium was generously provided by Mme Bernheim, President of the Fondation Emile Bernheim; the Fonds national de la Recherche scientifique belge; the Faculty of Philosophy and Letters at the Free University of Brussels; M. Raymond Vaxelaire, Managing Director of the Brussels department store INNO; the Direction générale de l'Enseignement supérieur et de la Recherche scientifique de la Communauté française de Belgique; the Direction générale de la Culture et de la Communication de la Communauté française; and the Canadian Embassy in Brussels. We wish to express our gratitude to them all, as well as to the participants in the colloquium, whose contributions to the discussion were essential for the development of these articles. Finally, we are grateful for the care and commitment which Angela Jackson of the University of Essex brought to her editorial work on many of the articles in this collection.

Geoffrey Crossick, Colchester
Serge Jaumain, Brussels

CHAPTER ONE

The world of the department store: distribution, culture and social change[1]

Geoffrey Crossick and Serge Jaumain

The way department stores have been approached by the historian has been transformed in recent years. Although the focus on businesses has not disappeared, department stores have come to engage the interest of historians with quite different agendas. It is, more precisely, *the* department store that has attracted attention, as if it were a single phenomenon whose meanings are undisputed. Departing from the more traditional business and economic approaches, the stores have come to be studied in relation to issues such as culture, consumption, gender, modernity and social anxiety. One is tempted to conclude that the department store has in recent years been explored less as an object of study in itself, and more for what it reveals about other matters of interest to the historian.

It was not always thus. Until the innovative work of Miller on the Parisian Bon Marché,[2] historical approaches to department stores tended to emphasise the dual themes of celebration and modernisation. They have been celebrated as businesses, with a long-established tradition of business biography, at times even business hagiography, concerned with the history of individual stores, and which often glorified the great figures of department store history, such as Aristide Boucicaut, Gordon Selfridge, William Whiteley and Emile Bernheim.[3] Other studies have stressed the role of the department store in the modernisation of retailing, introducing new methods into a distribution sector which seemingly lagged behind the pace of industrial change.[4]

Although these approaches have far from disappeared, the last decade or so has seen studies concerned not only with the internal functioning and commercial strategies of these establishments, but with their relationship to a larger cultural, economic and social environment.[5] Beyond such studies, however, a wider agenda has taken shape which is larger than that of even a more socially engaged business history, as historians of culture, consumption and gender have found in the department store a fruitful area of study. The cultural history of consumption, one of the fastest growing fields of historical inquiry, has found a world in which consumers, distributors and producers symbolically came together, and out of whose encounter emerged not only new methods of selling and to some extent production, but also what might for the first time be designated a 'consumer culture', one in which groups constituted by class and gender could find social definition through the acts of buying as much as of consuming. Gender history could hardly ignore the department store, which at the end of the nineteenth century appeared to be a feminine universe *par excellence.* The highly visible female shop assistant not only seized the attention of contemporary observers, but has attracted historians of female labour who have explained the internal organisation of the store itself, relations between employers and employees, and those between employees and what has been seen as a largely female clientele.[6] The department store now appears as not merely a huge sales hall, but as a meeting place, a site for female sociability and arguably also emancipation, where the absence of conventional boundaries engendered the contemporary anxieties which have themselves become an object of study. The study of women shoplifters is but the most explicit expression of the way the anxieties of contemporaries and the interest of historians have reinforced each other.[7] At no time did the department store evoke as much contemporary concern as between 1880 and 1914, its symbolic presence allowing it to stand for many of the social fears exercising European societies in these years. In these and other ways, historical research has passed from the celebration of the department store to a wider concern for the ways in which it represented, expressed, and perhaps shaped, changing aspects of the societies in which it appeared.

This research has largely focused on just four countries. The particular attention attracted by the USA mirrors the responses of businessmen themselves, especially during the inter-war period, when American retailing drew the owners and managers of stores from many parts of Europe to tour the major sites in New York and Chicago, seeking ideas which they could carry home. As relatively minor a figure as Frank Chiesman, from the south London suburb of Lewisham, toured US stores after the First World War, and the lessons he learned there strongly influenced the design and management of the store he rebuilt in the ensuing years.[8] For Europeans, however, the image of the great department store was born not in these glass palaces, but on the Left Bank of the Seine, for it is the Bon Marché and its successors across the river which have made Paris (rather than France as a whole) the second geographical focus of research. Increasing studies of Britain and Germany complete the picture,[9] for studies of the department store elsewhere have been few. Writings have been characterised by limited international comparison, for work has tended to confine itself within national boundaries,[10] by few recent syntheses,[11] and by a concentration on the period before 1914, to the relative neglect of the subsequent challenges. The heroic era of department stores has prevailed in the literature, when they seemed to announce the advent of modern consumer society, rather than the inter-war period in which they had to struggle for markets and identity in an era of *magasins à prix uniques* (single-price stores), or the post-war era of supermarkets and retail conglomerates. If historians have been drawn to the heroic era in which an Aristide Boucicaut or a Gordon Selfridge strode on the metropolitan stage, the neglect of the twentieth century detracts from a full appreciation of those founding decades.

Retail distribution constitutes an immediate point of intersection between economy, culture and daily life, and it is these intersections which the chapters in this book seek to explore. Some, drawing on a cultural history influenced by other analytical agendas, examine contemporary anxieties and contemporary representations, while others explore the architectural, business and geographical dimensions of these massive new retail establishments. As a whole, the articles gathered in this book take the department store not as an object of study in itself, but as a phenomenon whose exploration can lead the historian into other dimensions of social, economic and cultural life. In this way it is hoped to move towards a more balanced understanding of what was, for contemporary opinion, a phenomenon at once exciting and disturbing.

The department store as a phenomenon

The innovative role of the later nineteenth-century department store has become a commonplace of historical discussion. Yet the historian's regard is as liable to be seduced by these 'cathedrals of commerce'[12] as was that of the contemporary observer, with their impressive array of goods, and their extravagantly public style of both built architecture and window display. As Chapter 2 by Claire Walsh reminds us, however, we must define more clearly what we mean by the 'newness' of the department store. How well founded is the image of the revolutionary *grand magasin*, transforming commercial practice in a dramatic period of change, or have historians too readily adopted an image constructed by contemporary opinion concerned primarily to laud or to deplore what it saw as 'modernity'? Did contemporaries invent this specific phenomenon called the department store just as a section of contemporary Social Catholic opinion invented the *classes moyennes*?[13] Department stores existed, of course, just as the owners of small enterprise existed, but the department store was less novel and less homogeneous than contemporary debates lead us to expect. The parallel with the adoption of small enterprise by strands of late nineteenth-century conservative opinion is appropriate, not simply because those who praised small enterprise stressed the moral contrast between the independent family business and large capitalist retail establishments, but also because the department store became for some a symbol for other forces in contemporary society.

Attempts to unravel this 'phenomenon' of the department store might begin with the intellectual trajectory through which we ourselves initially encountered it. Our interest in the department store was born in neither business history nor the cultural analysis of consumption and gender. Instead, we separately encountered the department store through our interest in the petite bourgeoisie of small businessmen and women,[14] especially through the contemporary debates within which it appeared primarily as a caricature. For many small shopkeepers from the 1880s onwards, above all those organised in trade and political associations, the department store became the most powerful symbol of all that they hated, the forces of organised capital that were crushing independent small enterprise, and which they designated 'unfair competition'.[15] In France, Germany, The Netherlands and Belgium, independent shopkeepers sought from the state measures to control this new competition, demanding for example that taxation should be proportional to their turnover or to the number of specialist departments, in the hope that penal taxation would constrain further growth.[16] It was rare for such demands to elicit more than token responses, such as the limited reforms to the French *patente* tax in the 1890s, though Gyáni's chapter shows the range of controls imposed in Budapest. Governments were too attached to commercial expansion and the interests of middle-class consumers to interfere with the growth of department stores, though most German states did introduce some kinds of special taxes on them between 1899 and the First World War.[17] The first Padlock Law, introduced in Belgium in 1937, was perhaps the most severe restriction. Passed in part as a response to the success of the extreme right-wing Rexist movement in the 1936 elections, the Padlock Law forbade the opening or extension of establishments with multiple retail departments, without specific authorisation. The measure was more symbolic than effective.[18]

Small shopkeepers were not, however, uniformly hostile. Their awareness of more serious enemies may not have led to toleration but it certainly deflected criticism. An analysis of the evidence given to the Belgian National Commission on the Petite Bourgeoisie between 1902 and 1904 reveals that although 17 per cent of shopkeeper witnesses complained about the competition of department stores, 29 per cent denounced consumer co-operatives and fully 36 per cent the competition of what might seem an archaic target, the itinerant trader.[19] Belgian shopkeepers never formed anti-department store associations in the way that they did to oppose consumer co-operatives, moved by the level of competition and the political dimensions of co-operative stores.[20] Nevertheless, the principal French retailers' movement of the 1880s and 1890s, the *Ligue syndicale du travail, de l'industrie et du commerce*, took the department store as its main target.[21] The strength of anti-department store opinion in fact derived as much from political conjuncture and strategies as from any objective measure of their influence. After ignoring department stores in the 1920s, Belgian petit-bourgeois movements took to vociferously attacking them from 1933, influenced by German discourse as well as by fears that the socialists were seeking to win the support of shopkeepers by attacks on large-scale capital in retailing.[22] In any case, a good many of the more successful independent shopkeepers shared an unspoken admiration for department store owners, whom they saw as smaller retailers who had succeeded.[23] Unlike many a myth of the rise to wealth from humble beginnings, this one contained a good deal of truth. Most of the first wave of those who created Parisian department stores came from modest and often provincial backgrounds, and their careers began as the owners of small shops or as assistants in larger firms.[24] Other retailers welcomed the department store in their midst for more pragmatic reasons, for example those close to the Samaritaine in Paris who petitioned that the store be allowed to open on Sundays because it attracted shoppers to the area, while tradesmen in the vicinity of Whiteley's in west London were appalled at rumours in 1892 that the store might move elsewhere.[25] Indeed, far from being undermined by it, independent traders multiplied in the vicinity of the Bon Marché in Paris in the first decade of the twentieth century.[26] For all the noise made by retailer organisations, a noise which first alerted us to the department store as a phenomenon, independent shopkeepers were by no means uniformly hostile. Gaillard concluded that the quarrel between the *grands magasins* and the independent shop, which was to become a commonplace of Parisian life, took on dramatic significance only at times of financial, or we might add political, crisis.[27]

The hostility of retailer organisations may not have been commensurate with the share of trade taken by the new stores. Few business activities in later nineteenth-century Europe carried the emotional charge of the department store. Jefferys estimated that the proportion of retail sales in Britain accounted for by department stores in 1910 was no more than 2 to 3 per cent, while a German calculation of 2.3 per cent in

1913 was in the same range.[28] A study of Belgian department stores some 20 years later produced a similar figure of 3 per cent of retail sales, with the new *prix uniques*, the low-price establishments known in the USA as 'five and ten stores', not even reaching 1 per cent.[29] Pasdermadjian, from his perspective in the international department store association, estimated that Europe's stores in the 1930s accounted for no more than 5 per cent of trade.[30] The historian should not be surprised, not least the historian of the petite bourgeoisie. The political and cultural impact of a commercial phenomenon is not directly related to its economic weight, as the chapters in this book make clear. As Coles shows in his chapter, the rapidity of the growth of stores was one reason for their impact. These statistics should in any case be treated with caution. With the exception of Germany, European department stores sold little food, which constituted about half the retail market. If one focused solely on drapery, home furnishings and ready-made clothing – the spheres in which department stores were strongest – they will have accounted for a larger market share. Jefferys estimated for Britain that they accounted for 9.5–11.0 per cent of the clothing and footwear market in 1915, and between 13.0 and 15.5 per cent on the eve of the Second World War.[31]

The department store also appeared to us in a different guise, in the abundant literature of those who assumed the identity of the friends of small enterprise, amongst them sections of Le Playists and Social Catholics in France and Belgium, and *Kathedersozialisten* in Germany. They lauded small business as an alternative to a polarised class society, one which would still maintain the ideals of private property and private enterprise. The attempt to establish or re-establish a viable 'middle' in divided societies saw extensive activity to buttress small enterprise and to constrain those elements of organised capital which were seen as undermining it. The resulting catastrophist literature underlined the bleakest consequences of the department store: the uniformity and indeed debasement of taste in bourgeois consumption; the moral depravity induced by the department stores through the growth of shoplifting and the doubtful morality of young female shop assistants immersed in an atmosphere of excitement and ostentation; the destruction of family life not only for the armies of living-in employees but also for those middle-class women seduced by the stores into neglect of their familial responsibilities; the quest for luxury and acquisition rather than value and utility; and above all, for it must be remembered that we were reading this literature as students of the petite bourgeoisie, there was the threat to the survival of a middling group which was not only the guardian of honest moral values in society, but also represented for workers their one hope of social mobility.[32] For the Social Catholics and

Le Playists gathered around the *Société d'économie sociale*, the issue was straightforward: the social health of society required the saving of the social middle, represented by the small independent retailer, and the small shop was consequently idealised as the embodiment of those values whose destruction was symbolised by the rise of the department store. This moral critique was made clear in the speech by Frantz Funck-Brentano to the first International Congress of the Petite Bourgeoisie held in Antwerp in 1899. In the course of his keynote address, he told the harrowing tale of Mlle Marguerite Boulanger, a virtuous young woman destroyed by the power of the department store. She was accused of stealing a small piece of lace which had been caught up in her belongings, forced to endure a distressing interrogation in which she was stripped naked, and the search of her home while her elderly mother looked on in a state of shock. 'The next day,' Funck-Brentano told his audience, 'she died in atrocious pain, proclaiming her innocence ... and covered with the tears of her helpless mother, sister and brother.' This was more than a sad tale. It was evidence of the consequences of the disorganisation of society that followed when the old traditions of work, production and sale were lost.[33] In the critique of the morally corrosive influence of department stores, one was expected to see the reverse of the moral qualities of the *classe moyenne*, which was erected as an ideal with which to berate the undesirable aspects of modern life.

The department stores found articulate voices to defend them, stressing their role in the democratisation of fashion and consumption, the introduction of a new moral order into retailing through fixed and ticketed prices, and the incentives to national industry and trade. And in contradiction to the negative arguments of Du Maroussem and others,[34] they pointed to the beneficial impact of the stores on small workshops in their vicinity to which they put out not only manufacturing but also repair work. Few were more insistent than Georges d'Avenel, whose admiration was turned against the critics of large-scale retailing. 'Does the retailer exist for the public,' he asked 'or the public for the retailer?'[35] Yet even many of those who sought to defend small enterprise recognised the superior techniques introduced by department stores, and advised small shopkeepers to follow them and modernise their own retailing practices. The title adopted by the Belgian civil servant Hector Lambrechts was explicit: 'The business practices of large-scale retailing and their application to the small shop.'[36] The lessons which the modernisation of retailing offered the small shopkeeper were not always welcome, for it was modernity itself against which so many shopkeeper movements railed. The department stores were highly visible, through their architectural presence and their ostentatious publicity, and this very visibility was one reason why they became a symbol of

modernity in much of late nineteenth-century Europe: modernity in
design, in sales methods, in the application of new technology to the act
of retailing and to the art of attracting customers, as well as in much
else. The contrast with those forces which represented the modernisation of production is striking, for factories and mills were largely sheltered
from the public gaze by both distance and location.

Department stores, none the less, did not become symbols of modernity by locational chance. They benefited from the involvement of
large-scale capital to introduce the latest technical innovations as diverse as plate-glass windows, customer lifts, and cash registers. At the
same time they offered new ways of organising sales, relating to customers and employees, even of organising urban space. Space and
methods were explicitly intertwined, to create a new world of selling of
which those who designed the stores were conscious. Victor Horta, the
leading figure in the art nouveau movement of later nineteenth-century
Brussels and architect of the Innovation store, did not hide the motive
that lay behind his building plan. 'This was remarkably simple', he
explained. 'It was to grab the attention of those passing by the store and
to turn them into purchasers and, once inside the "cage", to compel
them to pass and to pause before the articles on display, no matter how
insignificant.' For, as he went on to argue, 'to facilitate sales and to
provoke the desire to buy are by no means the same thing'.[37] The sense
of bold innovation articulated by the department stores served to publicise the vision of modernity which the late nineteenth century came to
represent. Those who visited and shopped there encountered this expression of modernity in a tangible, public and almost daily form.
Indeed, the title of the main Belgian department store chain, Innovation, was chosen to express precisely that vision. If the historian might
protest that the department store merely drew on the wider changes in
which it was but a participant, and that much of the time it was no
more than adapting innovation found elsewhere, it was the first time
that so many of these had taken concrete form before a public gaze. It
was precisely because department stores were a symbol of this modernity that many independent shopkeepers felt threatened by them, and
that diverse moralists denounced the iniquities which they engendered.
Our engagement with these cathedrals of consumption is thus composed of that subtle blend of anxiety and admiration which is to be
found in Emile Zola's classic novel about the department store, *Au
Bonheur des Dames*, for which he prepared by observing closely and
over a long time the inner working of Parisian stores. [38] His compelling
description of the tragic fate of Le Vieil Elbeuf, the traditional and
outdated family drapery store which succumbed to its new competitor,
is balanced by his characteristic fascination with the modernity that *Au*

Bonheur des Dames represented. It is a tension strikingly absent from Duvivier's silent film version of the novel made in the 1920s, in which the diabolic horrors of the department store are set against the homely, if tired, values of the neighbourhood shop, in a simple Manichaean vision far from Zola's complex moral reaction to a world in change.[39]

However, we need to go beyond these representations of modernity and seek to relate them to the actual experience of retail change and the character of department stores. How extensive were the changes in business, employment and selling, and how far did these innovations spread through the urban system? And how were they experienced by those who worked and those who shopped in them? In responding to these questions, on many aspects of which research remains sparse, historical analysis can begin to assess the newness of the department store, and it can also explore why it assumed such symbolic weight, why it became the repository of so much enthusiasm and so much moralising. Such an approach will help to strip away some of the mythology which surrounds the supposedly revolutionary character of the department store by locating it within a larger framework of economic, social and cultural change in European societies.

The department store: a new world of retailing?

Is it possible to define the department store? Its most striking manifestation was architectural, although the notion of the purpose-built grand edifice fails to capture the piecemeal development which characterised most stores. As in architecture so more generally, there were no ideal types to provide a definition, but rather a heterogeneous collection of commercial enterprises with certain features in common. In terms of architectural grandeur, business organisation, character of clientele, publicity, range of merchandise and much else, not every department store was the Bon Marché. However, even if it is unwise to seek an exclusive definition of the department store, it will be useful to identify those features which made them distinctive.

Department stores have been distinguished from traditional retailing by their level of capitalisation, diversity of merchandise, methods of selling, and structure and styles of management, to which are conventionally added their social functions as 'cathedrals of commerce' redefining modes of consumption and providing new spaces for sociability. Any one of these could be found in earlier shops, but gathering them together constituted a major stage in the evolution of European retailing. As the chapters in this volume confirm, the department store's innovations were part of changing methods in a retail sector responding to shifting patterns of production on the one hand and of demand on the other. There was no moment at which a new phenomenon called the department store appeared. Examine, for example, the pictures of the Ville de Paris drapery store in rue Montmartre in 1843, with its external façade with huge bays, the corner entrance with a cupola, and the vast gas-lit and spectacular interior space for selling.[40] Nord has seen the Paris department store as 'heir to a merchandising tradition pioneered in the *passages*', the arcades built during the first half of the nineteenth century, innovative in their dramatic architecture, shopfronts and displays, and in their linking of theatre to merchandising.[41] The department store was the child, far more than the creator, of its era. Precursors can be found for each of the novel elements identified with the department store: diversity of goods in the popular early nineteenth-century bazaars, sociability in the exclusive shops of the later eighteenth century at which the ladies of the élite would gather to talk as much as to purchase,[42] or fixed and ticketed prices in the larger drapers of London and Paris. The apparent innovations which Pasdermadjian identified in Boucicaut's first small drapery store – low margins and high turnover, ticketed prices, free entrance and the right of exchange – were becoming commonplace amongst a new breed of city-centre retailers in many European capitals, and even some provincial towns.[43] What was new was their accumulation within a single highly capitalised and more rationally conceived enterprise.

Department stores everywhere were known for the range of produce that they sold, hence their English name which stresses the accumulation of goods in specialist sales units. Drapery was none the less the point of departure for most stores, and it long remained their core business. The explanations are various: drapers' shops had always sold a variety of goods, their expensive stock meant that they needed more capital than most retail trades, and they dealt in the textiles being transformed by industrialisation. Nevertheless, as a department store grew it rapidly increased the range of goods on offer. In a single decade after 1879 the number of departments in the Brussels Bon Marché grew from 18 to 32, and amongst those added were children's ready-made clothing, hats, perfumery, furniture, calicos and flannel, and travel clothing.[44] The splendour of the choice – Whiteley adopted the title of 'Universal Provider' with just that in mind – became a defining representation of the store, the subject of boasting and wonderment. A description in a guide to *Living London* (1903) captures well this sense of variety as one way in which stores represented themselves:

> When you have bought your medicines, your literature, your pictures, your saddlery, the latest bicycle and electric plant, flowers for the epergnes, bacon, eggs, and vegetables, fish, poultry, boots

and butter, you may, if you have time, step aside and sit for your photograph, having first made a special toilet, beginning with the bath and ending with the hairdresser and manicurist. Even then the 'stores' have not been fully explored!

In stores addressed to the rich, we are told, 'it is almost impossible to ask for anything which will not be promptly yours'. A house, furniture, greenhouse, animals, wedding trousseau, carpets, confectionery, and more.[45] Nevertheless drapery, together with ready-made clothing from the 1880s, remained central, for example accounting for 41 of the 52 principal departments in the Paris Bon Marché in 1906.[46] The importance which German stores attached to the sale of food was unusual, partly due to the limited growth of multiple retailing in the food trades there, but food departments gradually appeared elsewhere, not least where German firms expanded across national boundaries: by 1910 food accounted for 11 per cent of the turnover at Antwerp's Tietz store, a figure exceeded only by the household goods department.[47]

Between the 1850s and the First World War, the department stores of large capital cities prided themselves on their use of the most modern technology for building, equipment and sales. They were amongst the first to introduce pneumatic tubes to dispatch orders round the store, cash registers for on-the-spot transactions, lifts and escalators not only to transport customers between floors but to lead them through the theatre of the store, as well as experimenting with new construction methods and plate-glass windows to maximise display without as well as within. The new building which Jourdain built for the Samaritaine in Paris between 1905 and 1910 had electric awnings on the exterior to protect merchandise from the sun; steam heating ducts and electric conduits in each floor's exposed metal stanchions and girders; a pneumatic tube system for messages; motor-driven conveyor belts to transfer packages from the sales to the delivery area; and much more.[48] Department stores were becoming machines for selling,[49] with all that implied in terms of 'rationality' and a 'scientific' approach to marketing, advertising and selling, in the larger stores at least.[50] Zola's notebooks show his fascination with this aspect of the stores: the way a mail-order letter was dealt with, the way each dish was obtained by an employee in the dining-room, the way cash was handled and commission checked. Rational organisation directed to mastering operations made complex by their scale – that is what absorbed Zola's attention.[51] Whether these techniques to manage display, customers and transactions were matched by a real transformation of the methods used by sales staff is more open to doubt. Chessel's chapter suggests that French department stores during the inter-war years were far from the forefront of training in the new scientific sales methods being partly imported from the USA. In the department store, the skill of selling was now less the responsibility of sales personnel than of those who organised the space and the marketing programme. As was observed in 1932, the department store 'substitutes skilled advertising for skilled salesmanship'.[52]

The department stores offered new services, both to ease their customers' transactions and to make the act of shopping as agreeable as possible. Free entry with no obligation to buy was designed to remove all hesitation about going into the store, encouraging passers-by to inspect the vast range of merchandise as if in an exhibition hall, before deciding whether to become not merely observers but customers. No shop assistant or floor walker would harass those who entered, but were available to offer advice in response to the merest inquiry. To help the customer, prices were fixed, ticketed and even published widely through newspaper and other advertisements. As a final incentive to buy, home delivery and mail order were introduced together with a commitment to accept goods returned because the purchaser had changed her or his mind. The department store thus represented itself as a new style of retailing, one in which the relationship between customer and shopkeeper was more impersonal and therefore less threatening, and in which the range of leisure and rest facilities such as reading-rooms and restaurants, exhibitions and concerts, sought to present the experience less as trading and purchasing, more as relaxation and leisure, one reason for the magazines produced for female customers.[53] By the later nineteenth century increasing costs led to higher gross margins, which would pose problems for stores in the more bracing economic climate of the inter-war years, when novelty and fashionability were less compelling reasons to shop there.

The scale of department stores' massive regional and often national advertising engendered panic amongst independent retailers used to leaflets or small announcements in the local newspaper. Imaginatively illustrated publicity began to appear in the burgeoning press of later nineteenth-century Europe, though Weber's chapter on department store advertising in Ghent shows that its presence became most pervasive in the inter-war years. Newspaper advertising supported the mail-order catalogues which carried larger stores well beyond the boundaries of their own town, breaking the protection which distance had offered to an independent retailer's competitive position, though the tiny images that packed the pages of the catalogues could be a source of despair to advertising professionals.[54] No wonder that so many shopkeeper movements sought to defend locality and neighbourhood in the face of organised capital.[55] The Parisian Bon Marché distributed 1.5 million catalogues for its 1894 winter season, with 740 000 going to provincial addresses and 260 000 abroad. The consequence was to spread both the name of the largest stores and their sales. Georges d'Avenel reported in 1894 that the Louvre received each day 4 000 letters containing orders, and estimated that between 25 per cent and 40 per cent of the sales of the larger Parisian department stores were made by correspondence.[56] In 1905 Harrods launched a 24-hour telephone order service. Provincial stores could be just as invasive on a more local scale. Le Capitole in Toulouse offered motor van delivery of goods ordered from its catalogue within a 50 kilometre radius.[57] Mail order sustained customers on their holidays – the Galeries Lafayette had a regular motor delivery service running between Paris and Trouville in the early 1900s[58] – but they were even more important in spreading consumption practices and fashion beyond those who had personal access to the store, nowhere more strikingly so than in Imperial Russia. The Moscow department store Muir and Mirrielees had a mail-order service which reached throughout the Empire. Chekhov became so dependent on them for stationery, clothing and furniture after his move to Yalta that he named his two new mongrel puppies after the store.[59]

The history of the department store is also bound up with the heroic founding capitalist,[60] and the self-made manufacturer of the industrial revolution was reconstituted for a later age in which distribution and consumption had come to provide the stuff of legends. It is not only in the hagiographic histories that the great department stores appear to have been created by capricious and egotistical capitalist adventurers. They were often outsiders, above all the Jewish entrepreneurs prominent in the founding of early stores: the Galeries Lafayette in Paris, Innovation in Brussels, the Lewis chain in English provincial cities, and the Schocken, Wertheim and Tietz family chains in Germany.[61] The family's role in the launch of a new enterprise and in providing its first directors, each in a key post to assure close control over policy and management, was not exclusively the preserve of Jewish store owners.[62] Jewish control made an easy target for some organisations of independent retailers, encouraged by anti-semitic politicians. One grocery journal in Brussels wrote that small retailers were 'more deserving of the attention of elites than these Jacobs or Israelites arrived from who knows where'.[63]

The myth of the founding capitalist may have some roots in reality, but the geographical myth is less persuasive. The European department store was not limited to the great metropolitan capital cities whose most glittering examples dominate the literature, but spread in more modest incarnations through the urban system. The German case as described in the chapter by Coles may be exceptional in the extent to which department stores originated outside large cities, because the decentralised character of the German urban system was itself unusual, but he also shows how department store chains allowed stores to be established in medium-sized towns as well as in the suburbs of great cities. They began to resemble the multiple retailing companies which developed at this time, and with which they shared the characteristics of centralised purchasing and management, standardisation of employment, and tight control of the labour force, though in contrast to Germany only during the inter-war period did department store chains become significant in France and Britain.[64] Even without chains, however, the provincial diffusion of department stores offers us a somewhat different image, often more humble in style and market as well as in scale. Small-town stores could not buy on the scale needed to justify the low margins and high level of services that customers had come to expect, and it is not surprising that the inter-war period saw small-town and suburban stores become the branches of larger organisations such as Tietz in Germany, Nouvelles Galeries in France, Innovation in Belgium, and Debenhams in Britain. Mergers such as these became a valuable way of diffusing management skills through an increasingly differentiated sector.[65] The most challenging comparative question is why the phenomenon of the department store penetrated some countries so much more than others. Gyáni's chapter sees the slow growth of middle-class incomes and of urban culture as an explanation for their late appearance in Hungary. Italy in many ways constitutes a unique example, for the department store has remained of limited importance there, and before 1914 only Bocconi's chain based in Milan and the Mele store in Naples presented a real challenge to local retailers. A distinctive urban system and a distinctive shopping culture, together with low average incomes, offer a partial explanation, but a further factor may lie in the distinctive Italian chronology, for diversification as *prix uniques* took place before department stores had really flourished in the way that they did elsewhere.[66]

National diversity did not prevent the internationalisation of the department store. Although some chains crossed national frontiers – notably the German firm Leonard Tietz which opened stores in several Belgian towns – it was the phenomenon itself which became international, as department stores came to learn from each other. The writings about department stores and the travel of their directors diffused ideas so effectively that tourists would have found much that was familiar, as well as much that was new, about the stores they visited on their travels. The use of French names for stores all over Europe confirms the power of that example before 1914. The Louvre was common, but Bon Marché was the favourite, appearing in England on shop signs in improbable places such as Brixton in south London, Southport and Gloucester. David Lewis was so impressed by what he learned on a trip to Paris in the 1870s that he called his new Liverpool store 'Bon Marché' and painted its delivery vans in the same striped colours that he had seen in Paris.[67] By the inter-war years it was the USA which provided the main influence, something which had begun in London in 1909 when Gordon Selfridge opened his extravagant new establishment in Oxford Street on what were claimed to be American lines.[68] American marketing techniques were imported during the inter-war period, often following visits by department store directors, attentive to business methods in what was perceived as the most advanced country in terms of marketing.[69] In 1919 the future chairman of Barkers of Kensington went on an extensive tour of north American cities, and came back with many ideas about workforce management, marketing and architecture which all influenced the store's subsequent policies.[70] The chapter by Chessel shows the attempts to import American selling methods through the training of sales personnel, as well as the reticence with which these were welcomed, while Badel's chapter stresses the way Europe's own dynamic of development can be lost sight of in an exaggerated vision of American influence. The European experience remained the paramount influence, as contact amongst department store owners grew, facilitated by the International Association of Department Stores which was launched in 1931 by the directors of some of Europe's most substantial enterprises, one of its objectives being to diffuse best practice in sales and merchandise.[71]

One of the most striking importations from the USA was the *prix uniques*, the European version of the 'five and ten stores' launched by Woolworths and established across inter-war Europe. These were responses to the problems of high costs and low margins which department stores had inherited from the pre-war years and which now made them increasingly vulnerable. The new stores were directed at a socially inferior clientele far more attentive to prices and less concerned with service, yet nevertheless seeking a wide range of goods in a single establishment. They sold standardised objects of mass consumption, with a far smaller number of items than a department store might carry, and with prices conventionally rising in a series of clear steps, thus avoiding expensive ticketing operations. Selling was a minimal activity, and the mostly low-paid female assistants had only to collect the money and wrap the goods. The luxury and sociability of the department store may have been lost, but the principles of business were similar: rational organisation and the rapid turnover of stock bought cheaply through bulk orders.[72] The new *prix uniques* were initially competitors, but department store companies soon moved into the field in an effort to cut costs, maintain profits and exclude rival firms. The development of the *magasin à prix uniques* Sarma led the two great Belgian rivals, Bon

Marché and Innovation, to overcome their mutual hostility and form a
competitor company under the name of Priba. The collaboration was a
great success, and by the Second World War the newcomer's profit
exceeded that of Innovation.[73] *Prix uniques* were by the 1930s of prime
importance for department store companies, above all in Germany,
France and Belgium, allowing them to penetrate new lower middle- and
working-class markets.[74] In Italy, too, Rinascente (based on the older
Bocconi group taken over in 1917) launched Upim in 1928, and by
1940 there were 36 Upim branches compared with a mere 5 Rinascente
stores.[75] The department store in its classic form was ceasing to appear
as one of the great symbols of modern retailing, and was even beginning
to look like a tradition itself.[76] Financially better-off customers were
now more cost-conscious, especially in areas like ready-made clothing
where multiple retailers offered severe competition. A confidential report for London department stores in 1938 warned that management,
buying and selling, and store design all needed to be reorganised if the
stores were to survive.[77] Shopkeepers' associations, which had hitherto
attacked the department store as the symbol of modern consumerism
and organised capitalism, now turned their attention to the *prix uniques*
and multiple chains.[78] The development of *prix uniques* constituted the
first stage of a long-term process of reorientation of large-scale capital
within distribution. The department store may have become a traditional city-centre form of retailing, marginalised yet still patronised for
its traditional qualities, but it had played a crucial role in the evolution
of the modern distribution system.

The department store, the workforce and paternalism

Department stores are generally associated with new forms of organisation of the retailing workforce. The sheer size of the larger stores was
the most striking aspect: as early as 1877 the Bon Marché in Paris had
nearly 1 800 employees, a figure which had risen to nearly 7 000 in
1906, while by 1914, two of London's largest stores, Harrods and
Whiteleys, employed around 4 000 and 6 000 persons respectively.[79]
Their preferred personnel were generally young, unmarried[80] and, for a
long period, male. The last may be unexpected, for contemporary literature's obsession with the 'shop girl' occurred when the majority of
employees were in fact male. The prominence the stores gave to their
smiling female assistants, and anxieties about the apparent independence of these young women, made them one of the symbols of the
new-style retailing. Contemporary views were divided, with shop assistants being seen from one direction as standard-bearers for women's

labour, and from the other as being as frivolous and seductive as the world in which they worked, with consequences for their own moral standards and, by extension, for the moral ambience of the stores themselves.[81] Zola's portrait in *Au Bonheur des Dames* is no more than the most dramatic of such representations.

The reality was somewhat different. It is clear that male employees were more numerous. Although many worked in the wings – management, accounts, orders and dispatch, stores and delivery – a substantial number worked as sales staff. The feminisation of the sales workforce was not really achieved until the inter-war years, and as late as 1910 women were a minority of those employed even in sales and services by Parisian stores. They were hired as sales staff in just 16 of the Bon Marché's 52 departments. The pattern was uneven: if women constituted merely 30 per cent of sales and service employees at the Bon Marché in the years before 1914 and 25 per cent at the Louvre and the Bazar de l'Hôtel de Ville, they were 66 per cent at Innovation in Ghent.[82] It appears to have been the war and then the inter-war decades which saw the female department store assistant become more the norm. By 1921, 55 per cent of the 12 600 sales assistants in London stores were women, although it remains unclear how far female majorities existed in other cities.[83] Department stores liked to recruit their staff young, though whether this was because they would be easier to mould to the store's image, or because they were cheaper and easier to discipline, will have varied with the store and the functions. For young people from working-class backgrounds, work in a department store could represent upward mobility, but the majority of the workforce in larger stores appears to have come from lower middle-class families. The positions were much sought after, which enabled the stores to practice a rigorous selection process. Those seeking employment at the turn of the century in the Grand Bazar du Boulevard Anspach in Brussels had to present a written application, various educational certificates, evidence of a clean police record, and unimpeachable references, as well as having appropriate connections.[84]

The sales staff presented the ambiguities surrounding much white-collar employment: above all the encouragement of aspirations which social superiors found uncomfortable. In the case of department store sales personnel, mostly from skilled working- and lower middle-class backgrounds, the stores had to foster a sense of the ambitions of bourgeois life, the better to sell its paraphernalia, while discouraging any thoughts on the part of the assistants that they were the equals of their customers. As Susan Porter Benson has pointed out for US stores, the segregation of public space from more rudimentary employee space was one way of achieving that,[85] as were impersonal frameworks of discipline and bureaucracy. The department store's specialisation of functions was far from the multiplicity of tasks that fell to those working in small shops. Department store employment was characterised by precisely defined jobs integrated within a hierarchical organisation, and small breaches of the rules led to fines or dismissal. The bureaucratisation of selling created a rule-based environment, though as in most hierarchies superiors often appeared to those beneath them, and indeed were, more capricious and authoritarian than bureaucratic. At the end of the nineteenth century department stores would typically have a list of several dozen offences for which fines might be levied – indeed Whiteley's rule book contained 176 rules in 1887 – while dismissal was often with the shortest of notice, no more than 24 hours at Innovation in Verviers, for example.[86] The dangers of unemployment, with poor references in a field where excellent support was required, was one means of controlling the workforce. Miller has demonstrated that at the Bon Marché in Paris, 'firing was a tool that the Boucicauts used unhesitatingly and implacably in shaping their work force'.[87] Lesselier's reading of the files of Printemps led her to conclude that

> the *employée* [female sales assistant] was the child, the department heads and owners the father or the master: it was they who gave the orders and who punished, but even more so it was they who educated and inscribed on the minds and bodies of their employees moral precepts and the principles of obedience and discipline.[88]

Inspection, regulation and instability affected the whole workforce, but in particular the women over whom the sense of authority and tutelage seems to have been more strongly exercised.

There were more constructive ways of attaching the workforce to the enterprise. The most widespread was the commission paid to sales staff, often on the value of each sale, and which generally constituted the majority of an assistant's earnings. Commission was part of a wider structure of rewards and promotions which sought to bind each employee to the long-term success of the store, for until the mergers and new management techniques of the inter-war years, stores preferred to recruit internally to the management hierarchy. The consequence was competition amongst the workforce. Zola commented on the sales personnel in his notebooks that 'the dominant sentiment is the desire to make money; no affection, no camaraderie, just friction and the near hatred or jealousy which comes when interests are in conflict'.[89]

The distinctive work environment of excessive work, competitiveness and insecurity, led many before the First World War to denounce conditions and reject as hypocritical the more positive image about themselves which the department stores chose to diffuse. Belgian socialists described department store employees as 'black-coated proletarians' who 'do not even have the small protections which the *Conseils de Prud'hommes* provide for workers, nor those which have been provided through the social legislation of recent years'.[90] The picture that we derive from contemporary discussion is, as with most questions surrounding department stores, a contradictory one. For socialists and conservative social reformers alike, working conditions were iniquitous and exploitation rife. Yet the retailing sector as a whole was characterised by appalling conditions of labour and employment,[91] and if they differed in the stores it was for the better, not least in so far as overall earnings were concerned. The weakness of trades unions amongst department store employees was a characteristic of retailing as a whole. If the attempts to regulate workplace conditions and hours of labour focused on department stores, it was because they were the most visible sector of retailing and the most likely to make concessions, rather than because the circumstances of their workforce were inferior to those elsewhere in the retail sector.

Department store owners presented themselves in the guise of paternalist employers with canteens, medical services, pensions, leisure clubs and outings, insurance schemes and so on. The Boucicauts wove an impressive fabric of paternalistic concern at the Bon Marché, with at its heart a provident fund (1876) to provide a lump sum on retirement and a pension fund (1886), both non-contributory. At a more mundane level were the two free meals a day, educational courses, leisure clubs and free medical attention. Miller has shown the three concerns that motivated the Boucicauts: to create a stable and committed workforce, for the funds were available only after long service; to enmesh the employees within 'the family' of the store, in order to secure identity and longevity in a huge bureaucratic organisation; and to assure the middle-class values of the employees by rewarding good behaviour, providing access to middle-class culture, and ensuring that the paternalistic provision was directed at white-collar employees rather than manual workers.[92] Many were impressed by such policies. The annual meeting of the Le Playist *Société d'économie sociale* took a trip to the Louvre department store in 1891, one of the targets of the shopkeepers' movement, and the members were impressed by their tour, and by the clever speech by the Director who laid great emphasis on the possibility of *patronage* (paternalism under enlightened employers) offered by such businesses. He pointed to the good pay, retirement benefits, medical services, savings banks, canteens, and supervision by employers.[93] This was before the *Société* had learned that department stores constituted a threat to the small enterprise which that section of Le Playists had made the key to social stabilisation. The department store's potential for the reconstruction of relations between employers and workers seemed at that moment to present a more enticing vision than the myriad of small shopkeepers whom it threatened to displace.

These techniques for embracing the workforce within the enterprise had long characterised sections of continental European industry, especially amongst Catholic employers, and were less common in Britain.[94] The idea of a large family in a world without conflict was presented for external – and indeed internal – consumption, and a plethora of activities sought to reinforce that identity: fêtes were organised within the enterprise, employees celebrated key events in the life of the owners and their families, offices were decorated with photographs of the store's founders, family connections were an important factor in taking on new staff, and internal newspapers were published to report on the store's activities and its personnel. These practices were spreading elsewhere in large-scale retailing.[95] The sense of hierarchy, patriarchy and family will have particularly affected women employees, reproducing within the workplace the subordination many experienced in the private sphere.

As with all paternalistic systems, one is left reflecting not only on the gap between employer intentions and employee experience, but also on the contradictions in the largest enterprises between increasingly scientific and anonymous managerial styles on the one hand, and professions of personal concern and relations on the other. It is hard to resist the conclusion that by the early twentieth century the paternalist package primarily served the goals of labour control and public relations, as far as those not in management positions were concerned. For a long time, however, paternalist regimes reinforced by commission and internal promotion appear to have helped limit the number of workplace conflicts,[96] though there are too many other variables involved for such a conclusion to be secure. Not least amongst these is the instability of department store employment, which rendered paternalistic controls irrelevant to all but a minority who stayed for any length of time. A world of seasonal and unstable employment, above all for women assistants, fits ill with the paternalistic discourse of the proprietors, which described the experience of at best a small part of their workforce, and one that was disproportionately male.[97] The slow establishment of trade unions is hardly surprising,[98] and department store owners were reluctant to abandon the system of labour relations they had established. As Laurence Badel argues in her chapter, French department store owners in the inter-war years displayed a profound social conservatism to set against their commercial dynamism. This same reluctance to expose employees to outside influences helps explain the lukewarm attitude of store owners to the outside training of their workforce revealed in Marie Chessel's chapter, preferring as they did to see skill at selling as either a natural gift or the result of specific experience to be acquired within the store itself.[99]

The department store and the city

One reason for the impact of the department store was its effect on the organisation and representation of urban space. The architectural drama of the new stores was inescapable, both as urban presence, with the building itself serving as an advertisement, and through their often startling new interiors. Iron and steel, plate glass, new engineering methods and reinforced concrete all enabled the construction of open yet imposing façades, alongside airy and expansive interiors which encouraged people to enter and circulate. The interiors were designed to draw people on by means of light, staircases, and lifts. Department stores were just one part of a new urban monumentalism, as buildings of height and grandeur rose in the city skies where church spires and towers had once stood unchallenged – imposing town halls, railway stations and banks amongst them. Other retail forms were imposing themselves on the urban fabric during the second half of the nineteenth century, with the exuberance of new arcades such as in Brussels and Milan, as well as the more prosaic solidity of the co-operative store in provincial industrial towns. The impact of the department store none the less remained unique. The contemporary engravings reproduced in Marrey's impressively illustrated survey were drawn from a distance, often looking down from above, with the sheer mass of the building totally dominating the urban landscape, controlling the block and the streets.[100] Representations such as these sought to emphasise a defining feature of the stores: their urban monumentality.

Lewis Mumford observed, 'If the vitality of an institution may be gauged by its architecture, the department store was one of the most vital institutions in this commercial regime'.[101] Architectural patterns were shaped by audience as well as fashion. The Bon Marché's Left Bank location and its middle-class customers were matched by its re-strained façades and decoration, whereas across the river the exuberance of colour, materials and decor at Printemps was well-suited to its wealthier clientele and its location on tourist routes near the Opera.[102] None the less, architectural excitement was everywhere one of the stores' great appeals. Thus they moved between Second Empire classi-cism, renaissance, the distinctive art nouveau of the Corbin stores described by Coley in her chapter, or Frantz Jourdain's striking Samaritaine building in Paris; or in Germany, as James shows in her chapter, we can follow the generational contrast between Messel's distrust of commercial bourgeois culture, and Mendelsohn's buildings presented as an advertisement for modernity. We are left to ask whether the increasing assertiveness of German department store architecture was a response to the ambivalence of the country's urban élites to modern commerce, in contrast with its more ready acceptance in France. Yet beyond the shifting architectural idioms, the department store established itself as a distinctive and recognisable type, with many of the features introduced in Boucicaut's new Bon Marché building of 1872 repeated long after they had ceased to be necessary. Department stores not only had to compete architecturally with other buildings, they also had to give a clear signal of what they were. These signals were provided by features such as the great monumental stairs, devised initially to draw in reluctant shoppers, and which reached heights of magnificence at the turn of the century when consumer reticence had long passed; the splendid light courts which became mere design features with the advent of electric lighting; or the vast, raised corner rotunda.[103] For three-quarters of a century a department store, whatever its architectural style, had to look like a department store. The loss of confidence in that architectural form during the inter-war period perhaps coincided with a loss of confidence in the concept of the store.

Yet is it too narrow a perspective on the department store to require that it stand proud as an elegant new structure dominating the urban scene? In effect, that it be a magnificent purpose-built store, which explains the prominence accorded to the Bon Marché, arguably the first extravagant such construction in Europe, in the history of the department store. The purpose-built establishment – with its great breadth, imposing height, elaborate internal design – became the icon, an embodiment of newness and modernity, which has come to define our sense of what constituted a real department store. Yet there is another and more commonplace reality, for most department stores before the First World War were simply muddled accretions to existing buildings with the inconvenience and weakness of vision that accompanied such piecemeal development. Coley's chapter charts that balance between accumulated buildings and purposeful architectural design. The evolution of Barker's in London provides a good example of the former. In 1870 John Barker opened as a general draper in Kensington High Street, with a double-fronted shop and a dozen assistants. He steadily acquired other shops in the vicinity – for millinery and dressmaking, menswear and boys clothing, books, fancy goods, mantles, furniture, groceries, wines and spirits, and more. By 1893 he had amassed 28 shops, 42 departments and 1 000 employees, all combined into a single enterprise that lacked the grandeur of the purpose-built store.[104] Yet is was Barker rather than Selfridges or the Louvre which represented the norm.

The purpose-built store and growth by accretion were not alternatives in reality. Many a store started by piecemeal acquisitions until a whole site was occupied, when the store would be demolished and a new building erected, only for accretion to recommence as the grand new edifice itself proved insufficient. Fires often created the opportunity for major reconstruction which owners seized enthusiastically, providing they could raise the necessary capital.[105] On each of the occasions when it was destroyed in a fire – in 1872 and then again in 1888 – Fraser and McLaren's store in Glasgow was replaced with an even more splendid modern building.[106] The grand new stores built to impress may have received most of the attention, but they provide a distorted picture.

As distribution was separated from production in an increasing range of consumer trades, and as consumption itself became a social activity associated with leisure and entertainment, so consumer institutions centred on those parts of the city close to theatres and bourgeois street life such as the West End of London, or in Brussels the area between the Bourse and the Gare du Nord, close to the prestigious Théatre de la Monnaie. Nowhere was this more true than in Paris,[107] where much of the urban centre was reconstructed from the 1850s. The juxtaposition of Haussmann's rebuilding and the new department stores has made Paris the focus for so much writing on the subject, an imbalance that this volume can try to redress but from which it cannot escape. The Parisian stores seemed to depend on Haussmannisation: the interaction of new boulevards, prosperous apartment blocks, elegant bourgeois *flâneurs* and *flâneuses*, and these new cathedrals of consumption. In the words of Gaillard, 'the Paris of Haussmann is also the Paris of the *grands magasins*'.[108] There is some mythologising at work here. There was a long delay between the building of the boulevards and the new purpose-built department stores of the 1880s and 1890s, and the supposedly archetypal Bon Marché had in fact not been linked to the boulevard system at the time when it opened.

Central redevelopment was none the less of considerable significance, constructing the setting in which the stores' mix of theatre, architecture, fantasy and sociability could flourish. Department stores needed the clearing of space and rapid urban transportation systems carrying people rapidly to the centre, to create what has been called 'the extrovert city'.[109] The scope of retailing was now not the neighbourhood but the city as a whole. Without the opening up of the central space, without the department store as a place for encounters as much as for purchases, consumption as a generalised bourgeois leisure activity would have developed very differently. If the scale was not that of Haussmann's Paris, urban redevelopment repeatedly provided this space. London's great department stores tended to be located on the sites of somewhat earlier central reconstruction, but the Kensington Improvement Scheme of 1867 provided the street pattern of the district where Barkers as well as Derry & Toms were subsequently to open their stores. Berlin's

Kurfurstendamm was the setting for the new Kaufhaus des Westens. More modest programmes of street clearances and central redevelopment in provincial towns could have similar effects. The driving of rue de la République through Lyon's Presqu'île provided the setting for the A la Ville de Lyon store which opened in 1857. Birmingham's Corporation Street development, which took place under the municipal leadership of Joseph Chamberlain, provided the ideal setting for Lewis's new store, as did other schemes in Manchester and Sheffield.[110]

The interrelationship between the department store and the urban form needs closer comparative analysis, to establish the extent to which it was Paris in particular that was special, with its grand planned urban development and a handful of spectacular new department store buildings; or the centre of great capital cities in general that were special, distinguishing them from a mass of smaller towns. In this respect, as in so many others, we need to know more about the humdrum suburban and provincial enterprises.[111] We need to know more, for example, about the 18 department stores distributed across six towns in the English West Midlands in 1910 (which excluded the eight stores in the region's capital, Birmingham).[112] Suburban stores were significant only where substantial middle-class suburbia developed, which before the First World War was largely limited to Britain and Scandinavia, and it is therefore significant that Whiteley's, one of the most controversial of pre-war stores, was located not in the West End but in the west London suburb of Westbourne Grove.

Consumption, class and gender

The reawakening of interest in the department store has been closely related to the questions of consumption and gender which increasingly preoccupy social and cultural historians. A good deal of this work has derived from studies of the US experience, though care must be taken not to extrapolate too readily from north America to Europe. A further stimulus comes from the somewhat less fashionable concern for class. Although the last decade has seen a disenchantment with the study of the working class which had so long provided social history's vitality as a discipline, the European middle class has come to attract considerable interest. The role of consumption, and with it the department store which has become a symbol for the reconstruction of bourgeois consumption, is now stressed in the formation of a bourgeois identity whose roots have been increasingly presented as cultural more than economic. The department store has thus attracted those interested in some of the central concepts of contemporary social history, and the

litany can be completed by adding the nation. Ever since Veblen conspicuous and mass consumption has been linked to the distinctive social
structure of the USA, and has been seen as in some way formative of
American culture and identity.[113] Yet nation was not only relevant to
the analysis of American stores, for Auslander has shown how taste and
consumption were seen in contemporary discourse as constitutive of the
nation in Third Republic France – 'in shopping, constructing homes,
and producing everyday life, women were to make the nation'[114] – and
it is a theme explored further in the chapter by Tiersten.

Department store clienteles were more varied than the image of the
wealthy female customer would suggest. Indeed, wealthy bourgeois
élites continued to patronise exclusive specialist retailers long after the
advent of the department store. It is in any case unlikely that there were
enough such wealthy customers to go round, certainly in cities such as
London and Paris with plenty of stores. Each department store therefore had to identify its own segment of the market. Thus in Paris, the
Louvre has been described as opulent and conservative, the Bon Marché
as more middling and provincial in style, the Samaritaine as popular
and even working class, while Printemps directed itself at a younger
small- and middling-bourgeois clientele keen to display its modern
taste.[115] The contrast between stores with regard to their style, social
character of clientele and urban location was equally striking in London, for example between Whiteley's in Westbourne Grove and Harrod's
in Knightsbridge.[116] However enticing the prospect of creating a glamorous world for social élites, few stores could survive by serving such a
market. The others could create an illusion of elegance for their own
customers, but only once they had identified their market in social and
cultural terms. National differences such as those observed by
Pasdermadjian – who regarded Belgian, German and Swiss stores as
directed at a more popular clientele than those in other countries[117] –
were less significant than the variations amongst stores within a single
city or those between capitals and provincial towns. There were of
course exceptions: retail innovation in Moscow was dominated by the
Muir and Mirrielees store set up in the 1880s, drawing its custom from
right across the city's rapidly expanding professional, business and
managerial middle class.[118]

Even for Muir and Mirrielees, however, much rested on the growing
lower middle class of private and public sector white-collar workers,
schoolteachers and minor professionals whose own expansion in European labour markets coincided with the rapid growth of the department
store.[119] Indeed, as the civil service co-operative emerged in London
from the 1860s precisely to serve state employees, they attracted the
particular ire of independent shopkeepers for whom they combined the

two evils of department store and state employee, as did the parallel
Warenhaus für deutsche Beamte in Germany. The largest of such London
establishments was the Army and Navy Stores, founded in 1872, which
after an initial stage eschewing the provision of services soon adapted
into a full department store, whose turnover of over £3 million in 1898
reportedly made it the largest store in Britain.[120] Department stores in
general drew a substantial white-collar and lower-middle-class clientele,
and they were one source of lessons for these aspirant but insecure
groups on how to achieve a bourgeois lifestyle. As Perrot has observed,
'like fashion plates and catalogs, store windows became the best place
to school and train the public about its appearance'. He cites as an
example the importance of department store catalogues in France in the
spread of white as the colour for the bridal gown.[121] Mail-order catalogues not only created a massive postal trade for the stores, they also
served as guides to fashion and lifestyle for those who lived far from the
capitals as well as for the middle class who lived within them. In
1902–03, not only were 18 per cent of all the Bon Marché's sales
effected by mail order, a further 13 per cent were purchases made at the
store by provincials and foreigners and mailed to their clients.[122] This
was less the democratisation of fashion than its wider bourgeoisification.
Edinburgh department stores with their own dressmaking service thrived
by purchasing original model gowns from London and Paris fashion
houses and copying them for their own customers.[123] Department stores
were diffusers of culture and lifestyle as well as goods, for they attracted
mere visitors as well as purchasers, and with the much vaunted freedom
of entry these were by no means the same. Many went without any
intention of buying, including the *flâneuses* there merely to wander,
those referred to in Tiersten's chapter who loved to look and touch but
not buy, and who came to be called *palpeuses*. They were the inevitable
product of the department store's attention to spectacle and display, and
by the late 1880s the British trade press had given the name 'tabbies' to
such non-purchasing spectators.[124]

   It is therefore important to look behind the department store's image
as the expression of bourgeois indulgence or acquisitiveness, and to ask
who shopped at different stores, who visited them, and how their
displays and catalogues may have served to diffuse and homogenise
bourgeois culture. If we accept the central place of consumption in
bourgeois class formation, the diffusion of middle-class taste which
identified what it was to be bourgeois, then there is the danger that the
department stores' breadth of clientele generalised bourgeois taste to
such an extent as to undermine the clarity of the class. In Miller's
words, signalling the ambiguity not only of the department store but
also of the culturalist analysis of class, 'consumption itself became a

substitute for being bourgeois'.[125] The relationship between department stores and class identity is thus a conceptually awkward one that is in need of closer exploration. We must ask how far the department store did indeed shape and diffuse the bourgeois way of life, an argument most clearly articulated by Miller for the Bon Marché, and ask whether such a question can be effectively answered through an exploration of how the stores presented themselves in catalogues, publicity and display. We must be careful not to assume as achievement the image that stores liked to present of themselves. In any case, alongside the generalisation of taste which city-centre stores may have engendered, stands the fact that store location in segregating cities could segment customers in a way that encouraged cultural fragmentation as much as the reverse.[126] Research on the social base of different stores would also undermine the conception of the department store as an exclusively bourgeois institution: Lewis's of Liverpool who called themselves 'Friends of the People' to signal their intended market, or the French Dufayel chain with their extensive credit system reaching into popular urban *quartiers*, are examples of a working-class involvement with department stores which remains virtually ignored by historians.[127]

At the heart of the department store's representation lay a paradox: the goods offered to the aspirant consumer market were often mass-produced and aggressively priced, yet the culture being sold with it was one of luxury, indulgence and good taste. It was less the products which created the sense of elegance and good living than the department store setting in which they were sold. The display and context of the merchandise along with their publicity had to seduce, for the act of selling had been reduced in importance. As Sennett has argued, department store impresarios created 'a kind of spectacle out of the store, a spectacle which would endow the goods, by association, with an interest the merchandise might intrinsically lack'.[128] Spectacle and exhibition moved to the heart of the experience.[129] As early as 1855, Wylie and Lockhead's new store in Glasgow's Buchanan Street drew so many visitors in its early weeks that on Saturday afternoons they did no business and just admitted visitors wanting to view.[130] Gyáni notes in his chapter the same phenomenon at the Corvin store in Budapest. Theatrical images recur, for it was theatricality which gave meaning to the often mass-produced goods. 'Pass through the lamp and glass department', wrote one London observer at the turn of the century. 'It reminds one somehow of a scene in a pantomime, for there are numerous lights though it is noonday, and the flood of colour is rich and dazzling.'[131] Indeed theatre, and later film, offered the department store its approach to the spectator's experience: displays were treated as a sequence of tableaux, with recurrent motifs providing coherence.[132] The large stores excelled in their offerings of concerts, fashion shows, pageants and extravaganzas, merging the world of shopping and that of spectacle, as the chapter by Rappaport shows.

The department store's annual calendar, with its sequence of sales and seasonal events, such as those over the Christmas period examined in the chapter by Hosgood, created a ritualised structure for this culture of exhibition. Its annual sequence of rituals evoked the religious metaphor that recurs in contemporary comment. Thus a Paris store might have a white event in January, lace and gloves in February, coats and day wear in March, summer clothes in May, floor coverings in September, and so on.[133] Zola recorded the mesmerising effect of the annual white sale – 'exposition du blanc' – on his visit to the Bon Marché. 'The whole shop is white', he enthused in his notebooks, 'every department puts on display whatever it has that is white ... The banisters of the upper floors and the staircase are draped in white. All the piers are white. Curtains, socks. The name of the store is written in white socks ... Palaces, pavilions, arcades of ties ... '[134] Surviving photographs of window and shop displays from a modest English provincial store, Keddie's of Southend, confirm that such events were not confined to the great establishments: we can see a model of St Paul's Cathedral made entirely out of white handkerchiefs or a fully rigged ship constructed from white towels.[135] These events not only attracted custom, they also enabled the distinct seasonal cycles of different types of good to balance each other out, exploiting one of the business advantages of the multi-merchandise operation.

The result was to construct fantasy out of good business practice. In its cultural articulation and influence the department store should be linked to exhibitions as well as to consumption. Indeed, Parisian department stores used the term *exposition* in an ambiguous fashion, for both a display of newly arrived merchandise and a special event such as the sale of whites.[136] This was the era of the great international exhibitions in Europe's capital cities, whose ostentatious and exotic displays evoke parallel phenomena in department stores.[137] Their organisation of internal space was similar, not least because the same architects and engineers often worked on both. Boucicaut involved Gustave Eiffel in the design of his new store, while Frantz Jourdain used the pavilion for the perfume exhibition at the 1900 Exposition Universelle as a rehearsal for his new Samaritaine building.[138] The influence worked in the other direction too, as 'the ideology of the luxury store infiltrated the consciousness of site organisers' in 1900, and as art exhibitions began to learn display techniques from department stores.[139] Department stores regularly mounted special events to coincide with exhibitions. Barkers bought up all the choice food that the public had seen at the 1924

British Empire Exhibition in London, including two one-ton New Zealand cheeses, and transported them through the streets to their Kensington store on flag-bedecked open vans.[140] In the tourist itineraries constructed by late nineteenth-century guidebooks, the department store found its place alongside national monuments and artistic sites. Baedecker's 1912 guide to Berlin and its Environs advised tourists to visit the splendid interior of Wertheim's store, pointing out that 'visitors need not make any purchase'. Indeed, from the outset the Bon Marché organised guided tours of the building.[141]

'Through the windows of department stores', argued Jeanne Gaillard, 'the Parisian bourgeoisie discovered its new wealth and its new needs.'[142] Yet such claims must be treated with caution, for they privilege one element and one moment in the evolution of consumption. It is improbable that the department store itself transformed the world of consumption, as opposed to the way in which consumption was represented. The department store drew on, and was nourished by, wider currents of economic and cultural change: the spread of mass production from textiles to clothing, household goods, furniture; the development of newspapers, advertising and fashion magazines; rising real incomes, notably amongst the lower middle class; increasing mobility within large towns; and much else. Furthermore, those who find in the department store a new culture which attached multiple meanings to commodities and their acquisition should be cautious. McKendrick, Brewer and Plumb established the importance of consumption in the cultural world of the English eighteenth-century middle class, and a vigorous bourgeois consumer culture was a part of English industrialisation rather than some hedonistic decline from it during the later nineteenth century. Attaching a rich diversity of meanings to acquisitions appears less of a late nineteenth-century innovation than it once seemed.[143]

Shopping as a leisure activity, in contrast to the purposeful acquisition of goods, depended on many earlier innovations that were developed by the department store, above all the transformation of the personal relations between shopkeeper and customer into impersonal relations between strangers. Yet the fact that customers went to a department store to enjoy themselves, and that purchases were a price for that experience, finds parallels not only in the élite shops of eighteenth-century London and Paris, but at a more modest level in shops serving popular clienteles.[144] The nature of the pleasures may have differed, but entering a shop had rarely ever been solely about purchasing. The spectacle of the department store none the less offered a very different shopping experience, emphasised in publicity. Selfridge's early advertisements stressed that shopping, once part of the day's work, was 'an important part of the day's PLEASURE, a time of PROFIT,

RECREATION, and ENJOYMENT'.[145] The experience rested on stores' techniques for holding the visitor's attention and for persuading visitors to become customers. One consequence was the much publicised phenomenon of shoplifting, to which we shall return.

Contemporary discourse about the stores was suffused with moral ambiguity. Much of Miller's pathbreaking study of the Bon Marché revolves around the tension between on the one hand the extravagant, luxurious, bourgeois consumer world that the department store represented, with its bureaucratic functionalism and, on the other, the strand of bourgeois culture concerned with thrift, stability, authority, family and, especially in France, social relationships which eschewed the individualism of the market, a culture which the department store seemed to many to challenge. The new stores were insistently linked to the deformation of consumption and taste. In the words of the Social Catholic economist, Georges Blondel, 'these department stores ... serve to alter the customs of the population ... Amongst certain persons they provoke a sort of "hysteria for shopping"'.[146] For Lambrechts taste itself was transformed by the uniform and shoddy goods sold by the stores, and he predicted that the consequences would include 'the progressive perversion and elimination of all aesthetic senses and taste; the degradation of the personality, of individuality, in the absence of the food on which it might nourish itself; the disappearance of craft industries ... and the distinctive characteristics of the decadence of a nation, of a civilisation'.[147] Did the department store really play the significant role attributed to it both in such critiques and in the more positive publicity of the stores themselves? The department stores in their heyday sought to define culture and lifestyle, to assume an authority within a broad middle-class world in matters of fashion and taste. Abelson has argued for the USA that they 'assigned to themselves the role of new cultural authorities'.[148] Indeed, that role could be cited to defend the stores. The German liberal, Paul Gühre, argued that department store displays would raise public taste and teach people how to organise objects aesthetically.[149] The contemporary discourse surrounding the department store, whether from its critics or its friends, was certainly of interest, but it may lead us to overstate its influence as a motor of cultural and social change. This is true of consumption, and it is equally true of gender.

In late nineteenth-century discourse, the department store concerned women. It seemed to offer a privileged environment for female employees and for female customers, an environment whose apparent novelty provoked a growing sense of anxiety. Fears about the moral consequences of modernity came to focus on the department store in just the same way as did fears about the fate of the social middle. The symbolic power of the new phenomenon should not be underestimated. One source of anxiety was the *demoiselle de magasin*, the shop girl, representing the hope of social mobility for the daughters of the lower middle class on the one hand, and the moral depravity of these frenetic and seductive workplaces for social reformers on the other. Department store employees might progress within the store, but it was argued that they could not aspire to their own shop, home and family as could those employed in small shops. The accusation that few store assistants married was regularly repeated.[150] Furthermore, using fashionable pronatalist arguments, a Lyonnais shopkeeper newspaper denounced 'the encouragement to celibacy, because in department stores the assistants are housed separately, children are an obstacle, motherhood is impossible'.[151] The other source of anxiety was the deformation of bourgeois family virtue brought about by the enticements of shopping whose seductive powers drew women from their family duties, and at worst dragged them into debt and shoplifting.[152] It is a theme addressed in Tiersten's chapter on France. The sheer excitement of shopping, it was claimed, became a drug to which once responsible bourgeois wives became addicted. 'Eve's daughter enters the hell of temptation like a mouse into a trap ... As if from Charybdis to Scylla, she glides from counter to counter, dazzled and overpowered.'[153] These criticisms must be seen in the context of a pattern, dating from at least the early eighteenth century, of seeing women as the main force for profligate and impulsive spending on luxuries, in contrast to the sobriety of men who actually earned the money which was being spent. The critique of bourgeois women's behaviour that surrounded the department store was but one episode in a familiar story.[154]

Nowhere was the concern for the moral consequences of the excitement of shopping for vulnerable middle-class women more clearly and publicly apparent than in the debate about women shoplifting, a topic explored for Germany in the chapter by Spiekermann. Theft from department stores by middle-class women emerged as an issue of both social and scientific debate towards the end of the nineteenth century. The stores themselves were torn between on the one hand a desire to prevent theft, and on the other a fear of bad publicity which might seem to confirm the moral critiques of their establishments. Prosecutions of middle-class women were in fact not the norm. The need to explain apparently irrational behaviour, that is to say theft by persons who could have afforded to pay for the goods and indeed often had sufficient money in their purse to do so at the time, produced a focus on the physiological determinants of the behaviour in terms of characteristics deemed to be specifically feminine. At this point medical – especially psychological – opinion became paramount in absolving the women concerned of legal guilt. 'If the psychologist declares that the accused cannot be held responsible for their actions,' d'Avenel concluded, 'one can in good conscience close the affair.'[155] Doctors and psychologists seeking to establish the legal admissibility of scientific evidence collaborated with such strategies. A definition of women's physiology was constructed which used the deforming effects of female sexuality to explain acts of theft by bourgeois women. Medical argument linked the acts of theft to specific turbulence in the accused's body – menstruation, pregnancy, lactation, menopause, and so on. Yet, as O'Brien has shown, the medical explanation need not contradict those derived from a moral critique of consumerism. Women's weakness and susceptibility may have been physiological in origin, but it was the seductive excitement, the lights and the sensual displays, which drove them into what was for others a crime. The analyses of Alexandre Lacassagne in 1896, for example, did not reject the psycho-sexual explanation but laid emphasis on the dangers of consumerism.[156]

The images that recurred in debates about the department store derived as much from discourses of gender and class as they did from the sober realities of the stores themselves. As Rappaport has observed more generally of Whiteley's, the store was disturbing because it 'disorganised class, gender, moral and economic categories', by the mixed nature of its clientele and by ignoring the boundaries between public and private.[157] Yet historians have found in the stores an expression of shifting gender relations in the later nineteenth-century bourgeoisie. The department store has been placed in a new semi-public world of theatres, restaurants and retailing which signified new gender definitions in the bourgeois urban world. The critical eye of Hector Lambrechts detected this feature of the store, which 'is not a shop', he wrote, 'but a covered public square, to which one can go for all sorts of things, without having to even dream of buying ... It is truly a public square, dotted with a mass of stalls, while seeming to belong to everyone but the firm which owns it'.[158] The freedom of entry, the great architectural presence, the anonymity of the participants, and the theatrical style all placed the department stores in the public sphere. Yet middle-class women could avail themselves of salons and reading-rooms with domestic decor which implied some of the protections of the private sphere. Walkowitz has seen the music hall, theatre, museums, public transport and department stores of later nineteenth-century London as providing individual women with new sources of public freedom. The ideological division between a dangerous city centre and a secure domestic sphere could thus be softened, allowing a semi-public sphere to emerge for middle-class women. In Walkowitz's words, these women 'first established their urban beachheads around West End shopping and East End philanthropy'.[159]

The department store may thus be seen through one prism as offering emancipation for middle-class women, through another as a mere manipulator which created new consumer traps for them. The literature on which Hosgood draws in his chapter revolves around contemporary perceptions of these alternatives. Writing in recent years has come to stress the former, following the stimulus of Leach's work on the USA,[160] focusing on the freedoms which the stores offered middle-class women. Shopping and the creation of the domestic sphere had long been legitimate activities for bourgeois women, and the department stores drew upon women's established role by constructing a new world of shopping in which this role could be fulfilled. One version of this debate has revolved around women's engagement with modernity in the later nineteenth and early twentieth centuries. Wolff has argued that middle-class women were essentially excluded from the experience of modernity in those years by their location in the private, suburban and domestic world. Nava has disputed this view, claiming that theatres, department stores, trams and exhibitions constituted distinctive locations within which to seek the new emblems of status and individuality.[161] The Manichaean character of this debate should not distract us from the real ambiguities of the department store experience for bourgeois women, offering a feminine engagement with the public sphere, yet securing those new opportunities within a world of consumption which rendered it more legitimate.[162] As Tiersten has asked, was shopping just an ersatz public domain which actually served to exclude women from the 'real' public sphere?[163]

The debate within cultural studies echoes the literature of anxiety surrounding the department store before the First World War, as the chapters by Rappaport and Tiersten in this volume show. The fact that these were essentially male discourses explains the depth of the anxieties, but the redrawing of the gender boundaries of daily behaviour did indeed seem to constitute a threat. There were the fears of unplanned encounters in the space of the store, even worse the fears of illicit planned encounters with gentlemen friends, for the department store evoked the dangers of uncontrolled female sexuality. The sympathy for the suffragette movement displayed by several British department store proprietors only confirmed fears that the freedoms offered by the stores would extend beyond the sphere of consumption.[164] Whatever the reality, the department store was perceived as both empowering and demoralising in the decades before the First World War.

However, given the undeniable male presence in department stores, we must ask whether the discourses accurately described the stores' clientele. How insistently feminine was the department store? Many, such as the Belle Jardinière in Paris or Lewis's in Liverpool, traced their origins not to drapery or women's clothing but to menswear. When Lewis's Manchester store was opened in 1877, 'it was primarily intended, at this stage, for gentlemen rather than ladies'.[165] Department stores with more conventional origins had all moved into men's goods by the later years of the century, with men's clothing departments, tobacco and drinks. By 1914 stores had departments for heating, lighting and other small appliances which attracted male customers. Perrot has argued that by the late nineteenth century the stores had become teachers of fashion for men as much as for women, especially as expanding lower middle-class occupations created a market keen for instruction in middle-class mores.[166] If the department store was more mixed in its clientele than the discourses would lead us to believe, they served none the less to reinforce images of gender within consumption. They entrenched the styles, colours, interests and impulses that were seen to distinguish masculinity from femininity within the middle-class world.[167] The department store was a deeply gendered world, but it was never the overwhelmingly feminine one that the literature might at times lead us to believe.

The search for the true department store against which each pretender can be judged is mistaken, for it was too varied a phenomenon, and the department store is better understood within a process of change. A series of developments that had been transforming retailing through the nineteenth century flowed into the department store, which had then itself evolved into a plethora of other forms by the middle of the twentieth century. The department store shifted its character, towards chains, *prix uniques*, and so on. It is in this way unsatisfactory to define the 'true' department store and then test others against the ideal type and find them wanting.[168] Nevertheless, these innovations in retailing played an important part not only in distribution, but also in the cultural and social forces in which the process of distribution was embedded.

Was the department store new? At one level there is nothing new under the sun.[169] It is certainly the case that the problems, and indeed the shapes of solutions, articulated in the eighteenth and early nineteenth centuries and highlighted by Walsh in this volume, look in some ways familiar. What was new was not the needs and the responses to them, for these continued to evolve and were not themselves susceptible to sudden innovation, but rather a shift in the context of retailing: increasing mass production of consumer goods, increasing incomes especially in middling social groups, the level of capitalisation, and the potential offered by the reconstruction of urban space. The use of consumer goods to mark out 'distinction' was spreading more widely within the population, and the department store benefited from that, indeed in places orchestrated it. As a consequence, the department store became bound up with many of the most important dimensions of late nineteenth-century consumption, such as its feminisation, the depersonalisation of buying and selling, the emergence of modern marketing and advertising, and the development of retailing as spectacle.

The department store is a complex phenomenon which interlocks with so many themes of European development between 1850 and 1939 that its emergence as a major subject of historical research is not surprising. It is however striking that this emergence does not come primarily from an examination of the department store itself as a phenomenon in retailing history, though works in that area have contributed considerably to our understanding, but from historians fascinated by the attacks of the organised shopkeepers who so denounced them, and from historians wrestling with the concepts of modernity, consumption and gender. One sometimes wonders whether the department store – even with the solidity of its iron frame and plate-glass windows – is capable of taking the weight of analytical expectations heaped upon it. If at times one feels that one is learning more about the place of the department store in contemporary discourse than about what went on in the department store itself, more about its role in the culture of consumption than about the practices of purchasing and using goods in ordinary bourgeois lives, it remains the case that the department store has become a rich way of exploring many features of European cultural, social and economic change.

Notes

1. We are grateful to Lisa Tiersten and Erika Rappaport for their comments on an early draft of this chapter.
2. Michael B. Miller, *The Bon Marché. Bourgeois Culture and the Department Store, 1869–1920*, Princeton: Princeton University Press (1981).
3. See for example R. Lambert, *The Universal Provider. A Study of William Whiteley*, London: Harrap (1938), R. Pound, *Selfridge: a Biography*, London: Heinemann (1960) and Jacques Lacrosse and Pierre De Bie, *Emile Bernheim, Histoire d'un grand magasin*, Bruxelles: Labor (1972). For an example of how a business biography could advance beyond the early limitations of the genre, see A. Briggs, *Friends of the People: the Centenary History of Lewis's*, London: Batsford (1956).
4. For examples of these monographic studies of department stores, see M. Corina, *Fine Silks and Oak Counters: Debenhams 1778–1978*, London: Hutchinson (1978); A.P. Deslandes, *Historique du Grand Bazar d'Anvers (1885–1968)*, Anvers: Imprimeries générales anversoises (1972).

5. See, for example, F. Faraut, *Histoire de la Belle Jardinière*, Paris: Belin (1987); Konrad Fuchs, 'Zur Geschichte des Warenhaus-Konzerns I. Schocken Sohne. Unter besonder Berucksichtigung der Jahre seit 1933', *Zeitschrift für Unternehmensgeschichte*, 33, 1988, pp. 232–52; Philippe Verheyde, 'Les Galeries Lafayette, 1899–1955. Histoire économique d'un grand magasin', in *Comité pour l'histoire économique et financière de la France. Etudes et documents*, vol. V, Paris: Ministère de l'Economie (1993), pp. 201–53; Franco Amatori, *Proprietà e direzione. La Rinascente 1919–1969*, Milan: Angeli (1989).

6. One of the best examples of this new current of analysis is Susan Porter Benson: *Counter Cultures: Saleswomen, Managers and Customers in American Department Stores 1890–1940*, Urbana: University of Illinois Press (1986). See also Theresa McBride, 'A woman's world: department stores and the evolution of women's employment 1870–1920', *French Historical Studies*, 10, 1978, pp. 664–83.

7. See above all Elaine Susan Abelson, *When Ladies Go A-Thieving: Middle Class Shoplifters in the Victorian Department Store*, New York: Oxford University Press (1989). Also, Patricia O'Brien 'The kleptomania diagnosis: bourgeois women and theft in late nineteenth-century France', *Journal of Social History*, 17(1), 1983, pp. 65–77; Gail Reekie, 'Impulsive women, predictable men: psychological constructions of sexual difference in sales literature to 1930', *Australian Historical Studies*, 24(97), 1991, pp. 359–77, as well as Chapter 6 by Uwe Spiekermann in this volume.

8. Michael Moss and Alison Turton, *A Legend of Retailing. House of Fraser*, London: Weidenfeld and Nicolson (1989), pp. 302–03.

9. For Britain, see Dorothy Davies, *A History of Shopping*, London: Routledge and Kegan Paul (1966); J.B. Jefferys, *Retail Trading in Britain 1850–1950*, Cambridge: Cambridge University Press (1954); Alison Adburgham, *Shops and Shopping: 1800–1914*, London: George Allen and Unwin (1964); Gareth Shaw, 'The evolution and impact of large-scale retailing' in John Benson and Gareth Shaw, *The Evolution of Retail Systems, c.1800–1914*, London: Leicester University Press (1992), pp. 139–53; B. Lancaster, *The Department Store. A Social History*, London: Leicester University Press (1995). For Germany, see Siegfried Gerlach, *Das Warenhaus in Deutschland: Sein Entwicklung bis zum Ersten Weltkrieg in Historischer-Geographischer Sicht*, Stuttgart: Franz Steiner Verslag, (1988); Gareth Shaw, 'Large-scale retailing in Germany and the development of new retail organisations', in Benson and Shaw, *Evolution*, pp. 166–85.

10. An exception is Heidrun Homburg, 'Warenhausunternehmen und ihre Gründer in Frankreich und Deutschland oder eine diskrete Elite und mancherlei Mythen', *Jahrbuch für Wirtschaftsgeschichte*, (1), 1992, pp. 183–219. The one major work of international synthesis is H. Pasdermadjian, *The Department Store: its Origins, Evolution and Economics*, London: Newman (1954).

11. Though for Great Britain see Lancaster, *Department Store*.

12. The term was coined by Zola, who wrote that 'it was the cathedral of modern commerce, solid and light, made for a people of customers.' Emile Zola, *Au Bonheur des Dames*, originally published in 1883, Paris: Folio Classique edition (1980), p. 298. In his notebooks Zola had linked

the department store to a religious experience: Emile Zola, *Carnets d'enquête. Une ethnologie inédite de la France* (edited and introduced by H. Mitterand), Paris: Plon (1986), p. 184.

13. On the idea of the invention of the *classes moyennes*, see Geoffrey Crossick, 'Metaphors of the middle: the discovery of the petite bourgeoisie 1880–1914', *Transactions of the Royal Historical Society*, 6th series, 4, 1994, pp. 251–79, and *idem*, 'Formation ou invention des classes moyennes? Une analyse comparée: Belgique–France–Grande Bretagne (1880–1914)', *Revue belge d'Histoire contemporaine*, 26, 1996, pp. 105–38.

14. Research on the petite bourgeoisie has grown substantially in recent years. See Geoffrey Crossick and Heinz-Gerhard Haupt, *The Petite Bourgeoisie in Europe 1780–1914. Enterprise, Family and Independance*, London: Routledge (1995).

15. See above all Philip Nord, *Paris Shopkeepers and the Politics of Resentment*, Princeton: Princeton University Press (1986).

16. This was less true in Britain: Geoffrey Crossick, 'Shopkeepers and the state in Britain, 1870–1914', in Geoffrey Crossick and Heinz-Gerhard Haupt (eds), *Shopkeepers and Master Artisans in Nineteenth-Century Europe*, London: Methuen (1984), pp. 239–69. But see the independent shopkeeper protests against Whiteley's, which used local government bodies on which retailers were prominent as the basis for opposition: Lambert, *Universal Provider*, pp. 76–114.

17. Robert Gellately, *The Politics of Economic Despair. Shopkeepers and German Politics 1890–1914*, London and Beverly Hills: Sage (1974), pp. 42–4.

18. Peter Heyrman, 'Belgian government policy and the petite bourgeoisie (1918–1940)', *Contemporary European History*, 5, 1996, pp. 353–4; J.J. Boddewyn, *Belgian Public Policy towards Retailing since 1789. The Socio-politics of Distribution*, East Lansing: Michigan State University (1971), p. 54; Serge Jaumain and Lucia Gaiardo, '"Aide-toi et le gouvernement t'aidera". Les réponses de l'Etat à la crise de la petite bourgeoisie (1880–1914)', *Revue belge d'histoire contemporaine*, 20, 1988, pp. 417–71.

19. Serge Jaumain, *Les petits commerçants belges face à la modernité (1880–1914)*, Brussels: Editions de l'Université de Bruxelles (1995), p. 311. See also Ginette Kurgan-van Hentenryk, 'A la recherche de la petite bourgeoisie: l'enquête orale de 1902–1904', *Revue belge d'histoire contemporaine*, 14, 1983, pp. 287–332

20. S. Jaumain, 'Les classes moyennes belges de 1880 à 1914: "peur de rouge" ou peur des coopératives?', in Pascal Delwit and José Gotovich (eds), *La peur du rouge*, Brussels: Editions de l'Université de Bruxelles (1996), pp. 15–25.

21. See Nord, *Paris Shopkeepers*, especially ch. 6, pp. 261–301.

22. Heyrman, 'Belgian government policy', pp. 342–6.

23. For the example of Milan see Jonathan Morris, *Political Economy of Shopkeeping in Milan 1886–1922*, Cambridge: Cambridge University Press (1993), pp. 154–5.

24. Véronique Bourienne, 'Boucicaut, Chauchard et les autres. Fondateurs et fondation des premiers grands magasins parisiens', *Paris et Ile-de-France. Mémoires publiés par la Fédération des Sociétés Historiques et*

Archéologiques de Paris et l'Ile de France, 40, 1989, p. 259. For Boucicaut see Miller, *Bon Marché*, pp. 39–41. For Britain, Lambert, *Universal Provider*, chs 1 and 2, and Lancaster, *Department Store*, pp. 111–12. The observation was a commonplace at the time. See G. d'Avenel, *Le mécanisme de la vie moderne*, Paris: Armand Colin (1896), vol. 1, pp. 12–13, 21–22; Edmond Demolins, 'La question des grands magasins', *La Science sociale*, 9, 1890, p. 306.

25. J. Bernard and L. Hoffmann, 'Le petit commerce et les grands magasins', *La Réforme sociale*, 61, 1911, p. 301; Lambert, *Universal Provider*, p. 217.

26. G. d'Azambuja, 'Les grands magasins. Doivent-ils tuer les petits?', *La Science sociale*, 32, 1901, pp. 290–92.

27. Jeanne Gaillard, *Paris, la ville 1852–1870*, Paris: Editions Honoré Champion (1977), p. 540.

28. Jefferys, *Retail Trading in Britain*, p. 21; H. Aubin and W. Zorn (eds), *Handbuch der deutschen Wirtschafts- und Sozialgeschichte*, Stuttgart: Union Verlag (1976), vol. 2, p. 626.

29. Fernand Baudhuin, *Rapport de la Chambre Syndicale des Grands Magasins de Belgique aux Chambres Législatives*, Brussels: Vromant, 1934, cited by Jacques J. Dansette, *Les formes évoluées de la distribution*, Brussels: Pauli (1944), p. 100.

30. Pasdermadjian, *Department Store*, pp. 116–17.

31. Jefferys, *Retail Trading in Britain*, pp. 21, 61.

32. For an analysis of the French and Belgium literature see G. Crossick, 'Metaphors of the middle'. Examples of the contemporary literature are A. Feyeux, 'La question des grands magasins et des petits magasins', *La Réforme sociale*, 5, 1883, pp. 358–64; L. Goyard, *La crise du petit patronat et le syndicalisme*, Paris (1911); Bernard and Hoffmann, 'Le petit commerce'; Etienne Martin Saint-Léon, *Le petit commerce français. Sa lutte pour la vie*, Paris: Victor Lecoffre (1911); Georges Blondel, 'Le problème des classes moyennes. Aperçus français', *Bulletin de l'Institut international pour l'étude du problème des classes moyennes*, May 1908. From 1910 onwards, this bulletin divided its contents into regular sections. Alongside communications, official texts, parliaments, associations and education, was a monthly section headed 'Department Stores'.

33. Frantz Funck-Brentano in *Compte rendu sténographique du Congrès International de la Petite Bourgeoisie, tenu à Anvers le 17 et 18 septembre 1899*, Brussels: Oscar Schepens (1900), pp. 81–3.

34. Pierre du Maroussem, *La Question ouvrière. Vol. 2: Les Ebénistes du Faubourg Saint-Antoine*, Paris: Librairie Arth. Rousseau (1892).

35. Ibid., p. 2. See also Georges Michel, 'Une évolution économique. Le commerce en grands magasins', *Revue des deux mondes*, 1 January 1892, pp. 133–56.

36. H. Lambrechts, *Les procédés d'exploitation du grand commerce et leur application au petit commerce*, Paris: Extrait de la Réforme sociale (1910).

37. Victor Horta, *Mémoires* (edited and introduced by Cécile Dulière), Brussels: Ministère de la Communauté française de Belgique (1985), pp. 103, 110–11.

38. Zola, *Au Bonheur des Dames*. The 1886 translation into English as *The Ladies' Paradise* was reprinted in 1992 by the University of California

Press. For a selection from Zola's preparatory researches, see Zola, *Carnets d'enquête*.

39. *Au Bonheur des Dames*, directed by Julien Duvivier, 1929.
40. Bernard Marrey *Les grands magasins des origines à 1939*, Paris: Librairie Picard (1979), pp. 25–8. See Anatole France's memories of the wonders of the Deux Magots store he visited as a child just a few years later: Anatole France, *Le Petit Pierre*, Paris: Calmann-Lévy (1918), pp. 50–51.
41. Nord, *Paris Shopkeepers*, pp. 90–91.
42. Natacha Coquery, 'The aristocratic *hôtel* and its artisans in eighteenth-century Paris: the market ruled by court society', in Geoffrey Crossick (ed.), *The Artisan and the European Town, 1500–1900*, Aldershot: Scolar Press (1997), p. 107.
43. Pasdermadjian, *Department Store*, pp. 3–4. For the Newcastle store, Bainbridge, see Lancaster, *Department Store*, pp. 8–9. Miller is careful to place Bon Marché within the context of previous decades of commercial development, *Bon Marché*, p. 21.
44. Balance sheets of Bon Marché de Bruxelles 1879–1890: Archives du Groupe GIB in the Archives of the Université Libre de Bruxelles.
45. P.F. William Ryan, 'Scenes from shop and store London', in George R. Sims (ed.), *Living London*, London: Cassell (1903), pp. 140, 142.
46. Miller, *Bon Marché*, p. 51.
47. Calculated from the general accounts book of the Tietz store in Antwerp, in the Archives du Groupe GIB. For further analysis of this source, see Serge Jaumain, 'Les petits commerçants belges face à la modernité (1880–1914)', doctoral thesis, Université Libre de Bruxelles, 1991, vol. 3, annexes V.1–V.8.
48. Meredith L. Clausen, *Frantz Jourdain and the Samaritaine. Art Nouveau Theory and Criticism*, Leiden: E.J. Brill (1987), p. 250.
49. D'Avenel, *La méchanisme de la vie moderne*, p. 64.
50. Contemporaries wrote of the Parisian stores as machines functioning like 'a great steam engine' and 'with almost magical precision', Nord, *Paris Shopkeepers*, p. 62.
51. Zola, *Carnets d'enquêtes*, pp. 154–65.
52. P. Nystrom, quoted in Pasdermadjian, *Department Store*, p. 33.
53. See for example the periodical published by the Brussels Bon Marché, *La Mode-Bijou. Moniteur illustré publié par les Grands Magasins de Nouveautés Au Bon Marché* which appeared as early as 1882. For an interesting analysis of the diaries produced for women customers at Bon Marché in Paris, see Rachel Bowlby, 'Modes of modern shopping: Mallarmé at the *Bon Marché*', in N. Armstrong and L. Tennenhouse, *The Ideology of Conduct. Essays in Literature and the History of Sexuality*, London: Methuen (1987), pp. 188–92.
54. Marc Meulen, 'Les Ecoles des Hautes Etudes Commerciales et l'introduction du management en France', Thèse d'Etat, University of Paris X-Nanterre, 1992, p. 1099.
55. Nord, *Paris Shopkeepers*, ch. 6, pp. 261–301; Crossick and Haupt, *Petite Bourgeoisie*, pp. 164–5, p. 198 ff.
56. Miller, *The Bon Marché*, pp. 61–2; G. d'Avenel, 'Les grands magasins', *Revue des deux mondes*, 15 July 1894, p. 354.
57. R. de Boyer-Montégut, 'Enquête sur la situation des classes moyennes.

Toulouse et la Haute-Garonne', *La Réforme sociale*, 60, 1910, pp. 230–36.

58. P. Moride, *Les maisons à succursales multiples en France et à l'étranger*, Paris: Alcan (1913), p. 63.

59. Harvey Pitcher, *Muir and Mirrielees. The Scottish Partnership that became a Household Name in Russia*, Cromer: Swallow House Books (1994), pp. 141–9.

60. Valmy-Basse wrote in 1926 of men like Boucicaut and Hériot as 'draper's assistants of the heroic age': quoted by Aimé Dupuy, 'Les grands magasins et leur "histoire littéraire"', *L'information historique*, 1958, p. 112.

61. For Germany, where Jewish entrepreneurs were particularly prominent, see W.E. Mosse, *Jews and the German Economy: the German-Jewish Economic Elite 1820–1935*, Oxford: Clarendon Press (1987).

62. On the role of the family in the management of retailing enterprises, see Emmanuel Chadeau, 'Entre familles et managers: les grandes firmes de commerce de détail en France depuis 1945', *Revue du Nord*, 75, 1993, pp. 377–400.

63. Anon., 'Autour de la Semaine de la Poupé', *Le Moniteur de l'Epicerie*, 79, 1 March 1912, writing about the Tietz store in Brussels. For Paris, see Nord, *Paris Shopkeepers*, p. 169.

64. Shaw, 'Evolution and impact of large-scale retailing', p. 176; Jaumain, *Les petits commerçants*, pp. 52–6; Moride, *Les maisons à succursales multiples*.

65. Corina, *Fine Silks and Oak Counters*, pp. 94–104.

66. On the Italian case, see Vera Zamagni, 'Die langsame Modernisierung des italienischen Einzenhandels. Die Geschichte eines Sonderfalls in vergleichender Perspektive', in Hannes Siegrist, Hartmut Kaelble and Jürgen Kocka (eds), *Europaïsche Konsumgeschichte. Zur Gesellschafts- und Kulturgeschichte des Konsums (18. Bis 20. Jahrhundert)*, Frankfurt-am-Main: Campus Verlag (1997), pp. 705–16; Jonathan Morris, 'Les associations de détaillants en Italie à la fin du XIXe siècle', *Histoire, Economie, Société*, 16, 1997, p. 247.

67. Porter, 'The development of a provincial department store 1870–1939', *Business History*, 13, 1971, p. 66; Briggs, *Friends of the People*, pp. 36–8.

68. Lancaster, *Department Store*, pp. 68–81; Pound, *Selfridge*.

69. For Japanese parallels, see Nobuo Kawabe, 'The development of the retailing industry in Japan', *Entreprises et histoire*, 4, 1993, pp. 13–25.

70. D.W. Peel, *A Garden in the Sky. The Story of Barkers of Kensington, 1870–1957*, London: W.H. Allen (1960), pp. 60–71.

71. On the origins of this Association, Lacrosse and De Bie, *Emile Bernheim*, pp. 77–9. Amongst its Secretaries General were the authors of two significant works on the history of retailing, Henry Pasdermadjian and James Jefferys.

72. Roger Picard, *Formes et méthodes nouvelles des entreprises commerciales*, Paris: Recueil Sirey (1936), pp. 107–35.

73. Lacrosse and De Bie, *Emile Bernheim*, p. 97.

74. In Britain, however, it was Marks & Spencer, Woolworth and British Home Stores which captured the new working-class custom, rather than the department store companies.

75. Franco Amatori, 'Managers and owners in an Italian department store: La Rinascente from 1920 to 1970', unpublished paper to Colloquium on the Department Store in European Society 1850–1939, Brussels, September 1995.

76. Miller observes that by the 1920s the department store 'was no longer on the cutting edge of society', Miller *Bon Marché*, p. 236.

77. Moss and Turton, *Legend of Retailing*, pp. 149–56. For the major reorganisation of Printemps in Paris, see Meulen, 'Ecoles des Hautes Etudes Commerciales', pp. 1097–117.

78. The Swiss case has received only limited attention, but it is interesting to note the strong shopkeeper mobilisation against *prix uniques* in the late 1930s: Ingrid Liebeskind, 'Petit et grand commerce à Genève. Antagonismes et remous politiques', *Bulletin de la Société d'histoire et d'archéologie de Genève*, 19, 1988, pp. 21–81.

79. Miller, *Bon Marché*, pp. 43 and 46; Jefferys, *Retail Trading*, p. 330.

80. On unmarried status as a requirement for a large proportion of employees, especially women, see F. Parent-Lardeur, 'La vendeuse de grand magasin', in A. Farge and C. Klapisch-Zuber, *Madame ou mademoiselle? Itinéraires de la solitude féminine XVIIIe–XXe siècle*, Paris: Mayenne Montalba (1984), p. 97.

81. Claudie Lesselier, 'Employées de grands magasins à Paris (avant 1914)', *Le Mouvement social*, 105, 1978, pp. 109–26; Theresa McBride, 'A Woman's World'.

82. Lesselier, 'Employées', pp. 109–11; Livres du Personnel de l'Innovation de Gand, in Archives du Groupe GIB.

83. Sir Hubert Llewellyn Smith, *New Survey of London Life and Labour*, London: P.S. King (1933), vol. 5, p. 195.

84. G. Freddy, *Bruxelles inconnu. Etudes vécues*, Wavre: Librairie contemporaine (1904), p. 48. See also Zola, *Carnets d'enquêtes*, p. 207.

85. Benson, *Counter Cultures*, p. 207.

86. Isabelle Gatti de Gamond, 'Les demoiselles de magasin', in her *Question sociale, Morale et Philosophie*, Paris: V. Girard (1907), p. 214; Lambert, *Universal Provider*, p. 153. On dismissals, Archives du Groupe GIB, Fonds Innovation de Verviers, judgements of the Conseil des Prud'hommes de Verviers, 30 June 1916.

87. Miller, *The Bon Marché*, p. 83; see pp. 77–112 for an excellent study of the Bon Marché's labour management methods. For an alternative and laudatory contemporary vision, see Michel, 'Une évolution économique', p. 143.

88. Lesselier, 'Employées', p. 119.

89. Zola, *Carnets d'enquête*, p. 183.

90. Auguste Dewinne, *Les grands magasins*, Brussels: Imprimerie Veuve D. Brismée (1897), pp. 3 and 14. These articles had originally appeared in *Le Peuple*. The *Conseils de Prud'hommes* were legally established courts to resolve disputes relating to employment.

91. See for example Margaret G. Bondfield, 'Conditions under which shop assistants work', *Economic Journal*, 9, 1899, pp. 277–86; Wilfred B. Whitaker, *Victorian and Edwardian Shop Workers*, Newton Abbot: David and Charles (1973).

92. Miller, *The Bon Marché*, pp. 99–112.

93. J. Angots des Retours, 'Les Grands Magasins du Louvre', *La Réforme sociale*, 22, 1891, pp. 95–9.

94. But see the range of sporting and cultural clubs set up by Whiteley from the 1870s: Lambert, *Universal Provider*, pp. 150–51. See also Lancaster, *Department Store*, p. 142 ff.

95. See the large retail chains, such as Casino in France or Delhaize in Belgium: Michelle Zancarini-Fournel, 'A l'origine de la grande distribution, le succursalisme: Casino, Saint-Etienne 1898–1948', *Entreprises et Histoire*, 4, 1993, pp. 27–39; Serge Jaumain, *Les petits commerçants*, pp. 52–6.

96. Heinz-Gerhard Haupt, 'Les employés lyonnais devant le Conseil de prud'hommes du commerce (1910–1914)', *Le Mouvement social*, 141, 1987, pp. 81–99.

97. Of women taken on by Printemps in 1910, 60 per cent left within two years: Lesselier, 'Employées', pp. 111–12.

98. See Guy Moreau 'Entre classe ouvrière et petite bourgeoisie: les premières tentatives de syndicalisation des employés', in Ginette Kurgan-van Hentenryk and Serge Jaumain *Aux frontières des classes moyennes. La petite bourgeoisie belge avant 1914*, Brussels: Editions de l'Université de Bruxelles (1992), pp. 115–37.

99. For a similar reluctance in inter-war London, see Sir Hubert Llewellyn Smith, *New Survey*, pp. 160–62.

100. Marrey, *Les grands magasins*. An example is the grands magasins du Louvre in 1877, pp. 90–91.

101. Lewis Mumford, *The City in History*, Harmondsworth: Penguin Books (1966), p. 499.

102. Clausen, *Frantz Jourdain*, p. 213.

103. Meredith Clausen, 'The department store – development of a type', *Journal of Architectural Education*, 39, 1985, pp. 20–29.

104. Peel, *A Garden in the Sky*, pp. 35–43. For the same process in a Liverpool provincial store, David Wyn Davies, *Owen Owen. Victorian Draper*, Aberystwyth: Gwasg Cambria (n.d.).

105. Fires need not be beneficial. Whiteley's famously suffered five major fires in the 1880s, which severely disrupted trade as well as eating into capital: Lambert, *Universal Provider*, pp. 163–214.

106. Moss and Turton, *Legend of Retailing*, pp. 45–7.

107. Leora Auslander, *Taste and Power. Furnishing Modern France*, Berkeley: University of California Press (1996), p. 324.

108. Gaillard, *Paris, la ville*, p. 525.

109. Ibid., p. 528

110. Maurice Agulhon (ed.), *Histoire de la France urbaine. Vol. 4 La ville de l'âge industriel*, Paris: Seuil (1983), p. 465; Briggs, *Friends of the People*, pp. 60, 80–85.

111. Porter's brief study of Broadbents of Southport focuses primarily on finance and business organisation: J.H. Porter, 'The development of a provincial department store', pp. 64–71. For a useful brief survey of British provincial stores see Lancaster, *Department Store*, p. 25 ff.

112. Shaw, 'The evolution and impact of large-scale retailing', p. 143.

113. We are grateful to Erika Rappaport for drawing this point to our attention. For a recent exploration of this theme, see William Leach, *Land of*

Desire. Merchants, Power, and the Rise of a New American Culture, New York: Random House (1993).

114. Auslander, *Taste and Power*, pp. 377–413, quotation on p. 410.
115. Philippe Perrot, *Fashioning the Bourgeoisie. A History of Clothing in the Nineteenth Century*, Princeton: Princeton University Press (1994), pp. 66–7.
116. Lancaster, *Department Store*, p. 23.
117. Pasdermadjian, *Department Store*, p. 27.
118. Pitcher, *Muir and Mirrielees*, p. 136 ff.
119. See for example, Geoffrey Crossick (ed.), *The Lower Middle Class in Britain 1870–1914*, London: Croom Helm (1976).
120. J. Hood and B.S. Yamey, 'Middle-class co-operative retailing societies in London, 1864–1900', in K.A. Tucker and B.S. Yamey (eds), *Economics of Retailing. Selected Readings*, Harmondsworth: Penguin Books (1973), pp. 131–45. For shopkeeper criticisms, see the evidence to the Select Committee on Co-operative Stores, *Parliamentary Papers*, 1878–79, ix.
121. Perrot, *Fashioning the Bourgeoisie*, pp. 61, 78.
122. Miller, *Bon Marché*, p. 62.
123. S. Nenadic and C. Ranger, 'Women entrepreneurs in the garment trades: Edinburgh 1775–1891', ESRC End of Award Report, 1997, pp. 13–14.
124. Moss and Turton, *Legend of Retailing*, p. 71.
125. Miller, *The Bon Marché*, p. 185. See also Auslander, *Taste and Power*.
126. For an interesting American study of a kind not repeated for Europe, see Jeanne C. Lawrence, 'Geographical space, social space, and the realm of the department store', *Urban History*, 19, 1992, pp. 64–83.
127. Briggs, *Friends of the People*; Judith G. Coffin, 'Consumption, production and gender: the sewing machine in nineteenth-century France', in Laura L. Frader and Sonya O. Rose, *Gender and Class in Modern Europe*, Ithaca: Cornell University Press (1996), pp. 118–20.
128. Richard Sennett, *The Fall of Public Man*, New York: Vintage Books (1978), p. 144.
129. Miller noted the symbolic significance of the way the Bon Marché was transformed into a concert hall on special occasions: 'Spectacle and entertainment, on the one hand, the world of consumption on the other, were now truly indistinguishable.' Miller, *Bon Marché*, p. 173.
130. Moss and Turton, *Legend of Retailing*, pp. 36–9.
131. Ryan, 'Shop and store London', p. 140.
132. For Louis Haugmard's wider contemporary connections between cinematic images and consumption, see Rosalind H. Williams, *Dream Worlds: Mass Consumption in Late Nineteenth-Century France*, Berkeley: University of California Press (1982), pp. 78–84.
133. Perrot, *Fashioning the Bourgeoisie*, p. 62.
134. Zola, *Carnets d'enquête*, p. 166.
135. Photographs in the possession of the Keddie family. We are grateful to Sue Lomax, working on the Keddie store for her undergraduate project at the University of Essex, for drawing these to our attention.
136. Gaillard, *Paris, la ville*, p. 623.
137. For a parallel process in the USA, see Russell Lewis, 'Everything under one roof: world's fairs and department stores in Paris and Chicago', *Chicago History*, 12, 1983, pp. 28–47. While the sections on Chicago are interesting, little new is said about Paris.

138. Clausen, *Frantz Jourdain*, pp. 30–31.
139. Paul Greenhalgh, *Ephemeral Vistas. The Expositions Universelles, Great Exhibitions and World Fairs, 1851–1939*, Manchester: Manchester University Press (1988), p. 190; P. Mainardi, *The End of the Salon. Art and the State in the Early Third Republic*, Cambridge: Cambridge University Press (1993), pp. 144–6.
140. Peel, *Garden in the Sky*, p. 93.
141. Quoted in Warren G. Breckman, 'Disciplining consumption: the debate about luxury in Wilhelmine Germany, 1890–1914', *Journal of Social History*, 24, 1991, p. 503; Miller, *Bon Marché*, p. 169.
142. Gaillard, *Paris, la ville*, p. 525.
143. Neil McKendrick, John Brewer and J.H. Plumb, *The Birth of a Consumer Society: the Commercialization of Eighteenth-Century England*, London: Europa (1982); Amanda Vickery, 'Women and the world of goods: a Lancashire consumer and her possessions, 1751–81', in John Brewer and Roy Porter (eds), *Consumption and the World of Goods*, London: Routledge (1993), pp. 274–301.
144. Crossick and Haupt, *The Petite Bourgeosie*, pp. 118–19.
145. Quoted by Erika D. Rappaport, '"A new era of shopping": the promotion of women's pleasure in London's West End, 1909–1914', in L. Charney and V.R. Schwartz (eds), *Cinema and the Invention of Modern Life*, Berkeley: University of California Press (1995), p. 137.
146. Georges Blondel, 'Le problème des classes moyennes', p. 41.
147. Hector Lambrechts in *Les Classes Moyennes dans le Commerce et l'Industrie. XXIXe Congrès de la Société internationale d'économie sociale*, Paris, 1910, pp. 409–10.
148. Abelson, *When Ladies Go A-Thieving*, p. 51.
149. Breckman, 'Disciplining consumption', pp. 498–9.
150. For example see Feyeux, 'La question des grands magasins', pp. 361–2.
151. *L'Alliance*, November 1902.
152. For the protests at Whiteley's attempt to obtain a licence to sell wine and beer in his refreshment room to a largely female clientele, see Erika D. Rappaport, '"The halls of temptation": gender, politics, and the construction of the department store in late Victorian London', *Journal of British Studies*, 35, 1996, pp. 67 ff.
153. Pierre Giffard, *Les Grands Bazars*, 1882, quoted in Perrot, *Fashioning the Bourgeoisie*, p. 63.
154. For an excellent recent collection of essays on gender and consumption, see Victoria de Grazia with Ellen Furlough (eds), *The Sex of Things. Gender and Consumption in Historical Perspective*, Berkeley: University of California Press (1996). On the woman as archetypal consumer in late nineteenth-century French discourse, see Williams, *Dream Worlds*, p. 307 ff.
155. D'Avenel, *Le mécanisme de la vie moderne*, p. 75.
156. O'Brien, 'Kleptomania Diagnosis'; Abelson, *When Ladies Go A-Thieving*, and the article by Spiekermann in this volume.
157. Rappaport, '"The halls of temptation"', p. 61.
158. In *Les Classes Moyennes dans le Commerce et l'Industrie*, pp. 402–03.
159. Judith Walkowitz, *City of Dreadful Delight. Narratives of Sexual Danger in Late-Victorian London*, London: Virago Press (1992), pp. 45–9, quotation on p. 46.

160. William R. Leach, 'Transformations in a culture of consumption: women and department stores, 1890–1925'. *Journal of American History*, 71, 1984, pp. 319–42.

161. Janet Wolff, 'The invisible flâneuse: women and the literature of modernity', *Theory, Culture and Society*, 2, 1985, pp. 37–46; Mica Nava, 'Modernity's disavowal. Women, the city and the department store', in Mica Nava and Alan O'Shea (eds), *Modern Times. Reflections on a Century of English Modernity*, London: Routledge (1996), pp. 38–76.

162. In a more historically sensitive analysis, Rappaport stresses the way in which this public space was increasingly described and imagined as female space, certainly as far as London was concerned: Rappaport, '"A new era of shopping"', *passim*.

163. Lisa Tiersten, 'Redefining consumer culture: recent literature on consumption and the bourgeoisie in western Europe', *Radical History Review*, 57, 1994, p. 139.

164. Lancaster, *Department Store*, p. 192.

165. Briggs, *Friends of the People*, pp. 21 and 68; Faraut, *Histoire de la Belle Jardinière*.

166. Perrot, *Fashioning the Bourgeoisie*, pp. 71–4. Jefferys, however, was cautious about the department store's attraction for male shoppers between the Wars, *Retail Trading in Britain*, p. 313.

167. For the USA, see Leach, 'Transformations in a culture of consumption', p. 331.

168. For an example of the establishment of an ideal type of the department store, in this case with 11 defining characteristics against which upstart pretenders to the crown of being the first department store could be assessed, see Harry E. Resseguie, 'Alexander Turney Stewart and the development of the department store, 1823–1876', *Business History Review*, 39, 1965, pp. 301–22.

169. As Victoria de Grazia observed at the colloquium at which earlier versions of the chapters in this volume were first discussed, urging us not to deny innovation wherever it appeared merely because forerunners can always be identified.

CHAPTER TWO

The newness of the department store: a view from the eighteenth century

Claire Walsh

This chapter seeks to understand the nature of retailing in the eighteenth century in order to explore some of the definitions and assumptions that have been made about the emergence and the novelty of the department store in the nineteenth century. The chapter examines the design and display of mainly high-class shops in London through the course of the eighteenth century with some examples drawn from the early nineteenth century. It argues that the department stores of the nineteenth century should be understood as part of an ongoing process of retail development: seeds of the department store format (both structurally and in terms of sales method) can be observed in the large-scale and fast-selling shops of the late eighteenth century, and shopping as a social activity, including browsing and window-shopping, were well established at the beginning of the eighteenth century.[1]

Since the first publications on the history of retailing in the 1950s the development of the department store has been equated with 'revolutionary' new techniques in retailing, and retail historians continue to cite window displays, the display of goods in interiors, browsing and window-shopping, fixed prices and cash sales as key elements that mark a distinct break with the past and constitute the 'birth of modern retailing'.[2] The exact point at which these techniques are said to arrive has been debated, but they have never been shifted back before the nineteenth century.[3]

Taking up these ideas, social and cultural theorists have placed the department store at the very forefront of the 'retail revolution'. In order to define our present age as distinct and 'modern' they have seen the emergence of the department store as the analogue of 'industrial revolution', Marxist alienation and the beginnings of mass consumption.[4] For Miller the workings of French department stores mirrored the machinery of mass production, exploiting workers and consumers, the stores parading the multiplicity of goods created by the new factories in their lavish displays. Yet there is little empirical research evident to substantiate these views.

The emphasis placed by these theorists on the novelty and significance of the department store, with its massive scale, emphasis on display, dramatic interior design and freedom to browse, is very much a result of the construction of dramatic contrasts with a preceding age of supposedly 'primitive' retailing. Eighteenth-century shops have been characterised as dark and unappealing, as mere exchange points of goods for money.[5] Dorothy Davis has stated that the shopkeepers of the eighteenth century wasted no capital in 'fitting up shop-furniture to house and display goods'.[6] The assumption has been that in the eighteenth-century shop there was 'not much effort to attract customers'[7] and that goods were left to 'sell themselves'.[8] Working from this perception, the retail techniques of the department store have been accorded 'revolutionary' status and powers.[9] However, once efforts are made to build up a picture of eighteenth-century retailing, it becomes possible to reconsider the contrasts usually drawn between retailing techniques in the eighteenth and nineteenth centuries, and to become more precise about the impact of the department store.

The interior design of eighteenth-century shops

It is important to establish that purchasing through fixed retail shops was already a firmly established practice at the very beginning of the eighteenth century.[10] Fixed shops ranged from the simple conversion of a trader's front room to the establishments with sophisticated interior design which predominated in London's key shopping streets. In London, workshops, filled with the noise and dirt of manufacturing, were kept separate from the retail shop. The sales shop was no longer an area for displaying craftsmanship in action (indeed most retailers subcontracted work or bought wholesale); it was an area geared specifically to the specialised task of selling.[11]

While it has been assumed that elaborate display techniques and extravagant interior fittings were first deployed in nineteenth-century department stores, inventories of high-class London shops of the eighteenth century reveal the use of an impressive display of expensive interior fittings. These range from mirrors, glass display cases lining the length of the shop, mouldings with features such as festoons and cherubs, moulded and gilded cornices, and the arrangement of classical pillars or sculpted archways at dramatic points in the shop, often framing the customer's progression upstairs or into back shops.[12] Glass, an expensive commodity, could be used extensively throughout the shop,

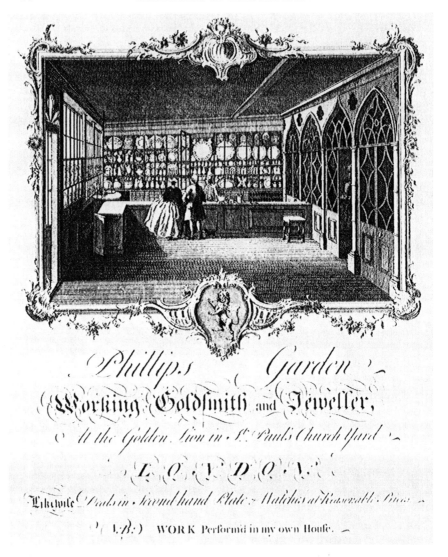

Phillips Garden

Working Goldsmith and Jeweller,

At the Golden Lion in St. Pauls Church Yard

LONDON

Likewise Deals in Second hand Plate & Watches at Reasonable Prices

(N.B.)   WORK Perform'd in my own House.

Plate 2.1   Trade card for Philips Garden, goldsmith, 1750s. (British Museum, Heal Collection)

not only in display cases, but in shop windows, internal windows, screens and skylights. The details of this kind of interior décor in inventories and contemporary descriptions accords well with depictions in trade cards and caricatures from the very beginning of the period. The trade card for a goldsmith, Philips Garden, from the 1750s (Plate 2.1) represents an idealised image rather than an actual shop and would have been used by several different goldsmiths. Idealisation served to impress potential customers but, by the same token, elements shown on the trade cards needed to be generally realistic to have credibility with consumers. These cards probably worked by representing perhaps far more elaborate design than present in the actual shop the card advertised, but consistent with high-class shop design of the time. The image represents a fashionable Gothic screen dividing front and back shop, a well-stocked window and a glass press behind the counter, all key elements of the goldsmith's battery of promotional devices and elements which created an influentially imposing interior. If the Gothic screen is meant to be glazed, glass appears as a predominant feature on all three visible sides of the shop. Inventories and plans make it clear that most goldsmiths had parallel glazed presses and so conventionally in shops constructed on these lines glass would entirely surround the customer.

The first room of London shops was typically long and narrow in comparison to present-day high street outlets, as they were based on the ground plan of terraced buildings, conventionally 14–16 feet wide. However, the types of decoration revealed in the inventories would have had considerable impact in shops this size. A screen from the 1780s in the height of fashion in the Neoclassical style (Plate 2.2) survives in a tobacconist in the Haymarket, dividing the fore and back shop, and provides some idea of the visual impact pillars, arches and glazed internal windows and doors would have made on customers as they entered by the shop door. As shopkeepers extended their shops further and further back into the building, arches and screens opened up the space, their gilded and moulded decoration made them much more important as grand design statements than as structural supports.

Along with structural embellishments were added elaborate furnishings, chairs and stools for customers, sometimes upholstered in velvet or leather, contributing to an air of comfort and deference intended to both flatter and detain customers. Mirrors and pictures appear on the walls, along with glass sconces, silk curtains, small tables, particularly in drapers' and china-sellers' shops, placing a premium on comfort and a domestic ambience.[13] The dramatic qualities of lighting were given particular attention in high-class shops. In drapers' and china shops the lamps, candlesticks and sconces, lit during the day behind fully stocked windows, reflected their light in the mirrors around the walls.[14] As Rouquet, a French visitor to London in 1755, commented:

> These shops they make as deep as possibly they can; the further end is generally lighted from above, a kind of illumination which, joined to the glasses, the sconces and the rest of the furniture, in regard to those passing by, is frequently productive of a theatrical effect, of a most agreeable vista.[15]

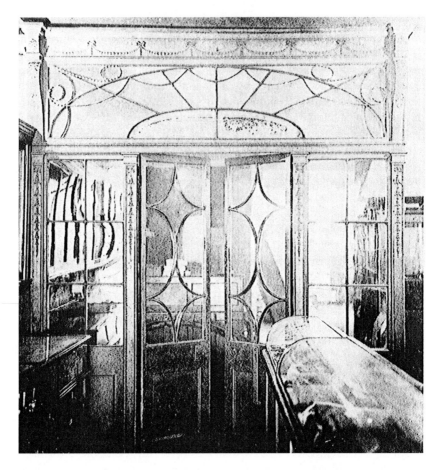

Plate 2.2 Shop screen in Freibourg & Treyer, tobacconists, Haymarket, London, 1780s. (British Museum, Heal Collection)

These carefully constructed interiors reflected or suggested the grand architectural gestures and fittings of wealthy private homes and lavish public interiors such as assembly halls and pleasure gardens. In the same way that to be seen at assemblies and the theatre was a mark of social status in the eighteenth century so, too, was making your purchases in the most fashionable shops – those which marked themselves out as distinguished and tasteful in their decoration, their selection of goods and the type of service they provided. The goods in these shops had their fashionable status created or enhanced to a large extent by the environment in which they were placed. Such trappings of high living were echoed on a lesser scale in smaller or more down-market shops, and the quantity and elaboration of fittings increased as the century progressed.[16]

The decorative elements used in shops created interiors which were dramatic, fashionable and class specific. They were designed to attract the right level of customer and to retain their custom, which they could do only if they could keep up with fashion and with competition from other shops. These grand gestures of interior design must have been changed frequently, as were shop fronts, according to the latest fashion trends. Two full-sized columns survive in the Museum of London from the interior of a pastry cook's from the end of the eighteenth century but, deceptively, the columns are made only of plaster. The fittings were as flimsy as props; the *Female Tatler* of 1709 described the drapers' shops on Ludgate Hill as 'perfect gilded theatres'.[17]

Just as department stores later evinced carefully constructed dream worlds, high-class shops of the eighteenth century created stage sets in which consumers could act out real or fantasy roles, in which they could perform to polite society, exploit the sensation of entering a temporary world of glamour and refinement, and in which they could become emersed in the drama of shopping and the dazzling show of the world of goods.

The display of goods

Little systematic study has been carried out on display techniques used in department stores and many interpretations are consequently impressionistic. The focus has been on the entrance areas and stairwells where grand style décor was combined with prominent and elaborate displays of goods. Cultural theorists have analysed this in terms of the arrival of a new visual culture, transforming people's shopping behaviour and their response to consumer goods.[18] However to reduce the issue to a simple conflict of a visual shopping culture versus a non-visual one is unproductive.

The emphasis placed on the novelty of the display of goods in department stores has arisen from the belief that goods in shops before the department store were accessible to customers only on demand, and that therefore goods must have been hidden out of sight. Dorothy Davis has stated of eighteenth-century shops that it 'does not sound as though shelves and cupboards and drawers were plentiful; it is more suggestive of brown-paper parcels heaped in back rooms and attics'.[19] While customers in many shops in the eighteenth century (but by no means all, as will be discussed later) were encouraged by staff to approach the counter where they could ask to be shown the full range of stock, this does not mean that goods were out of sight, and obviously this was not the case in nineteenth-century shops both before and contemporary with department stores. There was a strong emphasis on visual enticement in eighteenth-century shops.

Not only were goods on display on racks, shelving and in glassfronted presses (sometimes lined with velvet), in glass display cases and on moveable showboards, they were also openly displayed around the shop. Caricatures represent special items being hung from hooks, and cloth was contrived to flow down to the floor making the most of its tactile appeal and visual qualities, suggestive of the flamboyant displays of cloth in nineteenth-century department stores (Plates 2.3 and 2.4). Goods were not 'left to sell themselves' in the eighteenth century: customers' attention was drawn to them by their position or display fitting, and the décor of the shop articulated sophisticated social and cultural messages which were intended to be associated with the goods on sale.

Displays in shop windows were equally important as visual enticements. Although eighteenth-century shop windows were subdivided by glazing bars, the size of expensive glazed windows made an impression on contemporary commentators as did the richness of the displays behind them, even though goods tended to be pressed up against the individual panes of glass rather than arranged in a three dimensional display. Sophie Von La Roche visiting London in 1786 was impressed by 'the fine shops, which jut out at both sides of the front doors like big, broad oriels, having fine large window-panes, behind which wares are displayed, so that these shops look far more elegant than those in Paris'.[20]

Drapers were by far the most innovative in their window displays and in the use of dramatic displays outside their shops, often being remarked on for their technique of hanging lengths of cloth on either side of the shop door.[21] The absence of sheet glass before the 1850s did not mean that goods were not displayed or that customers were not attracted to them. The lack of this sort of evidence in the past has lead historians to overemphasise the novelty of these techniques in the midnineteenth century. Jefferys claimed that before the department store:

> Window display was practically unknown outside some of the shops in the larger towns. Symbols of the trade or a few articles showing the type of shop were often placed in the windows, but the use of bottle glass in the windows frequently obscured even these ... in the great majority of instances the retailer relied upon his reputation and skill to attract his custom rather than on any bright or elaborate display.[22]

Along with the assumption that window displays were unimportant has gone the assumption that consumers did not indulge in window-

Plate 2.3 Caricature, 'A Milliner's Shop', 1787. (British Museum)

Plate 2.4 Promotional illustration for Harding, Howell & Co., *Ackermann's Repository*, 1809. (British Library)

shopping in the eighteenth century. Clearly both assumptions must be revised. Window-shopping was an important activity and window displays considerably impressed consumers. In 1786 Sophie Von La Roche talked of goods displayed 'in such abundance of choice, as almost to make one greedy',[23] and Joanna Schopenhauer in 1803 of 'the brilliant displays of precious silverware, the beautiful draperies of muslin ... behind large plate-glass windows, the fairy-tale glitter of the crystal shops, all this bewitches the visitor'.[24]

Once they had gone inside and had approached the counter, customers in eighteenth-century shops continued to assess goods visually, but they also employed tactile and verbal skills to inform themselves about the stock on offer, feeling the quality of the goods and questioning the sales staff. Their purchasing decisions would be based on the use of all three faculties. While department stores did achieve particularly eye-catching displays, it would be wrong to ignore the fact that nineteenth-century customers also assessed goods using tactile and verbal skills, particularly as in department stores they were encouraged, or even pressured by floor walkers, to approach counters and engage with shop assistants who were eager to initiate the sales process.[25] Only where large items in a limited range were concerned might decision-making be based mainly on visual comparison. The balance to a predominantly visual assessment seems to have shifted only in the twentieth century.

Illustrations of departments within department stores which sold small items reveal a similar arrangement of counter and customer space as in eighteenth-century shops, with customer seating in front of the counters and stock organized on shelves behind them from which staff could bring down a selection of goods (Plate 2.5, compare with Plate 2.4). The architectural setting is more spacious and grandly conceived and the displays more lavish, but the sales procedure is still counter- and service-orientated. While this is not the arrangement of all departments, this central component of retailing in the nineteenth century is often ignored in descriptions which emphasise only the fact that display existed without considering the kind of sales process used.

The fact that selling in department stores was based on deferential service and advice is important to bear in mind. The level of the market at which nineteenth-century department stores targeted themselves varied depending on their location, but they drew in the main on the lower middle and upper middle classes. As commentators observed the phenomenon of increasing consumption, the term 'democratic' was often applied to department stores during the nineteenth century, but the term is not accurate in characterising department store strategies or their actual use.[26] The design of shop fronts and entrance halls, the use of

Plate 2.5 The silk and robe department, Harrods, diamond jubilee publication, 1909. (Harrods Ltd, Company Archive)

doormen and floor walkers, the price and quality of stock were all powerful non-verbal messages which worked to limit the customers who crossed the threshold to the department store's chosen market. This market was considerably broader than those of smaller shops but certainly did not encompass all classes. Cultural theorists have been reluctant to reject the concept of democratisation which fits neatly with the concept of the arrival of 'mass' consumption in an industrial age. Michael Miller has recognised that this term is superficial and misleading, but is unwilling to abandon the concept, concluding that, although it was only the bourgeoisie who went in, the Bon Marché 'opened its doors to everyone'.[27]

These points are not meant to suggest that change had not taken place between the eighteenth and nineteenth centuries but are used to emphasise themes of continuity which stress changing processes rather than revolutionary breaks. The other area of continuity between the eighteenth and nineteenth centuries is in methods of manufacturing. Central to historians' interpretations of the novelty of the department store and association with the advent of 'mass' consumption is its much proclaimed link to mass production, where the scale of department store sales is tied to revolutionary industrial change.[28] The large body of recent work on industrialization in the eighteenth and nineteenth centuries now shows that mechanisation affected the production of consumer goods only slowly, having gradual effect especially after 1850.[29] Many department stores retailed products that were not produced by machine, and instead were made in small batches using subcontracting systems. Large shops and department stores from the 1830s through to the 1860s were already selling a broad range of goods under one roof before mechanised production had any significant effect on their stock. Non-mechanised manufacturing systems (subcontracting and putting out as well as small plants) used in the eighteenth and first half of the nineteenth century were highly successful at meeting increasing demand and rapid fashion change.[30] Mechanised production and the emergence of the department store as a 'machine for selling' cannot be tenably linked.

'Obligation to buy' and shopping as a social activity

It is claimed that customers entering eighteenth- and early nineteenth-century shops were under an obligation to buy and could not browse at will. Miller has stated that 'the idea of "shopping" was, for all practical purposes, non existent, as entry into a shop entailed an obligation to make a purchase'.[31] Many eighteenth-century shops were based on service as a key sales device, encouraging customers to approach the counter in order for them to have full access to the stock and to be talked through the process of selection. This does not mean, however, that customers were obliged to buy. Retailers complained vociferously that customers would 'swim into my shop by shoals, not with the least intention to buy, but only to hear my silks rustle'.[32] Joanna Schopenhauer, observing shopping practices in London in 1803, stated that shopping meant

> going into at least twenty shops, having a thousand things shown to us which we do not wish to buy, in fact turning the whole shop upside down and, in the end, perhaps leaving without purchasing anything. It is impossible to admire sufficiently the patience of the shopkeepers, who endure this nonsense without ever dreaming of showing annoyance.[33]

Customers knew that the tradition of deferential service ultimately worked in their favour. Rouquet characterised the retailer–customer relationship in 1755 as one where 'the seller always stoops; the purchaser always assumes an imperious air'.[34] It is clear that an obligation to buy did not exist even though shop staff might place considerable pressure on customers through their sales patter.

One of the commonly held beliefs in recent literature on the department store is that shopping as a social activity did not exist before the advent of the department store. In Miller's opinion not only did 'shopping' not exist, 'nor was any attempt made to turn buying into a pleasant or convenient experience'.[35] Once attention is given to the design of shops in the eighteenth century, however, it becomes clear that shopping before the department store was not simply a matter of exchanging goods for money. The interior decoration and comfortable trappings, the display of goods and attentive service were not only seductive and detaining but made shopping a pleasurable leisure activity, and one that could be the means of defining social status. It is evident that in the eighteenth century shopping was a prominent social activity. For well-off women in particular, shopping was a regular, accepted pastime, carried out with friends, principally for entertainment. Malcolm, writing in 1808, describes middling-class ladies (as well as the aristocracy) spending their days 'shopping in Hackney or other coaches in the morning, Visits, Musick, or Reading, occupy the space from breakfast at nine, ten, and eleven, till four, five, or six o'clock ... '.[36]

Men certainly derived immense pleasure from making their purchases in the eighteenth century, but they did not go on regular shopping outings with groups of other men. Women commonly shopped in pairs, in groups, and on their own. This they did both with and without male escorts.[37] The preponderance of references to women shopping in groups throughout the eighteenth century and retailers' references to the importance of catering to the needs of female consumers may suggest that the design of high-class shops was gendered, providing furnishings that had particular appeal to female consumers.

There has been a tendency in cultural theory to equate the supposedly new selling techniques of the nineteenth century with new, passive responses on the part of consumers. Rosalind Williams in *Dream Worlds* is convinced that before the mid-nineteenth century 'goods were obtained mainly through barter and self production' and 'shopping was restricted to occasional fairs',[38] and therefore that the new display and advertising techniques of the department store were 'powerful'.[39] In her thesis the extravaganzas of display and decoration in department stores had the power to induce 'numbed hypnosis' and 'pushed' the consumer to buy, whereas previously people were not or could not be persuaded to spend.[40] Display and advertising are seen as the instruments which could manipulate an unsuspecting public into soaking up the increased output from the factories of the industrial revolution. This concept of the power of retail display has had a widespread impact, influencing work on twentieth-century consumption such as Elizabeth Wilson's *Adorned in Dreams: Fashion and Modernity*, where twentieth-century consumers are characterised as mere victims of display's manipulative power.[41] Shopping in the nineteenth century and onwards is thus constructed as primarily a passive spectator experience rather than as a process involving negotiation, assessment and skill.

However, quite clearly, visual enticement in department stores was part of a long-standing retail tradition. Shoppers in the eighteenth century had to contend with all the manipulative techniques that also faced the consumers of the nineteenth century: the lure of quantities of goods attractively displayed, the use of exotic references in displays, the seductive ambience of pleasing and dramatic interiors, the management of the flow of shoppers through the shop, and the pressure of artful sales patter. Eighteenth-century consumers cannot be regarded as simply passive victims of these manipulative ploys. Customers did not enter the shop as innocent, first-time buyers; they had previous experience of other shops, and had usually visited several in pursuit of a particular purchase in order to make comparisons of goods and service. Joanna Schopenhauer defined shopping as 'going into at least twenty shops' in an afternoon.[42] Even allowing for exaggeration this points to the comparative nature of shopping. Consumers, to varying degrees, and with varying ability during their lifetimes, learnt how to negotiate or interact with the selling process. They employed their critical faculties in making their purchase, weighing up price, style, availability, service, trustworthiness, variety, proximity of the shop and the pleasure they would gain from it. And the manipulative intent and psychological power of shop design was recognised and understood by contemporaries. Abbé Prévost said of the shopkeepers in Bath in 1734 that they were: 'Dealers in all kinds of Jewels, delicacies, and gallantries, taking advantage of a kind of enchantment which blinds everyone in these realms of enjoyment, to sell for their weight in gold trifles one is ashamed of having bought after leaving the place'.[43] Consumers of the nineteenth century must, likewise, have been as aware of, and as experienced in dealing with, these manipulations as were the consumers of the eighteenth century. A more enlightened view of the skill involved in shopping would also place the role of women consumers in a more constructive light. Shopping can be seen as active and productive rather than as passive and frivolous. Shopping was an activity which offered women autonomy, power and pleasure.

Showrooms and browsing

A linchpin in historians' claims for the newness of the department store is the issue of browsing. The nature of browsing in the eighteenth century has been misunderstood in just the same way as the notion of 'obligation to buy'. Whether browsing was encouraged in eighteenth-century shops, as in department stores, was very much a matter of the internal arrangement of the shop and the sales method that was used. Prosperous high-class shops in the eighteenth century, even though they were heavily service orientated, had begun to set aside areas where customers could browse at their leisure, handle goods that were on open display and converse with staff and other customers. Although in operation earlier, by mid-century these areas were being referred to as showrooms and had become a common feature of high-class shop design.[44]

A standard design format had developed for the showroom. The ideal showroom was on the first floor, secluded from the bustle of the street and the counter area below, in a large well-lit, and finely decorated room. If it were on the top floor of the building or built into a rear extension, a skylight could be introduced providing a dramatic effect as well as diffuse light.[45] Siting on the first floor usually provided large windows overlooking the street, direct access to the shop below and a more open space, contrasting with the narrower shop area lined with counters. Skylights were a hallmark of the well-appointed showroom and they appear in many of the showrooms illustrated in Ackermann's promotional prints of the early nineteenth century (Plate 2.6). Skylights were expensive and dramatic and brought these elements to the experience of shopping.

Plate 2.6   Promotional illustration for Morgan & Sander's, *Ackermann's Repository*, 1809. (British Library)

The showroom was a room away from the sales area, with its counters and busy shop staff, where goods were openly displayed and could be examined at the customer's leisure (Plate 2.6). Obviously the only shops that entertained this design feature were those with enough space and capital to do so. In the eighteenth century a showroom indicated an up-market shop, not only because their decoration was expensive to provide, but also because showrooms were incredibly wasteful in terms of space and selling time. Although much stock could be placed on display, plenty of room had to be allowed for customers to move around freely in attractive and expensive surroundings, or sit down if they wished, but without the customer being in direct negotiation with staff who might encourage a sale. This, however, worked in the favour of high-class shops as a mark of refinement in contrast to the pushier techniques of some of the lower-class or fast-selling shops of the period. Service was, nevertheless, available in the showroom if required. Staff were on hand to offer information or advice and proprietors would offer to guide customers through the showrooms of a shop.[46] In the showroom, instead of the intense sales patter of pushier shops, polite conversation, perhaps about manufacturing methods or the antique style, ensued. The art of retailing here was to make salesmanship sound like a discussion of taste.

While small shops possessed little space, they could choose to echo the polite approach of the high-class shops, offering customers the use of the family parlour adjacent to the shop with its sociable atmosphere. Shoplifting cases brought to the Old Bailey reveal that customers were frequently invited to sit down in the parlour to take refreshment when they were out shopping, a practice continued in the tearooms of the department store.[47]

Not only can the design motifs of eighteenth-century showrooms be seen to have a correlation with the dramatic spaces of department stores, but the concept of using space for different shopping activities – areas for browsing and areas for processing sales – can also be compared. In the department store display and browsing areas were integrated with counter selling and this might be seen as a conflation of the two methods of selling – the fast processing of payments over the counter and the leisurely perusal of goods – into the same area. Indeed architectural plans reveal this reorganisation of selling space in smaller shops during the early years of the nineteenth century.[48] The fact that these ideas filtered down to lower-class shops shows how widespread and influential were developing ideas about retail techniques, and this points to department stores' exploration and reworking of established ideas rather than their break with the past.

Large-scale and fast-selling shops

In order to understand not only pre-established retail techniques drawn upon by department stores, but also the chronological development of department stores as a retail type, it is important to consider the size and layout of the larger shops in the second half of the eighteenth century. Most shops in London's prime shopping streets were the size of only a few rooms at the beginning of the century, but by the second half of the century they covered several floors of the building. Usually hemmed in on either side by other businesses, they expanded backwards and upwards.[49] Even very successful multi-storied shops remained, in the main, long and thin because of the problems of buying out adjacent shops.

In the nineteenth century clearing banks, unavailable in the eighteenth century, helped with the problem of financing expansion, as did increased business from progressively larger premises. Nevertheless it is still notable that most nineteenth-century department stores grew by the slow, piecemeal addition of surrounding buildings rather than being purpose built. While incorporating these *ad hoc* additions, these stores underwent considerable restructuring to present uniform fronts and coherent internal spaces. The advantages of iron frame (later steel frame) building techniques available after 1850 allowed transformations in overall size and internal spaces, and the construction of atria and sweeping staircases produced dramatic effects on a new scale.

To a great extent it is the drama of these expansive internal spaces which has lead cultural historians to interpret the department store's effect upon consumers as 'overpowering'. The impression such spaces made, however, must be considered in terms of whether this was an initial encounter for the consumer, and whether consumers were already acclimatised to the experience, especially if they were acquainted with buildings of similar architectural style such as theatres and museums.

As a strategy, however, the technique of enticement through design and display was explored particularly imaginatively and capital intensively in the case of the department store, whereas most high-class shops of the eighteenth century emulated, but struggled to meet, the architectural extravagances of assembly halls and top class domestic architecture. They did not possess the same symbolic importance in the city as department stores, although by the late eighteenth century certain shops had gained reputations as tourist attractions. The iconic status of the department store within the urban milieu must have had an affect on the way consumption was seen and thought about. In both periods consumption was criticised and moralised, and in both periods consumers engaged with consumption as a form of pleasure, practical function and self-definition. However, in the nineteenth century shops sought to celebrate and include urban life, whereas eighteenth-century shops sought to exclude the street in a conscious attempt to signal refinement.

Despite financial and physical constraints on expansion in the eighteenth century, this does not mean that the desire to expand did not exist, nor that the imagination for large-scale internal planning was not present. We have evidence of a few shops achieving massive proportions in the late eighteenth century, dwarfing the main body of retail outlets as did department stores. These shops managed to operate on an enormous scale by renting pre-existing single structures of the right size.

Importantly, the buildings chosen were usually aristocratic mansions. Wedgwood began renting the seventeenth-century mansion of the Portland family, Portland House, in 1774 for £120 per annum. This was a massive sum for the period, but Wedgwood had been prepared to pay as much as £400 per annum for a suitable location. Wedgwood had secured not only the grandest and largest house in the street, four storeys high and with a huge frontage 54 feet long, with space for numerous showrooms, but also a house which provided all the right social connotations to promote his wares and draw in socially elevated customers. The house had already had its reputation established as a fashionable social and leisure venue. It had been used regularly for assemblies, masques and concerts, and had been refurbished in the 1760s especially for these events. Several of the rooms were to be used as showrooms, but Wedgwood was particularly attracted by the 'Great Room' on the first floor which ran the full width of the house with its seven windows, and he immediately planned to add a gallery to it, in the style of the most up-to-date Parisian shops. Ninety classical pillars lined the Gallery and one hundred and three the room below. A grand staircase, flanked with four large pedestals for urns, led up to the Great Room.[50]

In the same way, the drapers Harding & Howell in 1796 took over the most distinguished private residence on Pall Mall, Schomberg House, another seventeenth-century mansion, and James Lackington, the bookseller, moved into a mansion in Finsbury Square at some point before 1790. All these shops operated on a significantly increased scale and with a sense of dramatic interior display which aligns them with the kind of structural distinctiveness that department stores possessed in the nineteenth century.

Wedgwood's and Harding & Howell's shops ostensibly displayed aristocratic pretensions and they certainly needed to establish their fashionability by attracting the social élite, but they also operated on such a large scale that the main body of their clientele was drawn from a broader social group which included the upper middling sort. In Lackington's case he drew on a very broad customer base, promoting his shop from the outset in terms of reasonable prices and large stocks without pretensions to aristocratic refinement.[51] Yet the interior design of his shop, revealed in Ackermann's promotional print of 1809, shows increased space and grand proportions deployed in an overtly dramatic manner, utilising aristocratic grand style in a highly theatrical way (Plate 2.7).

These large-scale shops of the late eighteenth century did not operate in the same social context as department stores, and their customer base cannot be compared directly with those of department stores which drew predominantly on a middle-class clientele, but it is important to recognise that a process of transformation in the market is observable at this level of retailing which looks forward to the department store. Historians of the early-modern period have traced the gradual expansion in the market for consumer goods from the late seventeenth century onwards, particularly for the middling sort for whom goods increasingly played a role in social and self-definition.[52] Throughout both the eighteenth and nineteenth centuries different types of retail outlets were adapting and marketing themselves at these expanding markets at different social levels.[53] The emergence of department stores in provincial England in the 1830s and 1840s, which has received very little attention from cultural historians, forms part of the response to this gradually expanding market. While the department stores of the 1880s catered for a different clientele to the large-scale shops of the 1780s, they were both broadening their appeal to wider sections of society. At the same time they were encouraging changing patterns of shopping, fostering participation in more experiential forms of shopping by a broader public.

The 'mansion style' shops of the late eighteenth century were responding not only to a changing social climate, but also to a changing retail climate. Exchange of retail ideas is observable throughout the century, particularly between retailers of different product types,[54] but also between shops trading at different levels of the market. In the late eighteenth century these large-scale shops seem to be absorbing retailing techniques deployed by large fast-selling shops aimed at a broadly based customer group.

Fast-selling shops in the eighteenth century retailed huge quantities of ready-finished stock at reasonable prices and in standardised quantities.[55] Significantly, these shops dealt only in cash transactions, long before the mythical period of 'modern retailing'. Profit came from the high turnover of competitively priced goods. In all probability along with cash sales went fixed prices for goods. The usual procedure of

Plate 2.7 Promotional illustration for Lackington, Allen & Co., *Ackermann's Repository*, 1809. (British Library)

haggling over prices was a time-consuming and skilled business requiring close supervision of any staff by the shopkeeper. For these fast-selling shops, needing a high turnover and a quick throughput of customers, fixed prices would have been one way of speeding up the sales process. Without the need for close supervision of staff, large numbers of shop assistants could be employed and the number of transactions increased. It seems that resources in these shops were concentrated on the fast processing of payments over the counter.[56] There seems to have been little attempt at exclusivity, with the wording of advertisements signalling bonanza shopping rather than gentility. Fast-selling shops used pushier sales patter and emphasised quantity and choice through profusive, flamboyant displays of goods, displays which would often spill over the boundaries of the shop and into the street. 'An Old Draper' in his reminiscences of the 1820s described the efforts of a Whitechapel shop geared to fast sales to draw customers in from the street: 'we made a very large and flaring show of goods upon every possible occasion, piling stacks up outside the door ... at times we even had a length of stuff let down from the top story [sic] window to the bottom so as to attract notice and attention.'[57]

Both Wedgwood's and Lackington's shops took up this method of quantity selling for fixed prices and combined it with the enticing properties of the high-class shop and showrooms. Both sold by fixed prices and cash only and used a large body of staff to process sales, again pointing to their concern with high turnover rather than aristocratic selectivity. Insistence on cash sales was unusual for a high-class shop in the late eighteenth century, but it would have mitigated against the financial risk involved in retailing on such a large scale. Certainly, to survive in retailing, both Wedgwood and Lackington needed a huge turnover of stock and a healthy cash flow, and they had plenty of evidence around them of the financial success of London's fast-selling shops. It seems that high-class retailing, when it operated on a very large scale, naturally reached the point whereby other, slicker, management systems were more appropriate than more traditional genteel retailing techniques. The use of numerous showrooms led inevitably to the use of large numbers of staff and a shift away from haggling and to the development of an intensive sales processing area with numerous counters below the showrooms of the kind seen in fast-selling shops. Because the largest high-class shops were also the most sociably fashionable, such techniques would be accepted rather than scorned.

It is this combination of broad appeal, reasonable prices, show areas and grand style design which is such a feature of nineteenth-century department stores. Potentially it was the cross-fertilization of large-scale high-class approaches to retailing with large-scale fast-selling middle market methods which paved the way for the development of the department store.

While it is not known whether Harding & Howell traded for cash only, it could easily be claimed that their shop in Pall Mall, opened in 1796, fits the criteria, in a structural sense, of an early department store. Having bought one-third of Schomberg House, the business acquired the other two-thirds and restructured the interior. The ground floor was redesigned into five departments separated by glazed mahogany partitions. Upper floors were reached by the original grand staircase and there was a refreshment room on the furnishing fabrics floor. The departments included furs and fans, haberdashery, jewellery and ornamental articles, perfumery, millinery and dress, small furniture, and foreign manufactures.[58] The promotional illustration of the interior of Harding & Howell from 1809 (Plate 2.4) reveals the combination of counter selling within a grandly designed sweep of showrooms with considerable customer space, skylights, columns and glazed screens.

Conclusion

Many of the assumptions made about the dramatic rise of the department store and its novelty in the nineteenth century need to be rethought once a clearer picture emerges of retailing in the eighteenth century. Many of the techniques credited as new to the department store can be seen to have had a long-standing history. Window-shopping, browsing, the use of seductive display and interior design to enhance the appearance of goods, and shopping as a social activity were all in operation throughout the eighteenth century. Large-scale shops of the late eighteenth century combined fixed-price cash sales with browsing, dramatic design, carefully managed customer space, counter and show areas and different levels of salesmanship, and, while operating in a different social context, these point to changing processes within retailing and within consumers' shopping patterns which look forward to the department stores of the nineteenth century.

Rather than searching for a revolutionary break with the past at some point in the nineteenth century, it is more effective to consider the subject in terms of elements of continuity and change. Continuity can be seen between the eighteenth and nineteenth centuries in the desire of retailers to market their goods and manipulate their customers. There is continuity in the ability of customers to negotiate manipulation and the sales process, approaching the task of shopping with knowledge and experience. In both periods consumers engaged in shopping as a social and leisure activity, and in both periods consumers were impressed by novel innovations but also became acclimatised to them. In the eighteenth century shops were welcoming spaces for the women whom they had already consolidated as consumers, a tradition that was to be continued and nurtured by department stores.

Change lies in the areas of scale, levels of capitalization, social context, building technology and the volume and types of goods on sale. These areas of change have their own developmental history involving retail innovation, cross-fertilization and stages in expansion or adaptation. The ways these significant changes impacted the development of the department store and retailing in general still need to be explored in depth rather than being naturalised as the marks of 'modernity'.

Notes

1. This work arises from my MA dissertation 'Shop Design and the Display of Goods in the Eighteenth Century', Royal College of Art, 1993, and work towards my PhD at the European University Institute in Florence on 'The Culture of Shopping in London, Paris and Amsterdam in the 17th and 18th Centuries'.
2. The classic text introducing these ideas is James Jefferys, *Retail Trading in Britain 1850–1950*, Cambridge: Cambridge University Press (1954).
3. The earliest date given for this change is *c.* 1815 in Alison Adburgham, *Shopping in Style*, London: Thames and Hudson (1979).
4. For example David Chaney, 'The department store as a cultural form', *Theory Culture and Society*, 1, 1983, pp. 22–31; Michael Miller, *The Bon Marché: Bourgeois Culture and the Department Store, 1869–1920*, London: Allen and Unwin (1981); Rosalind Williams, *Dream Worlds: Mass Consumption in Late Nineteenth-Century France*, Berkeley: University of California Press (1982).
5. For example Chaney has asserted 'Retail shops until the last quarter of the nineteenth century were so small and the production of goods such a personal business that the extended process of negotiating a transaction was only embarked upon if both sides felt reasonably confident that a successful outcome could be reached.' Chaney, 'Cultural form', pp. 22–31.
6. Dorothy Davis, *A History of Shopping*, London: Routledge (1966), p. 193.
7. W. Hamish Frazer, *The Coming of the Mass Market 1850–1914*, London: Macmillan (1981), p. 110.
8. Michael Winstanley, *The Shopkeeper's World 1830–1914*, Manchester: Manchester University Press (1983), p. 58.
9. For example Miller, *Bon Marché*, p. 30, 'a retail revolution' from 'small shop to department store'.
10. Lorna and Hoh-cheung Mui, *Shops and Shopkeeping in Eighteenth Century England*, Montreal: McGill-Queen's University Press (1989)
11. This is clear from the study of inventories. Surveys of shopkeepers inventories are taken from Orphans Court (OCI), Corporation of London

Record Office (CLRO) for the period 1695–1732, (Working Trades List C) and from Probate 31 (P31), Public Record Office (PRO) for the period 1742–90.

12. P31 and OCI inventories, see also George Braithwaite, PRO Chancery Masters Exhibits C105/5 Part I. Other inventories reveal the increasing elaboration of fittings throughout the century – PRO and OCI

13. P31 and OCI, see for example William Marford, draper CLRO OCI 3178.

14. OCI, with the exception of goldsmiths in this period who traded by natural light.

15. Bernard Denvir, *The Eighteenth Century: Art, Design and Society 1689–1789*, London: Longman (1988), p. 44.

16. Evidence from P31 inventories.

17. Quoted in James Pellor Malcolm, *Anecdotes of the Manners and Customs of London*, London (1808), p. 133.

18. Chaney, 'Cultural Form', p. 23, and Laermans who states 'The coming of the department stores drastically changed the character of the act of buying and selling', and that department stores developed the 'technocracy of the eye', Rudi Laermans, 'Learning to consume: early department stores and the shaping of the modern consumer culture 1860–1914', *Theory, Culture and Society*, 10, 1993, pp. 79–102, quotations on pp. 86 and 82. According to the Ewens 'shopping became a perceptual adventure', Stuart and Elisabeth Ewen, *Channels of Desire*, New York: McGraw-Hill (1982), p. 68.

19. Davis, *History of Shopping*, p. 193.

20. Sophie Von La Roche, *Sophie in London*, trans. Clare William, London: Jonathan Cape (1933), p. 83.

21. For example witness accounts in Old Bailey Proceedings (OBP).

22. Jefferys, *Retail Trading*, p. 4.

23. Roche, *Sophie in London*, p. 87

24. Joanna Schopenhauer, *A Lady Travels: Journeys in England and Scotland from the Diaries of Joanna Schopenhauer*, trans. and ed. R. Michaelis-Jena and W. Merson, London: Routledge (1988), p. 138.

25. Laermans has asserted that the freedom to browse in department stores meant they 'could no longer even rely on the sales talk that traditionally accompanied the act of selling and buying'. Laermans 'Learning to consume', p. 90.

26. The classic reference is to the novel by Émile Zola, *Au Bonheur des Dames* (1883), set in the 1880s.

27. Miller, *Bon Marché*, p. 165.

28. For example Jefferys, *Retail Trading*, Chaney, 'Cultural form', Miller, *Bon Marché*.

29. See in particular Raphael Samuel, 'Workshop of the world: steam power and hand technology in mid-Victorian Britain', *History Workshop*, 3, 1977, pp. 6–72.

30. John Styles, 'Manufacturing, consumption and design in eighteenth-century England', in J. Brewer and R. Porter (eds) *Consumption and the World of Goods in the Eighteenth Century*, London and New York: Routledge (1993), pp. 527–54.

31. Miller, *Bon Marché*, p. 24.

32. *The Plain Dealer*, quoted in Daniel Defoe, *The Complete English Tradesman*, New York: Burt Franklin (1970) p. 64.
33. Schopenhauer, *A Lady Travels*, p. 151.
34. Quoted in Denvir, *Eighteenth Century*, p. 44.
35. Miller, *Bon Marché*, p. 24.
36. Malcolm, *Anecdotes*, pp. 486–8, see also p. 133 and Schopenhauer, *A Lady Travels*, p. 105.
37. Examples in the Old Bailey Proceedings are numerous, for example see OBP Feb 1715 p. 4 and OBP Feb 1780 p. 180.
38. Williams, *Dream Worlds*, pp. 2 and 9.
39. Ibid., pp. 66–7, Miller, *Bon Marché*, ch. 1, pp. 19–47.
40. Williams, *Dream Worlds*, p. 67.
41. Elizabeth Wilson, *Adorned in Dreams: Fashion and Modernity*, London: Virago (1985).
42. Schopenhauer, *A Lady Travels*, p. 151.
43. A.F. Prévost quoted in A. Barbeau, *Life and Letters at Bath in the Eighteenth Century*, London: William Heinemann (1904), p. 80.
44. The term is first recorded in 1617, *Oxford English Dictionary*, R. Cocks, Diary, 2 Jan 1617.
45. See Whittwick's and Papworth's architectural drawings (RIBA), and descriptions in Roche, *Sophie in London*, pp. 100–102 and 111–12.
46. For example Roche, *Sophie in London*, pp. 237–9.
47. For example OBP, April 1780, pp. 267–8.
48. For example the redesign of Dabb, Rundle & Brown's shop on Fish Street Hill, Plymouth by Whittwick in the 1820s, RIBA.
49. Lease plans CLRO.
50. 1790 inventory reproduced in Una des Fontaines, 'Portland House: Wedgwood's London showrooms 1774–94', *Proceedings of the Wedgwood Society*, II, pp. 136–48.
51. James Lackington, *Memoirs of the First 45 Years*, 1795.
52. Brewer and Porter (eds), *Consumption and the World of Goods*, especially Styles, 'Manufacture, consumption and design', p. 540.
53. In the eighteenth century the most notable of these were the fast-selling shops and in the nineteenth century co-operatives, branch shops and the 'monster shops' of the 1820s.
54. Claire Walsh, 'Shop design and the display of goods in eighteenth-century London' *Journal of Design History*, 8, 1995, pp. 157–76.
55. Evidence from newspaper advertisements, Burney Collection, British Library, 1740s onwards.
56. Robert Owen, *The Life of Robert Owen Written By Himself*, London: Charles Knight (1971), p. 13 and evidence from inventories OCI.
57. Anon., *Reminiscences of an Old Draper*, London (1876), pp. 18–19.
58. Adburgham, *Shopping in Style*, p. 81.

CHAPTER THREE

Department stores as retail innovations in Germany: a historical-geographical perspective on the period 1870 to 1914

Tim Coles

The evolution of German department stores before the First World War has stimulated a great deal of academic attention.[1] Among this literature three themes have been prevalent. The physical form of a department store in terms of its architecture and interior design has been approached repeatedly, in particular with respect to the great Berlin stores.[2] The central argument of this work was that the commercial success of a department store was directly related to its form in terms of architectural style and interior design.[3] Alongside studies of the form of retail space are accounts which deal with the organisation of a department store business. Despite their very descriptive nature, these are systematic dissections of the methods used to operate the more successful stores and were designed to highlight the innovatory techniques they adopted.[4] Finally, considerable attention, in particular at the turn of this century, was devoted to the evaluation of the importance of department stores within the political economy of Germany. Interest dwelt on the interrelationship between their commercial success, their impact on small-scale forms of retail organisation, the development of a distinctive *Mittelstand* movement and the introduction of progressive department store taxation (*Warenhaussteuer*).[5]

The great fascination with the department store, especially that shown by contemporary commentators, stems from the fact that it was a new and highly innovative form of retail organisation. In its physical form, organisation, operation, level of success and impact on the retail system it was unique. As a result of the new ideas it employed, the department store developed rapidly to possess one of the pivotal positions within the German distribution system before the First World War. In spite of this status, the location of early German department stores has not been explored fully. This is a surprising omission when it is considered that the geographical position in the market is of considerable importance in determining the success of a business.[6] This shortcoming is addressed here by way of an examination of the historical geography of the emergence of this retail innovation prior to the First World War. A brief sketch of the temporal pattern of growth in the department store sector is followed by discussion of its spatial dimension with special reference to settlement preference and spatial pattern.

The origins and rise of the German department store

Georg Wertheim operated from the first German department store business in Stralsund in 1876. From this date, the growth of the department store sector in terms of the number of stores was continuous, if not uniform in rate. In fact, during the final quarter of the nineteenth century there were two discrete periods, each of which exercised a great influence on the growth of the sector. In the period from 1875 to 1885, the earliest businesses were established, including those which belonged to the most important entrepreneurs in the sector: Leonhard Tietz in 1879, Oskar Tietz in 1882, Rudolph Karstadt in 1881 and Thomas Althoff in 1885. Indeed, of the four important businesses operating before the Nazi seizure of power in 1933 only Schocken had been established outside this period in 1901.[7]

The earliest department stores were rather small-scale simple affairs and hardly the large-scale twentieth-century 'cathedrals of consumption'. Instead, most commonly they occupied a single shop and sold a combination of piece goods, linens, woollens, haberdashery and, after 1880, ready-made clothing.[8] In character they were little more than diversified Spezialgeschäfte (speciality shop retailers) but were crucially different from their shop competitors in terms of the operational principles and characteristics they adopted: the elimination of the middleman in the purchasing process, purely cash sales to consumers and a pricing system of 'low mark-up, high turnover' to generate higher volumes of sales and levels of profits – all broke with the traditional practices in the retail system.

Steady growth in store numbers occurred throughout the 1880s but was overshadowed by a period of more accelerated growth which began in 1890. This continued until the outbreak of the Great War by which time there were approximately 400 stores operating throughout Germany.[9] Much of the growth in store numbers after 1900 was due to the rise of small, tax exempt stores with annual sales of less than 400 000 Marks. In 1905 there were 22 such stores in operation in Prussia whereas by 1911 this number had almost trebled to 65. The accelerated growth in the department store sector after 1900 is also revealed by the value of store trade which continued to rise sharply. Thus, between 1905 and 1911 taxed sales in Prussia increased from 176 to 296 million Marks or by 68 per cent,[10] clearly demonstrating the growing appeal of department stores within Wilhelmine society.[11] Moreover, one of the characteristic developments associated with the growth of the department store sector before the First World War was the increasing volume of sales per store.[12] This is shown most clearly in the case of the largest, most conspicuous stores. For example, the turnover of Wertheim's Leipziger Straße store in Berlin doubled to reach 60 million Marks in the six years from 1899.[13]

The original basic 'expanded *Spezialgeschäft*' form of department store continued to appear during the 1890s. However at this time it was joined by stores which Lux describes as 'embryonic department stores', whose principal differences from their predecessors were a much larger store size and a greater range of goods on offer.[14] The larger premises which these stores occupied were derived from one of two sources: larger buildings which were directly converted for the purpose of retailing from other uses, or islands of land which had been built up from smaller parcels and which were subsequently redeveloped into large-scale retail functions. Typical of the former method was Oskar Tietz's conversion of a Munich office building to accommodate the latest Hermann Tietz store in 1890.[15] By contrast, over a period of 16 years Wertheim accumulated the necessary plots to develop the Leipziger Straße store to a total floor area of approximately 14 500 square metres in 1912.[16]

The 1890s were however a bridging point between earlier, relatively more 'primitive' stores and the most functionally complex or 'complete department stores' as termed by Lux. These stores dominated almost exclusively developments after the turn of the twentieth century.[17] They were housed in purpose-built accommodation, were of the greatest size, and stocked the widest ranges of products and goods, while offering a multitude of secondary services aimed at giving the customer the most complete shopping experience possible.[18]

Alongside the changing characteristics of internal business organisation, it is important to note that during the first decade of the twentieth century there were clear signs of fracture in the department store sector. The size of businesses and their spatial remit began to vary dramatically. Growth in the number of stores was no longer solely dominated by the establishment of new, independent, single store businesses. Instead branches of department store chains made an increasingly significant contribution to the overall number of stores, although single store outlets still constituted the majority of the total.[19] However, Hirsch recorded that in 1910 52 department store businesses operated a total of 186 stores in chain organisations.[20] The process of chain development had begun in the 1880s under the initiative of Wertheim, Oskar Tietz and Rudolph Karstadt among others, but did not take off fully until the 1890s.[21] Even within the group of 'chain-developing' department store businesses there was a clear polarisation between those which had nurtured a small chain (of one to five stores) and those which had developed more aggressively to build much larger chains (of ten to fifteen stores).[22]

Investigation into the geography of early department stores is hampered by the absence of comprehensive catalogues which detail the locations of businesses.[23] Unfortunately, therefore, fragments of information published in accounts which often deal with a completely different field of enquiry must be used as source material. This is less than satisfactory as, in general, such literature favours documentation of the larger, more successful businesses at the expense of the smaller, independent ones. Despite this shortcoming, there are two distinct spatial dimensions to the growth of early German department stores in terms of their changing settlement preferences and spatial pattern.

Settlement preference

The demographic size of the locations in which the earliest department stores were established is surprising. Instead of an initial location in the largest, most developed consumer markets to exploit growing pools of demand, many of the earliest department stores were established in settlements of an opposite nature. Of the first generation of department store businesses only Messow & Waldschmidt, with the opening of their store in Dresden in 1876, established their first store in a *Großstadt*, or urban centre with a population in excess of 100 000.[24] By contrast, very many of the early businesses established stores in relatively inconspicuous, small towns (Table 3.1). Admittedly, they experienced the effects of industrialisation but they were, nevertheless, consumer markets of restricted potential as the population of each town was low. It is remarkable that, with the exception of Hermann Tietz, each of the 'start-up' locations of businesses in Table 3.1 was also the home town of the founder.

During the 1880s isolated forays were made by the pioneers to establish stores in the larger German consumer markets. For example, Wertheim was quick to colonise the largest market in the country, Berlin, with the opening of a store in Rosenthaler Straße in 1885.[25] while Hermann Tietz founded its first store in Munich in 1889. In general, however, such stores represented an anomaly as businesses continued to concentrate on small and medium-sized towns. For example, Karstadt

Table 3.1   The settlement characteristics of the towns in which the five pioneers of the German department store established

Organisation(s)	Town	Population*	Characteristics
Wertheim and Leonhard Tietz	Stralsund	29 492	Harbour and diversified manufacturing centre
Karstadt	Wismar	15 260	Trade centre, especially for grain. Growing industry based on shipbuilding, machinery, chemicals and textile stuffs
Hermann Tietz	Gera	27 118	Reuß principality residence. Trade and production centre ('Klein-Leipzig'). Woolwares, musical instruments, tobacco wares and machinery manufactured
Thomas Althoff	Dülmen	4 304	Relatively inconspicuous crossing-point of railway lines with beer breweries, machine and linen factories, dye and iron works

*   Population in 1880

Source: Adapted from S. Gerlach, *Das Warenhaus in Deutschland. Seine Entwicklung bis zum ersten Weltkrieg in historisch-geographischer Sicht*, Stuttgart: Franz Steiner Verlag Wiesbaden GmbH (1988), p. 42.

opened stores in Lübeck (1884) and Neumünster (1888) during the 1880s, neither of which had a population in excess of 50 000 people.[26] The location of department stores in small and medium-sized towns was a characteristic which lasted until the end of the century: of 51 towns in which at least one department store was recorded as operational in 1899, 27 had fewer than 50 000 residents, 13 had a population of 50 000 to 100 000 and only 11 had more than 100 000 people.[27] Thus, over half of all towns in which department stores functioned were situated towards the base of the urban hierarchy while only 21 per cent were to be found in the *Großstädte*, which experienced the full impact of the dual processes of industrialisation and urbanisation. Some of the larger organisations, among which Karstadt and Althoff are the clearest examples, followed strict programmes which involved the establishment of stores in smaller towns, rather than the *Großstädte*. Until the outbreak of the First World War, Karstadt was engaged in the colonisation of the smaller and medium-sized towns of northern Hannover, Mecklenburg-Schwerin, Mecklenburg-Strelitz, Pommerania and Schleswig-Holstein, no territory among which is recognised by Tipton as having a particularly strong economy.[28] During the 1890s Karstadt opened stores in the relatively small, obscure towns of Heide (1893), Mölln (1895), Preetz (1893) and Eutin (1896).[29]

Despite the persisting predilection for relatively smaller urban centres the first signs of change in locational emphasis occurred during the 1890s. An increasing number of businesses began to make concerted efforts to open stores in *Großstädte* as well as in those urban areas experiencing explosive rates of demographic growth. In this decade Hermann Tietz completed its coverage of the three largest cities in Germany by opening a store in Hamburg during 1897, and a store in Berlin was commissioned which finally opened in 1900.[30] Leonhard Tietz also had similar interest in developing within large consumer markets. In 1890 he moved the head office of his business to Elberfeld and opened further stores in the Rhineland region in Cologne (1891, 1895), Remscheid (1891), Aachen, Mainz, Düren and Düsseldorf (all 1892).[31] Thomas Althoff undertook a similar operation in the north of the Rhine-Ruhr region and Münsterland, opening stores at Recklinghausen (1893), Essen (1894), Münster (1896) and Duisburg (1899).[32] Each was quite a perceptive move on two counts: firstly, to exploit the rapid development of consumer markets as a result of accelerated industrialisation and demographic growth; and secondly, to obtain a secure foothold in the market before competitors had a chance to establish themselves.

The process of opening stores in large cities flourished before the outbreak of war. Karstadt opened new stores in Hamburg, while Althoff located in Dortmund and Leipzig and Leonhard Tietz opened a new store in rapidly emerging Düsseldorf. The degree to which there had been a change in the locational preference of department stores is remarkable when compared to the previous decade: of 81 towns with over 50 000 residents and in which a department store was operating in 1909, only 40 had a population of between 50 000 to 100 000. Instead, the majority of towns in which department stores operated were now *Großstädte* and 19 even had a population in excess of 200 000. Thus, the number of department stores in *Großstädte* had quadrupled while the largest settlements in the urban hierarchy (with over 200 000 residents) had become heavily favoured locations.[33]

The rise in popularity of the *Großstadt* was primarily a result of a change in settlement preference of businesses. However, to some extent it was also a function of demography and statistical definition. Many of the towns in which department stores were located were of a relatively small size at the beginning of the 1890s. Around the turn of the century they experienced dramatic demographic explosions and found themselves catapulted into the *Großstadt* classification. For example, Gelsenkirchen which was home to the stores of Gebr. Sinn & Co and Alsberg experienced just such an explosion[34] when between 1871 and 1910 its population increased tenfold.[35] It increased from 36 935 in 1900 to 169 530 in 1910 and thereby achieved *Großstadt* status in under a decade.[36]

The new trend of store establishment in larger urban centres reflects the fact that such locations were better equipped to support department stores. It was not just an issue of the higher raw demand in large cities, but also increased consumer dependency and inflated per capita demand. This is confirmed by Prigge's data which reveals a proportional relationship between settlement population and the amount spent per store.[37] However, explanation of the locational preferences of the department store is not restricted exclusively to market characteristics or, more particularly, to the location of demand. Instead, a combination of store-related factors, such as general operating characteristics, together with the individual conditions affecting entrepreneurs (often idiosyncratic in nature), were of far greater importance in determining the changing locational trends of early department stores. For instance, the introduction of innovatory methods by the department stores did not receive immediate acclaim. Working-class patronage was not immediately forthcoming because department stores strictly applied the principle that all transactions be settled immediately in cash at admittedly lower resale prices. During the third quarter of the nineteenth century it was common practice for consumers of all classes to pay by credit in the so-called *Borgwirtschaftsystem*.[38] Many consumers from the petite bourgeoisie and working class did not have the necessary disposable income to be able to shop in the early department stores. In addition, considerable reticence and hostility was shown to the department store by consumers from the aristocracy and the *Bildungsbürgertum*.[39] Some members of the educated, upper middle class of Wilhelmine Germany were ashamed to be caught shopping in department stores. Anecdotal evidence of the Hermann Tietz store in Munich reveals how many well-to-do ladies from families of high social standing told assistants that they were shopping there 'on behalf of the servants' and insisted that all purchases were packed in ordinary, anonymous, brown paper bags rather than those bearing the company motif.[40]

Indeed, the rejection of the department store as a retail organisation by many prosperous consumers from the aristocracy and bourgeoisie continued well after the turn of the century. This rejection reflected much wider social and cultural tensions within Wilhelmine urban society between two groups: on the one hand there was the *Bildungsbürgertum* (the educated, prosperous, upper middle classes) for whom luxury was a symbol of their position in society and good taste was acquired through education, personal development and hard work; and on the other, the new urban middle classes among which were *Angestellten* (white-collar workers), the *nouveau riche* and, to some extent, the petite bourgeoisie, for whom consumption and luxury were a symbol of aspiration as well as social and economic achievement.[41] This group had bourgeois aspirations and money, or more correctly disposable income, which offered them the means of achieving their ambition. This philosophy proved distasteful to the established upper middle classes of urban society who were fearful of the march towards modernity and the erosion of high culture that this entailed. They were particularly anxious about the rise of mass-produced goods, their perceived poorer quality and the willingness of the new urban middle classes to acquire them. Moreover, for this second group, the quality of an item did not appear as important as the very act of consumption which almost served to confirm their new-found social status.

Department stores represented an interface between the philosophies of the two groups which proved difficult to reconcile. Indeed, department stores encouraged social mixing as a means of improving the performance of a business. Conscious efforts were made to market stores in such a way as to cater for all types of demand.[42] In the case of the more prosperous consumers this was achieved through the development of a complete shopping experience which integrated the highest quality products, shopping environment and peripheral service functions, and which emphasised shopping as a leisure activity. By contrast, department stores also encouraged and exploited mass production and distribution in order to attract customers from the lower middle and working classes. A democratisation of consumption evolved in which higher-quality goods became available to the relatively less prosperous through price reductions secured as a result of economies of scale and bulk purchasing. Furthermore, consumers could now enter a high-class shopping establishment without any intention to buy, but merely to browse. This allowed consumers of all classes access to high-quality shopping experiences which had once been the sole preserve of the more prosperous. Thus, as Stresemann records, in Berlin

> the elegant civil servants' wives from West Berlin or from Charlottenburg are to be found in the crowds, just as the wives of the artisans or workers from the North and the East, who at all times when they attend Wertheim put on their best clothes which are usually reserved for celebrations.[43]

In the case of Wertheim, class distinction was maintained by the strictures of store employee–customer etiquette.[44] Store managers issued strict guidelines as to how, when and where customers from different social classes should be addressed. However, for many of the more prosperous consumers this still proved unacceptable. Instead, as Steindamm describes for Berlin, they preferred to shop, as always, in the more serene, elegant *Spezialgeschäfte* which stocked far wider ranges of goods and lines of products which were, in addition, of much superior quality.[45] Thus, the success of the department store sector *per se* and the individual stores was to some degree a function of the extent to which social and cultural prejudice could be overcome in retail space as much as the consequences of sound business practices. In one sense, therefore, the department store played an important role in fashioning middle-class culture in Wilhelmine urban society; through consumption they encouraged the expression of the aspirations and position of the new urban middle classes; moreover, through the goods and products supplied stores initiated a shift away from traditional perceptions of taste, luxury and culture.

Department stores were not warmly received by small-scale shop-keepers, many of whom were suspicious of their potential impact on their own businesses. Moreover, they were doubtful of the new methods, some of which had not been previously tried in Germany either on their own or in combination with each other: cutting out middlemen, a system of lower mark-up, greater stockturn, exclusively cash sales and comprehensive advertisement campaigns all challenged conventional business training which emphasised a more conservative, less risky approach to retailing.[46] As a consequence, the early businesses, some of which were financed by sceptical parents who had experience of the retail trade, received only relatively limited capital with which to indulge their experiments. For example, Oskar Tietz had a capital of only 1 000 Marks to begin the Hermann Tietz group while just 1 000 Taler was made available to Rudolph, Ernst and Sophie-Charlotte Karstadt to establish their business, and this only in the form of a loan. Their father was deeply sceptical of the potential success of the business.[47]

The fact that many of the early department store entrepreneurs located their business in their home towns (or regions) strongly suggests that they were keen to capitalise upon their intimate knowledge of local market conditions and consumer habits.[48] Again this is extremely important when viewed in the context of the early difficulties and levels of competition described above. As a result of these factors, pioneering stores had great difficulty generating suitable or substantial rates of return. Thus, it was absolutely critical that entrepreneurs neither misjudged their market nor collected 'shelf warmers', both of which could have increased their costs, decreased their profitability or, ultimately, spelled their closure.

Characteristics of low capital investment, intimate knowledge of local markets and consumer resistance may help to explain why smaller-scale settlements were initially favoured. However, this does nothing to resolve the question of store development in relatively larger towns and cities in the early phase of the growth of the sector. As previously noted, in 1899 there were 24 cities in which stores were located and which had local populations in excess of 50 000, some of which had been colonised by the large chains such as Barasch, Leonhard Tietz, Hermann Tietz and Knopf. However, many department stores in large cities were the sole retail outlets of their respective businesses. In the case of the chains, there were very sound reasons for opening branches in large cities, among which were the larger, heterogeneous, more fluid markets. Precisely such a reason prompted Wertheim to move to Berlin in 1885 and Tietz to Munich in 1889. Unfortunately, in the absence of more detailed archival material for the smaller independent businesses, it is not possible to comment more definitely on the decision-making process behind store location. It is true that many entrepreneurs such as Messow & Waldschmidt in Dresden, Barasch in Breslau, and Knopf in Stuttgart considered the use of department store principles in large towns as an ideal method through which substantial sales and profits could be generated. However, this, in turn, raises the question of why more businesses did not establish in the larger, more diversified, *Großstadt* markets at an earlier date. This may relate to the innovatory nature of the department store and the overall economic climate in which the first stores were established. Many early department stores were vulnerable to consumer mistrust. In large urban environments this vulnerability was exposed to intense competition not just from a multitude of better positioned, well-patronised *Spezialgeschäfte* but also the more specialised, long-established, large-scale organisations such as *Kaufhäuser* (large-scale specialty stores). If Berlin is taken as an example, any department store locating there in 1880 would have faced competition from 56 shops selling cotton wares, 158 ladies wardrobe, 346 men's wardrobe, 96 children's clothing, 290 linen, 257 manufactured and fashionable clothing, 179 hosiery and 198 selling cloth.[49] In addition there were at least four large *Kaufhäuser* with good reputations: Jordan founded in 1839, Gerson in 1839, Hertzog in 1839 and Israel in 1843.[50]

Such competition would have made it extremely difficult for fledgling department stores to gain a secure foothold in a larger urban market. It also suggests, as work on American stores has emphasised, that the growth of the store was a direct function of the commercial ability of the entrepreneur.[51] Only the better financed, well-managed, more experienced and ambitiously inclined department store entrepreneurs could have functioned effectively to secure a foothold in this type of market. Indeed, Wertheim's move to Berlin is an important example of this. Wertheim opened its first store in the city's Rosenthaler Straße in 1885. This was a very favourable location on the periphery of the Central Business District and also had access to consumers of the petite bourgeoisie and working classes in the adjacent suburbs of Spandauer Viertel, Königsviertel, Oranienburger Vorstadt and Rosenthaler Vorstadt. The next Wertheim store was opened in Louisenstadt (Kreuzberg), Berlin's largest district, and very close to Moritzplatz, a principal node in the public transport system and near to the well-known Lubasch Bazaar. This resulted in a bitter struggle between the two stores in which Wertheim eventually prevailed.[52] The financial strength derived from the success of the Rosenthaler Straße store ultimately proved to be the foundation stone for the establishment of subsequent stores in Oranienstraße and in Leipziger Straße.

The implication of this argument is that there were simply too few businessmen in the early phase of department store growth who were capable of operating in the large-market environment. However, one should also recognise that capital investment, the requirement for which was often substantial in large-scale markets, was required alongside entrepreneurial ability to launch a store business. Early stores which were operated on the largely untested assemblage of department store principles were considered risky ventures by financiers, contemporary economic commentators and their owners. For example, Karstadt was formed by Rudolph Karstadt with his brother, Ernst, and sister, Sophie-Charlotte. After the first year, Ernst and Sophie-Charlotte were worried that the business was badly underperforming and they would never be able to repay their father's large loan. Rudolph bought them out and in the second year carried forward a modest 20 000 Marks. Karstadt had to wait a further two years before he had the necessary financial strength to launch his first branch in Lübeck.[53]

The prevailing economic climate at the time of the establishment of the early stores further compounded the air of scepticism. The earliest stores were opened during the Great Depression which began in 1873. Many banks had suffered badly during the crash of 1873 and its aftermath through misguided decisions. In the period which preceded the crash, banks had too readily invested in speculative ventures, many of which were badly planned and managed, overreliant upon invested capital, and which collapsed during the financial crisis.[54] As a consequence of the crash, banks were extremely reticent to invest in early department stores. After all, these were speculative business ventures with a not insignificant risk of failure and limited earning potential for the banks. In this sense department stores were untested retail organisations in highly competitive urban retail systems, and the generation of high turnover in the early years of the business was debatable given consumer ambivalence to cash sales. Furthermore, investment portfolio calculations undertaken by Tilly indicate that high rates of return were not be found in trade for the period 1883 to 1913.[55] Restrictions on the availability of capital did not continue indefinitely until the First World War. Around the turn of the century banks were increasingly prepared to invest large amounts in department store businesses, in particular those already well financed and operating ambitious expansion policies with demonstrably high profit levels. For example, by the third phase of its expansion in 1906 the Wertheim store on Leipziger Straße had mortgage liabilities of 12 million Marks at a rate of between 3.4 per cent and 4.1 per cent, while in 1910 the Kaiser Bazar in Berlin had liabilities of 4.7 million Marks at 4.75 per cent.[56] This emphasises Tilly's thesis: namely, that banking assistance during the industrialisation period was aimed at those businesses already in a sound financial position.

Ultimately, the exact location of an early department store was a result of decision-making processes made by their owners in which businesses factors were not always the most important consideration, but rather personal circumstances. Thus, Wismar was chosen as the starting-point of the Karstadt empire, although it lay 31 km from the family's home town of Schwerin. Rudolph Karstadt could not establish his business in Schwerin as it would have represented direct competition to that of his father, who was not in any case warmly sympathetic to the revolutionary methods employed by his son.[57] More extreme conditions underpinned Oskar Tietz's decision to establish the Hermann Tietz business in Gera in 1882 instead of Stralsund and Prenzlau, which were towns in which his immediate unsympathetic family and uncles lived respectively. Tietz discovered a cheap method of making lace which formed the basis of his business. Gera was chosen because as a weaving town there was the necessary quantity of cheap woollen seconds required for the process. Moreover, it was close to Plauen im Vogtland where Tietz had found an artisan prepared to undertake the process.[58]

The spatial pattern of department store location in Germany before 1914

The dispersed pattern of the earliest department store businesses is clear, and this persisted until the outbreak of the First World War. Stores were widely distributed from Aachen in the west to Königsberg in the east, and

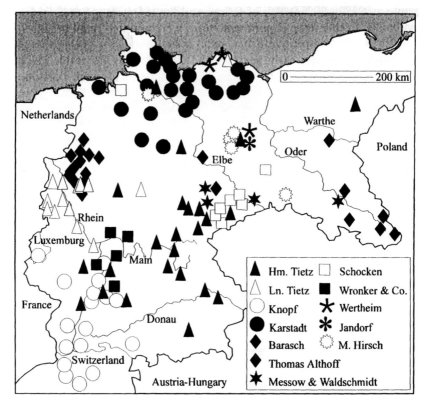

Figure 3.1 The location of stores of the major German department store chains in 1914

Source: Adapted from S. Gerlach, *Das Warenhaus in Deutschland. Seine Entwicklung bis zum ersten Weltkrieg in historich-geographischer Sicht*, Stuttgart: Franz Steiner Verlag Wiesbaden GmbH (1988); J. Wenicke, *Das Waren- und Kaufhaus*, Leipzig: Gloeckner (1913); Karstadt A-G, Essen (ed.), *Karstadt Magazin, Jubiläumsaugabe, 1881–1981*, 2/81 (1981); K. Fuchs. 'Zur Geschichte des Warenhaus-Konzerns', *Zeitschrift für Unternehmensgeschichte*, 33(4), 1988.

from Hamburg in the north to Munich in the south.[59] Figure 3.1 confirms the general characteristic of dispersion but indicates that there were distinct concentrations of stores within this pattern. However, by the turn of the century, stores had begun to gravitate towards the more industrialised, economically advanced areas of the country such as the Rhine Valley, Ruhrgebiet, Saxony, Silesia and Berlin.

The development of extensive independent department store chains appears to underpin this distribution. There were two elements to the process of chain growth: its timing and spatial pattern. Business expansion through branch openings began in the middle to late 1880s but proceeded at a much faster rate in the 1890s. By 1900 many businesses had created quite extensive networks by two contrasting methods. The first involved the development of a department store chain which was concentrated either exclusively or predominantly upon a single urban area but was still able to become a large business (*Großbetrieb*) inspite of a restricted spatial focus.[60]

This type of chain was present in Berlin before 1914. The firm A. Jandorf & Cie. opened its first store at the corner of Spittelmarkt and Leipziger Straße during 1892. During the next 15 years Jandorf pursued an active policy of branch establishment but solely within Berlin. Six further stores were established in total culminating in the Kaufhaus des Westens which opened in 1907. Similarly, Wertheim came to concentrate almost exclusively upon trade in Berlin. Wertheim opened its first store in Stralsund in 1876, quickly followed by a second branch in Stralsund (1880) and one in Rostock (1884).[61] The greatest impetus to the growth of their business came when the four Wertheim brothers moved to Berlin, where they opened their first store in 1885. Thereafter followed the establishment of four further department stores in the city including the company's flag-ship, the largest department store in Germany, on Leipziger Straße which was responsible for approximately a third of department sales in Prussia in 1905.[62]

Nevertheless, only relatively few businesses chose to take this path towards network expansion.[63] Instead, and of greater importance to the development of a wide distribution of department stores, more businesses chose to develop a decentralised network of stores extended over a wide spatial area. First evident in the mid-1880s and continuing until the First World War, intra-regional network expansion policies were most keenly pursued by firms during the 1890s.[64] In general, store networks were cultivated which concentrated upon the region in which the earliest store of the chain was opened (Figure 3.1). In the 1880s and, more importantly the 1890s, department store owners were most interested in developing strong intra-regional chains of stores in order to capture regional sales and create *de facto* local sales monopolies. A consequence of the development of such networks, as well as the foundation of new, independent, often smaller department store businesses, was to confirm the continued predilection for smaller and medium-sized towns as the location of department stores during the 1890s and 1900s.

Major chains were nurtured firstly by businesses within a single part of the country and markets elsewhere in the country were initially left to other businesses to exploit. As a result of this, particular firms became associated with distinct parts of Germany (Table 3.2). It is important to note that regional networks were more frequent by this stage than is suggested by Table 3.2. Moreover, overlap amongst chains certainly

Table 3.2   The regional specialisation of large department store chains in Germany before 1914

Organisation	Spatial Preference
Gebr. Barasch	South-Eastern Germany (Silesia)
Fried. & Alsberg.	Ruhrgebiet and Münsterland
Karstadt	Northern Germany, particularly Schleswig-Holstein
Geschwister Knopf	South-western Germany, Alsace, Luxemburg and Switzerland
Messow & Waldschmidt	'Mitteldeutschland' (especially Leipzig, Dresden and Breslau)
Schocken Söhne	South-eastern Germany (Saxony and Niederlausitz)
Gebr. Sinn & Co.	Ruhrgebiet
Hermann Tietz	'Mitteldeutschland' initially, later southern Germany
Leonhard Tietz	The Rhineland (Rhineprovinz and Rhinehessen)
Theodor Althoff	Münsterland and Ruhrgebiet
Wertheim	North-eastern Germany and Berlin
Wronker & Co.	Central Germany (Rhine and Main confluence)

Source: Adapted from S. Gerlach, *Das Warenhaus in Deutschland. Seine Entwicklung bis zum ersten Weltkrieg in historisch-geographischer Sicht*, Stuttgart: Franz Steiner Verlag Wiesbaden GmbH (1988); J. Wernicke, *Das Waren- und Kaufhaus*, Leipzig: Gloeckner (1913); Karstadt A-G, Essen (ed.), *Karstadt Magazin. Jubiläumsausgabe, 1881–1981*, 2/81 (1981); K. Fuchs, 'Zur Geschichte des Warenhaus-Konzerns', *Zeitschrift für Unternehmensgeschichte*, 33 (4), 1988.

existed and the degree of overlap increased proportionally as the process of network expansion continued into the twentieth century. The location of department stores in the Rhine-Ruhr region at the outbreak of war indicates quite intensive competition as four regional chains overlapped (Table 3.3). Further comment on either of these issues is however restricted by the shortcomings of the data source. Many more firms than those actually listed may have pursued this type of expansion policy but their business activities are not systematically documented. It seems reasonable to argue that regional network development and levels of overlap were greater than displayed here.

After 1900 a new, more conspicuous dimension to department store chain expansion was in evidence, although this may be detected as early as the middle to late 1890s. Established, ambitious, large-scale businesses attempted to penetrate consumer markets not just in their home regions but countrywide. Instead of the adoption of an expansion policy which was solely intra-regional in context, well positioned firms also

Table 3.3   The location of branches of department store chains in the Rhine-Ruhr region of Germany prior to the outbreak of the First World War

Location	Business(es) present
Aachen	Leonhard Tietz A-G, Kaufhaus 'Hammonia' GmbH
Barmen	Leonhard Tietz A-G
Bonn	Leonhard Tietz A-G
Cologne	Leonhard Tietz A-G, Gebr. Alsberg, Gebr. Sinn & Co.
Dortmund	Thomas Althoff, Meyer & Günther
Duiburg	Thomas Althoff
Düren	Leonhard Tietz A-G
Düsseldorf	Leonhard Tietz A-G, Gebr. Hartoch
Elberfeld	Leonhard Tietz A-G, Gebr. Alsberg
Eschweiler	Leonhard Tietz A-G
Essen	Gebr. Sinn & Co., Thomas Althoff, Kander GmbH
Gelsenkirchen	Gebr. Alsberg, Gebr. Sinn & Co.
Gladbeck	Thomas Althoff
Hagen	Gebr. Sinn & Co.
Krefeld	Leonhard Tietz A-G, Gebr. Sinn & Co.
Lüdenscheid	Gebr. Alsberg
Mönchen-Gladbach	Gebr. Abraham
Recklinghausen	Thomas Althoff
Remscheid	Leonhard Tietz A-G., Thomas Althoff
Solingen	Gebr. Alsberg

Source: Adapted from J. Wernicke, *Das Waren- und Kaufhaus*, Leipzig: Gloeckner; Karstadt A-G, Essen (ed.), *Karstadt Magazin. Jubiläumsausgabe, 1881–1981*, 2/81 (1981); S. Gerlach, *Das Warenhaus in Deutschland. Seine Entuicklung bis zum ersten Weltkrieg in historisch-geographischer Sicht*, Stuttgart: Franz Steiner Verlag Wiesbaden GmbH (1988).

pursued inter- or even multi-regional expansion policies. Local regional polices were becoming increasingly inadequate in the battle to increase sales. The most valuable local markets had been identified and tapped. For a company to continue to grow, new sources of sales had to be found. Hermann Tietz had concentrated on southern Germany since first moving into Munich in 1889. It consolidated its position by expanding into Saxony and by taking both Hamburg (1897) and Berlin

(1899/1900) by storm.[65] Thomas Althoff, whose empire was based on the north-west of Germany, broke with his tradition by opening a store in Leipzig in 1914.[66] More spectacular than each of these cases was Leonhard Tietz's forays from the Rhineland into the neighbouring countries. From 1900 he developed a network of branches in the Belgian towns of Antwerp, Mechelen, St Nicolaas, Bruges, Brussels and Liège. These were united in 1908 under the title Societé Anonyme Grands Magasins Leonhard Tietz and from 1912 Tietz also participated in the Dutch department store business of De Bijenkorf N.V. Amsterdam.[67] As a direct consequence, this accentuated the extent to which large department store chains came into regular, direct competition with one another. Competition between major players had existed in the 1890s but following the turn of the century colonisation in new, remote markets, previously the almost exclusive domain of a single, albeit competitor, firm brought large chains into more intense direct conflict.

The clusters of department stores which were strategically positioned throughout the country corresponded with regional patterns in the economic geography of Germany and location of urban centres at the time. High concentrations of department stores were certainly located in those regions which performed most strongly in the German economy. Unlike France, where economic development was centred predominantly on Paris which occupied a position of massive importance in the national economy, economic growth in Germany was far more polycentric in nature. Demand was not concentrated in Berlin in the way to be found in many other European capitals.[68] The economic development of Germany was driven by the performance of a number of discrete regional economies, each of which Tipton recognises as unique in nature.[69] The concentration of department stores reflects the location of the most successful regional economies and, within those, the largest and most successful urban economies. Highly urbanised regions with large pools of demand to be satisfied were very favourable locations for department store entrepreneurs.

However, the clusters of stores reflected the emerging structure of the urban hierarchy not just through a reaction to demand but also to the services that were available in urban centres, especially larger ones.[70] Department stores had to create considerable linkages with local ancillary services in order to be able to operate effectively in urban retail systems. The headquarters of German department store chains were located in the major regional centres and at nodal points within the national transportation system. This allowed a business the greatest access to the functions so important to its commercial success: large-scale wholesalers, communications, transport links, warehousing, local producers, legal and financial services, and the regional press for advertisement purposes. Figure 3.1 reveals that many branches of chains were located in large urban environments which surrounded the major regional centres in which their headquarters were present. This allowed greater economies of scale to be achieved in an organisation through closer co-ordination of central purchasing and advertising, legal and financial transactions, warehousing and the minimisation of distribution costs.[71]

The popularity and persistence of the intra-regional scale of chain expansion can also been viewed as part of a cautious approach to the development of business, both in the short and longer term, which many department store owners adopted. At an early stage, many businesses faced difficulties in the development of a strong backbone to their trade, and the opening of branches was necessary for a business to grow because in many cases the sales potential of the start-up location was soon reached. By concentrating on the development of a chain within a single region, often the home region, a department store owner aimed to use intimate knowledge of the local markets to maximise the growth potential of his business. Early in the development of an intra-regional chain owners looked to open a branch only in a settlement with a similar demographic, economic and social profile to the original start-up location. Owners saw considerable advantages to the subsequent development of their business in towns which mirrored the start-up location in terms of the size of the market as well as the quality and value of demand. This allowed the expanding business to operate more efficiently as demand could be judged more accurately, the correct goods and products could be purchased at the more competitive rates which were offered to greater bulk purchases, and superfluous stock could be minimised. Furthermore, the concentration on a single region in the formative years of a business meant that potentially harmful competition with other large chains could be avoided, and strong local monopolies could be achieved which would form the basis of expansion on a wider spatial scale. This helps to explain why Karstadt and Althoff chose to develop their businesses in small and medium-sized towns situated in the economic backwaters of Schleswig-Holstein and the Münsterland respectively.

Intimate knowledge of, and strategic location within, the markets of key urban centres was also used as a safeguard to guarantee the continued growth of a department store business. The size and value of urban markets certainly did vary within a region, often sharply so in terms of fashion trends, taste and per capita spending. As the process of business growth continued in the medium term, owners gradually shifted the emphasis in the selection of towns for new stores away from those with a very similar profile to the start-up location. Instead, urban centres were increasingly chosen which had different functional characteristics and where there were, in turn, subtle differences in the characteristics of indigenous demand. A shortcoming of the early concentration on towns with similar profiles was that these businesses were very sensitive to the variations in consumption and the value of demand engendered by the performance of the local economy. For this reason the Leonhard Tietz department store business, whose central aim was to capitalise on the large pools of demand to be found in the industrialising Rhineland region, carefully selected locations for its branches to minimise the damaging effect of local economic fluctuations: thus, Mainz, Coblenz and Düren were chosen to take advantage of the demand of a large agricultural population within their hinterlands, while Aachen, Krefeld and Barmen were selected to exploit the demand of strong textiles towns, with Cologne and Düsseldorf offering great sales potential through the large number of people engaged in the wholesale trade, transport and the free professions.[72]

In fact, a method which combined risk reduction and greater profit generation provides the link between the earlier intra-regional and later inter-regional network expansion policies. Increased store location in large cities, greater overlap with other business networks in the same region and the creation of inter- or multi-regional networks during the 1900s all represent logical steps forward from earlier more conservative network management schemes. For an established business to grow it had to continue to generate ever greater sales and hindrances to growth had to be overcome. No published evidence exists to suggest that the establishment of inter-regional chains was a result of a decline in the share of sales which a business enjoyed within a regional market. Rather, chain expansion was part of a profit maximisation process in which ever increasing sales and greater profit levels were continually strived for. No longer were the small, medium or, in some cases, large-scale urban centres in the base region capable of supporting the ambition or growth of a business. Increasingly, larger markets with greater sales potential and raw demand were targeted in regions which were often remote as well as highly urbanised and economically developed. These markets had to have equivalent, if not more favourable, consumer profiles than those in the base region.

The process of colonising large remote regional consumer markets was an aggressive strategy and it was not without high risk. Investment in new stores was high without guarantees of success but conversely often with strong direct competition. In large cities such as Berlin, Hamburg, Frankfurt am Main, Leipzig or Munich the ability to support many stores was a function of a market with a complex social structure.[73] In these cities stores existed side by side and market segmentation resulted from a process of selective targeting. A niche in the market was identified and a store attempted to capitalise on the demand and sales potential it offered. A store then geared itself completely to the market it aimed to serve. In general, a turn of the century store was aimed at consumers of the lower middle class, although through its prices, goods and choice, it could gravitate in varying degrees towards two poles: working-class demand or patronage from the well-off, most exclusive circles. An identifiable system of market segmentation existed in Berlin among the department stores on the important Leipziger Staße.[74] A complete and precise assemblage of store attributes both determined the exact customer profile of a store and served to perpetuate its perceived image in the urban retail system (Table 3.4). When Tietz opened its first store in 1900 two competitors were in close attendance: Wertheim attempted to market itself as the most exclusive store in Berlin, while Jandorf aimed more towards the working classes. Tietz fashioned his business to attract customers from the 'social middle ground'.

The picture of chain expansion painted so far is one of demand-driven network expansion and business growth. It is one which describes a correlation between chain expansion and the development of urban

Table 3.4   A comparison of the department stores located on Leipziger Straße in Berlin before the First World War

Name	Wertheim	Hermann Tietz	A. Jandorf & Cie
Situation	Western End at the Leipziger Platz.	Central position at Dönhoffplatz.	Eastern end at the Spittelmarkt.
Typical custom	Persons of good standing, high society.	The comfortable middle class.	The better-off working class.
Quality of items	The best items to middle-quality wares.	Mainly medium quality, without the very best and cheap or simple goods.	Predominantly cheaper goods with some medium-quality items.
Store attributes	Façade and interior decoration the epitome of artistic taste. Show windows artistically arranged too.	Exterior presentation splendid and elegant without the beauty that above all Wertheim had. Elegant show windows.	Aesthetically not rating with either Wertheim or Tietz. Functional use of façade to display 'wares, wares, wares'. Not as elegant.

Source: P. Göhre, *Das Warenhaus*, Frankfurt am Main: Rütten and Loening (1907), pp. 90–93.

and regional economies. However, the exact location of branches was not always dictated by such clear demand-led logic or firm business acumen. Instead, personal factors often had a considerable role to play in the final choice of a location for a new department store. This is illustrated by anecdotal evidence of the deliberations of the Tietz family over their next ambitious project to follow the opening of their Hamburg store in 1897. With the great success of the Hermann Tietz store in Munich impetus towards expansion was great. Oskar Tietz, co-owner and chief executive of the company, wanted to expand the business by establishing a new store in London. Hermann Tietz, co-owner and under whose name the company traded, wanted as an American national to know nothing of this. Instead he believed that the only suitable location outside Germany was the USA – more precisely Baltimore, Pittsburgh or San Francisco. Oskar Tietz's wife did not want to leave Germany at all and protested amid tears. As a compromise Berlin, the single most important German retail market, was chosen.[75]

Conclusion

The development of the German department store from retail innovation to the most conspicuous organisational form in the retail system was rapid and accompanied by a distinctive geographical dimension. Smaller settlements were favoured as early locations, only to be replaced by larger *Großstädte* at the turn of the century, while regional store networks were more numerous than those with a national remit. The evolution of the department store had very widespread ramifications for the development of retailing in Wilhelmine Germany. Not only did it bring about a change to the culture of retailing which involved the introduction of new sales, marketing and managing techniques, it also led to a change in the culture of consumption. Department stores represented an interface between the cultures of different consumer groups in urban society. They were a very sensitive gauge of consumer behaviour and taste and often served to accentuate tensions between consumer groups. Throughout its development, the department store exploited demand available from, and geared its operation towards, those groups of consumers willing to shop in a store. When viewed separately, the importance of the attitude, mentality, cultural background and aspirations of the consumer are as important in the historical geography of the German department store as traditional demand and supply-side explanations, perhaps even more relevant. Indeed, the importance of the consumer as an agent of change in German retail history, although clearly demonstrated here, has been understated in the published literature. Instead, attention has focused especially on the rise of the *Mittelstand*, the middle-class socio-political interest group in German society, and has dwelt almost exclusively on the ability of the large-scale retailer to determine change in the retail system and the *Mittelstand's* opposition to this.[76] Although, their impact may have been considerable, the retail process, by definition, involves a final purchase by a consumer. Clearly, therefore, research into the importance of consumers as agents of retail change in Germany is still at a preliminary stage. It must represent a priority in the future so that the true legitimacy of the *Mittelstand's* interpretation of retail change, and the extent to which they should have turned their attention towards consumers, not retail organisations, can be assessed.

Notes

1. See the comprehensive bibliographies of department stores which accompany; Einzelhandelsinstitut der Universität Köln (ed.), *Bibliographie des Einzelhandels 1883–1933*, Stuttgart: C.E. Poeschel (1935); Siegfried Gerlach, *Das Warenhaus in Deutschland. Seine Entwicklung bis zum ersten Weltkrieg in historisch-geographischer Sicht*, Stuttgart: Franz Steiner Verlag Wiesbaden GmbH (1988); and Uwe Spiekermann, *Warenhaussteuer in Deutschland. Mittelstandsbewegung, Kapitalismus und Rechtsstaat im späten Kaiserreich*, Frankfurt am Main: Peter Lang (1994).
2. A. Wiener, *Das Warenhaus*, Berlin: E. Wasmuth (1911); K.K. Weber and P. Guttler, 'Die Architektur der Warenhäuser', in Architekten- und Ingenieur-Verein zu Berlin (ed.), *Berlin und seine Bauten. Teil VII. Bauten für Handel und Gewerbe. Band A. Handel*, Munich, Berlin and Düsseldorf: Ernst and Sohn (1978), pp. 29–70. Weber and Guttler's systematic review is compiled from the massive body of literature published on the Berlin stores and is an excellent bibliographical reference work on department store design.
3. Salman Schocken, 'Warenhausbauten', *Das Kaufmann und das Leben. Beiblatt für Handelswissenschaft und Handelspraxis*, bks 1 and 3, 1913/14, pp. 1–8, 33–41.
4. The most representative of this genre are, Paul Göhre, *Das Warenhaus*, Frankfurt am Main: Rütten and Loening (1907); and Leo Colze, *Berliner Warenhäuser*, reprinted in Berlin: Fannei and Walz (1989). Göhre describes the Wertheim store on Leipziger Straße while Colze concentrates on the Kaufhaus des Westens.
5. Gustav Stresemann, 'Die Warenhäuser, ihre Entstehung, Entwicklung und volkswirtschaftliche Bedeutung', *Zeitschrift für die gesammte Staatswissenschaft*, 56, 1900, pp. 696–733; P. Messow, *Die Schäden im Detailhandel und die Warenhäuser*, Dresden: no publisher (*c.* 1900); Richard Büchner 'Warenhaussteuer', in L. Elster, A. Weber and F. Wieser (eds), *Handwörterbuch der Staatswissenschaften*, Jena: Gustav Fischer (1928), vol. 8, 4th edn, pp. 888–96; Robert Gellately, *The Politics of*

Economic Despair. Shopkeepers and German Politics, 1890–1914, London: Sage (1974); Spiekermann, *Warenhaussteuer in Deutschland*.

6. This argument is emphasised in the many studies that deal with the development of the American department store. See for example, F.W. Ferry, *A History of the Department Store*, New York: Macmillan (1960); J.C. Lawrence, 'Geographical space, social space, and the realm of the department store', *Urban History Yearbook*, 19, 1992, pp. 64–83; K.C. Klaasen, 'T.C. Power & Co.', *Business History Review*, 66, 1992, pp. 671–722.

7. David Bernstein, 'Wirtschaft. II. Handel und Industrie', in S. Kaznelson (ed.), *Juden im deutschen Kulturbereich. Ein Sammelwerk*, Berlin: Jüdischer Verlag (1962), p. 187; Konrad Fuchs, 'Zur Geschichte des Warenhaus-Konzerns I. Schocken Söhne. Unter besonderer Berücksichtigung der Jahre seit 1933', *Zeitschrift für Unternehmensgeschichte*, 33(4), 1988, pp. 232–52.

8. Käthe Lux, *Studien über die Entwicklung der Warenhäuser in Deutschland*, Jena: Gustav Fischer (1910), p. 9.

9. Johannes Wernicke, *Das Waren- und Kaufhaus*, Leipzig: Gloeckner (1913), p. 28.

10. Gellately, *The Politics of Economic Despair*, p. 44.

11. Stresemann, 'Die Warenhäuser', p. 714; Robert Gellately, 'An der Schwelle der Moderne. Warenhäuser und ihre Feinde in Deutschland' in, A. Peter (ed.), *In Banne der Metropolen: Berlin und London in den zwanziger Jahren*, Göttingen and Zürich: Vandenhoeck and Ruprecht (1993), pp. 131–56, see here p. 140.

12. Lux, *Studien*, p. 21.

13. Heidrun Homburg, 'Warenhausunternehmen und ihre Gründer in Frankreich und Deutschland oder eine diskrete Elite und mancherlei Mythen', *Jahrbuch für Wirtschaftsgeschichte*, 1992, pp. 183–219, see here p. 208.

14. Lux, *Studien*, p. 10.

15. Georg Tietz, *Hermann Tietz. Geschichte einer Familie und ihrer Warenhäuser*, Stuttgart: Deutscher Verlagsanstalt (1965), p. 40.

16. Peter Stürzebecher, *Das Berliner Warenhaus. Bautypus, Element der Stadtorganisation, Raumsphäre der Warenwelt*, Berlin: Archibook-Verlag (1979), p. 188.

17. Lux, *Studien*, p. 10.

18. See the catalogues of secondary services listed in Göhre, *Das Warenhaus*, pp. 47–51 and Colze, *Berliner Warenhäuser*, pp. 22–31.

19. Lux, *Studien*, p. 15.

20. Julius Hirsch, *Die Filialbetriebe im Detailhandel*, Bonn: Marcus and Weber (1913), p. 196.

21. Gerlach, *Das Warenhaus in Deutschland*, pp. 44–6; Karstadt A-G, Essen (ed.), *Karstadt Magazin. Jubiläumsausgabe, 1881–1981*, 2/81 (1981), pp. 16–17, 20–22; Göhre, *Das Warenhaus*, p. 98.

22. Lux, *Studien*, p. 15.

23. Fairly comprehensive catalogues are presented by Göhre, *Das Warenhaus*, Hirsch, *Die Filialbetriebe*, and Wernicke, *Das Waren- und Kaufhaus*, but these are by no means inclusive of every store in operation at the date of publication. Moreover, there are some differences between the sources in terms of classifcation. Although care must be taken with their use, these

lists nevertheless provide a representative sample upon which to base an examination of the historical geography of department store location.

24. Wernicke, *Das Waren- und Kaufhaus*, p. 26.
25. Stürzebecher, *Das Berliner Warenhaus*, p. 13.
26. Karstadt, *1881–1981*, p. 13.
27. F. Huber, *Warenhaus und Kleinhandel*, Berlin: J. Guttentag (1899).
28. Frank B. Tipton, *Regional Variations in the Economic Development of Germany during the Nineteenth Century*, Middletown (CO): Wesleyan (1976).
29. Karstadt, *1881–1981*, p. 17.
30. Stürzebecher, *Das Berliner Warenhaus*, p. 32.
31. Gerlach, *Das Warenhaus in Deutschland*, pp. 39–40, 44–5.
32. Karstadt, *1881–1981*, p. 20–22.
33. Paul Prigge, 'Die Warenhaussteuer im Jahre 1909 oder 1909/10', *Statistisches Jahrbuch deutscher Städte*,18, 1912, pp. 213–23.
34. Wernicke, *Das Waren- und Kaufhaus*, p. 26.
35. Wolfgang Köllmann, 'The Process of Urbanisation in Germany at the height of the industrialisation period', *Journal of Contemporary History*, 4, 1969, pp. 59–76. For the statistics see p. 65.
36. The *Dortmunder Adreßbuch*, Dortmund: Crüwell, (1912), 47th edn, provides a useful catalogue of the *Großstädte* in Germany and the rest of the world with relevant rates of population expansion.
37. Prigge, 'Die Warenhaussteuer'.
38. Friedrich Hübner, *Zur Lage des Kleinhandels*, PhD. dissertation, Heidelberg: K. Rössler (1902).
39. Gellately, 'An der Schwelle der Moderne', p. 140.
40. Tietz, *Hermann Tietz. Geschichte einer Familie*, pp. 30–31.
41. Warren G. Breckman, 'Disciplining consumption: the debate about luxury in Wilhelmine Germany, 1890–1914', *Journal of Social History*, 24, 1991, pp. 485–505; Jennifer Jenkins, 'The Kitsch Collections and *The Spirit in the Furniture*: cultural reform and national culture in Germany', *Social History*, 21, 1996, pp. 123–41.
42. Gerlach, *Das Warenhaus in Deutschland*, p. 52 ff.
43. Stresemann, 'Die Warenhäuser', p. 714.
44. Göhre, *Das Warenhaus*, p. 43.
45. Johannes Steindamm, *Beiträge zur Warenhausfrage*, Berlin: E. Ebering (1904), p. 20.
46. Hübner, *Zur Lage des Kleinhandels*.
47. Tietz, *Hermann Tietz. Geschichte einer Familie*, p. 24; Karstadt, *1881–1981*, p. 10.
48. Gerlach, *Das Warenhaus in Deutschland*, pp. 42–3.
49. *Berliner Adreß-buch für das Jahr 1880*, 12th edn, Berlin: W. and S. Lowenthal (1880).
50. H. Schnedler, 'Kaufhäuser', in Architekten- und Ingenieur-Verein zu Berlin (ed.), *Berlin und seine Bauten. Teil VIII. Bauten für Handel und Gewerbe. Band A. Handel*, Berlin: Ernst (1978), pp. 89–128, see here p. 91.
51. Klaasen, 'T.C. Power and Co'; Lawrence, 'Geographical Space'; Laujlianen, R., 'Defense by expansion: the case of Marshall Field', *Professional Geographer*, 42, 1990, pp. 277–88.
52. Simone Ladivig-Winters, *Wertheim. Geschichte eines Warenhaus*, Berlin: beibra (1997), p. 18ff.

53. Karstadt, *1881–1981*, p. 13.
54. Richard Tilly, 'German banking, 1850–1914: development assistance for the strong', *Journal of European Economic History*, 15, 1986, pp. 113–52.
55. Ibid., pp. 132, 135.
56. Göhre, *Das Warenhaus*, p. 63; Julius Hirsch, *Das Warenhaus in Westdeutschland*, PhD. dissertation, Bonn, Naumburg an der Saale: Lippert and Co. (1909), p. 33.
57. Karstadt, *1881–1981*, pp. 8–12.
58. Werner Mosse, 'Terms of successful integration. The Tietz family, 1858–1923', *Yearbook of the Leo Baeck Institute*, 34, 1989, pp. 131–61. A description of the process is given on p. 134.
59. Wernicke, *Das Waren- und Kaufhaus*, pp. 28–30.
60. Gerlach, *Das Warenhaus in Deutschland*, p. 44.
61. Stürzebecher, *Das Berliner Warenhaus*, pp. 182–90.
62. Homburg, 'Warenhausunternehmen', p. 208.
63. Gerlach, *Das Warenhaus in Deutschland*, p. 44.
64. See the example of the Schocken business which followed an intra-regional policy from 1901 to 1914 and was probably the best known business to attempt this strategy after the turn of the century: Konrad Fuchs, 'Zur Geschichte des Warenhaus-Konzerns', p. 233.
65. Gerlach, *Das Warenhaus in Deutschland*, p. 45.
66. Karstadt, *1881–1981*, p. 23.
67. Bernstein, 'Wirtschaft', p. 189; Homburg, 'Warenhausunternehmen', pp. 211–12.
68. Homburg, 'Warenhausunternehmen', pp. 213–14.
69. Tipton, *Regional Variations*.
70. The emergence and changing spatial pattern of the urban hierarchy and urban functions in Germany during this period has been considered in detail in H.-H. Blotevogel, 'Faktorenanalytische Untersuchungen zur Wirtschaftsstruktur der deutschen Großstädte nach der Berufszählung 1907', in, W.H. Schröder (ed.), *Moderne Stadtgeschichte*, Stuttgart: Klett-Cotta (1979), pp. 74–111, and *idem* 'Kulturelle Stadtfunktionen und Urbanisierung. Interdependente Beziehungen im Rahmen der Entwicklung des deutschen Städtesystems im Industriezeitalter', in H. J. Teuteberg (ed.), *Urbanisierung im 19. und 20. Jahrhundert. Historische und Geographische Aspekte*, Köln: Böhlau (1983), pp. 143–85.
71. Julius Hirsch, *Die Filialbetriebe*, pp. 197–202.
72. Ibid., pp. 195–6 and Hirsch, *Das Warenhaus in Westdeutschland*, p. 22.
73. Gerlach, *Das Warenhaus in Deutschland*, p. 51.
74. Göhre, *Das Warenhaus*, pp. 91–3.
75. Tietz, *Hermann Tietz. Geschichte einer Familie*, p. 55.
76. Gellately, *The Politics of Economic Despair*.

CHAPTER FOUR

'Doing the shops' at Christmas: women, men and the department store in England, *c.* 1880–1914

Christopher P. Hosgood

According to one French observer the English were always 'at it'. The editor of the *Lady's Pictorial* agreed that by the early twentieth century 'it' had become a national pastime, enjoyed all the year round, and all the more significant because it attracted men and women in 'a kind of informal rendezvous that is distinctly cheering'.[1] Not all observers, and certainly not all Englishmen, were as charitable about shopping habits. We shall see that Clarence Rook, a prolific journalist who developed a misogynistic rhetoric sustained in part by attacks on what he identified as women's irrational love of 'doing the shops', shopping was representative of the adversarial relationship between men and women. Earlier, in 'What I Hate about Women', a series which appeared briefly in, of all places, the *Lady's Pictorial* in the mid-1880s, 'A Bachelor' ridiculed the pettiness of the female mind. The column was supposed to be amusing, but was really insulting and patronising to women, and it was soon dropped. None the less, it is significant that the author chose shopping as the topic of his first article:

> And now, as to shopping. Does not the very sound of the word make your mouths water, and the young blood rush into your cheeks, and make your bright eyes brighter, and I know you would like to rush upstairs and 'put on your things' and 'go shopping'! And yet, he concluded spitefully, you none of you really want anything.[2]

How can such conflicting views of shopping – as a battleground to some, as a locus of festive sociability to others – be reconciled? Rook and his kind are important because their writings illustrate the extent to which shopping had acquired an added social resonance by the late nineteenth century. This examination of the experience of shopping, most particularly in December and January, and its impact on the relationship between women and men, is a part of a larger study which is grounded on the premise that shopping was an important and vibrant component of Victorian popular and middle-class culture. For many people shopping was a means to an end; shopping became an important social signifier because it provided access to public space, and consequently shopping, and the way in which it was represented, was employed by various groups as a means of either extending or limiting public influence and authority. Of course the late nineteenth century was not the first occasion when shopping assumed a social significance. One has only to read Sala's mid-century reportage,[3] or read the literature of the Lord's Day Observance Society or the testimony of witnesses before the 1847 Select Committee on Sunday Trading (Metropolis)[4] to understand the importance of late Saturday night and early Sunday morning shopping to the cultural life of 'outcast London'. However, by the latter decades of the century the difference was that a variety of groups, recognising the importance of shopping in the consumer age, attempted to use it to their own wider political advantage. Shopping became quite literally a means of staking a claim to space and thus shops became contested cultural territory. Furthermore, by the early twentieth century there is no doubt that individuals could legitimately go out shopping without buying. Shopping was more than proof that individuals subscribed to a consumer culture, new or old, it was also at its most elemental level an excuse to get out and about. Which allows a new cultural reading of the tired joke concerning a wife's response to her husband's query: 'How are you getting on with your shopping? Wife: Oh splendidly! Let me see, we've been to fifteen shops, and I haven't bought a thing yet.'[5]

Judith Walkowitz, and more recently Erika Rappaport and Bill Lancaster, clearly demonstrate that by the 1870s and 1880s shopping in the West End had become for women both a pleasurable activity and an important method of gaining access to a public territory which, if not formerly denied them, had not always been easily accessible.[6] While not for a moment denying the significance of this work in identifying the origins of women's public liberation, it must be said that the precise mechanics through which women accumulated authority by 'doing the shops' remains unclear. Both Christopher Breward[7] and Rappaport suggest that retailers consciously created respectable, attractive environments complete with rest-rooms and restaurants, thereby making it safe for middle-class women to go shopping. Such an interpretation is compelling, but does not really suggest that women participated as active agents in their emancipation. Conversely, Rachel Bowlby reminds us that while shopping did provide a legitimate opportunity to leave the family home, it did not necessarily provide the wider liberation that may have been expected. Bowlby, heavily influenced by Freud, suggests that the creation of willing consumers also promoted women's seduction by a male dominated advertising, fashion and retailing community, so that by 'just looking' into the shop windows women were reinforcing their narcissism.[8] Thus we might conclude that women, seduced by the attractions of the shop, were deflected from more important political issues. In other words while shopping did enable women to escape the domestic sphere, it did not automatically empower them with moral authority. Indeed, it left them open to the taunt from men that they were simply parading and massaging their petty vanities. However, while there can be no doubt that the advertising and fashion industries did attempt to commodify women in the nineteenth century,[9] it should not be thought that shoppers were always pliable and gullible consumers to be manipulated at will.

It is important to remember that shopping was not a new experience for women, unique to the late nineteenth century. While the British consumer culture clearly evolved over the years, shopping had long been a part of the urban environment. As Claire Walsh has shown, eighteenth-century retailers were well versed in the art of seducing customers; they went to considerable trouble and expense, particularly by investing in lavish shop fittings, to create a comfortable shopping environment.[10] None the less the venue was transformed as retailers constructed bigger and more ornate shops. Careful planning by innovative retailers keen on promoting their shops as havens from the earthiness, squalor, or danger of the street represented a new, or at least more frequently employed, phenomenon. By the late nineteenth century such luxury was commonly extended into the less exclusive social and cultural world of the department store. The elegant, often ostentatious domestic trappings of the emerging department stores were surely a novelty to many customers; the luxury associated with the most exclusive West End shops was incorporated into the design of new high street and suburban drapers, such as Whiteley's. Indeed, the successful seduction of women customers tempted to enter the shop was in part due to the creation of an environment in which goods formed only one part of the attraction. With their palatial interiors, lush carpeting and draperies, grand staircases leading to viewing galleries, not to mention liveried (to the extent that they were neatly, respectably and uniformly dressed) staff, department stores offered those shoppers who felt any claim to middle-class gentility the opportunity to participate in a cultural experience which both confirmed (in their own minds) their social rank and reinforced their membership in the consumer culture.

This calculated attempt to attract women into a domestic environment is significant because it stands as evidence that the new shopping experience did not automatically afford women public emancipation. Certainly it allowed women an opportunity to venture into the city centre or high street, territory more commonly associated with men's public space. Such a public presence was in itself troubling to some observers. Consider Clarence Rook's remarkable topographical study of London, published as *London Side-Lights* in 1908. Underpinning his descriptions of the metropolis is a palpable tension between the London of women, which he classifies as Bayswater and the West End, and the London of men, Fleet Street and the City. He concludes that the barrier between the two worlds could ultimately be explained as 'a question of shops'.[11] Indeed, while travelling along Fleet Street he delights in the realisation that there are no butchers, no grocers, no drapers and no milliners.

> There is probably no woman living who has ever bought a frock in Fleet Street or the Strand. These streets, stretching along to the City, are the last outposts of masculinity. They were built for man, and they are man's preserve. But now and again the incursion of woman is insistent and triumphant ...[12]

Given that the City is built for men, he laments the presence of 'a curious little wedge of femininity shoved into the stronghold of man, a little curve around the [St Paul's] Cathedral, barred to vehicular traffic, a thoroughfare blocked by the wedge of women who are looking into the drapers' windows'.[13] Who can doubt that for Clarence Rook the enemy was literally and figuratively at the gates of the city!

However, women's growing public presence was potentially compromised by a new interpretative twist to the shopping agenda. By the latter decades of the century there was a real and symbolic distinction between marketing – that is, the acquisition of necessities – and shopping – that is, the accumulation of consumer goods, most particularly fashionable items for personal use. So whereas shopping in mid-century required the women to venture out into an earthy, volatile and potentially dangerous environment, it can be argued that *fin-de-siècle* shopping was actually a more sanitized activity which provided women with less contact with the public sphere. A safe urban presence was acquired or provided at the expense of some public authority. Due to a combination of forces, such as the marketing techniques of retailers attempting to develop a broader customer base amongst the growing middle class and more affluent sections of the lower middle class, as well as the availability of cheaper plate glass which enabled more attractive window advertising, women were identified, collectively and individually, as being consumed by a desire to consume. Shopping, which women had recognised in mid-century as a legitimate opportunity for public engagement, had actually been compromised as a liberating activity. It is this process that explains why women, looking to recapture the spirit of freedom represented by shopping, were so attracted to the Christmas season as an opportunity to reassert their public authority. Quite simply Christmas shopping was a way of countering the charge that shopping was indicative of the all-consuming power of female vanity. Women could, and most certainly did, legitimately claim that they were shopping exclusively for others at Christmas and as a consequence countered the charge that shopping was by definition an example of feminine indulgence.

So did this public freedom provide opportunities for a more far-reaching emancipation or did it create new means of inhibiting their economic and social position? This is a complex question because its resolution depends on successfully negotiating an interpretative distinction between the reconstruction of the shopping experience, and the identification of various representational responses to the shopping phenomenon. To confuse matters further, I have no doubt that the way in which shopping was represented in the popular press shaped not only the popular perception of shopping but also the very act of shopping itself. With these caveats in mind I would like to consider the question by examining two related issues. Firstly, the impact of this new opportunity for public engagement on women's attempt to emancipate themselves from their husband's authority. 'Doing the shops' became a highly ritualised affair which reflected important developments not only in retailing and consumer culture but also in the relationship between men and women, and particularly husband and wife. Christmas shopping in particular offered more than an opportunity for women to extend their public freedom; very cleverly they turned to their advantage their knowledge of the commodity culture. In the anonymity of the shopping crowd women also discovered a shared experience. Shopping provided many with their first opportunity to exercise public authority over their husbands. Moreover, I wish to suggest that in order fully to understand Christmas shopping we need also to examine the post-Christmas sale season; these two seasons were intimately connected. My second goal, is to explain why men were represented as occupying a subordinate and dependent social role and why women shoppers were represented, particularly at the sales, as irrational and vicious consumers seduced by the heaping counters of merchandise; women's behaviour was so uncivilized that, by implication, they were not worthy of citizenship. This chapter argues that the way in which the shopping experience was represented by the press reflects an attempt to undermine, in the age of the 'new woman' and the 'sex wars', very real gains by women. I will argue that many of the features of traditional popular culture – including inversion and excess – were invoked so that by around 1910, far from reinforcing women's public emancipation, shopping had come to symbolise a new, albeit public, separate sphere. Shopping was an activity which witnessed a tremendous struggle between men and women, both at the representational and experiential levels. My hope is to identify the mechanics of a vibrant but double-edged shopping culture which may have provided women with an opportunity to gain moral authority but also provided men with an opportunity to undermine women's emancipation. Certainly Christmas was never the same and requires us to reconsider the old adage that Christmas represents a time of goodwill between men ... and women.

The Christmas carnival

The classic mid-Victorian Christmas was profoundly private. By that I do not mean that the whole experience was acted out in the home, although a good deal of it was, but that public activity – such as attending church or carol-singing – served only to reinforce the devotion to the family. Shopping played very little part in this dramatic episode. Quite simply, beyond the excitement of the market on Christmas Eve, it is difficult to find much of an association between shopping and Christmas. However, while in the realisation Christmas remained essentially a family affair, in the anticipation it became increasingly public. The growing popularity of exchanging gifts allowed women, who assumed responsibility for a good deal of the shopping, a worthwhile dividend on their investment of time and energy. 'Doing the shops' became a central feature of Christmas celebrations in the 1880s, 1890s and early 1900s; it was perhaps the most visible sign of the secularisation and commercialisation of the mid-Victorian Christmas ideal. A clearly defined Christmas shopping season emerged late in the century; over a relatively short period it expanded from the few days it took to acquire provisions for the mid-century Christmas dinner, to a sustained and progressively dramatic six-week period by the 1890s. This reflected the newly popular concern for the purchase of Christmas gifts, novelties which could be bought well in advance of Christmas Day.

This new association of Christmas with the purchase of presents is important because it is evidence of a new consumer culture which was seeking to establish itself at this time. Historians examining the nineteenth-century Christmas in Britain and North America have been heavily influenced by social anthropologists such as Marcel Mauss; the result is that there is a considerable body of literature on the significance of the gift exchange in modern society. Giving gifts acts as a means of sustaining a social relationship as it represents giving something of oneself to others, in expectation of some sort of response in order to redress the debt relationship which has been initiated either by a present or a thank-you.[14] Thus the notion of the Christmas present as one of the central features of the nineteenth-century Christmas has helped to create our interpretation of the festive season as one characterised by the worship of the family rather than the community.[15] The process by which the gift was acquired has been largely ignored, presumably because it was assumed to have had little significance to the larger theatre of Christmas. Thus, father's role of Santa Claus is documented, whereas mother's role in acquiring the presents in the first place has been considered too commonplace to engage interest. That is a shame because it was this process, shopping, that proved so important to women in their search for the means of extending their authority not only within the family but, perhaps more importantly, within the community. When we recognise that Christmas was not just about the giving of gifts but also about the acquisition of gifts, we will understand that Christmas was not just a family affair, it comprised some important features which were distinctly public and which were controlled by women.

This extension of the shopping season to accommodate the important task of acquiring gifts was significant to women because it represented one important way by which they could reclaim a public street presence. To the extent that Christmas shopping provided women with a legitimate role as consumers, untainted by any charge of irrational, compulsive, narcissistic behaviour, it represented a victory for women. Both in action and rhetoric women's role as Christmas shoppers promoted a healthy new image of the woman shopper. She was now characterised by correspondents in the women's press as a model consumer, prepared to sacrifice her health and sanity so that the family could enjoy Christmas. Significantly, the long shopping season was justified by the need to shop frugally by scouring the stores for the best prices, at further benefit to the family. Braving the elements and the crowds, dodging traffic, queuing at the shop counter and at the cashier's wicket, enduring Christmas bazaars, were part of an experience which denied the view that shopping was necessarily narcissistic. In this sense shopping was an empowering experience for women.

Coincidentally, representations of Christmas shopping featured more regularly in the popular press by the 1890s. This popular interest in shopping is significant because it produced a stereotype of the assertive woman Christmas shopper as one who achieved public authority during the Christmas shopping season, but who was subsequently ridiculed in a vicious attack on her irrational shopping habits. In the 1870s and early 1880s, when shopping for Christmas novelties first began to gain popularity, men were still positioned at the forefront of the celebrations which marked the Christmas season. There was no assumption that novelty consumerism would allow women to win new ground. Representative of this is a wonderful illustration entitled 'Father Christmas of

To-Day' which appeared in *The Penny Illustrated Paper* in 1880. The paterfamilias is seen returning home – strong, powerful, omniscient – with presents and Christmas paraphernalia about his person. With one hand he places a new bonnet on his wife's head, with the other he displays to the family a magnificent turkey. In his city suit, accented by cape, top-hat and bushy white beard, there can be no doubting his command of the situation.[16] Such an image of Santa can be contrasted to one appearing in the *Lady's Pictorial* 15 years later in an illustration entitled 'Santa Claus Up-to-Date'. By now the image of the benevolent father arriving home has been replaced by the purposeful woman entering a carriage, followed by a male servant weighed down by presents, after a successful day at the shops.[17]

By the 1890s woman came to occupy the central role as family provider at Christmas – the force behind Santa. Significantly, men do not disappear from the process, but increasingly they are represented as subordinate to women during the Christmas shopping season. Men become beasts of burden, cruelly loaded down with their wife's purchases, and pathetic hangers-on, ready to do their wife's bidding. Men were emasculated at Christmas, stripped of their authority – publicly humiliated. In popular comics women seeking 'ideal husbands' were advised to choose one who liked to shop, that is one who would docilely follow in her path: 'You will find him very useful if managed judiciously'.[18] Quite apart from carrying parcels husbands were good for tipping porters and squabbling with cabmen. In a delightful cartoon which appeared in *Punch* in 1904, the husband, Archie, is seen struggling down the staircase of the 'Grand Bazaar' loaded down with numerous precariously balanced parcels. His wife, at the foot of the stairs, peremptorily shouts up to him: 'Make haste, Archie. Don't dawdle. We shall be frightfully late.'[19] *Punch*, which so successfully captured the spirit of this representational shopping inversion, began to depict men, and husbands most particularly, as a stock character – as 'The Submerged Sex'. In one such cartoon a husband is so loaded down with packages that he can hardly stand up, let alone see where to walk. Yet as he struggles along his wife imperiously commands: 'For goodness sake, John, put your hat on straight; here come the Hyphen-Smiths.'[20] In a comic ditty from *Tit-Bits* a similar spirit of public subordination is invoked:

> My wife's a whale for shopping,
>   and when Christmas time comes around
> She took the biggest basket and got early on the ground.
>
> I'm basket carrier in chief – she dumps the goods on me,
> Till I become at midnight's hour a walking Christmas-tree,
> A Harrod's Stores, a Pickford Van, or C.P., if you choose,
> Until I wish that someone else was walking in my shoes.[21]

The very act of carrying a parcel in public became a 'social sin' for men, a sign of weakness. 'If you must have your luggage about you, take a cab, man, take a cab!' scolded a smart man who came upon his younger brother in Bond Street carrying a parcel so small it could hang from one finger.[22] This spirit of inversion subtly insinuated itself into the most innocent representations of domestic Christmas shopping scenes, as in a lavish double page illustration which appeared in the Christmas number of The Sphere in 1907 called 'The Joys of Anticipation'. At the centre of the scene is Mother, clearly animated by a successful day at the shops, who cannot wait to show off her purchases to the governess. Unbeknownst to Mother, her two daughters are at the top of the stairs peeking over the banister attempting to catch a quick glimpse of the presents. Father is relegated to the open front door in the background where, as a peripheral figure, he supervises the arrival of a rocking horse.[23]

Christmas found men reduced to minor roles as surrogate Father Christmases; they are depicted putting toys into stockings hung over bedposts, while women look on from the doorway to see that father does not muck it up – as he does in one famous illustration in the London Illustrated News. Significantly, and there is appropriate ironic inversion in this, men are represented at their most pathetic when they venture out Christmas shopping into women's public space without a woman chaperone. At least in the homage to the existence of Father Christmas men are represented as loveable and kindly. When in the shop they are ridiculed as incompetents. Frequently they are accused of leaving their shopping too late, so there is little choice, 'with the result that they seldom buy satisfactorily'.[24] More often they prove themselves simply incapable of making the appropriate purchases. A typical seasonal story of a father's doomed attempts to master shopping appeared in the Pall Mall Gazette in 1909; on this occasion father set off with good intentions to simplify present buying by shopping scientifically, thereby illustrating the extent to which women exaggerated the trials of shopping. Foolishly he arrived at 'Sellem's' in the West End with a list of names attached to a corresponding list of presents – one shop, one list, one day of strategic shopping and the whole business was over for another year. One can imagine the women readers, privileged by their intimate knowledge of the pitfalls that lie ahead, laughing at the innocent abroad in the shop. Although intimidated by the staff he is determined to stand up to them. 'I was not going to give in without a fight. I was strengthened by the thought that after all, these people were my servants ...' Quickly beguiled by the young female shop assistant to abandon his choices in favour of alternative presents, he returns home to find himself in disgrace, no longer to doubt the authority of the fit and proper person – his wife.[25]

In another illustrated episode a young husband decides to buy his wife a Christmas present without first consulting with her. After making his purchase – a walking stick – he experiences a number of disasters on the way home. He pokes an elderly lady with the present, whereupon she humiliates him by threatening, as a crowd congregates on the street, to turn him over to the police for assault. He takes refuge in a restaurant, where he accidentally sweeps the contents of a table on to the floor with the stick when he turns to greet a friend. Finally, after arriving home he is ridiculed by his wife for buying a walking stick which is three months out of fashion. 'Was there ever anything to equal the stupidity of a man?'[26] The sheepish husband had been persuaded to make a purchase by the pretty but crafty young shop assistant who successfully sold off her old stock. This episode is important because it provides a clue to an important element in any attempt to understand the origins of women's authority at Christmas – their appreciation of the subtleties of fashion, particularly in the form of Christmas novelties.

Why were men represented as submitting to this ritual subordination at Christmas? Not surprisingly the accounts of men's contributions to the Christmas shopping ritual suggest a certain fatalism – an acceptance of the inevitability of their surrender to women's will at Christmas. This fatalism underpins a poem submitted to *Tit-Bits* by Mr J.R. Earnshaw of Cheadle, Cheshire in 1891:

> See the postman with the bills, Christmas bills;
> How the sight of them my heart with consternation fills;
> How they tumble, tumble, tumble
> In my letter box each day,
> In a vast chaotic jumble,
> With a deep sepulchral rumble,
> That fills me with dismay.[27]

Yet such a fatalistic demeanour was adopted because the popular press' representation of men as pathetic dogsbodies during the Christmas shopping season, and the subordination it implied, was intended as a temporary condition. Indeed, the whole point of ridiculing men and elevating women was to establish an appropriately exaggerated and hence presumably unbelievable situation, which could then be exploited by illustrating the true nature of women shoppers after Christmas. As the pendulum swung in favour of women's authority at Christmas, so afterwards it would swing back in favour of men when the sales began. Women were only conferred public authority in the popular press because the social reality, that is their continued subordination, would soon be revealed.

Consequently, when we consider Christmas shopping we must recognise that women did employ their new public skills to good advantage.

However, we need also to differentiate carefully between women's experience, that is the mechanics of shopping, and the subsequent
representation of that experience. While Christmas shopping did provide women with an opportunity to extend their public authority, it also
allowed men an opportunity to trivialise this achievement by invoking,
particularly through its representation in the popular press, the traditions of popular culture. Specifically we see in the representation of the
Christmas shopping experience evidence of lingering traditional rituals
of public inversion. Such inversion demanded the temporary suspension
of traditional relationships – in this case through the subordination of
men and the elevation of women before Christmas, followed by the
journalistic humiliation of women after Christmas – thereby prompting
a form of theatrical conflict which released social tension and acted,
following the subsequent righting of the balance, to maintain the *status
quo*. The treatment of shopping in the press during the Christmas
season can be seen as one part of a stylised attempt to contain women's
authority. Popular press accounts of shopping were so pervasive that
eventually, when superimposed upon the true experience, representation and reality were mingled in the public mind.

Sales fever

Having won control of the streets at Christmas through their selfless, or
so they avowed, commitment to the purchase of novelties for family
and friends, women had to be careful not to fall from grace in the post-
Christmas winter sale season. Significantly, although seasonal sales had
long been part of the retailing calendar, it was only in the 1880s and
particularly in the 1890s that sales were more closely associated by men
with the irrational woman shopper. In other words this view did not so
much develop in conjunction with women's take-over of the shopping
streets in the 1870s, as it accompanied the ritualised inversion later
associated with Christmas shopping. The press's developing critique of
women's supposed predilection for sales might appear innocuous but
was in fact potentially extremely damaging to women's newly won
position. Interestingly, an article in 1894 clearly identifies Christmas
Day as the moment when men can question women's shopping authority. A husband and wife are out for a Christmas Day walk when
Angelina realises that her favourite bonnet shop is just around the
corner. "'Oh, I forgot! it will be shut. How hateful!" Edwin: "Cannot
you do without shopping for one day?" Angelina: "Three days! Sunday,
Monday, Tuesday! If it weren't for the January sales after, I would go
mad!"'[28] Back-handed compliments about the ability of women to shop

all day, exhausting the patience of any poor family member, particularly a husband, who might accompany them, were symptomatic of a broader attempt to portray women as compulsive shoppers who were not, by extension, to be taken seriously. Comic periodicals begin at this time to include a growing number of shopping quips, cartoons and jokes pursuing this vein of attack. A cartoon titled 'She Wanted Some Change', which appeared in *Skits* in 1891 is representative. The scene depicts a husband and wife seated at the breakfast table. 'Wife: "My dear, I am going shopping, and want a little change." Husband: "All right; but as you are always shopping, I don't see where the change comes."'[29] More sinister were the attempts to explain compulsive shopping habits by classifying women as potential kleptomaniacs, whose aberrant behaviour was driven by an innate desire to acquire – or consume – rather than by need.[30] Tales of wealthy women who were discovered to have rooms full of stolen merchandise, none of which was needed or ever used, were in currency as early as the 1870s. On one occasion it was reported that a 'kleptomaniac', the wife of a wealthy London businessman, was discovered to have a huge store of stolen goods, all neatly labelled 'from so-and-so's' hidden in a secret room.[31]

The sale season presented the press with its best opportunity to strip women of some of the respect and authority they had accumulated during the rough and tumble of the Christmas shopping season. Women were vulnerable to attack, or so the tenor of press articles generally implied, because the sale season saw them scrambling for items to sate their own petty cravings. During the Christmas shopping season women had assumed much of their moral authority on the weight of their claim to be shopping for others – that is purchasing presents for family and friends. Indeed, it was women's determination that children enjoy the celebrations that provided the justification, if one was required, for their getting out and about even during tempestuous times, such as the Boer War or the constitutional crisis of 1910. 'As usual' observed the editor of the *Lady's Pictorial* 'it will largely rest with women to make the best of things [at Christmas] ... They will not let children lose one of the pleasures of Yuletide.'[32]

The January sales, which by the late nineteenth century equalled and perhaps surpassed the summer sales in importance, were dominated by the huge clearances of women's fashion items which had to be sold, so the trade claimed, to make way for the new seasonal fashions. The reality, which was that drapers bought stock purely for the sales, was unimportant. What was important from a male perspective was that women were fighting and, as we will see, very occasionally dying, in order to possess a bargain price on a dress, coat, hat or pair of gloves. Male condescension was expressed in newspaper and trade journal comments which mocked and belittled women's supposed enjoyment of sales generally. In the tongue-in-cheek tradition a journalist with the *Pall Mall Gazette* casually remarked on 30 December that the upcoming sales season represented the 'beginning of a strenuous time for many women … '.[33] More scornful was the commentary in *The Draper*: 'A tremor ran through the world of women with the dawn of the week. "First Monday in July – After Season Sales begin" was their waking thought, and it thrilled them.' The 'masculine world' had 'simply to accept the inevitable and pay'.[34] However hypocritical *The Draper*'s position, given the financial gains its commercial readers were expecting to make as a result of the sales, its position does illustrate the extent of the ebb and flow of moral authority during the seasonal shopping calendar; the long-suffering male appears, but now as the philanthropist who humours his wife's excesses, because it suited his domestic agenda, rather than as the hen-pecked husband. Men, threatened by women's growing presence on the streets, reacted by belittling women's new shopping experience. Shopping was characterised as the 'always forgiven vanity of the lovely sex. All women are constantly hungering with a Corinthian hunger for some new things with which to add to the charms Nature has bestowed upon them'.[35]

It has to be said that the tenor of criticism changed over the years. In the 1880s and 1890s when sale behaviour was first ridiculed on a regular basis, women were represented as innocent but silly victims, who were often more sinned against than sinning. Women's weakness was that they could not control their propensity to buy, buy, buy. Typical of this view was a full front-page illustration in *Snap-Shots* in 1895 titled 'Selling Off Winter Stock'. Inside a large drapery/department store the shop men, depicted as foxes, can be seen rubbing their hands in anticipation of the approaching customer/victim. Outside, the female shoppers, depicted as geese, view the bargains displayed to tempt them into the shop. Dresses, hats, jewellery, and other tempting bargains are all individually located in the middle of leg-hold traps. The final insult is registered on the sale tag which reads 'All greatly reduced – from 50/- to 49/11 3/4'.[36] Perhaps, you might think, the viewer could anticipate a happy ending; perhaps the women decided against entering the shop. Unfortunately the shoppers' fate was sealed; the subtitle, 'The Annual Game of Fox and Geese', makes the outcome all too clear!

However, a more venomous critique of women's sale behaviour can also be identified; women were further represented as cunning and duplicitous – conniving as well as pushy. The low cunning associated with women shoppers is evident in a story which appeared in *Tit-Bits*. The audience is told of a woman who, upon examining a bonnet she had ordered, feigned shock at what she called a 'simply horrid' affair, and indignantly informed the assistant that though she could hardly expect to be charged the agreed upon price, she would condescend to pay 15s. 6d. As soon as she had left the shop she exclaimed to her friend how thrilled she was with a bonnet that was 'simply ravishing'. As she explained, if she had admitted her true feelings to the assistant the price would have remained at a guinea.[37] This story illustrates the developing male contention that women shopped because of an inherent deviousness which was partially slaked by bargain-hunting. 'The prime secret of ladies' love of shopping lies in their propensity for bargaining.'[38] Unable to resist the temptations of the remnant table, so it was argued, women bought articles for which they had no need, just because they felt they were getting a bargain.[39] This view was constantly reinforced by jokes in the popular press. For example in *Tit-Bits* a piece titled 'An Irresistible Bargain': 'Mrs Nuwife: "I bought a lovely bottle of medicine to-day, warranted to cure St. Vitus's dance. I only paid 2s. 6d. for it." Her hubby: "but neither of us have that disease." Mrs Nuwife: "I know, but it was marked down from 3s."'[40] Or: 'Husband: "Why do your clothes cost you twenty pounds more this year than last? Aren't things cheaper?" Wife: "Yes, dear; that's just it. There are so many more bargains."'[41] Or, again in *Tit-Bits*, a short quip: 'Through an error of the clerk, the sign read thus: "A great bargain! Last one left. Formerly five shillings now offered for eight." And Mrs. Bargainbuyer paid eight shillings for it, and went home happy.'[42] This tradition of belittlement culminates with Ernest Denny's monologue on 'The Gentle Art of Shopping'. In the sketch an unnamed woman shopper explains her motives for attending the sales. The important point, of course, being that this is actually a male interpretation of the female perspective. In one passage the woman addresses the audience:

> If you'd only seen what I got for nine pounds ten! ... Why, I simply couldn't tell you *what* I bought! But, I know they were all *enormous* bargains! ... I beg your pardon? ... Did I – *what*? ... 'Did I want any of those things?' ... Now *isn't* that just like a man? ... 'Did I want them?' ... Well, what if I *didn't* ... It's quite possible I *may* want *any* of them ... before the end of the summer.[43]

This notion that sales created a temporary loss of reason, manifested in an unseemly scramble for merchandise, strengthened in the early years of the twentieth century. After 1900 observers refer more frequently to the violence which they associated with sales fever. Even fairly innocent commentaries on the opening of sale season employed the language of war and the military. For example, one writer observed that Peter Robinson's winter sales 'are so popular that the premises are literally besieged from the moment of opening on the first and following days, so that it is the early bird that will fare the best'.[44] It became a journalistic commonplace to pepper accounts of sales with descriptions of ladies 'elbowing', 'pushing' and 'ejaculating' at each other: 'no one is expected to have any good manners during "after season sales".'[45] Indeed, one of the most popular jokes in the drapery trade ran: When is a lady not a lady? Answer: When she attends a sale.[46] A Bond Street draper's contemptuous diary entry demands little comment: 'I have a sale on to-day in my shop, and there is something about the crowds of women that reminds me of a farmyard.'[47] In cartoons, shops were increasingly depicted as the venues for consumer conflict – as battle zones. Only the strong or devious survived; thus, for example, little old ladies, hopelessly lost, were buffeted by the crowd, and swept away until they came to rest in the relative safety of a lift, which then whisked them away to another floor, and more confusion.[48]

The one event most responsible for reinforcing the British public's association of sales with violence was the so-called 'Battle of Louisville' when one shopper was crushed to death during a remnant sale in Kentucky, USA. On a Saturday in October 1906 a riot broke out when thousands of women 'besieged' a large department store. The crush became so great that no business could be conducted, and frustrated shoppers began to pull a number of valuable costumes to pieces. In response the police attempted to close the doors to stop more customers adding to the congestion. However, their plan backfired when a shout of 'Stop thief' rang out and three women fainted, precipitating a fresh panic. The police finally succeeded in emptying the store and clearing the surrounding streets of the crowd, though not before 12 women had been hospitalised: of these one later died of internal injuries sustained in the stampede, one broke an arm, one broke a collar bone and one lost a portion of her scalp.[49] Clarence Rook, the journalist who so frequently used shopping as a literary opportunity to belittle women, commented on the 'battle': 'There is nothing easier than to taunt a whole sex ... with a fondness for a bargain.' However, with an uncharacteristic display of sympathy, he refrained from caustic comment on this occasion. His restraint was only temporary, and he returned to the issue of shopping two months later by posing a question that puzzled him greatly:

> Whence comes the woman's passion for a bargain? During those weeks at the turn of the year, I have been shoved off the pavement by rabid ladies in High Street Kensington; and I have seen the bargain sales in Chicago. The women of the world are struggling to get a remnant at cost-price.[50]

To another columnist the events in Louisville served principally to focus public opinion on women's alleged sale behaviour, and the result was simply to reinforce existing stock jokes. It didn't matter that the excitement and clamour of a sale never approximated that which could be found in any male institution such as a mart or stock exchange: 'Women will be represented as violent, rapacious, thievish ... .'[51]

Punch made great fun of the sale season and the supposed undercurrent of violence it engendered. Indeed, so common had the expectation of the mayhem accompanying sales become by 1910 that one of the magazine's most successful jibes played on the absence rather than the presence of mayhem. 'Improbable Scenes'. Number VII, 'At A Bargain Sale', depicted two women shoppers, in the most genteel of shopping circumstances, each politely requesting, with a bow no less, the other to go ahead of them at the counter; the sense of the absurd was nicely set off by the approving smiles of the other women shoppers who patiently queued for their turn.[52] The viewer, in the post-Louisville climate and conditioned to recognise the unlikelihood of such illustrated events unfolding, was unwittingly seduced into reinforcing their image of women's behaviour at a typical sale. The presence of mayhem was parodied the following year in a cartoon which very cleverly intertwined the two male strategies for ridiculing women and the sales – that is the false economy and violence they were supposed to entail. On this occasion the 'Female Economist', in need of some material to cover a footstool, is seen getting up at 4 a.m., in order to join the queue at 5 a.m., so that she can then join the 'battle of the remnants'. In the central panel, which illustrates the 'battle', women are seen fighting over pieces of material, literally engaged in a tug-of-war so that they can save 2s. 4½d. The final insult occurs in the concluding panels when the 'Female Economist' is seen in a restaurant where she recovers from her ordeal by ordering a meal costing 22s. 6d.[53] As a final example of the popular press's association of mayhem and violence with the sales a cartoon appeared in *Punch* inspired by a notice posted in an unnamed London department store which invited customers to walk through the shop with the same freedom they could expect in the British Museum. In other words they need not fear being cajoled into buying by overanxious assistants and as they deliberated could expect to linger over the items for as long as they liked. In *Punch*'s interpretation of events as they unfold at the store the women, and they are all women bar one, are seen stampeding through the aisles in order to be the first to get at the sale items. The first arrivals are indiscriminately pulling sale articles off the displays. In the rush children are being hauled off their feet and, to emphasise the reality of a gendered shopping crowd, the one man present is trampled underfoot by the crowd as he tries to escape.[54]

Why was women's shopping behaviour represented so viciously? In part it must surely feature as part of the process invoked by men, and those who supported traditional patterns of authority, to place the male/female relationship back on a proper footing after the inversion of the 'Great Christmas Carnival'. The ridiculing of women bargain-hunters was an attack on their newly won public authority and also an attempt to undermine and denigrate the character of the shopping crowd. Women's public position and behaviour was being compromised, their supposedly irrational behaviour publicised, at the very moment when other questions about women's political emancipation were being debated. This was surely no coincidence. The attacks on shopping also represented an attempt to rehabilitate men, who were portrayed as long suffering yet understanding of women's weaknesses. An early example of this can be found in a cartoon found in *The Penny Illustrated Paper*. What, demanded the caption, were men called who could summon up the energy and patience either to accompany their wives on bargain-hunting expeditions to the shops, and/or condone the expense? The answer: 'Heroes of Every-Day Life'.[55] Thus the 'Submerged Sex' of December had been transformed into benevolent and knowing men who condescended to humour their wives' or daughters' fickle nature. Perhaps then it can be said that in February, once the last of the sales were over and the excitement of Christmas was a distant memory, the engagement between men and women should not be considered as primarily a struggle with winners and losers, but as a complex and ritualised form of renegotiating female/male relationships. On the one hand both Christmas shopping and the sales provided women with very real social and economic benefits; however, when we examine the manner in which these shopping experiences were represented in the popular press we can identify a different process at work. So successful was the invocation of the traditions of popular culture – that is, the representation of the temporary subordination of men or the world turned upside down, followed by the very obvious righting of that world in the sales season that followed – that women's victory in the shop was quite literally used against them by those who would maintain traditional gender relations. Shopping came to be viewed – by feminists as well as other observers – as a leisure activity that symbolised middle and lower middle-class women's co-option by the commodity culture.

Notes

1. *Lady's Pictorial*, 23 November 1912, p. 828.
2. Ibid., 23 October 1886, p. 360.
3. George Augustus Sala, *Twice Around The Clock, or the Hours of the Day and Night of London*, London: Houlston and Wright (1859), p. 155;

George Augustus Sala, *Gaslight and Daylight with Some London Scenes They Shine Upon*, London: Chapman and Hall (1859), p. 361.

4. See for example Society For Promoting the Due Observance of the Lord's Day, *Quarterly Publication*, January, 1845, pp. 43–4; *Report from the Select Committee on Sunday Trading (Metropolis)*, P.P. (Parliamentary Papers) 1847 (666) vol. IX, p. iii.

5. *Tit-Bits*, 23 December 1899, p. 301.

6. Judith Walkowitz, *City of Dreadful Delight: Narratives of Sexual Danger in Late-Victorian London*, Chicago: University of Chicago Press (1992); Erika D. Rappaport, '"The halls of temptation": gender, politics, and the construction of the department store in late Victorian London' *Journal of British Studies*, 35, 1996, pp. 58–83; Bill Lancaster, *The Department Store: a Social History*, London: Leicester University Press (1995).

7. Christopher Breward, *The Culture of Fashion: a New History of Fashionable Dress*, Manchester: Manchester University Press (1995).

8. Rachel Bowlby, *Just Looking: Consumer Culture in Dreiser, Gissing and Zola*, New York: Methuen (1985), pp. 20–32.

9. See Thomas Richards, *The Commodity Culture in Victorian Britain, Advertising and Spectacle*, Stanford: Stanford University Press (1991).

10. Claire Walsh, 'Shop design and the display of goods in eighteenth-century London', *Journal of Design History*, 8, 1995, pp. 157–76.

11. Clarence Rook, *London Side-Lights*, London: Edward Arnold (1908), p. 11.

12. Ibid., p. 11.

13. Ibid., p. 12.

14. See John Beattie,"'Tis the season to be jolly – why?', in *New Society*, 1, 1962, pp. 12–13; Pamela Shurmer, 'The gift game', *New Society*, 18, 1971, pp. 1242–4. More recently see Daniel Miller (ed.), *Unwrapping Christmas*, Oxford: Clarendon Press (1993).

15. Gavin Weightman and Steve Humphries, *Christmas Past*, London: Sidgwick and Jackson (1987), p. 15.

16. *The Penny Illustrated Paper*, 11 December 1880, p. 369.

17. *Lady's Pictorial*, 7 December 1895, p. 881.

18. *Punch*, 18 December 1897, p. 285.

19. Ibid., 12 October 1904, p. 423.

20. Ibid., 18 December 1913, p. 491.

21. *Tit-Bits*, 22 December 1909, p. 316.

22. *Punch*, 4 March 1908, p. 178.

23. *The Sphere*, 23 November 1908, pp. 20–21.

24. *Lady's Pictorial*, 21 December 1912, p. 1042.

25. *Pall Mall Gazette*, 22 December 1909, p. 4. It must be said that there is an interesting subtext to this 'Christmas Shopping' story. The author, C.C.L. Ionides, pokes fun at the traditional British department store practice of employing shop walkers and assistants whose duty it was to wait upon the customer, not allowing them to leave (if at all possible) without making a purchase. By the end of the day the male shopper in this story is reduced to skulking around the store in a desperate attempt to avoid the assistants. Careful readers would have recognised 'Sellem's' as Harrod's – identified by the reference to Harrod's famous moving inclined passage to the upper floors.

26. *Lady's Pictorial*, 29 December 1888, p. 756.

27. *Tit-Bits*, 19 December 1891, p. 190.
28. *To-Day: A Weekly Magazine-Journal*, 22 December 1894, p. 198.
29. *Skits*, 1 August 1891, p. 5.
30. Elaine S. Abelson, *When Ladies Go A-Thieving: Middle-Class Shoplifters in the Victorian Department Store*, New York: Oxford University Press (1989). See also Chapter 6 by Spiekermann in this volume.
31. *The Warehouseman and Draper's Journal*, 16 December 1876, p. 585.
32. *Lady's Pictorial*, 26 November 1910, p. 870.
33. *Pall Mall Gazette*, 30 December 1910, p. 9.
34. *The Draper*, 12 July 1902, p. 973.
35. *The Warehouseman and Draper's Trade Journal*, 19 July 1884, p. 486.
36. *Snap-Shots: Humerous Pictures and Amusing Reading*, 19 January 1895, p. 1.
37. *Tit-Bits*, 27 December 1890, p. 178.
38. *The Warehousemen and Draper's Trade Journal*, 19 July 1884, p. 486.
39. *The Draper*, 11 July 1903, p. 925.
40. *Tit-Bits*, 13 June 1896, p. 181.
41. Ibid., 12 August 1893, p. 325.
42. Ibid., 25 July 1896, p. 289.
43. Ernest Denny, *The Gentle Art of Shopping: some Sidelights on the 'Sales'*, London: Samuel French (1919), p. 6.
44. *The Sphere*, 29 December 1900, p. 390.
45. *The Draper*, 12 July 1902, p. 973.
46. Ibid., 25 July 1903, p. 992.
47. Charles Cavers, *Hades! The Ladies! Being Extracts from the diary of a Draper*, London: Gurney and Jackson (1933), p. 248.
48. See for example *Punch*, 8 January 1913, p. 27. A lift attendant misunderstands an old lady's request to be taken to 'I-I-Iremungry' and takes her instead to the restaurant on the top floor.
49. This account is taken from *The Draper's Record*, 27 October 1906, p. 219; *The Draper*, 27 October 1906, p. 1267.
50. *The Reader*, 12 January 1907, p. 308.
51. Ibid., 5 January 1907, p. 289.
52. *Punch*, 7 December 1910, p. 14.
53. Ibid., 11 January 1911, p. 27.
54. Ibid., 2 August 1911, p. 77.
55. *The Penny Illustrated Paper*, 21 June 1890.

CHAPTER FIVE

Marianne in the department store: gender and the politics of consumption in turn-of-the-century Paris[1]

Lisa Tiersten

> The creation of these great bazars has given birth to new forms of moral corruption ... nowhere to be found in Balzac's *Comédie Humaine*.
>
> Ignotus[2]

In a recent landmark ruling protecting free speech in shopping malls, the New Jersey Supreme Court argued that commercial space has emerged as the *de facto* civic public in late twentieth-century America.[3] The court's decision points to the long-standing tension between civic culture and the liberal marketplace, one which surfaced as paramount in the late nineteenth century as democratic market societies were established in the West. In the last quarter of that century, models of public life steeped in traditions of civic humanism and inscribed in the political order in France, Britain, Germany and the USA clashed with the liberal ethos of *laissez-faire* and individual competition enshrined in the burgeoning consumer marketplace.[4] Conflict between civic and commercial culture, between the public citizen and the marketplace individual, was complicated, moreover, by the feminisation of the consumer sphere in the *fin de siècle*.

This chapter examines the conflict between civic and marketplace publics as it shaped the discourse on women consumers in late nineteenth-century France. During this period, the department store developed as a controversial new arena for bourgeois women.[5] Although etiquette experts, department store architects and social commentators were uncertain whether the *grand magasin* was a new form of public or private space, many agreed that the presence there of unchaperoned middle-class women posed a threat to the social order. In the accounts of various commentators, the new department store was said to seduce women away from the moral sanctuary of the home and, by cultivating their baser instincts of egotism, vanity and pleasure-seeking, to inure them to maternal and wifely sentiment and render them indifferent to the concept of social duty. According to critics across a broad political spectrum, the modern marketplace was so dangerous precisely because it provided women with the kind of financial and psychological independence that undermined their nurturing, dependent roles within the family.

For proponents and critics of the Republic alike, more was at stake in this debate than the definition of gender roles. Their concerns about women consumers, I wish to argue, cannot be separated from fundamental political and ideological anxieties about the corruption of republican virtue by private passions: about the contradiction, in spite of their mutually supporting roles in practice, between the Republic and the marketplace.[6] This contradiction was born of the uneasy, shifting compound of liberal individualism and civic values contained within French republican ideology and practice throughout the nineteenth century. In contrast to Britain and the USA, where liberalism as both an economic and social doctrine was more widely accepted, as well as to Germany, where a strong state precluded the triumph of *laissez-faire*, France's relationship to liberal thought and practice was complicated by the persistence of corporatist and communitarian currents in republican ideology.[7] As a consequence of these tensions, the notion of the civic public itself was in many ways an unstable construct, and its instabilities were accentuated by the advent of political democracy and a mass marketplace in the late nineteenth century. The *fin-de-siècle* economic take-off of the department store thus coincided with, and was nourished by, the establishment of a liberal Republic in 1877, but its success was predicated on capitalist principles in certain ways inimical to republican ideals.[8]

As the bourgeois order faced the task of reconciling the commercial sphere with the civic ethos of the Republic, the disciplining of the self-interested shopper and the controlling of the unsupervised urban spaces they frequented came to be seen as a crucial part of this project. In the political realm, radical republican reformers, centrist republicans, reformist Social Catholics and Le Playist Catholics alike extolled the disinterested bonds forged within the affective realm of the family as the corrective to the rampant individualism perceived to be corroding modern French life.[9] In the commercial arena, entrepreneurs, store managers and publicists sought to align the consumer marketplace with the Republic through policies and rhetoric representing the department store as a public-minded civic institution. Through store design and publicity, they sought to situate the act of consumption within the stable, disciplinary framework of the family, and thereby to transform shopping from an interested pursuit to a disinterested one. In political and social rhetoric, the family was ascribed a privileged role in the moralisation of the marketplace; in commercial discourse, women were cast as its primary agents. By forging rhetorical links between the commercial public and the bourgeois family, the department store itself took on the role of civilising the consumer, in this way adapting itself to the social politics of the Republic.

The department store, the city, and the *flâneuse*

For the critics of big commerce, the advent of the department store signalled a change not simply in the structure of commercial life, but in the very nature of the relationship of the individual to society.[10] The putative decline of the city as a communitarian public arena and the proliferation of new, undisciplined public spaces were lamented by critics as a by-product, at least in part, of the materialism, democratisation and individualism bred by the reign of big commerce. Jeremiads decrying the collapse of politeness and saturated with nostalgia for a fictional past abounded in the late nineteenth-century bourgeois press. In one such narrative, the journalist Octave Uzanne glorified the bourgeois order before the department store as a pre-commercial paradise in which Darwinian laws of competition were unknown. In his eyes, community had disintegrated into individualism, and individualism into egotism and the rule of personal desire. 'Politeness ... is dead', he wrote, 'it is disappearing more every day in our little egotistical, Americanized world, in which everyone thinks only of himself, his own pleasure, his own feelings ... .'[11]

Where women were concerned, the dangers of excessive individualism were perceived to be particularly potent. For conservatives in particular, women's increasing presence in the public arena – linked in part to republican legislation of the 1880s – could only result in the abandonment of the *foyer* and the corruption of pristine interiority.[12] In a sharply accusatory speech to a prominent women's organization in 1911, the best-selling Catholic novelist Henry Bordeaux voiced the view of many foes of the regime that the public persona of the modern woman had utterly supplanted her private identity:

> The housewife of today has her office or her laboratory. She publishes or she invents. She goes to court or to the hospital ... One rarely finds her at home; she is always out and about ... busy running all over the city. Her husband, if she has the time for one, is nothing but a prince Consort ... the greatest of all arts, the culinary art ... has been morally abandoned ... Her egotism is revolting ...[13]

Women in the public world of work were often perceived in the popular imagination to be deficient in domestic virtue. But unlike the world of work, a sphere that closely bordered the civic public and subscribed to 'masculine' values of discipline and order, the introduction of women into the commercial public threatened the bourgeois order by drawing them into a dangerous network of unregulated desires where the purposes of self-interest and pleasure-taking could easily overrun the dictates of social duty and propriety. This phenomenon was considered particularly severe in the French setting. An English observer suggested that the problem of the wayward female consumer was essentially a Parisian one, rooted in a love of finery enflamed to obsession by the advent of the department store:

> That some of these [Parisiennes] really like their husbands and have a sort of fondness for their children is not at all impossible, but as it is extremely difficult to associate indoor love with outside vanities, the former are pretty often abandoned in order to be better able to attend to the latter.[14]

The ultimate consequence of unregulated consumption was not simply the erosion of the structure of the French family, but the devastation of the French population. 'Aspirations to luxury ... ', as one doctor put it, 'have enfeebled the maternal impulse and promoted depopulation'.[15]

As both embodiment and symbol of the unregulated commercial public, the department store was the target of much popular invective directed against the moral degradation of the modern city and the modern woman.[16] In contrast to the small boutique, which simulated domesticity with salon-style fitting rooms replete with house plants, paintings and fireplaces, the department store was designed to signal a radical departure from the domestic and the mundane. Not only did the *grands magasins* bill themselves as 'sensational attractions', but tourist guides to Paris of the period listed them among the most fascinating of the city's spectacles. As colossal, architecturally modern structures strategically situated on the big boulevards synonymous with Haussmann's new 'open city', department stores were constructed as monuments in the modern urban landscape.[17]

The perception of the department store as an extension of the city street was accentuated by the lure of its opulent window displays and its policy of free entry. Unlike the boutique, which kept its wares discreetly out of sight, the department store used huge plate-glass windows brimming with enticing commodities to ensnare the female passer-by. Crossing the threshold of the *grand magasin*, the *flâneuse* became a browser, with no obligation to strike up a conversation with sales personnel or other customers or even to make a purchase. She could continue her urban promenade unmolested through the vast spaces of the department store, circulating freely, a spectator rather than a participant. The very scale of the place, the sense of open space seemed to make the store a city in itself; one cartoon in the popular press suggested that internal omnibus lines be installed to help weary and bewildered customers to navigate the stores' expanses.[18] The similarity between the bustling, turbulent street and the store was further underscored by the fact that male customers kept their hats on inside store precincts. Although etiquette experts tended to object to the disrespect for ladies implicit in the gesture, they conceded that it was unavoidable in public.[19] They also worried intensely about the confusion of the consumer with the 'public woman' and warned that the solitary shopper could be easily mistaken for a loitering prostitute by a zealous store inspector.[20]

The anonymity of the department store, like that of the modern metropolis, was said to create a competitive public of self-seeking autonomous strangers: an illicit public far from the civic public of the republican imagination. To critics, the lack of personal contact, structure, and supervision in the department store was precisely what allowed for the possibility of feminine deviance. Whereas shopping at the small boutique entailed personal, ritualised interactions requiring civil behaviour, the department store made no such demands. One observer insisted that women who were perfectly polite at the couturier metamorphosed into rude, aggressive shoppers in the department store:

> [They] become utterly transformed the moment they find themselves unknown, in the presence of an anonymous shop assistant, amid ready-made merchandise, in galleries as accessible as the street. In this setting, a woman makes impossible demands and shows impatience that she would not dream of revealing to the couturier ... her needs must be gratified instantly.[21]

The juxtaposition of the uncivil shopper with machine-made commodities draws attention to the multiplicity of ways, both moral and aesthetic, in which urban commercial space violated civic ideals of social responsibility and personal authenticity.

The department store's reputation as a subversive environment was transformed in the early 1880s when media attention was drawn to the scandalous phenomenon of well-to-do women shoplifters, causing the stores to be identified by numerous commentators as a crucible of new urban pathologies.[22] Shopping became part of an emergent medical paradigm of French decline, according to which the nation's degeneration was understood as an organic phenomenon.[23] As the republican language of virtue became inflected by the rhetoric of biological vigour, feminine self-interest was sometimes reformulated as psychological perversion; in the words of one journalist, bourgeois shoppers were subject

to 'new styles of neurosis'.[24] Yet, although the causes of women's behaviour were sometimes differently construed, the consequences of their
exercise of private passions in the public realm were perceived to be the
same: the spectre of bourgeois women roaming the city's streets freely in
pursuit of pleasure imperilled their domestic virtue and challenged bourgeois male authority at home and in public.

Not only were the spectacularly displayed commodities in the department store said to whet the dormant appetites and incite the prurient
desires of the kleptomaniac, but the shopper was easily wrought to
frenzy in the presence of unruly crowds.[25] Like Poe's celebrated man of
the crowd, whose vocation it is to follow the flow of the crowd with no
fixed destination or stable identity, the individual shopper was caught
up in the mass of consumers.[26] Her psychic disorientation was manifest
in her transfigured appearance: just as the crowd man's 'chin fell upon
his breast, while his eyes rolled wildly from under his knit brows',[27] the
faces of shoppers emerging from the department store were reported by
a medical expert to 'wear a bizarre expression. Their pupils are extraordinarily dilated ... and they have dark shadows beneath their eyes'.[28]

According to theorists such as Gustave LeBon, the crowd became a
single organism, possessed of an independent will and governed by
unconscious, irrational impulses.[29] Thus crowd hysteria invoked images
of violent revolution and democratic demagoguery that were anathema
to republican conceptions of public order and individual rationality.
Both the detached, independent *flâneuse* and the shopper as a neurotic
particle in a disturbed mass – one an example of excrescent individuality and the other of the dissolution of the self into the group – represented
deviant forms of identity, each lacking the proper balance between self
and society inscribed in the civic order.

If LeBon suggested that women's innate suggestibility made them
especially susceptible to the crowd's thrall,[30] others argued that the
pathological passions of the individual female consumer were aroused
by the department store's use of manipulative marketing techniques.
The journalist Pierre Giffard observed that the top department stores
had only one goal: 'to seduce women'.[31] Similarly, Octave Mouret, the
owner of Zola's fictional department store, Au Bonheur des Dames,
'tried to think of every possible way to satisfy women, to give them
what they might want, to envelop them with a caress ... he considered
gallantry and a flattering air as the first rule of thumb'.[32] In general,
men were considered by these critics to be beyond the reach of 'the vast
spider's web' woven by the department store.[33] While men sought to
improve their condition through the discipline of hard work, commentators claimed, women indulged their gossamer dreams in the department
store. Giffard insisted that the male shopper was somehow always able

to control his impulses: 'You resist ... temptation ... because you are a man.'[34]

For those who saw women as the victims of entrepreneurial exploitation, the department store consumer was a shopping addict and an impulsive spendthrift. Accounts of shopper fanaticism often verged on the ridiculous: a magazine article related the story of a woman who went to the department store intending to buy a few hairpins and returned home with a living-room full of furniture;[35] in a medical study, a doctor presented the case of a gravely ill patient who died on her way to a sale at the Galeries Lafayette. 'It was not that she wanted to buy anything in particular', he wrote, 'but rather that she desperately needed the atmosphere of the department store.'[36] But for those who believed the shopper to be deliberately eluding male authority, as in countless Madame Bovary narratives in the women's press, the consumer was a ruthless schemer who would go to any lengths to dupe her husband when it came to gratifying her desires: thus, in a *feuilleton* of 1880 by the Catholic novelist Mathilde Bourdon, a stockbroker's wife drove her hardworking husband to bankruptcy, theft and, finally, to hard labour in prison because of her uncontrollable lust for redecorating.[37] Giffard described a life and death struggle between the department store's profit motive and shoppers' rapaciousness: 'On the side of the department store, intoxicating displays, the shimmer of fabrics, dazzling mirages, irresistible seductions ... which bedazzle women ... . On the side of those weak creatures, incessant theft and the trickery of returned merchandise.'[38] Nevertheless, his final verdict insisted on the fundamental culpability of women. 'If I had to choose ... one guilty party', he wrote, 'I would choose women a priori ... .'[39]

The spendthrift reportedly became an adulteress or part-time prostitute when her husband proved unable to satisfy her consumer appetites. The department stores were said to promote this behaviour not only by seducing shoppers into yielding to their desires, but also by withholding the credit readily available at the boutique. Without credit, department store detractors claimed, shoppers were forced to resort to sexual commerce (or theft) to obtain the objects of their desires. As if this were not enough, opportunities for anonymity, combined with the lushness of the atmosphere, were observed to make the department store an ideal site for adulterous trysts and other erotic misdemeanours. 'The department store', wrote one commentator, 'closes its eyes to the amorous ... intrigues which fill its galleries daily.'[40]

The bourgeois adulteress took her place beside the male sexual transgressors – fortune-seeking adventurers, voyeurs, exhibitionists and molesters – said to flock to the department store's unmonitored spaces. In the files of the store inspector, the female analogue to the molester was described as the *palpeuse* or caresser: the woman who titillated herself by stroking and fondling the merchandise. In his work on shop-lifters, Dr Paul Dubuisson described the shopper's pleasure in fondling commodities: 'She finds herself ... in an extraordinary atmosphere which assaults all her senses ... . And she not only has the right to look at all these riches, she is also allowed to touch them, to fondle them at her leisure ... .'[41] The *palpeuse*, objected one journalist, 'derives [her] pleas-ure for free, by simply looking and touching'.[42] The point was that the consumer not only sought to indulge herself, but that she had no sense of social obligation; the undisciplined consumer's pursuit of 'free' pleas-ure, like the rapacious capitalist's pursuit of profit, knew no bounds and observed no rules. Speaking before a women's group in 1911, a newspaper editor pinpointed the consumer problem as women's refusal to brook any opposition, legal or moral, to the gratification of their desires: 'There is something which women ... detest. It is the law, that is to say, any obstacle ... . They desire so passionately when they desire ... that nothing will make them say: It's impossible, it's against the law.'[43] The female consumer, in other words, was a hazard to the civic Repub-lic because she was so likely to indulge her private passions at the expense of the public good.

Civilising consumption

Although the Republic of the 1880s enshrined the liberal individual, by the 1890s the social strife and economic dislocation of the era had already engendered a crisis of liberal individualism.[44] Thus, the bour-geois Republic openly joined forces with big commerce in this period, but it did so within the context of a corporatist, rather than a liberal *laissez-faire*, framework. Outside of the republican mainstream, in re-formist movements such as Social Catholicism and in Catholic Le Playist circles, the rhetoric of liberal individualism was supplanted by that of social interdependence and co-operation. Under the aegis of the radical republican Solidarist movement of the 1890s, moreover, republican reformers such as Léon Bourgeois sought to chart a middle course between the collectivism of the socialists and the unchecked individual-ism of the liberals: to accept capitalism, but to regulate its abuses.[45] In its attempt to anchor the individual more firmly in social context, without ever denying the importance of the individual self, the Solidarist movement constituted a kind of republican reckoning with what were perceived to be the failures of liberal individualism, both in economic and political terms: an attempt to infuse the Republic with the moral vigour of the civic humanism privileged by Rousseau and other 'backward-looking' Enlightenment republicans.[46] Thus, ambivalence about the social relations of the marketplace were voiced not only by conservative critics, either of modernity in general or of the Republic in particular but, rather, in political debates about republican virtue and individual autonomy, in commercial debates about the nature of selling and in social debates about gender roles. Doubts and anxieties were voiced from within the heart of the liberal bourgeois Republic.[47]

Although the primary focus of social concern was restive workers, the politics of class overlay the politics of gender and bourgeois identity.[48] Bourgeois women who used consumer culture to stake out their own identities and spaces, independent of male authority, were also the target of a critique of the destructive impact of individualism. This critique was vitiated, however, by uncertainty about whether the birth of the commercial public spelled the 'fall of public man', or the rise of a new public forum. It was not fully clear to contemporaries what kind of self operated in such a context and what the relationship was between that self and an anterior, 'private' self. According to republican definitions of the public, the self-interestedness of shopping behaviour seemed to make the marketplace a private domain: women lost control over their socially correct façades and reverted to their 'true' uncivil selves. On the other hand, consumer culture and its commodities offered a whole new range of possibilities for theatrical self-display and feminine posing. In either case, the visibility of bourgeois housewives in this arena not only posed challenges to male authority but, more fundamentally, called into question the meaning of republican citizenship; whether women in the marketplace became more authentic or more false, the female consumer clashed with the republican ideal of the virtuous public self. As burgeoning consumerism seemed to transform Paris into a female city of chic and fashion, an arena of individual and private pleasure, bourgeois men fought to reclaim the city as a masculine sphere of public virtue and order. The image of the feminine commercial public as chaotic, irrational and hyper-individualistic was constructed against that of the presumably rational, orderly and social nature of the masculine civic public,[49] and debates about female individuality converged with debates about urban life and the boundaries between public and private.

Department store advocates to a large extent shared the anxiety of critics about the problems of controlling the consumer. Thus store owners, publicists, and defenders did not deny the existence of shopping disorders or breaches of civility in the consumer public, but took the position that individual pathology, rather than the commercial environment, provoked this behaviour and that, in fact, shopping was a constructive outlet for bourgeois women's potentially dangerous impulses. For the hedonist poised on the brink of destruction, shopping was a pleasurable and benign distraction from the more serious crime of adultery. For the morally sound *mère de famille*, it was a sphere in which she acted for the benefit of her family and the nation. In the discourse of the department store, the commercial public and the civic public were portrayed as interpenetrating, mutually supporting spheres, and the *grand magasin* as a staunch supporter of feminine domesticity and a bulwark of the Republic.

The department store's attempt to reconcile commercial with civic values was pursued in a variety of ways. Entrepreneurs such as Boucicaut of the Bon Marché and Chauchard of the Louvre were civic-minded men well known for their active philanthropic efforts. Through innovative policies of business paternalism, moreover, they demonstrated that they operated not only as profit-seeking capitalists, but also as civic-minded employers responsible for the well-being of their employees. They also sought energetically to publicise these policies to their customers. A Bon Marché publicity pamphlet of 1889, for example, used the metaphor of a bee hive to characterise the relationship of employees to enterprise: 'every bee enjoys the honey that has been produced (and) ... in return for his zeal and his efforts, obtains security in the present and for the future and the hope of becoming rich'.[50] According to the same pamphlet, it was the department store's ability to bring satisfaction to everyone which made it a socially progressive institution: 'The merit [of the Bon Marché] ... is that the prosperity of the establishment is founded not only on the devotion, but also on the contentment of fellow workers of all classes'. Store policies were presented as rooted in the social contract, not capitalist exploitation.

However much the stores portrayed themselves in their advertising as avatars of progress, their appeals to modernity were often tempered by the invocation of tradition.[51] The careful balancing of change and tradition can be seen, for example, in an advertisement announcing the turn-of-the-century renovation of the Belle Jardinière department store: customers were assured that they would find improvements, but would encounter 'neither a new spirit nor new methods'.[52] Similarly, a Bon Marché pamphlet emphasised the compatibility of commercial modernity with republican values: 'Time, which modifies all things, will no doubt lead to changes in [our] ... commercial ... organisation; but no matter what these transformations may be, our future will never be beyond the influence of ... work and honesty.'[53]

If department store retailers sought to represent the stores as a civic institution in relationship to its workers and to the larger society, they figured the *grand magasin* as a family, a home and an extension of the domestic interior in relation to their female customers. Thus entrepreneurs sought to domesticate the department store environment and to represent shopping as a family activity. In providing amenities such as correspondence rooms, newspaper reading rooms, cafeterias and play areas for children, the department store tried to create domestic (and civic) spaces within its precincts, and to potentially expand the consumer clientele to include husbands and children. The store's home-like atmosphere and ability to cultivate the consumer's domestic sentiment were emphasised in numerous advertisements. An advertisement for the Bon Marché, for example, in the form of a letter from a customer, literally conflated domestic space with the commercial environment:

> I feel so pleasantly at home at the Bon Marché! Sometimes I actually forget that I'm not in my own house. The atmosphere is one of honesty, order, regular activity ... and that comfort ... which is the ... charm of the French *foyer* ... Why do I love the Bon Marché? Because it is a big family and I am a part of it.[54]

Advertising not only played down the urban character of the store environment, but also underscored the probity of shopping by portraying consumption as a domestic responsibility. In a promotional piece for the Pygmalion, for example, a shopper wanders enraptured through the store, lost in oblivion, but the crucial factor is that she is not alone: her young daughter accompanies her on the entire expedition.[55] The child's presence not only added innocence to the picture, but cast the mother in the role of indulgent parent rather than vain pleasure-seeker. Without denying the individualistic component of consumption, the advertisement and many others like it suggested that no real conflict existed between feminine vanity, the tenderness of the wife and mother, and the duty of the bourgeois citizen.

Advertisements also implicitly linked consumption to female citizenship by portraying the shopper as the guardian of the nation's artistic prestige and, consequently, of its economic and political power. In an advertisement of 1904 for a sale of silk fabric, the Pygmalion department store lavishly thanked its customers for their support of French workers: 'Ladies, we give you our deepest gratitude. It is you, sovereign *Parisiennes* ... with your taste for beauty and refined luxury, who have combined the useful with the beautiful and performed a true act of patriotism in supporting a national industry which sustains thousands of modest workers'.[56] This vision of consumer nationalism often went beyond the purchase of French over German or English products, to the cultivation of a distinctly personal style: a woman's duty to the bourgeois Republic lay in aesthetic self-expression. Although consumption remained an exercise of individuality, its wider goal was to further the public good through the cultivation of French taste.

In fact, if department store critics argued that the marketplace had the capacity to corrupt and deform feminine identity, defenders claimed that it had the power equally to fashion women into dutiful wives and citizens.[57] Although most advertisements tended to emphasise the harmlessness of the pleasure of impulse spending, women's magazines and advice literature of the *fin de siècle* made strenuous attempts to discipline consumers by trying to instil in them the habit of budgeting. Budgetary guidelines urged women to spend according to plan rather than impulse and for others rather than for themselves. The etiquette expert Louise d'Alq's rule of thumb was to spend on the 'interior' before the 'exterior': one spent first on rent and household maintenance, second on the upkeep of husband and children, and last on pleasure.[58] 'Is it possible that a woman whose household is in disorder', she wrote, 'could possibly enjoy the "pleasures" of a theatre box or a trip abroad ... bought with money ... indispensable to the household?'[59] Similarly, in the very same speech in which Henry Bordeaux reviled the modern woman, he idealised the *femme de foyer* who preserved her domestic persona in the public sphere: 'She will save for the interior the treasures of tenderness that other women waste in the outside world .... More organized, she will have more time. More balanced, she will know how to choose better .... Able to forget herself, she will think more of others.'[60]

In educating women to be smart shoppers, the department store claimed its ability to transform the would-be bourgeois homewrecker into a domestic paragon, a role model to the working classes, and a boon to the economy. The consumer was not an apostate, but a representative of the family, a conduit between the private and the public; through her, the ethos of the bourgeois home could civilise the marketplace. Consumption, in these terms, became a distinctly feminine form of exercising bourgeois citizenship, and the fact that the denizens of the commercial public were bourgeois women offered an opportunity to shore up male authority at home and in the public realm.

However, the new feminine forms of citizenship implicitly proposed by the department store were not analogous to traditional masculine forms. Late nineteenth-century Frenchwomen's roles as consumer-citizens, such as they were, were essentially extensions of their more entrenched republican roles as mother-citizens.[61] Entrepreneurs, publicists, and social scientist proponents of the department store sought to downplay the consumer's individuality and to fashion a socially constructive image of her civic role to align themselves with republican politics, particularly the Solidarist politics of the 1890s and early 1900s. None the less, although department store defenders sought increasingly to underscore the consumer's social usefulness toward the end of the century, the figure of the consumer-citizen was virtually always mediated by that of the mother. The existing paradigm of republican citizenship for women was thus sustained, rather than challenged, by department store models.

On the other hand, the purview of the consumer-citizen did surpass the purely domestic limits of the mother-citizen in one important way; in France more than elsewhere, women's roles as consumers bore a more nationalist tincture because of their roles as trustees of French aesthetic capital. The Republic's symbolic and material investment in protecting what might be termed the French aesthetic patrimony directly involved the republican *femme de foyer*, to whom this patrimony was entrusted; and the aesthetic mission of republican housewives could be and was linked by market-makers to women's role as consumer. Department store display constituted nothing less than a new branch of art proclaimed one enthusiast: consumers' exposure to the department store's high aesthetic standards resulted in the refinement of the public taste.[62] Other advertisements cast the department store as the shopper's humble servant. Thus, a catalogue of 1910 for the Pygmalion department store proclaimed:

> our Album ... will serve ... to demonstrate that French taste has not degenerated over the past century ... that it is ... still worthy of its former renown, its uncontested supremacy. The Frenchwoman is still the queen of the world. To preserve her superiority ... (she) must rely on those zealous servants who seek to fulfil ... her most subtle desires in the domain of art and fashion.[63]

Although similar claims were made by department stores in other nations in this period, they had particular resonance in France because of the widespread perception of national decline. Only part of the concern over French decay is reducible to the apocalyptic mood of the *fin de siècle*; part of it was legitimate concern over France's considerable economic and demographic lag behind both old and new competitors. Material rivalry was closely related to cultural contest: the German decorative arts movement associated with the Werkbund, for example, threatened the French reputation for aesthetic superiority at its very core, in the world of artisanal production. In the view of many concerned about France's putative aesthetic slide, women had an obvious role to play in rehabilitating the French reputation for taste through sober and artful consumption. According to the foes of big commerce, this task could only be accomplished by avoiding the *camelote* sold by the department store; advocates, by contrast, claimed the department store as the best possible venue for constructive, tasteful consumption. This was not only because of the beauty of department store merchandise, but because of the revolution of *bon marché*; in the words of the economist Georges Michel, 'thanks to its reduced prices, the department store has been able to develop the public taste and to permit the great democratic masses to procure objects which, until now, have been within the grasp of the privileged classes alone'.[64] In their rhetoric of class conciliation, defenders of big commerce thus actively adopted the republican language of social peace and solidarism.

The republicanisation of the marketplace at the turn of the century was perhaps best epitomised by a full-page advertisement of 1912 allegorising the expansion of the Bazar de l'Hôtel de Ville. In it, a fleshy, robust Marianne wearing a Republican *cocarde* proffered consumer goods – a box of pearls, a pair of shoes and two hats – to three small children, dressed respectively in the costumes of a stevedore, a policeman and a bourgeois citizen in frock-coat and top hat.[65] The department store's Marianne was thus the mother who tended her children by seeing to their material comforts, she was the nation seeing to its economic future and she was the consumer protecting its standards of taste. The image of the children representing different social classes and gazing wondrously at the goods, moreover, clearly suggested that the growth of the marketplace and the diffusion of goods promised not fractious individualism, but a Republic of social peace and plenty. Marianne – a mother first, but also a consumer and a citizen – was its emissary.

Notes

1. I am grateful to Geoffrey Crossick, Victoria De Grazia, Perry Friedman, Serge Jaumain, Cat Nilan, Ingmar Nyman, Erika Rappaport, Peter Scholliers and Lars Trägårdh for their helpful comments and suggestions.
2. Ignotus, 'Les grands bazars', *Paris divers*, Paris (1881), n.p.
3. Joseph P. Sullivan, 'Court protects speech in malls', *New York Times*, 21 December 1994, p. 1.
4. The republican conceptions of public life to which I refer are sometimes conflated by historians with Habermas's notion of the public sphere. The Habermasian public sphere, however, differs significantly from republican conceptions of the civic public, the latter rooted in nostalgia for the classical past and characterized by a rejection of the marketplace and values of liberal individualism. These models of public life, however, like the Habermasian public sphere, functioned as normative ideals within social and political discourse, rather than as social realities. Nevertheless, in nineteenth-century Paris, the ethos of the civic public was perceived to be embodied in such venues as bourgeois clubs and voluntary associations, public squares, municipal institutions such as museums and in more traditional, supervised commercial locales such as small boutiques and theatres. On the relevance of the Habermasian public sphere to French politics, see Keith Michael Baker, 'Defining the public sphere in

eighteenth-century France', in Craig Calhoun (ed.), *Habermas and the Public Sphere*, Cambridge, MA: MIT Press (1992), pp. 181–211.

5. Recent research has emphasized the role played by the commercial public as a site of female activity and explored the kinds of problems engendered by this association. See, for example, Judith Walkowitz, *City of Dreadful Delight: Narratives of Sexual Danger in Late-Victorian London*, Chicago: University of Chicago Press (1992), and Erika Rappaport, "'A new era of shopping": the promotion of women's pleasure in London's West End, 1909–1914', in Leo Charney and Vanessa Schwartz (eds), *Cinema and the Invention of Modern Life*, Berkeley: University of California Press (1995), pp. 130–55.

6. On relations between the regime and big business, particularly on Opportunist and Radical Republican indifference to shopkeeper protest against the department store in the late 1880s and 1890s, see Philip G. Nord, *Paris Shopkeepers and the Politics of Resentment*, Princeton: Princeton University Press (1986). According to Nord, the Boulangist movement of 1889 marked the crucial turning-point when mainstream republicans abandoned the interests of small retailers in favour of big commerce.

7. While historians such as Patrice Higonnet and Jennifer Jones justifiably have claimed that Rousseau's impact on French republicanism has been overemphasized, I would argue, with Philip Nord and Ronald Aminzade, that Rousseauian civic values (including hostility to the marketplace and to competitive individualism) remained a force in French politics well into the late nineteenth century, coexisting in uneasy tension with liberal values of individualism and economic competition. Higonnet himself argues that the corporatist ethos remained powerful in France, despite the rhetoric of individual rights enshrined in 1789, and suggests that, from the outset, republicans were fundamentally unable to connect individualism with concern for the public good. Nord suggests that the Third Republic inherited these contradictions, particularly since radical republicanism, with its strongly Rousseauian tincture, continued to play a crucial political role. Patrice Higonnet, *Sister Republics: The Origins of French and American Republicanism*, Cambridge, MA: Harvard University Press (1988); Jennifer Jones, 'Repackaging Rousseau: femininity and fashion in Old-Regime France', *French Historical Studies*, 18, 1994, pp. 939–67; Ronald Aminzade, *Ballots and Barricades: Class Formation and Republican Politics in France, 1830–1971*, Princeton: Princeton University Press, (1993); Philip G. Nord, 'Republicanism and utopian vision: French Freemasonry in the 1860s and 1870s', *Journal of Modern History*, 63, 1991, pp. 213–29.

8. Department store commerce expanded exponentially during the 1860s and 1870s, so that by 1877 the stores were economic giants. According to Philip Nord, 'the Bon Marché's gross earnings, seven million francs in 1863, had shot up to sixty-seven million by 1877', *Paris Shopkeepers*, p. 77. Business continued to grow apace during the 1880s and 1890s, and the stores' success was made visible by architectural expansion and the diversification of product lines.

9. Social Catholics specifically targeted the department store as a threat to the stability of the family. For an excellent discussion of their critique of big commerce, see Geoffrey Crossick, 'Metaphors of the middle: the

discovery of the petite bourgeoisie 1880–1914', *Transactions of the Royal Historical Society*, 6th series, 4, 1994, pp. 251–79.

10. Critics included small retailers and artisans, *boulevardiers* and *flâneurs*, a wide range of journalists, writers, artists, social scientists, and cultural critics, and, in the realm of politics, Social Catholics, and Catholic Le Playists. But they also numbered among them Opportunist and Radical Republicans who, although committed to supporting the business community, worried along with everyone else about the centrifugal forces of individualism unleashed by the marketplace.

11. Octave Uzanne, *La femme et la mode*, Paris: May et Motterez (1892), p. 226.

12. The passage of the Sée Law creating girls' *lycées* in 1880 and the reintroduction of divorce in 1884, for example, were said to promote women's independence.

13. Henry Bordeaux, 'L'école des femmes', *Le bulletin du Foyer*, pp. 15–17 (Conférences Littéraires et Cours Pratique d'Economie Domestique pour les Jeunes Filles et les Jeunes Femmes du Monde. Extracts of a speech given to *Le Foyer*, 11 February, 1911), Archives de la Seine: D 40Z Collection Bouteron.

14. William Marshall, *French Home Life*, London: William Blackwood and Sons (1883).

15. Foveau de Courmelles, *Modes féminines et dépopulation, ext. de la Revue Mondiale*, 1 November, 1901, pp. 284–85.

16. Nord's *Paris Shopkeepers* offers the best account of the department store as a prime target for critics of Haussmannisation.

17. Jeanne Gaillard has written the most comprehensive analysis of Haussmann's transformation of Paris from a closed city of separate neighbourhoods into a network open to the circulation of traffic, people, and goods that altered the bourgeois conception of boundaries between public and private. *Paris, la ville 1852–1870*, Paris: Honoré Champion (1977). See also Nord, *Paris Shopkeepers*.

18. Anon., *Actualités: Ah Mame Chopin!* Musée Carnavalet, Moeurs PC 130–37.

19. See, for example, Louise d'Alq, *Le nouveau savoir-vivre universel*, 3 vols, Paris: Bureaux des Causeries Familières (1881), vol. 1, pp. 173–4.

20. D'Alq, *Le nouveau savoir-vivre*, vol. 3, p. 217. On the conflation of the prostitute and the fashionable woman, see also Marianna Valverde, 'Fashion and the fallen women in nineteenth-century social discourse', *Victorian Studies*, 32, 1989, pp. 169–88, and Walkowitz, *City of Dreadful Delight*.

21. Arsène Alexandre, *Les reines de l'aiguille*, Paris: Théophile Belin (1902), p. 175.

22. On the topic of shoplifting, see Patricia O'Brien, 'The kleptomania diagnosis: bourgeois women and theft in late nineteenth-century France', *Journal of Social History*, 17, 1983, pp. 65–77. See also Chapter 6 by Uwe Spiekermann in this volume.

23. This rhetorical shift has been aptly noted by Robert Nye in his book *Crime, Madness, and Politics in Modern France: the Medical Concept of National Decline*, Princeton: Princeton University Press (1984).

24. Ignotus, 'Les grands bazars,' n. p.

25. For Zola, for example, the Bon Marché's yearly white sale was the site of

mob hysteria. Emile Zola, notes for *Au Bonheur des Dames*, p. 164, Bibliothèque Nationale: NAF 10277.

26. Edgar Allan Poe, 'The Man of the Crowd', in James Harrison (ed.), *The Complete Works of Edgar Allan Poe*, New York: AMS Press (1965).

27. Ibid., p. 142.

28. Ignotus, 'Les grands bazars,' n. p. The journalist claimed to cite a celebrated physician.

29. These theorists included the social psychologist Gustave LeBon, the novelist Paul Adam, and the syndicalist-socialist Georges Sorel.

30. Gustave Le Bon, *Psychologie des foules*, Osnabruck: Zeller Verlag (1982). Original edition 1895.

31. Pierre Giffard, *Les grands bazars: Paris sous la Troisième République*, Paris: Havard (1882), p. 14.

32. Zola, notes for *Au Bonheur*, p. 11.

33. A. Coffignon, *Les coulisses de la mode*, Paris: Librairie illustré (n.d. [*c.* 1890]).

34. Giffard, *Les grands bazars*, p. 298.

35. Anon., 'Deux sous d'épingles', *Agenda de la Maison des Magasins Réunis* (1913), p. 7, Bibliothèque Historique de la Ville de Paris: 4°Z 211.

36. Paul Dubuisson, *Les voleuses de grands magasins*, Paris: A. Storck et Compagnie (1904), p. 42.

37. Mathilde Bourdon, 'Histoire d'un agent de change', *Le journal des Demoiselles*, 1, 3 January–4 September 1880.

38. Giffard, *Les grands bazars,* p. 240.

39. Ibid., p. 299.

40. Coffignon, *Les coulisses,* p. 194. Even if the consumer did not actually commit adultery, the act of shopping carried salacious overtones for many observers. For the popular novelist Henri Boutet, the consumer's agitation, her rapture upon making a purchase, and the surge of remorse she felt afterward tellingly mimicked the emotional cycles of the adulterous wife. *Almanach pour 1899: Les heures de la Parisienne*, Paris: Melet (1899), pp. 56–7.

41. Dubuisson, *Les voleuses*, p. 41.

42. Ignotus, 'Les grands bazars,' n.p.

43. Fernand Laudet, 'Exposition de l'oeuvre du Foyer', *Le bulletin du Foyer*, pp. 10–11, AS: D 40Z. *Le Foyer* offered a course in law intended to combat this very problem.

44. As Philip Nord writes, 'the first years of the Third Republic ... placed the highest premium on the individual of outstanding ability ... . But liberal individualism was under siege at the end of the century ... corporatist thinking enjoyed a revival in the nineties', in *Paris Shopkeepers,* p. 480. In Maurice Agulhon's words, by the 1890s, 'French society ... staked less on a "law of the jungle" capitalism than on sound, straightforward capitalism', in *The French Republic, 1879–92*, Oxford: Blackwell (1993), p. 52. Similarly, Judith Stone suggests that a combination of economic woes and social disharmony during the 1880s engendered a thoroughgoing reconsideration (although not a repudiation) of the tenets of classical liberalism in the 1890s. *The Search for Social Peace: Reform Legislation in France, 1890–1914*, Albany, NY: State University of New York Press (1985), p. 25.

45. See, for example, Agulhon, *The French Republic*, ch. 2.

46. The phrase is T.H. Breen's, from his essay 'The meanings of things: interpreting the consumer economy in the eighteenth century', in John Brewer and Roy Porter (eds), *Consumption and the World of Goods*, London: Routledge (1993).

47. For example, the French trade literature on advertising in the 1890s is replete with doubts about whether the primary purpose of advertising is to sell things or to enhance French aesthetic prestige. See the journal *La publicité moderne* for examples of these debates.

48. Recent research suggests that, although republican reformers such as the Solidarists were more concerned with repulsing the socialist threat than they were with controlling bourgeois women, some of the same concerns that shaped debates about workers informed debates about women. See Judith Coffin, 'Social science meets sweated labor: reinterpreting women's work in late nineteenth-century France', *Journal of Modern History*, 63, 1991, pp. 230–70; Elinor Accampo, Rachel Fuchs, and Mary Lynn Stewart (eds), *Gender and the Politics of Social Reform in France, 1870–1914*, Baltimore: Johns Hopkins University Press (1995). Philip Nord argues convincingly, moreover, that masculine roles were as shifting and contested within the bourgeois interior as feminine roles were in the public realm in *fin-de-siècle* France. Philip Nord, 'Republican politics and the bourgeois interior in mid-nineteenth-century France', in Suzanne Nash (ed.), *Home and Its Dislocations in Nineteenth-Century France*, Albany: State University of New York Press (1993), pp. 193–214.

49. It was also constructed, of course, against the image of the rational, orderly and virtuous feminine domestic realm.

50. A. Cucheval-Clarigny, *Les grandes usines de Turgan: Les magasins du Bon Marché* (1889), pp. 43–4, BHVP Actualités: 120 Bon Marché.

51. For an analysis of the Bon Marché's complex relationship to traditional and modern social and economic values, see Michael Miller, *The Bon Marché: Bourgeois Culture and the Department Store, 1869–1920*, Princeton: Princeton University Press (1981).

52. La Belle Jardinière publicity (n.d. [early twentieth century]), AS: D 39Z.

53. Cucheval-Clarigny, *Les grandes usines*, p. 44, BHVP Actualités: 120 Bon Marché.

54. 'Pourquoi j'aime le Bon Marché', Bon Marché publicity (1921), BHVP Actualités: 120 Bon Marché.

55. Pygmalion publicity (11 November 1907), n.p., BHVP Actualités: 120 Pygmalion.

56. *Exposition des soieries*, Pygmalion publicity (1904), n. p., BHVP Actualités: 120 Pygmalion.

57. As one publicity textbook put it, 'The advertiser ... knows that he can create new desires, or transform those that exist', Octave-Jacques Gérin and C. Espinadel, *La publicité suggestive: Théorie et technique*, Paris: Dunod et Pinat (1911), p. 21.

58. Louise d'Alq, *Le maître et la maîtresse de maison*, Paris: Bureaux des Causeries Familières (1882), p. 118.

59. Ibid., p. 118.

60. Bordeaux, 'L'école des femmes', p. 22.

61. As Elinor Accampo, Rachel Fuchs and Mary Lynn Stewart argue, this was the only possible relationship between women and the French state in the *fin de siècle*. On gender and republican citizenship, see Accampo, Fuchs

and Stewart, *Gender and the Politics of Social Reform* as well as Judith Stone, 'Republican ideology, gender, and class: France, 1860s-1914', in Laura Frader and Sonya Rose (eds), *Gender and Class in Modern Europe*, Ithaca and London: Cornell University Press (1996), pp. 238–59.

62. Gilles Normand, *Les Entreprise modernes. Le Grand commerce de détail*, Paris: Librairie Perrin, (1920), pp. 19–23.

63. *Carnet d'artiste. Les Soieries au XIIIe siècle. L'Exposition du 4 avril 1910*, p. 2, Pygmalion publicity, BHVP Actualités: 120 Pygmalion.

64. Georges Michel, 'Une évolution économique: Le commerce en grands magasins', *Revue des deux mondes*, 109, 1 January 1892, pp. 133–56.

65. Bazar de l'Hôtel de Ville publicity (1912), AS: D 18Z. The figure of Marianne appears not infrequently in department store advertising around the turn of the century, thus invoking an iconographic connection between the nation and the marketplace.

CHAPTER SIX

Theft and thieves in German department stores, 1895–1930: a discourse on morality, crime and gender

Uwe Spiekermann

Shoplifting today is a mass phenomenon, which in 1994, resulted in 579 274 cases being reported to the German police. However, the actual number of these crimes committed in Germany is perhaps 25 times greater, creating an estimated annual economic loss of 2 billion DM.[1] A hundred years ago, people did not know how to react to this phenomenon, although in certain well-read circles there would have been an awareness of the novel by Karl Gutzkow entitled *The Wizard of Rome*, which was written towards the end of the 1850s and described the conviction of a rich woman for theft from a fashion shop. Many people would have read Emile Zola's *Au Bonheur des Dames* (1882), a work in which shoplifting becomes a symbol of the seductive power of the modern type of Parisian department store. However, only specialists would have known Victor Mataja's book *Large Stores and Retail Trade* (1891), in which the author refers to the situation in Paris once again, this form of theft as yet remaining undifferentiated from common crime in Germany. At this time, both brawls and theft were part of everyday life and were more likely to result in the perpetrator being beaten up than reported to the police. In addition, theft from small shops was complicated not only by the presence of the proprietor and the shop assistant, but also by the broad shop counter which acted as a simple and effective deterrent.

By the end of the 1890s, the situation in Germany had changed dramatically. 'Today one can read about thefts in department stores everywhere.'[2] From the 1890s onwards, the department store had gained ground in Germany as a new form of business enterprise.[3] Apart from profound changes produced in the retail trade, the advent of the department store also resulted in new, and sometimes criminal, behaviour patterns particularly amongst female customers. Whilst shoplifting today is regarded with reluctant tolerance as an unavoidable evil, German people at that time reacted with a mixture of fascination and amazement to this strange form of crime which did not correspond to their norms of bourgeois virtue.

This chapter investigates the early history of shoplifting within the context of the intellectual cultural environment in Germany after the turn of the century. Before exploring the different manifestations and interpretations of the new phenomenon of 'department store theft', its empirical significance should be considered. The first group to criticise the new form of business enterprise was the shopkeeper movement. In their view, the business ethics practised by department stores were immoral and, as such, were both an expression and the origin of criminal action. Journalists and economists offered explanations which were less straightforward. They argued that the department store operated as a selling machine, using – or indeed abusing – the female psyche. The social responsibility for theft was already under discussion but, under the influence of the new sciences of psychiatry and criminology, blame was now individualised. Department store theft was considered to be not only the product of woman's body and her sexuality but also of mental disease and inferiority, which was regarded as part of woman's nature. This 'scientific' view, the product of male prejudice, served as the basis for an understanding of department store theft which was both new and unromantic. By the 1920s department store theft had lost its exceptional status and had become one more petty crime amongst others.

The quantitative development of department store theft in Germany

It is impossible to investigate the precise number of department store thefts in Germany around the turn of century, because the data published at that time are not sufficiently consistent. German crime statistics before 1977 were published as undifferentiated data, using only general categories. In criminal law, department store theft did not differ in any way from ordinary neighbourhood or street larceny. All these offences were considered as different forms of 'simple larceny' and therefore those convicted were punished by imprisonment.[4] In cases of 'repeated simple larceny' the punishment quickly increased in severity, possibly amounting to several months or even up to a year in prison, but rarely more than that. An examination of these crime statistics, containing only the number of convicted thieves within the general categories, reveals that department store theft certainly did not increase the total number of cases of 'simple larceny'. On the contrary, the annual total decreased slowly but continuously, with the exception of the years of war and inflation. The statistics also show that the number of thefts committed by women decreased much more than the number committed by men. This occurs particularly in the case of 'repeated simple larceny', which probably took place more often in department stores than in any other location. This unbalanced pattern of development is significant and relates to issues of gender and department store theft which will be examined in more detail.

Nevertheless, the decrease in official crime statistics must not lead to the mistaken belief that the new phenomenon of department store theft was negligible. A regional analysis of the relevant court records shows, for example, that the proportion of women in all cases of 'simple larceny' was at least 10 per cent and that this trend was rising.[5] This percentage, if extrapolated to apply to Germany as a whole, would produce a figure of approximately 2 000 female department store thieves each year. Considering the relatively small scale of the problem indicated by these figures, can a study of this phenomenon be justified?

It can be argued that there are three reasons which make such a study worthwhile. Firstly, if evidence from unofficial sources is also taken into account, a distinctly different impression of department store theft will emerge. Contrary to the pattern followed by the development of 'simple larceny', the absolute figures clearly rose from the turn of the century until the beginning of the First World War. In 1898, nearly a hundred shoplifters were taken to court by the Berlin department stores. In 1907, this number was reported for the last few days before Christmas alone.[6] In 1909, 'several hundred thefts' were noted by the West German company of Leonhard Tietz, and at the same time it was mentioned that these 'were not as widespread in west Germany as, for example, in Berlin'. It was estimated that the value of all the goods stolen at Wertheim would be 'enough to run an ordinary department store'.[7] The increase in thefts did not match the growth in department store turnover, which rose from 50 million Marks in 1900 to approximately 500–600 million Marks in 1913,[8] but it is clear that department store theft did increase within the overall crime statistics. This trend continued during the first years of the First World War but, contrary to the development of larceny as a whole, department store theft rapidly lost significance after 1916 because supplies of goods for the department stores were unavailable.[9] After the First World War, the number of offences increased enormously again. 'In 1921, according to a police report, more than 1 000 thefts occurred in one of Leipzig's biggest department stores. The value of the missing goods reached more than 750 000 Marks.'[10] It was only with the stabilisation of the German currency that these figures decreased, finally settling by the end of the 1920s at a level probably slightly below that of the pre-war period.[11]

Secondly, it is necessary to examine why the development of department store theft was not reflected in the official crime statistics. The reason lies principally with the department stores themselves. Not only the customers, but also the thieves were treated in a relatively generous way. The department store detectives who from 1898, were employed to guarantee the internal security of the salerooms, always took the particulars of the thieves but, although they sometimes photographed them and ensured that the stolen goods were paid for, they normally did not hand the culprits over to the police. Persistent offenders, professional thieves and gangs were the only exceptions.[12] Generally, department stores refrained from making official announcements because they feared that any association with crime might harm their business.[13] For this reason, the official statistics revealed only a fraction of the thefts discovered, which again were only a small part of all the offences occurring. As a result, the official statistics did not reflect the real situation. Department store theft could only be counted when it was discovered, reported to the police and punished accordingly, leading to the inevitable conclusion that there were a great number of crimes which were not reported.

Thirdly, it can be argued that the ensuing discourse on theft and thieves in German department stores was one which was taking place without a sound empirical picture of the new phenomenon and therefore could not be 'objective'. A study of this phenomenon will not reveal 'facts' concerning a special form of crime, but can lead to a greater understanding of the contemporary assessment of the department store, of the subsequent consequences and of the perception of female crime by male experts. Many contemporary articles and books illustrate how people at the turn of the century merely equated this new form of retailing with a new form of crime. This consciousness formed a mental reality in its own right and in some ways gives a better impression of contemporary values and priorities than empirical information ever could. Although department store theft was an important criminal offence, its historiographic significance clearly consists in a discourse on morality, crime and gender, which, at the same time, mirrored the mentality of German society.

Business immorality and personal immorality: the perspective of the petit-bourgeois movement

Today, the significance of the department store as a new and innovative form of retailing is widely accepted. However, a hundred years ago, Germans were unable to recognise and define the department store in a modern sense. It was quite difficult to distinguish between the former bazaars, large shops and hire purchase companies, between consumer co-operatives for civil servants and mail order houses with salerooms. The problem of differentiation was even more difficult because German department stores originally sold mainly cheap and mass produced articles using loud and blatant advertising. This explains why the petite bourgeoisie, which dominated the retail trade, concentrated its energy, at least till 1896, primarily on competing with hawkers and consumer co-operatives. The department stores were not seen as a threat but rather as objects of scorn and mockery.[14] The traditional retail traders had seen the appearance of many unusual kinds of retailing, frequently of a transitory nature as in the case of the one-price bazaars, and it was presumed that this would also be the fate of the department stores. The petite bourgeoisie backed a policy of 'quality' instead of 'trash', they preferred polite service to the anonymous treatment of customers: 'The retailer should advise the public; as an expert he should point out that one thing will suit you whereas another item might not be appropriate for your particular household. In this respect, retailers will always be good advisers for their customers.'[15]

But these expectations were unrealistic and when, in 1897, a new architectural style came to symbolise the dynamic expansion of department stores, the petit-bourgeois movement began a systematic campaign against the new competitor, whose strategy appeared both unfair and immoral. The petit-bourgeois movement was especially angry about the 'loss leader' system, which meant that goods were offered at cost price or even lower. In the eyes of the retailers, this was only a sales gimmick. The department stores tried to present themselves as a cheap source of goods, but they used 'business practices, which would have created outrage in former times'.[16] In reality, however, goods were not cheaper, and the quality undoubtedly compared unfavourably with the usual range offered by an old-established retailer. The petit-bourgeois movement never considered the department stores to be an equal competitor, but as illegitimate interlopers denying small retailers their rightful property.[17] This 'criminalisation' of department stores was an important basis for the public and political confrontations which followed. The prohibition and 'strangulation' of the department stores was demanded in Germany and many special taxes and state restrictions were introduced.[18]

During this conflict, newspaper articles on department store theft were seized upon by leading representatives of the petit-bourgeois movement. They could easily be integrated into the existing debate, and the well-known thefts in Parisian department stores had already been interpreted as a symbol of the increasing immorality in public life.[19] It became clear that in Germany, too, a gradual moral decline had begun. The collective departure of department stores from traditional business practices led directly to individual deviance: 'Opportunity makes a customer – it also makes a thief. These great bazaars and chain stores lure the customer into buying and stealing those masses of goods which are so enticingly arranged; they have made many a vain and over-dressed woman into a thief.'[20] The department stores helped to make this kind of crime an everyday phenomenon. Both the working class and the middle class were affected. The petit-bourgeois movement argued that the department store undermined the unwritten laws of traditional and patriarchal society and that their existence therefore challenged the moral consciousness of the German nation.[21] Fighting against the new competitor meant fighting for the ethical ideals of the German people, it meant resisting the reprehensible influences of the scheming Americans and the artificial French.[22] Whilst the supposed decline of the middle classes caused by the department stores had to be prevented by the State, the struggle against the risk posed by female thieves had to be individualised: 'Craftsmen, merchants and peasants! Keep your wives and daughters away from those stores, for otherwise you may get them back, roasted by (hell) fire or denounced as thieves.'[23] An alteration in the behaviour of women was seen as instrumental in helping men gain victory over their opponents. In this discourse, the German woman was seen as a moral force that must be protected against all the temptations which led her to theft. The German family was imagined as a bulwark against the immorality of department stores, an immorality that could also be seen in the stores' pretence of support for single women when in reality the seductive charms expected of female shop assistants in order to achieve sales were but the first step towards prostitution.[24] The early petit-bourgeois movement thus stressed, in a way that was inevitably coloured by its own ideology and preju-dice, two important points which were to influence the future discourse on department store theft, firstly, the role of woman as the most frequent department store customer and, secondly, the social consequences of modern consumer society.

Woman: a creature subject to temptation

At the end of the 1890s, all the participants in the discussion agreed that the growing importance of the department stores resulted from their attractiveness to women. Such 'amazing creations like the huge department store are made of the flesh and the blood of woman. That is the secret of their success'.[25] An understanding of the predominantly male line of argument suggests that the department store combined two female stereotypes for commercial purposes, the picture of the caring wife and mother on the one hand, and the image of the vain and fashionable woman on the other.

Initially, the woman was always attracted by the low prices and special offers which were the constant theme of advertisements. Thus, shopping in the department store seemed to be the sacred duty of a woman who was supposed to run her household as economically as possible. The 'loss leader' system was criticised so severely by the lower middle-class movement because it exposed the ambiguities of the commercial economy. On the one hand, it intensified price competition and challenged the regulated economy to which the petit-bourgeois movement was committed. On the other, it helped women play their household role by saving their husband's income. This was the main reason why these companies started to open food halls on their upper floors in 1892. Fresh food, as well as mass-produced food, was offered at exceptionally low prices.[26] The department store appeared to meet in a reasonable fashion the need for irregular purchases, such as textiles and furniture. The emphasis on low prices in this new kind of retailing thus connected with the attachment to thrift in a traditional system of values, an attachment acceptable not only to housewives but also to many underpaid single women.

Women, 'addicted to cheapness'[27] as it was put at the time, found themselves confronted by the modern high-powered sales techniques of the department store, which had never previously been experienced in such a concentrated form. The department store owner now

> has the woman caught in the trap. Now he can trust in the allure of a thousand ringed fingers tempting her to buy something, and he can be certain that even the most thrifty of housewives, who has come because of an unprecedented bargain, will go home weighed down with items she does not need.[28]

The female customer entered into an aesthetically constructed world of merchandise; she was led into a new, hitherto unknown relationship with goods for sale. In contrast to the medium-sized fashion shop, where most of the products were carefully kept either on shelves or in cases and boxes which were taken out only on request, the department store's goods were openly displayed, available for the customer to see without any obligation to buy. The nature of shopping changed, as the vastness and splendour of the new stores gave it a new quality. The department store as a whole however, continued to be divided into a number of smaller departments which were managed independently with individual tills, the old-fashioned counter now becoming merely a small cash desk. Shop assistants were plentiful, attending to the goods and maintaining direct contact with the female customers. Self-service did not exist, the customer had to point out the desired product to the saleswoman, get a receipt in order to pay at the corresponding till and then finally receive the chosen item. This system had been practised by the hire purchase bazaars since the early 1880s, but they had only offered a limited choice of products, and it was the department store that presented a wide range of goods in a new and seductive fashion. The department store was originally created to exploit the need for basic requirements, only to abuse those needs subsequently in order to encourage mass consumption. The aim was to create new needs, to stimulate the desire for something new, something more.[29] Women in particular were confronted with the conventional image of the beautiful and elegant woman, an image most middle-class women could imitate only through considerable financial sacrifices. Once established, these new requirements began the process which forms the basis for mass consumption and affluence in the present day. The 'loss leader' system lost its significance for new companies from the turn of the century, as the act of shopping itself became the essential experience. It became an expression of the new lifestyle characterised by modern mass consumption.[30] In using tempting displays to stimulate the desire to purchase, the department store represented the increasing importance of means over ends.

This system directed at the stimulation of needs required new inner restraints, because of the fundamental discrepancy between an individual's resources and his or her potentially inexhaustible demand. These restraints had to rest on individual self-discipline, and on the ability to recognise the constraints of household expenditure, when faced with a world of exciting goods for sale. Self-control was often unsuccessful. Many people outside the petit-bourgeois movement argued that the department stores' powers of seduction were the main reason for the increasing number of thefts there:

> Desire is stimulated by the quantity and variety of the products exhibited before the public. This same desire is further excited by the fact that, particularly at peak business hours, nobody watches over the goods placed so temptingly close to the customers. Theft is aided by the mass of customers who, albeit unknowingly, thus become accomplices.[31]

However, the question of whether it was the department stores themselves that were responsible for the thefts became less important after the turn of the century. The reasons for this change were not only to be found in the fact that many paid less attention to criticisms presented by the petit-bourgeois movement or in the increasing social acceptance of the department store from the late 1890s. It was also pointed out that people did not steal in department stores alone but also at markets and fairs.[32] The changing social character of shopping was mentioned as well as a greater sense of discipline in spending and the lower frequency of theft amongst working-class women.[33] But the main argument seemed to be that German department stores, in contrast to their French counterparts, sold only for cash. As a consequence, indebtedness was virtually eliminated.

The second important argument against department stores' responsibility for theft was the existence of internal control measures, which had been improved steadily since 1898: 'Some of these great bazaars ... have set up their own police service and have employed private detectives, especially women, who patrol the shops in various disguises, to watch the customers and catch thieves when necessary.'[34] During peak business hours, regular policemen were also employed to guard the salerooms.[35] Detectives and shop assistants were instructed to be vigilant and keep a watchful eye on the customers. At the same time, the first internal security devices were introduced. Glass display cases established a new kind of separation without destroying the visual impact, the supervision by employees was improved with the help of mirror systems and, finally, valuable goods were kept securely.[36] Nevertheless, in comparison with the measures suggested by criminologists and psychologists, these precautions still seemed inadequate while some rationalisation measures, such as the establishment of central cash register systems from 1905 to 1906, served to diminish the effectiveness of supervision. In spite of all these measures, theft remained an evil that was tolerated by the owners of the department stores. They sought primarily to minimise the social consequences by treating the thieves leniently. The experience of shopping was considered more important than the prevention of theft by individuals. Delinquency was reluctantly accepted as an aspect of mass consumption: 'If we opposed an institution merely because it was unable to prevent theft, there would be only one radical means at our disposal: that is to say, the abolition of property.'[37] The dialectical connection between department stores and theft was recognised, but contemporary opinion supported the view that 'theft does not depend on the place of the crime, it is the thieves themselves who must be watched'.[38]

These thieves were mostly women, a surprising fact when statistics reveal that female crime was only one-fifth of the total.[39] Shops in general and department stores in particular were amongst the few public places where a woman was able to move freely, unaccompanied by her husband. The strong interest in female department store thieves has always been an expression of a male desire to control women and also an indication of male interest in what was supposed to be 'real' female behaviour. It soon became apparent that the actual events, rather than being recorded accurately, were being integrated into a system determined by what was considered to be the norm and that this revealed more about the way men thought than it did about offences committed by women. This observation applies to the numerous scattered statements of middle-class critics, economists and contemporary journalists. It is applicable to an even greater extent in the case of the 'scientific' remarks of psychologists and experts on crime, which can only be understood as part of a discourse characterised by public prejudices and a very specific perception of reality. Science was in this respect an instrument of social power, not of enlightenment. The female thief was reduced to her gender, she was not perceived as an individual but as an object. She was considered a passive, but nevertheless an emotional and highly excitable, creature. Whilst the nature of man was accepted as being predominantly intellectual and rational, woman was reduced to her body, and was thus understood as a form of weak-willed reaction to external stimuli. A female thief once said that 'she had seen a large assortment of things lying on a table in a muddle. She thought someone had whispered into her ear, "Take it, take it!" Highly excited, she had felt compelled to pick up and conceal some children's clothes without thinking what she was doing'.[40] The offence was tempting not because of the stolen goods but because of the circumstances in which they were acquired. In this sense, the means were perhaps more important than the ends.[41] Female department store theft seemed to be a collective epidemic that was hard to fight because of women's compulsion to steal and because guards and security devices could be ignored:

> There were hundreds of women recognisable by their big, loose coats and their even more suspicious looking 'capes', who came to the department stores all the year round, year after year, just to steal. They looked around to see if some of the employees of a particular department were anywhere near or if they were momentarily idle, and whether or not the crowd was large enough for them to carry out their plan unseen. Normally they carried some so called 'pseudo purchases' with them, and while the shop assistant delivered the bargains to the till, the offenders stole a considerably more valuable item. Shortly afterwards they would disappear without paying.[42]

From the beginning, this phenomenon was of interest to neurologists because most thefts seemed to be aimless and the kind of goods which were stolen appeared to be so utterly arbitrary.[43] Initially they believed that department store theft might be a specifically female form of a physically compulsive act, which resulted from an excessive demand on the senses caused by the enormous range of goods offered at the department stores. Although this was still seen as a necessary condition, the main reason seemed to lie in the essence of woman.[44]

However, this simple stimulus-response model was not considered to be completely satisfactory. It was obvious that many female department store thieves lived in sound financial circumstances, and that they therefore did not steal out of any real material necessity. Whilst poor living conditions and the intention to improve their situation were arguments enough to explain those offences committed by working-class women, the general seductive power of the department store alone was not sufficient to explain theft committed by middle-class women.[45] Neurologists and legal experts therefore asked themselves whether female department store theft might not be interpreted as, on the one hand, an expression of a kind of disease, presumably of a mental nature, or on the other hand, a product of female sexuality. Both ideas were based on a changing attitude towards the nature of woman. During the nineteenth century, medicine had assumed the physical inferiority of woman, but specific psychological features were increasingly added to this model which came to depend less on physical factors alone.

Diminished responsibility: the pathologisation of department store theft

The discourse relating to department store theft has always contained an element of astonishment. Theft seemed to be an atavistic element in the well-organised world of the German middle classes, the 'emergence of a long forgotten period in mankind's history, when the naked urge to take everything that could be useful was justified by nature'.[46] If department store theft had been occurring a few decades earlier, neurologists probably would have diagnosed kleptomania. However, in contrast to this earlier view of kleptomania as a disease of the wealthy, psychiatrists in the 1890s were beginning to deny the existence of an independent pathological mania for stealing, provided that there were no other symptoms of mental disease.[47] Psychiatrists, consulted in cases of theft by wealthy women, and reluctant to send them to prison, most frequently diagnosed neurasthenia, a chronic form of mental fatigue, or a specific form of hysteria. Both of these diagnoses held a common view of theft as a kind of impulsive act which could not have been caused by the temptations on offer in the department stores alone. Department store theft was usually interpreted as a criminal act, committed in a state of impaired consciousness, but rarely as a compulsive act. This also applied to cases of female thieves who suffered from prolonged mental problems such as mental deficiency. Whenever psychiatrists published an article on the phenomenon of department store theft, their discussion went beyond narrowly medical issues. The behaviour of female thieves was always attributed to a mental disease, such as 'pathological confusion'. In the same way that middle-class retailers would not initially accept department stores as equal competitors, psychiatrists would not classify theft committed by wealthy women as ordinary crime. Only organised gangs or so-called professional thieves were thought of as 'real' offenders. Established experts were not willing to accept the notion of a scandalous new kind of crime, that is to say a theft committed without any apparent material necessity. Instead, department store theft was excluded from what was called the 'normal' behaviour of middle-class citizens. Psychiatrists believed that most female thieves were inferior beings in a moral, as well as a physical and psychological, sense. The discourse on temptation promulgated by the petit-bourgeois movement, journalists and economists, revealed the participants' prejudices against both the business practices of the department store and women. The pathologisation of department store theft by psychiatrists was an expression of their own hopes and fears rather than the result of careful analysis. Thus, most of the case studies dealing with female department store thieves tell us more about the power of scientific definition than about the reasons for a particular crime.

Neurasthenic women, most of them in their twenties or thirties, were frequently physically and emotionally exhausted by several pregnancies, diseases or tragic events:

> They had shown physical signs of serious anaemia and clear symptoms of emotional fatigue long before they committed the offence. They had complained about headaches and were hardly capable of doing their housework; they did not sleep well and had to rest frequently during the day. Contrary to their former frame of mind they became careless in carrying out their duties; they tended to be moody and irritable and, occasionally, could not force themselves to do their work; when time pressed, they carried out their duties hastily and superficially ... . These women had never shown any signs of hysteria, nor had hysteria run in their families, they had on the contrary always been particularly good-natured, diligent and well-behaved people ... . All these women showed similar behaviour patterns: they pulled themselves together reluctantly to do their shopping, during this time they also went to the department store where they actually bought some goods and, whilst waiting in a queue, 'lifted' certain other items, which were usually inexpensive. All the persons examined ... offered the same excuse: because of the crowd and the bright lights they had become dizzy and had taken those items without thinking ...[48]

In contrast, hysteria in women seemed to be a direct result of woman's physical nature:

Almost every case shows hereditary disease of varying severity in the family; it can be proved that symptoms of hysteria, of a lasting or of a periodic kind, had been diagnosed long before the theft. Apart from the well-known symptoms of sudden rage, the disorders essentially connected with menstruation are attacks of acute anxiety and restlessness, of dizziness and a transient disturbance of consciousness. From the beginning, some patients did not remember their offence at all. When they were arrested, they were so utterly taken aback that they did not know what to say to the accusation of having stolen the items found on them. Some confessed to having stolen everything, although they had a receipt for part of the goods.[49]

However, the diseases diagnosed by psychiatrists were not always recognised by criminologists and lawyers. German criminal law at that time did not acknowledge the existence of a grey area between health and disease. In order to reach the verdict of 'not guilty', Article 51 of the German penal code insisted that consciousness must be disordered to such an extent that the accused was incapable of making a decision of their own free will. However, this kind of diminished responsibility did not occur in most cases of neurasthenic and hysterical women.[50] As a result, the majority of psychiatrists would appeal to the courts for leniency for their clients. However, following the conviction of a thief, a psychiatrist would only be able to bring about a reduction of the prison sentence, they could not prevent it. The introduction of a new legal term of 'diminished responsibility', which had been under discussion for some time in more general terms, appeared to be an acceptable solution. The offender had to be considered more thoroughly as an individual, temporary disorders had to be acknowledged, and a prison sentence could be replaced by a fine if desired.[51] However, this phenomenon must be examined within a wider context than the modern reform of criminal law. The fundamental inferiority of woman's nature was also stressed. It was argued at the time that this infantile creature, inferior both physically and psychologically, required a special status within the criminal law because, unlike a male criminal, she could not be considered responsible for her offences.[52] Professional motives were also relevant. 'Diminished responsibility' was a plea which was inevitably connected with an extensive psychiatric report, and it was suggested that all female department store thieves should be examined by psychiatrists.[53] Although thieves who were discovered but not reported were often handed over to their families to be handled privately, frequently by a type of 'house arrest', the intention was that psychiatry, because of its greater flexibility, could take over the role of the institutions of criminal law in cases of reported theft.[54]

But despite intensive debates at the beginning of the twentieth century and during the late 1920s, a plea of 'diminished responsibility' was not legally acceptable in a criminal case. The definition seemed too vague and society's traditional demands for protection of property, personal security and the deterrent impacts of law were of paramount importance.[55] More moderate assessments of department store theft also failed, as the scientific discourse had already begun to adopt new concepts before the First World War. Department store theft was no longer seen as simply an expression of mental disease, it was also increasingly being regarded as a crime related to sexuality. After the First World War, Article 51 of the German penal code was applied less frequently to department store theft and the usual appeal to the courts for leniency gradually came to be based on a comparison with other forms of 'simple larceny', rather than on pathological evidence.[56]

Environment and stimulation: the sexualisation of department store theft

Despite an understanding of department store theft as the expression of a mental disorder or disease, the explanations given for this criminal offence were neither satisfactory nor reassuring. A problem remained, considerable numbers of women were stealing from busy department stores and hoarding the stolen items at home. These women were not deprived materially and consequently did not need the stolen goods at all. The pathologisation of department store theft merely provided a description without being able to show realistic possibilities of controlling the phenomenon. After the turn of the century, new hypotheses were investigated in which particular attention was given to the sexual background of this type of offence.[57]

The basis for this discourse was the seductive power, not only in an asexual sense, of the department store itself. Department stores were regarded as 'the clip joints of trade' by many retailers and any kind of purchase there gave rise to sexual allusions: 'Our female population, is so ripe for seduction (amusement), with respect to purchasing of course, for women seem to buy completely unnecessary little things so very often.'[58] The atmosphere in the salerooms was tense and sparkling and the presence of so many well-dressed women of marrying age was often referred to as an attraction in its own right.[59] The department store was part of the commercialisation and rationalisation of society, an expression of technical and organisational efficiency. At the same time, however, it also contained the opposite, namely the 'craving for sexual satisfaction; a kind of desire often lost in the worries of everyday life'.[60] In department stores people were not looking for goods alone, they were also looking for one another. Dressing in fine clothes and shopping had a larger purpose.

When this interpretation was taken into consideration, occasional observations on the remarkably high proportion of menstruating, pregnant or menopausal female thieves in the total number of department store thefts came to seem more important. This information was originally noted by French neurologists, but it was soon acknowledged in Germany too.[61] Some psychiatrists even thought that thefts 'were committed almost exclusively under the influence of menstruation or, rather, of the ovulation process. Some of the female offenders were a few months pregnant, one of them was eight months pregnant'.[62] The small number of these cases, had led to scepticism before the First World War, but the data were later seen to indicate the psychological character of department store theft in psychiatric terms. Some experts claimed that 63 per cent of the total of all female thieves were menstruating women, others cited a figure of 88 per cent.[63] As menstruation and pregnancy were regarded as times of higher sexual stimulation and arousal, it now seemed possible to classify department store theft as a special form of female sex crime. Whilst in the nineteenth century menstruation had been regarded as a characteristic of woman's physical inferiority, it now became the physical basis of abnormal behaviour. In 1908, Wilhelm Steckel, a Viennese psychologist, became a decisive influence in inspiring the discussion on the sexualisation of department store theft. He thought that the 'root of all cases of kleptomania was frustrated sexuality'.[64] According to Steckel, this could easily be demonstrated by looking at the choice of objects stolen. These were either sharp objects, like pencils or umbrellas, or things into which something could be inserted, such as stockings, gloves, rings or fur coats. Unimpressed by the variety of these goods, Steckel insisted that all these things were symbols of male and female genitals. Female department store thieves thus appeared to be 'frustrated women who lacked the courage or the opportunity for sexual satisfaction ... . What we are faced with is a transfer of emotions from sexuality to crime'.[65] This interpretation resulted in a new explanation for the problem of department store theft which had far-reaching implications. It was no longer the multitude of different mental diseases that had to be investigated, but rather the sexuality of the thieves, and the way in which this predominantly female sexuality provided a common link between all the offences.

The former pathological approach was not altogether ruled out by the new explanation but it gradually lost its former significance. As female department store thieves had been considered as being 'subject to all kinds of nervous and psychotic diseases',[66] the experts were greatly relieved that the offence could now be understood primarily as a result of sexual problems between the sexes. Even though menstruation was only a periodic event, the psychoanalytic explanation had long-term significance which also removed from the department stores the burden of responsibility for the thefts. Despite the fact that the erotically charged atmosphere of the department stores was considered a catalyst for the offences and although menstruation was the most likely time for theft, the fundamental reasons seemed to be of a more individual nature. As the pattern was always the same, that is to say a so-called 'transfer', new opportunities for individual therapy and general prevention were opened up. Female thieves were still considered prisoners of their bodies, and more specifically, of their sexuality, but instead of the fatalist diagnosis of physical and intellectual inferiority, this new view of the condition as a merely temporary deviation allowed for the possibility of individual recovery. In addition, this view supported changes in the field of criminology which argued that it was no longer only degenerates, people with hereditary diseases or 'born' criminals that were predestined for offences, but that any human being was capable of theft under certain circumstances.

This new interpretation was however, only accepted very gradually and was frequently mixed with the older ideas of the economically tempted woman or the thief suffering from diminished responsibility.[67] It was supported by new observations, which suggested that single women 'committed whole series of thefts just to get sexual satisfaction'.[68] This was the other side of the sexual explanation in which department store theft seemed to be an act of compensation directly aimed at sexual abreaction, at orgasm.[69] In this interpretation the great number of customers did not function as the thief's protection but as the basis of her sexual satisfaction. Although various new approaches and techniques such as psychoanalysis managed to produce a more detailed picture of the phenomenon, they too regarded the problem as basically one of sexuality. The notion of a 'desire for weakness' and the idea of 'socio-ethically weak individuals' are representative of this approach:

> The female thief identifies with the great mass of customers and seeks to get them in some way to act against the big store. Occasional suggestions of this kind are to be found amongst educated people. They constitute a kind of sexual compensation and should be seen as a form of sadism (even sabotage). Sadistic motives and the accumulation of stimuli are thus combined: a thirst for adventure and a sadistic desire to sabotage![70]

Although psychiatrists at the turn of the century were still investigating the motive for theft, their successors in the 1920s considered such a search to be a waste of time. They had freed themselves from the idea that department store theft had to have a rational explanation. It now seemed merely an act in which people surrendered to the demands of their sex drive. The extraordinarily high share of female thieves thus became plausible, because 'men have more opportunities to abreact in a natural and necessary way'.[71] In the late 1920s, the original attitude towards department store theft was regarded as outdated because the new interpretation of theft as a sexual crime had invalidated its significance: 'Interpreted in this way, the concept of department store theft has completely lost the significance and legitimacy it once held.'[72]

The trivialisation of department store theft

Both the pathologisation and the sexualisation of department store theft were expressions of its increasing individualisation. At the turn of the century, the image of the seduced woman contained various notions, for example, the seductive power of the department store, theft as a challenge to femininity and threats to the ideal of a household economy capable of living within its means. However, as time went by, although retaining a certain relevance, these different aspects gradually diverged. Problems resulting from the tempting offers available in department stores provoked a demand for 'education of the public mind'[73] which remained largely unanswered. At the end of the first decade of the twentieth century, the department stores were losing their exceptional market position in Germany: 'The aura has gone, at last the customers have realised that department stores do not give anything away, and it has became a business like any other.'[74] Not only the large stores, but also the particular shops catering for the middle classes, copied the main business principles of the department stores by renovating and extending their salerooms and by lowering their prices with the help of bulk purchasing. Although the department stores increased their market share, alternatives appeared which presented equally good opportunities for consumers. Although we lack research on consumer behaviour during this period, it is clear that during the successive periods of rising prices between 1900 and 1914, the pressure on bourgeois real income left less money for such products as clothing and furniture which lay at the heart of department store sales. The contrast with the preceding period of rapidly growing real income between 1895 and 1900 is clear. However, the competitors of the department stores achieved equality in more than just economic terms. After the turn of the century, shoplifting gradually increased in these shops too, though its significance was limited.[75] Nevertheless, department store theft gradually lost its position as an offence outside the definition of common crime. Simple shoplifting could no longer be regarded as exceptional. This attitude was reinforced by the store owners, who commented relatively rarely on the problem of theft.[76] In contrast to what was then the current inclination of expert commentators to pathologise these offences, department store owners stressed that all thieves acted consciously. They believed that the main motive for thieves was the desire to enrich themselves whilst harming the stores.[77] Although this belief had been heard only intermittently before the First World War, the old ideas gradually lost their influence during the slow transition from department store theft to shoplifting and from pathologisation to sexualization. In 1920 it was said that the experts writing at the turn of the century,

> primarily described theft by economically well-situated individuals of high social positions; it was said that they concentrated on the uncontrollable desires resulting from pregnancy, as well as all kinds of hysteric tendencies, neurasthenic deviations and monomanic conditions, solely in order to explain department store theft by members of those groups. This appears today as an outdated approach. Department store theft itself continued, but as the large store became more popular and the sale lost its function as a social event, it was stripped of its romantic aura.[78]

At the same time, a change occurred in the groups of offenders which attracted particular attention. Instead of middle-class women aged between 20 and 40, the case studies now focused on younger people from both middle-class and lower-class backgrounds.[79] Although this was in part the result of a genuinely increasing share of younger and lower-class people in department store theft from the beginning of the twentieth century, it was also seen as a logical consequence of adolescence, a phase of rapid sexual change when a higher crime rate was to be expected. The discourse about crime thus shifted after about 1900, focusing on groups other than middle-class adult women, but it is not clear that the composition of department store thieves had changed as substantially as had the discourse.

The behaviour of these young thieves was clearly different from that of older offenders. Although studies revealed the intellectual deficiency of some offenders, the primary motive for the offence was material benefit, as the store owners pointed out. Thus the 'myth of indiscriminate theft'[80] was called into question. Further research in the mid 1920s led to criticism of the classic psychiatric perspective on department store theft. The serious problems of supply, above all food supply, in the decade of crisis from 1914 to 1923, combined with social insecurity amongst the old middle classes, led to the new concept of a dual motivation for female department store thieves. They seemed 'to act according to the principle of killing two birds with one stone. The enrichment motive joined the sexual motive, and then gradually replaced it'.[81] Consequently, department store theft was eventually stripped of its former exceptional status. As a sexual offence it was still an expression of specifically female criminality but, as a common crime for the purpose of personal material benefit, it lost its former sense of mystery and became an explicable offence. Department store theft, trivialised in this fashion, became just another ordinary crime.[82] The new concept of dualism was supported by German criminologists, male and female alike, at least until the 1970s, when it was challenged by the sociological approaches and critical contributions of the new feminist movement.[83] The discussion surrounding shoplifting as a mass phenomenon continues to reflect experts' particular concern with the sexual dimension of the offence, demonstrating the longevity of past ideologically charged interpretations.

Voyeurs of crime

This study has concluded with the trivialisation of department store theft in the late 1920s, when it became the mass phenomenon that we know today. With the assistance offered by the spread of self-service, the banal nature of the offence means that shoplifting is today virtually ignored except by researchers and those whom it directly concerns. The question of why people steal without any apparent necessity does not arouse public interest, even though the scientific discussion is more intense now than ever before. In 1900, the situation seems to have been different, for people were fascinated by both the new department stores and theft from them. Newspapers carried not only advertisements for the stores but also reports on thieves who had been apprehended and their remarkable offences. These escapades include the case of a woman who hid in a department store in order to be locked in overnight, only to be caught the next morning with her hoard of stolen goods because she had fallen asleep after drinking too much alcohol,[84] and that of the ecstatic woman whose hand grabbed the forbidden fruits like a flash of lightning and who thus lost her honour.[85] Reports of new ingenious techniques of theft were excitedly followed by the readers and the imaginative ploys of the criminals provoked amazement.[86] There was also a novel which was serialised in one of Germany's leading magazines. It told the story of a respectable man whose aristocratic fiancée slipped a piece of jewellery into his pocket without his noticing. He was caught and only saved from a prison sentence by a saleswoman who in due course became his devoted wife.[87] Nevertheless, department store theft was only briefly a topic of general public interest and, despite a considerable number of articles, an in-depth discussion of the phenomenon did not materialise.

The German middle classes became voyeurs who observed the incidents only to heap unreserved condemnation on the offenders. The public debate had little or nothing to do with reality. Only unusual stories were discussed, many of them imaginary or at least embellished. This public representation hardly differed from the way in which department store theft was later interpreted by the various specialists, who reinterpreted it according to their own ideas and took popular prejudices as the basis for scientific research. Whilst the department stores seemed for a while to represent the fulfilment of their customers' desires, the phenomenon of department store theft seemed to confirm the worst contemporary fears. As the department store gradually receded as an object of public fascination, so the discourse on department store theft grew less intense. The public had made its peace with the phenomenon long before science trivialised it. Only the most spectacular cases attracted public attention and even those were instantly forgotten once a new and more interesting topic arose. New ways had to be found to express new anxieties, such as fear of escalating crime, of the economic disintegration of society or of the fundamental nature and sexuality of woman. At the same time, the department stores were constantly employing new strategies, promising that their existence was of public benefit and promoting the notion of happiness as a purchasable commodity. From this period onwards, it becomes easy to identify many of the characteristic preoccupations and marketing strategies of our own times.

Notes

1. Data from *Polizeiliche Kriminalstatistik Bundesrepublik Deutschland. Berichtsjahr 1994*, Wiesbaden: Bundeskriminalamt (1995), p. 167; Jörg Michaelis, *Kriminologisch-kriminalistische Aspekte des Ladendiebstahls unter besonderer Berücksichtigung des Warenhausdiebstahls*, Frankfurt am Main: Peter Lang (1991), pp. 18–19.

2. *Mittheilungen des Zentral-Verbandes Deutscher Kaufleute (MZVDK)*, 9, 1898/99, no. 9, p. 7.

3. In my earlier study of department stores, I define them as capitalistic retail trading companies, dealing in different kinds of goods in uniform sales departments: Uwe Spiekermann, *Warenhaussteuer in Deutschland. Mittelstandsbewegung, Kapitalismus und Rechtsstaat im späten Kaiserreich*, Frankfurt am Main: Peter Lang (1994), p. 29. Using a wider definition, department store history in Germany would start in the 1830s and 1840s, when large shops had been founded especially in Berlin (Gerson, Hertzog, Israel, Jordan, Mannheimer). Uwe Spiekermann, *Geschichte des modernen Kleinhandels in Deutschland 1850–1914*, doctoral thesis, University of Münster, 1996, pp. 188–91, 311–12.

4. A. Leppmann: 'Ueber Diebstähle in den grossen Kaufhäusern', *Aerztliche Sachverständigen-Zeitung*, 7, 1901, p. 33.

5. Precise data can be found in Alfred Sauer, *Frauenkriminalität im Amtsbezirk Mannheim*, Breslau: Schletter (1912), p. 82.

6. Paul Dehn, *Die Großbazare und Massenzweiggeschäfte*, Berlin: Trowitzsch and Sohn (1899), p. 33; Leo Colze, *Berliner Warenhäuser*, 3rd edn, Berlin: Herman Seemann Nach. (1908), p. 72.

7. All quotations from Julius Hirsch, *Das Warenhaus in Westdeutschland; seine Organisation und Wirkungen*, Leipzig: A. Deichert Nachf. (1910), p. 116. See also Leo Katzenstein, 'Die Warenhausfrage', *Jahrbücher für Nationalökonomie und Statistik*, 85, 1905, p. 497.

8. Julius Hirsch, 'Die Bedeutung des Warenhauses in der Volkswirtschaft', in *Probleme des Warenhauses*, Berlin: Verband Deutscher Waren-und Kaufhäuser (1928), p. 60.

9. Kurt Boas, 'Über Warenhausdiebinnen, mit besonderer Berücksichtigung sexueller Motive', *Archiv für Kriminal-Anthropologie und Kriminalistik*, 65, 1916, p. 103, n. 1; Helenefriderike Stelzner, 'Warenhausdiebstähle der Jugendlichen und deren Äquivalente', *Zeitschrift für die gesamte Neurologie und Psychiatrie*, 62, 1920, p. 217.

10. Erich Wulffen, *Das Weib als Sexualverbrecherin*, Berlin: Dr P. Langenscheidt (1923), p. 77. Sebastian v. Koppenfels, *Die Kriminalität der Frau im Kriege*, Leipzig: Ernst Wiegand (1926), p. 36.

11. Schütz, 'Zum psychologischen Verständnis des Taschen- und Warenhausdiebstahls', *Archiv für Kriminologie*, 79, 1926, p. 245 (refers more to department store thefts than pickpocketing); Hans Bernd Thiekötter, *Die psychologische Wurzel und strafrechtliche Bewertung von Warenhausdiebstählen*, Bochum-Langendreer: Heinrich Pöppinghaus (1933), p. 1. Theft by department store employees began at the turn of the century but increased quickly, despite different types of supervision. See 'Unredliche Verkäuferinnen', *Deutsche Handels-Wacht*, 8, 1901, p. 36; Udo Baumgarten, *Die Bedeutung der Warenhäuser für die deutsche Volkswirtschaft*, Borna-Leipzig: Robert Noske (1911), p. 108; *Die Organisation des Warenhauses A. Wertheim*, Berlin: Zeitschrift "Deutsche Confection" (1907), pp. 19–20 and esp. Stelzner, 'Warenhausdiebstähle', p. 209. In South Germany this development was probably different (see Hermann Körner, *Die Warenhäuser. Ihr Wesen, ihre Entstehung und ihre Stellung im Wirtschaftsleben*, doctoral thesis, Heidelberg, Tübingen: Hermann Kirschner (1908), p. 147). Department store theft in Germany never acquired as great a significance as in the USA or in France. See 'Warenhaus-Diebinnen', *Archiv für Kriminologie*, 78, 1926, p. 200. Victor Mataja, *Großmagazine und Kleinhandel*, Leipzig: Duncker and Humblot (1891), p. 68.

12. Baumgarten, *Bedeutung*, p. 108; Colze, *Warenhäuser*, p. 74.

13. Hans Gudden, 'Die Zurechnungsfähigkeit bei Warenhausdiebstählen', *Vierteljahrsschrift für gerichtliche Medizin und öffentliches Sanitätswesen*, III. ser. 33, 1907, suppl. vol., pp. 64–5.

14. Werner Rubens, *Der Kampf des Spezialgeschäftes gegen das Warenhaus (mit besonderer Berücksichtigung der Zeit von 1918 bis 1929)*, Köln-Ehrenfeld: Max Klestadt (1929), p. 13.

15. *Stenographische Berichte über die Sitzungen der Bürgerschaft zu Hamburg im Jahre 1901*, Hamburg (1902), p. 452 (Blinckmann).

16. Dehn, *Großbazare*, p. 27.

17. See for example 'Ein Brief an die Feinde der Waarenhäuser', *Hamburger Fremdenblatt*, 1898, no. 51 fr. 02.03., 4th suppl., Staatsarchiv Hamburg (STA Hbg.) 331-3 Politische Polizei (PP) S 6750, vol. 1.

18. Spiekermann, *Warenhaussteuer*. Käthe Lux, *Studien über die Entwicklung der Warenhäuser in Deutschland*, Jena: Gustav Fischer (1910), p. 3, draws a direct line between department store theft and new laws against department stores.

19. *Stenographische Berichte über die Verhandlungen der durch Allerhöchste Verordnung vom 22. December 1897 einberufenen beiden Häuser des Landtages. Haus der Abgeordneten*, vol. 3, Berlin (1898), p. 2038 (Brockhausen). Cf. 'Die Umsatzsteuer im preußischen Abgeordnetenhause', *MZVDK*, 8, 1897/98, no. 11/12, pp. 1–2; Johannes Steindamm, *Beiträge zur Warenhausfrage*, Berlin: E. Ebering (1904), pp. 13–14.

20. Dehn, *Großbazare*, p. 33. E. Suchsland, *Schutz- und Trutzwaffen für den gewerblichen Mittelstand in seiner Notwehr gegen die Konsumvereine und Warenhäuser*, 2nd edn, Halle an der Saale: Buchhandlung des Waisenhauses (1905), pp. 67–8.

21. *Stenographische Berichte* (1902), p. 709.

22. See for example Robert Wilhelms, *Die Waarenhäuser und ihre Bekämpfung*, Strassburg im Elsaß: Schlesier and Schweikhardt (1898), p. 5.

23. E. Suchsland, *Die Klippen des sozialen Friedens. Ernste Gedanken über Konsumvereine und Warenhäuser*, 6th edn, Halle an der Saale: Buchhandlung des Waisenhauses (1904), p. 30. Liberal critics took over this argument from the petit-bourgeois movement and called for the adequate education of all wives, see *Stenographische Berichte über die Verhandlungen der durch die Allerhöchste Verordnung vom 23. December 1895 einberufenen beiden Häuser des Landtages. Haus der Abgeordneten*, vol. 2, Berlin (1896), p. 1601 (Eynern). Working-class women were rarely mentioned in this discussion. They were considered to be hardly able to listen to reason, to be bad customers or lost to the consumer co-operatives.

24. 'Zur Warenhausfrage', *Deutsches Blatt*, 1899, no. 4 fr. 14.01., suppl., STA Hbg. 331-3 PP S 6750, vol. 2; Hermann Nickel, 'Die Warenhäuser als Zerstörer des Familienlebens', *Deutsches Blatt*, 1903, no. 93 fr. 21.11., STA Hbg. 331-3 PP S 6750, vol. 3. The employment of unmarried women was mentioned in *Stenographische Berichte über die Verhandlungen des Preußischen Hauses der Abgeordneten, 20. Legislaturperiode, I. Session 1904/05*, vol. 1, Berlin (1904), p. 1322 (Hammer). Moral danger was the theme of 'Das Loos der weiblichen Angestellten in den Waarenhäusern', *MZVDK*, 11, 1900, no. 12, p. 4; J. Henningsen, *Beiträge zur Warenhausfrage!*, Hamburg: Deutschnationale Verlagsanstalt (1906), pp. 13–14; Regina Schulte, *Sperrbezirke. Tugendhaftigkeit und Prostitution in der bürgerlichen Welt*, Frankfurt am Main: Syndikat (1979), pp. 99–102.

25. *MZVDK*, 9, 1898/99, no. 5/6, p. 15. Valid statistics or estimates on the real share of women customers of the department stores did not exist, but figures of 90 per cent or 99 per cent (Georg Buß, 'Das Warenhaus. Ein Blick aus dem modernen Geschäftsleben', *Velhagen & Klasings*

Monatshefte, 21(1), 1906/07, p. 612) were definitely an overstatement. Male theft was not investigated or discussed.

26. Uwe Spiekermann, 'Rationalization as a permanent task: the German food retail trade in the twentieth century', in Adel P. den Hartog (ed.), *Food Technology, Science and Marketing. European Diet in the Twentieth Century*, East Linton: Tuckwell Press (1995), pp. 200–220.

27. 'Einfluß der Frauenwelt', *MZVDK*, 7, 1896/97, no. 13, p. 3.

28. 'Tietz und Wertheim', *Die Zukunft*, 32, 1900, pp. 537–542, here p. 542.

29. J. Wernicke, 'Der Streit ums Warenhaus', *Deutsche Wirtschafts-Zeitung*, 8, 1912, col. 929.

30. Even opponents were attracted by the luxury of department stores. Franz Heise jr, 'Ein Stündchen im Warenhause. Betrachtungen', *Deutsches Blatt*, 1904, no. 143 fr. 28.05., suppl., STA Hbg. 331-3 PP S 6750, vol. 3.

31. Leppmann, 'Diebstähle', p. 5. Cf. 'Berliner Gesellschaft für Psychiatrie und Nervenkrankheiten. Sitzung vom 10. Dezember 1900', *Archiv für Psychiatrie und Nervenkrankheiten*, 35, 1902, p. 264 (Rothmann); 'Diskussion über H. Gudden: Über den Geisteszustand bei Warenhausdiebstählen', in *Verhandlungen der Gesellschaft Deutscher Naturforscher und Ärzte. 78. Versammlung zu Stuttgart*, vol. 2, Leipzig: F.C.W. Vogel (1907), p. 334 (Haenel).

32. Adolf Braun, *Die Warenhäuser und die Mittelstandspolitik der Zentrumspartei*, Berlin: Expedition der Buchhandlung Vorwärts (1904), p. 8.

33. Körner, *Warenhäuser*, pp. 34–6; Leopold Laquer, *Der Warenhaus-Diebstahl*, Halle an der Saale: Carl Marhold (1907), p. 38; Thiekötter, *Wurzel*, pp. 34–5. For an opposite view see Magnus Biermer, 'Warenhäuser und Warenhaussteuer', in *Handwörterbuch der Staatswissenschaften*, 3rd edn, vol. 8, Jena: Gustav Fischer (1911), p. 600.

34. Dehn, *Großbazare*, p. 33.

35. *MZVDK*, 9, 1898/99, no. 11, pp. 5–6.

36. Hans Gudden, 'Die Zurechnungsfähigkeit bei Warenhausdiebstählen', *Neurologisches Centralblatt*, 25, 1906, p. 922; Emil Raimann, 'Über Warenhausdiebinnen', *Monatsschrift für Kriminalpsychologie und Strafrechtsreform*, 13, 1922, p. 317; Wulffen, *Weib*, p. 77; Thiekötter, *Wurzel*, p. 1.

37. Braun, *Warenhäuser*, p. 8.

38. 'Diskussion über H. Gudden', p. 334 (Kron).

39. *Kriminalstatistik für das Jahr 1903*, Berlin: Puttkammer and Mühlbrecht (1906), esp. pp. II.30–II.60.

40. Longard, 'Die geminderte Zurechnungsfähigkeit', *Monatsschrift für Kriminalpsychologie und Strafrechtsreform*, 3, 1906/07, p. 89.

41. W. Försterling, 'Genese einer sexuellen Abnormität bei einem Falle von Stehltrieb', *Allgemeine Zeitschrift für Psychiatrie und psychisch-gerichtliche Medizin*, 64, 1907, p. 951.

42. Laquer, *Warenhaus-Diebstahl*, p. 36.

43. Gudden, 'Zurechnungsfähigkeit', p. 922.

44. P.J. Möbius, *Ueber den physiologischen Schwachsinn des Weibes*, 9th edn, Halle an der Saale: Carl Marhold (1908), pp. 76–80.

45. Breckman's aphorism 'Bourgeois women were analyzed, working-class women criminalized' (Warren G. Breckman, 'Disciplining consumption:

the debate about luxury in Wilhemine Germany, 1890–1914', *Journal of Social History*, 24, 1991, p. 496) is neat but incorrect.

46. Schleich, C.L., quotations in Laquer, *Warenhaus-Diebstahl*, p. 6.
47. Eugen Wilhelm, 'Ein Fall von sogenannter "Kleptomanie"', *Archiv für Kriminal-Anthropologie und Kriminalistik*, 16, 1904, pp. 160–64.
48. Leppmann, 'Diebstähle', p. 32.
49. Gudden, 'Zurechnungsfähigkeit', pp. 66–7.
50. Nevertheless some neurologists spoke of the 'temporary diminished responsibility' of women, e.g. Karl Birnbaum, 'Die kriminelle Eigenart der weiblichen Psychopathen', *Archiv für Kriminal-Anthropologie und Kriminalistik*, 52, 1913, pp. 364–77, esp. p. 377.
51. A. Leppmann, 'Gutachten über die strafrechtliche Behandlung der geistig Minderwertigen', in *Verhandlungen des Siebenundzwanzigsten Deutschen Juristentages*, vol. 3, Berlin: J. Guttentag (1904), pp. 136–52, esp. pp. 140–41; Gudden, 'Zurechnungsfähigkeit', p. 69 (Strassmann); Rudolf Ganter, 'Der Warenhausdiebstahl', *Die Gegenwart*, 1911, pp. 64–5.
52. Paul Julius Möbius, 'Pariser Warenhaus-Diebinnen', *Illustrierte Zeitung*, 120, 1903, p. 250. Cf. 'Diskussion über H. Gudden', p. 335 (Gudden).
53. Laquer, *Warenhaus-Diebstahl*, pp. 26, 35.
54. Raimann, 'Warenhausdiebinnen', pp. 320–21 pleaded for the care of thieves within the family.
55. For counter-arguments see Longard, 'Zurechnungsfähigkeit'.
56. The changing discourse has been reflected in Wulffen, *Weib*, p. 75; Schütz, 'Verständnis', p. 251; Thiekötter, *Wurzel*, pp. 38–46.
57. The background of the new discourse was formed by the establishment of modern sexology by Bloch, Ellis, Forel and Hirschfeld and by the new psychoanalytic sexual theory by Freud.
58. 'Stenographischer Bericht über die 12. General-Versammlung des Zentral-Verbandes deutscher Kaufleute', *MZVDK*, 10, 1899/1900, no. 1, p. 6 (Ledermann).
59. See for example Joseph August Lux, 'Das Warenhausfräulein', *Geschlecht und Gesellschaft*, 9, 1914, pp. 44–8.
60. Lothar Eisen, 'Psychologie des Warenhauses', *Geschlecht und Gesellschaft*, 8, 1913, p. 390.
61. The first 'extensive' (56 cases) examination was carried out by Legrand de Saulle, see Mechtild Rotter, 'Die Frau in der Kriminologie', *Kriminalsoziologische Bibliographie*, 6, 1979, vol. 23/24, p. 98, n. 3. The relationship between menstruation and department store theft was also emphasised by Paul Duboisson, *Die Warenhausdiebinnen*, 2nd edn, Leipzig: Hermann Seemann Nachf (1904), pp. 135–46. For Germany cf. Boas, 'Warenhausdiebinnen', esp. pp. 113–14.
62. Gudden, 'Zurechnungsfähigkeit', p. 66. Birnbaum, 'Eigenart', p. 366, observed 'that the criminal impetus was absent beyond this phase'.
63. Cf. Koppenfels, *Kriminalität*, pp. 7–8; Käthe Schmitz, *Die Kriminalität der Frau*, Bochum-Langendreer: Heinrich Pöppinghaus (1937), p. 58. Contrary to this view: Wulffen, *Weib*, p. 76.
64. Wilhelm Stekel, 'Die sexuelle Wurzel der Kleptomanie', *Zeitschrift für Sexualwissenschaft*, 1908, p. 589.
65. Ibid., p. 596.
66. Boas, 'Warenhausdiebinnen', p. 116.

67. Urgent proofs of this were Birnbaum, 'Eigenart'; Boas, 'Warenhausdiebinnen'.

68. A.H. Hübner, *Lehrbuch der forensischen Psychiatrie*, Bonn: A. Marcus and E. Webers (1914), p. 665. Kurt Boas, 'Über Hepephilie. Eine angebliche Form des weiblichen Fetischismus', *Archiv für Kriminal-Anthropologie und Kriminalistik*, 61, 1913, pp. 103–32, discussed this problem in connection with fetishism.

69. Schütz, 'Verständnis', p. 251.

70. Schlör, 'Zur Psychologie des Taschen- und Warenhausdiebstahls', *Die Umschau*, 31, 1927, p. 348.

71. Schütz, 'Verständnis', p. 252.

72. Schlör, 'Psychologie', p. 347. Raimann, 'Warenhausdiebinnen', esp. p. 306, criticised this form of sexualisation.

73. *Stenographische Berichte über die Sitzungen der Bürgerschaft zu Hamburg in Jahre 1897*, p. 2055 (Arendt).

74. Deutsche Confektion fr. 07.06.1898, quotations in J. Wernicke, *Wandlungen und neue Interessen-Organisationen im Detailhandel*, Berlin: Herm. Walther (1908), p. 29.

75. Cf. J. Wernicke, *Kapitalismus und Mittelstandspolitik*, Jena: Gustav Fischer (1907), p. 564.

76. At least until 1920, department store theft was not mentioned in the annual report of the Association of German department stores.

77. Konfektionär fr. 22.11.1906, quotations in Laquer, *Warenhaus-Diebstahl*, pp. 25–6.

78. Stelzner, 'Warenhausdiebstähle', p. 216. The thieves were furthermore considered as psychopathic, but not mentally ill; see Thiekötter, *Wurzel*, p. 18.

79. Already Laquer, *Warenhaus-Diebstahl*, pp. 27–9, mentioned this important group of thieves.

80. Stelzner, 'Warenhausdiebstähle', p. 212.

81. Schütz, 'Verständnis', p. 250.

82. From a background in sociopsychological approaches see Sophie Kunert, *Straffälligkeit bei Frauen, ihre Entstehung und Beschaffenheit*, Leipzig: Johann Ambrosius Barth (1933), pp. 35–43.

83. See Schmitz, *Kriminalität*; Clemens Ameluxen, *Die Kriminalität der Frau seit 1945*, Hamburg: Verlag für kriminalistische Fachliteratur (1958), pp. 16–18; Wolf Middendorf, 'Die Kriminalität der Frau im Wandel. Historische und kriminologische Aspekte', *Zeitschrift für die gesamte Strafrechtswissenschaft*, 91, 1979, pp. 192–223; Michaelis, *Aspekte*. In general see Dietlinde Gipser, 'Kriminalität der Frauen und Mädchen', in Hans Joachim Schneider (ed.), *Die Psychologie des 20. Jahrhunderts, vol. XIV*, Zürich: Kindler (1981), 437–51.

84. 'Was in den Großbazaren Alles gestohlen wird', *Das kleine Journal*, 1898, no. 352 fr. 22.12., STA Hbg. 331–3 PP S 6750, vol. 1.

85. Buß, 'Warenhaus', p. 612.

86. *Die Organisation*, pp. 17–19; Klaus Strohmeyer, *Warenhäuser. Geschichte, Blüte und Untergang im Warenmeer*, Berlin: Klaus Wagenbach (1980), pp. 166–72.

87. Margarete Stahr, 'Aus dem Warenhaus!', *Illustrirte Zeitung*, 121, 1903, pp. 39–40, 77–8.

CHAPTER SEVEN

Selling dreams: advertising strategies from *grands magasins* to supermarkets in Ghent, 1900–1960

Donald Weber

Despite the recent upsurge of interest in the history of the department store, the problem of definition remains unsolved.[1] It is of crucial importance to reach an understanding of the nature of this institution which played a central role in the transformation of consumer habits. In a recent review of new studies on the history of consumption, it was pointed out that 'recognition of the dynamism of earlier retail environments; the extent of consumers' pre-existing skills ... and the sophistication of earlier consumption cultures, blurs distinctions between department stores and earlier shops'. It has also been claimed that recent studies 'draw attention to consumers' own practices and knowledge at the expense of advertising images, as sources of the meaning of objects'. The same author argues for a 'greater integration of manipulationist and voluntarist accounts of consumer culture'.[2] It is therefore clear that the history of the *grands magasins* should extend beyond the study of the institution and its commercial practices, and be situated within a wider economic and cultural context.

Firstly, however, it must be recognised that no dichotomy existed between the new commercial strategies of the stores and the cultural preferences of their bourgeois customers. The history of the *grands magasins* has modest beginnings: their direct predecessors were small clothing shops, drapers, stores for household goods and furnishings for interior decoration, and also small traders in crystal and chinaware, in other words, those establishments which sold goods that were considered fashionable. Fashion can be regarded as a pattern which emerges as many individuals attempt to gain pleasure from new experiences, such as the wearing of a new dress, but with no central authority imposing the criteria for novelty.[3] It had been recognised that if this desire for novelty, characteristic of modernist Western culture, could be directed towards the possession and use of new objects, a promising source of profit would be realised. Small traders were already aware of this principle and had been putting it into practice since the eighteenth century.[4] As a result, a new dimension had been added to the old process of commercial exchange, that is to say desire. Goods could be emotionally promising besides being rationally useful, and seduction therefore became as good a commercial strategy as conviction.[5] These changes were occurring at a time when there was an increase amongst that section of the population modernist enough to long for novelty, materialist enough to project this upon objects and prosperous enough to be able to afford them, in other words, a section of the emerging nineteenth-century bourgeoisie. The successful commercialisation of their modernist lifestyle is known today as the consumer society. The specific historical role of the *grands magasins* is a direct result of their capacity to create a 'dream marriage' by combining modernist bourgeois culture with commercial mass production.[6] The department store and the bourgeoisie enjoyed an interactive relationship: bourgeois modernism was shaped out of a romantic heritage in an era of profound technological and commercial changes which included the development of the department stores. In their turn, they adapted to the preferences of their customers, while at the same time fulfilling a role in the broader environment of institutions and practices that helped shape bourgeois culture.

Secondly, the department store should be considered within the context of the whole of the retail sector within a changing economy. The central feature of the *grand magasin* was its concentration of capital, enabling the store to enjoy the advantages of economies of scale. The rapid rise of department stores in the second half of the nineteenth century reflected increasing urbanisation and the development of new methods of urban transport.[7] As such, the emergence of the big city store, offering a diversified range of goods, was not the invention of an ingenious tradesman, but was rather a function of the social phenomenon of a more densely concentrated and mobile population operating on a capitalist basis within a free market. To take full advantage of the concentration of capital, the new commercial firms needed to address the whole of the urban population, either by relying extensively on publicity (*grands magasins*), by constructing a chain of stores spread over the city (*maisons à succursales*), by offering the possibility of mail order (*ventes par correspondance*), or by a combination of the above. Technically, before the breakthrough of methods for preserving food such as canning or refrigeration, only the chain stores, dealing in smaller quantities of goods and situated nearer to the customers, could successfully deal with perishable products.[8] In contrast, the other establishments were effectively more suited to the sale of fashionable products as a result of their reliance upon publicity for marketing goods.

By the 1930s the field of retailing in Belgium had been divided into no fewer than nine types of institution. Traditional shopkeepers still dominated in numerical terms, along with various types of itinerant traders and local markets. Exploiting the new possibilities for an economy of scale were, as noted above, both the chain stores and the department stores. Mail-order enterprises can be included as a separate category, although this sector was largely controlled by the department stores. Both the chain stores and the department stores were facing competition from supermarkets and so-called fixed-price stores (*magasins à prix uniques*); both would try to take over the new institutions with a varying degree of success, even if this involved the fundamental transformation of their businesses. Also dealing with economies of scale but on a non-capitalist basis, were the co-operatives, which were primarily socialist attempts to establish a counter-economy, and to a lesser degree, the so-called *économats*, outlets retailing to employees which were set up within businesses or administrative organisations.[9] By this time, competition between the small shopkeepers on the one hand, and department stores and co-operatives on the other, had become serious enough to persuade the government to introduce restrictive measures. However, even the most complex typology would be inadequate to categorise the entire range of commercial initiatives in the retail sector. The department store was never an isolated institution with clearly defined features. Most companies combined both old and new techniques and would fall midway on a scale of continuously changing retailing methods.

Thirdly, the department store should be considered from a longer chronological perspective than merely from the era of the *Belle Epoque*. By extending the history of the department store into the twentieth century it becomes possible to clarify the nature of the development of these new sales enterprises. In general terms, it is possible to identify three stages of expansion in the evolution of Belgian department stores during the twentieth century. The first wave of expansion was geographic in character. Following the lines of continuing urbanisation, the stores appeared outside the capital in smaller cities and new regional centres. The immediate result of this was a conflict with local shops which were still growing to become *grands magasins*. At an intermediary stage, to cope with local competition and to prepare for further expansion, the main department stores began to adopt the structure of a limited liability company. Financial groups were invited to bring in new capital. The second wave of expansion was, in essence, social. The department stores opened up new chains of fixed-price stores, offering common goods for daily use, thereby addressing a much broader section of the population, in particular, consumers from the working class. This development reflected the growth of disposable income in the first decades of the twentieth century.[10] Another intermediary stage followed during which the stores made the initial moves in a process which was to result in the eventual merger of many companies in order to concentrate capital and to prepare for further expansion. The third wave of expansion was commercial in nature. By opening up food departments in their chains of fixed-price stores, thereby turning them into supermarkets, the department stores entered the vast area of food marketing in an attempt to take over the entire retail sector. This was made possible only by a structural change affecting the internal economy of the household, where the introduction of the refrigerator took place at the same time as the trend towards smaller families, the rise in numbers of working wives and increased mobility due to the motor car. As a result of this, the nature of the department stores changed profoundly. Expanding into smaller towns, lower strata of customers, and the quite unfashionable food sector, the dream marriage of modernist bourgeois culture and commercial goals faced divorce. As the stores entered the era of the supermarket, the argument for the necessity to maintain low prices gained in importance, to the detriment of lifestyle arguments, a transition which was clearly reflected in the increasingly materialistic publicity efforts.

Finally, it should be noted that part of the debate surrounding the definition of the department store has been obscured by the fact that they have been considered primarily from a national perspective. Without denying the influence of regional customs, the essentially urban nature of these institutions must not be overlooked. The advent of the *grand magasin* was never a French, American, British or German phenomenon, but common to the whole of the Western industrialising, urbanising, capitalist world. The bourgeois founders belonged to a cosmopolitan social class and had capital available for investment. The environment of the department store, *grand magasin* or *Warenhaus*, was the city, not the nation,[11] and the character of the phenomenon should be regarded as urban rather than national.

It is therefore necessary to examine the twentieth-century evolution of the *grands magasins* from an urban perspective. Instead of the almost legendary companies of the major European capitals, a smaller provincial town somewhere in Europe was deliberately selected. Ghent was chosen, the third in size of the five main Belgian urban agglomerations. This study focuses on two aspects of the phenomenon. Firstly, the institutional aspect will be considered through the presentation of an overview of the department stores at a local level and their transformations during the period 1900–1960; and secondly, aspects of their changing nature will be examined through an analysis of their advertisements in local papers. To be included for consideration the following criteria were applied: the stores must have been calling themselves a *grand magasin*: they must have offered goods of various kinds, e.g. clothing and furniture; they must have functioned on a turnover basis through organising regular special sales (*solden*); and they must not have been stores where the food department predominated (*Delhaize*), or been co-operative societies (*Vooruit*).[12]

From *grands magasins* to supermarkets

Ghent, as a provincial town of less than 250 000 inhabitants, was never really regarded by the department stores as a likely location for the generation of high profit margins. However, as one of the five main urban environments in Belgium, Ghent can be regarded as representative of the situation at a local level. Before the First World War, only the Grands Magasins aux Nouveautés à l'Innovation, one of the three major *grands magasins*, was established in Ghent. Department stores were still primarily operated at a local level. The oldest of the Belgian department stores, Au Bon Marché, was firmly established in Brussels and, with branches in Liège and Antwerp, had covered the best of the Belgian market. Nevertheless, since their bourgeois customers were becoming increasingly mobile, it was decided to advertise in the local papers in Ghent at regular intervals. The Grand Bazar du Bon Marché in Antwerp was the successful second initiative of the founder of the Maison Universelle in Ghent. However, until the *grands bazars* of Liège and Brussels linked in a limited liability company with their colleagues in Antwerp and Ghent in 1920, the Maison Universelle would never quite realise its potential. This does not mean that Innovation was the only competitive department store in Ghent before 1920. On the contrary, it faced relatively severe competition from several local stores.

Apart from the Maison Universelle, founded in 1882 and predecessor of the later Grand Bazar,[13] six local competitors were to be found in Ghent, claiming to be *grands magasins*. All of them were founded in the nineteenth century, and were still in existence after the First World War, although by that time none continued to operate as department stores. In 1909 each of them was presenting itself as a *grand magasin*, offering goods of different kinds, and taking part in clearance sales at the end of the season. Following the example set by the Brussels store, the Bon Marché, several of them tried to gain a commercial advantage by imitating the names of famous French *grands magasins*. Local department stores developed initially from small shops, run by ambitious young tradesmen. By the end of the 1920s, financial companies were prepared to become involved and were eager to participate in the lucrative department store business. Despite this, not one of these local stores survived the crisis years of the early 1930s and the sharp competition with the department stores from Brussels.

The local department stores emerged from four different backgrounds. Firstly, the most common origin of a department store was the drapery shop. The Grands Magasins aux Nouveautés was founded in 1909 when O. Dupont took over E. Boulet's small drapers,[14] which dated back to 1890.[15] By 1929 however, it had resumed its former modest proportions. Similarly, K. Ledant's fashion shop, the Grand Louvre, founded around 1884,[16] proudly presented itself as the Grands Magasins du Louvre in 1909.[17] The intentional confusion with the French department store of the same name was not to prove beneficial however, as the shop declined after the First World War. A second type of establishment to develop as *grands magasins* were the haberdashery shops. In Ghent only the Van Gheluwe haberdashery, in business since early 1866,[18] attempted to become a department store. S. Van Gheluwe had advertised his establishment as the Grands Magasins au Beffroi in 1909,[19] but he died soon afterwards. The shop continued under the ownership of O. Gevaert and by the end of the 1920s, still remained competitive. A third type was the chinaware and crystal shops. The Grands Magasins Réunis Ad. Dangotte originated in 1883,[20] when Adolphe Dangotte took over his father's business, a chinaware and crystal shop which had first been mentioned by the local almanac in 1863.[21] Adolphe Dangotte added household tools and furniture to the store's stock. In 1914 the shop was transformed into a limited liability company,[22] dealing with 'all activities connected with decorative arts and furnishing'. It still existed after the First World War, but seemed to have withdrawn from the department store category. Finally, by 1929 two more stores had arrived in the locality. Both were credit houses (*maisons de crédit*),[23] dating back to the beginning of the twentieth century. Vlaamsch Crediethuis Frankenhoff et Co., produced a frequent but simple type of informative communication which perhaps can not be defined as advertisements. La Providence on the other hand, run by C. Vanex, seemed determined to corner the market by advertising abundantly. This final category of companies was of significance as it illustrated a new interest in the retail sector on the part of the financial world, coinciding with the transformations which the department stores in Brussels were undergoing during this period. However not one of the local stores achieved a breakthrough in extending their market from a local to a national level.

Unfortunately for the local department stores, Ghent was inevitably dominated by stores from other Belgian cities, in particular from the capital, Brussels. The Bon Marché, owned by the family Vaxelaire, was the first Belgian *grand magasin*, in business since François Vaxelaire and his wife took over a store from the Thiéry brothers in 1866. Its home base was in Brussels, and with branches opening between 1881 and 1886 in Liège and Antwerp, the business expanded to cover the major cities in Belgium. The store prospered and by the turn of the century it had overtaken all its competitors. The Vaxelaires appear to have become a little overconfident, for the Bon Marché ceased to exhibit any degree of innovative enthusiasm. This notion of innovation was the key concept expressed in the name of the Grands Magasins aux Nouveautés à l'Innovation, founded in 1897 by Jules Bernheim and the Meyer brothers, and located immediately adjacent to the Bon Marché in the main street of Brussels. The store presented a dynamic image, addressing a broad range of customers and opening no fewer than seven branches in the following decade, including branches in the towns of Liège, Ghent and Antwerp. A rather complex early history was associated with the third main department store of the period. In 1885, Grand Bazar was the name of the Antwerp store of Adolph Kileman, the founder of the Maison Universelle in Ghent in 1882. It was also the name of August Tiriard's store in Liège, founded in 1885, and of the limited liability company founded on his initiative on the Boulevard Anspach in Brussels two years later.[24] In the years to come, these three companies were to become financially intertwined.

One factor common to all these stores was that they did not develop from smaller shops, but were founded directly as department stores.[25] By the beginning of the twentieth century they had already undergone a first wave of expansion: the Bon Marché had three branches, while Innovation had seven and the Grands Bazars four. This type of expansion continued throughout the century.

In 1920, certain important developments were to prepare the department stores for a second wave of expansion. Firstly, Bernheim succeeded in taking over the giant Brussels department store of German origin, Tietz, defeating its opponent the Bon Marché with what was presented as a non-negotiable bid of 36.5 million francs.[26] In preparation, financial groups from Brussels bought shares in the store when the new limited liability company was formed.[27] Nevertheless, Bernheim's Innovation was almost ruined, and struggled for several years to overcome its debts. When it finally succeeded, the reborn Innovation probably equalled the size of the Bon Marché. A second event took place during the same year when Victor Tiriard succeeded in linking his Grands Bazars of Liège and Brussels to those of Ghent and Antwerp by taking an important share in the newly founded limited liability company, Grands Bazars Réunis Anvers-Gand.[28] The Bon Marché was rather late to react to these developments, turning into a limited liability company as late as 1927.[29] Having attracted new capital, the department stores were ready for a new type of expansion.

A new formula was being prepared for the department stores. The magic word was *prix uniques*. The principle of *prix uniques* was to concentrate on basic products which were always certain to sell in very high quantities but with low profit margins. General expenses were kept to a minimum by the use of simple architecture and a high level of self-service.[30] In other words, the new stores were radicalising the rational principles of sales organisation that had been established by the *grands magasins* in the previous century. However, whereas the *grands magasins* had concentrated on luxury articles, thereby addressing the needs of wealthy bourgeois as the most obvious market, the *magasins à prix uniques* offered simple products for daily use, attracting a much broader section of the population. *Prix uniques* were not a European invention. Their origins were to be found in the American fixed-price stores, such as Woolworth's Five and Dime. Despite the fact that the products initially offered for sale were all within a specific low price range, it seemed only a matter of time before the new stores would overlap with the *grands magasins*. By the 1930s most European countries had a chain of fixed-price stores.[31] The first initiative in Belgium came from Jean Van Gijsel, who established Sarma, a limited liability company, in 1928.[32] The creation of Sarma, as a fourth big name in the world of the Belgian *grands magasins*, caused some consternation, as both Bernheim and Vaxelaire fully understood the possibilities inherent in the new formula. Vaxelaire's Bon Marché was the first to react, founding its own fixed-price store in 1929, while Bernheim attempted to establish an international structure around Innovation.[33] However, both failed and, as neither seemed capable of formulating an answer to the Sarma challenge, the old rivals decided in 1933 to merge their supermarket initiatives into Prisunic-Priba.[34] During this period, despite the absence of Grands Bazars on the new marketing scene, Prisunic-Priba found it hard to compete successfully with Sarma, above all because the policy-makers of the old *grands magasins* found it difficult to adapt to the new methods and apply the *prix uniques* principle in a consistent way. As the creator of a brand new company, Jean Van Gijsel was unaffected by this type of indecision.

However, before open warfare broke out between the department stores, the Belgian government decided to intervene. The international economic crisis of the early 1930s had intensified the complaints of the traditional sector of small shopkeepers against the new retail structures, forcing the governments of several European countries to introduce restrictive measures.[35] The *Loi de Cadenas* (Padlock Law) was passed in early 1937, forbidding any expansion of department stores. This restriction was not lifted until the end of 1960.[36] It served to slow down department store development and expansion, although the stores often showed themselves capable of creatively circumventing the prohibitive measures.[37]

Gradually, department stores began to introduce food departments into their fixed-price stores, thereby entering a third wave of expansion. By 1960, the sector of the market served by the department stores had become somewhat simplified. Firstly, Sarma had not realised its potential for a breakthrough into the market dominated by the three main stores. Jean Van Gijsel had left the board of directors to join the Grands Magasins de la Bourse, the only independent *grand magasin* remaining from former days. Despite cautious co-operation, Sarma-Bourse remained in fourth place. The three main stores, the Bon Marché, Innovation and the Grands Bazars, had left all their competitors behind, but their ranking order now differed from 1929 (Table 7.1).

Whilst the Grands Bazars had achieved a great deal, becoming the leading department stores by 1959, and Innovation had managed to maintain its second position, the Bon Marché had lost its leading position and was now unable to challenge the positions held by the other two. It was therefore not surprising that the Grand Bazars were the stores which achieved the breakthrough in the transformation of the

Table 7.1   The main *grands magasins* in Belgium compared 1929–59

	Capital*	Balance*	Gross Profit*	Branches
1929				
Au Bon Marché	40	216	9	4
A l'Innovation	75	210	18	10
Grands Bazars	48	194	14	6
1959				
Au Bon Marché	200	1 413	67	5
A l'Innovation	600	1 969	93	12
Grands Bazars	370	2 364	61	19

*   Millions of Belgian francs.

Figures for the *Grands Bazars* are the combined results for Grands Bazars Réunis Anvers-Gand, Grand Bazar du Boulevard Anspach (Brussels) and Grand Bazar de la Place St.-Lambert (Liège). *Recueil des actes*, 25 December 1929, pp. 3889–90 (A l'Innovation, situation on 31 July 1929) and 28 June 1930, p. 5319 (Au Bon Marché, situation on 31 December 1929); *Recueil financier*, 37, 1930, pp. 1157, 1159, 1447 (Grands Bazars, situation on 31 January 1930), and 66, 1959, p. 4001 (Au Bon Marché, situation on 31 July 1959), p. 3971 (A l'Innovation, situation on 31 July 1959) and pp. 2861–73 (Grands Bazars, situation on 31 January 1959).

grands magasins into supermarkets, perhaps to some extent due to the fact that the complex structure of the Grands Bazars affiliation had slowed down the development of their own chain of supermarkets. In 1960 the Grand Bazar d'Anvers[38] decided to break away from the main group to form G.B. Supermarchés.[39] While the Grands Bazars of Liège and Brussels drifted away as the affiliation was falling apart, the Antwerp bazar was creating its own success story. The merger in 1968 of the old Grand Bazar d'Anvers within its own supermarket chain[40] was to mark the symbolic and final end of the era of the *grands magasins*. As a result of this increasingly successful competition, the former rivals, Innovation and the Bon Marché, inevitably merged. The newly created Inno-BM was worth 1.5 billion francs in 1969,[41] but as their supermarket chain Priba-Unic was still relatively unprofitable, within a few years they had again lost their leading position to the rapidly growing G.B. Entreprises.

However, the department stores were not the only type of retail companies. There were also the *maisons à succursales*, loosely affiliated chains of food stores, and the co-operative societies, mainly established by the socialist movement in an attempt to create a counter-economy. One of the former, Delhaize-De Leeuw, had no intention of allowing G.B. Entreprises to take over the entire retail market, including the food sector. Very soon, G.B. Entreprises considered it wise to merge with the former competitors of Inno-BM, creating GB-Inno-BM in 1974.[42] Finally, in 1987, Sarma, which had been taken over in 1969 by an American multinational, J.C. Penney, was to join the ranks of GB-Inno-BM. A coalescence was taking place: as the *grands magasins* had expanded according to the supermarket/*prix uniques* principle, they had achieved the domination of a greater part of the retail market in all its sectors, but had also lost their former modernist identity. Only the purely commercial principle remained, 'the bigger you are, the more you get', which resulted in a process of generalised amalgamation.

Department store advertising in local newspapers

As the stores expanded the eagerness to advertise paradoxically diminished. Publicity fever reached a high point in the late 1920s.[43] There has probably never been more advertising in Belgian history than during these years, with the possible exception of the 1990s. The four main department stores were facing severe competition on two fronts, both from the old local shops, in their last attempt to gain a share of the market held by the *grands magasins*, and from new companies on a national scale, as the ever growing consumer market had attracted the

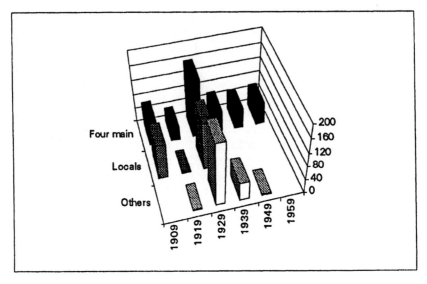

Figure 7.1   Numbers of department stores' advertisements in two Belgian local newspapers, 1909–59[44]

attention of those with capital. Amongst this latter group (category 'Others' in Figure 7.1) the most outstanding enterprises were the Etablissements Louis Van Goitsenhoven, owned by an industrialist operating on a relatively modest scale and specializing in cinema, gramophones, photography etc., and also Aux Variétés, a chain with no fewer than 24 branches in 1929, owned by the De Baerdemacker family. The pattern of development for advertising which reaches a peak in 1929 is more easily understood if the difficulties resulting from war, both in the first half of 1919 and the second half of 1939 are taken into consideration, as publicity efforts during these periods were almost entirely absent. The diminished advertising activity after 1929 is mainly due to the reduced pressure of competition. The local stores were being forced out of the market, soon to be joined by the remaining competitors of the old *grands magasins*, with the notable exception of Sarma. In Brussels however, the competition remained fierce through the entire period.

In 1909, local publicity was still dominated by the local stores, to the detriment of the Bon Marché and Innovation (Figure 7.1). However, by 1929 local advertising had decreased to one-third of the advertising market. A decade later it was virtually non-existent, as department stores in Ghent outgrew the local market. The four main department stores were facing a new challenge from 1929 onwards, the market having been divided into three sectors, with local stores, the four main

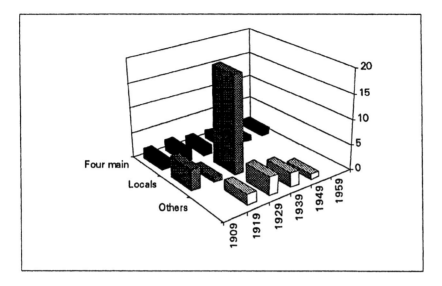

Figure 7.2 Frequency of publication of each department store advertisement (Ghent, 1909–59)[45]

grands magasins, and the other department stores all having equal shares. By 1939, however, the big four had recaptured a major part of the market, and after the Second World War they shared a virtual monopoly in department store advertising. As the Bon Marché did not have a branch in Ghent, and Sarma, according to the *prix uniques* principle, was less inclined to maintain an image through advertising, from 1929 onwards the main competitors in the advertising market were Innovation and Grand Bazar. The dominance of Grand Bazar seemed established by 1959, reflecting the commercial success of the store. The remarkable entry into department store publicity of the first *maison à succursales*, Delhaize, took place in 1959, their numerous large advertisements being almost exact copies in style of those which had previously been used by the former *grands magasins*.

A notable difference between the main department stores and their competitors on both the local and the national level becomes obvious when comparing the frequency of the publication of a single advertisement (Figure 7.2). The long-term commercial success of the department stores can be understood through a more detailed examination of their advertising strategies. The principal *grands magasins* took care to adapt their advertisements to the specific commercial occasion which required publicity, thereby giving the public a broader range of reasons to buy, whereas their competitors used more generalised advertisements which were published repeatedly, without variation.

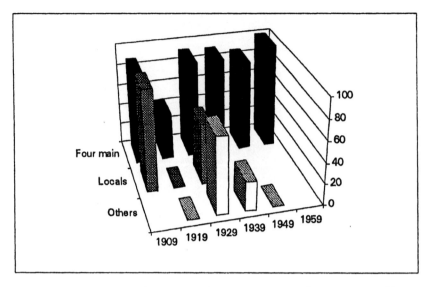

Figure 7.3 Percentage of large-size department store advertisements (Ghent, 1909–59)[46]

The frequency rate for advertising of the four main department stores is remarkably consistent throughout the period 1900–1960, with the average appearance of each advertisement always fewer than three, whereas the others scored averages of up to 20. After the Second World War advertisements published more than once became the exception.

Similar conclusions can be reached from a closer examination of the size of advertisements (Figure 7.3). The advertisements appear to decrease in size when a store became unable to meet the challenge from competitive forces. This occurs in the case of local stores after the First World War, with national competitors after the Second World War and with Sarma in 1959. Generally speaking, however, the department store advertisements were large, illustrating the importance that was attributed to advertising. By 1959 the publication of a small advertisement had become almost unthinkable to the department stores.

The *grands magasins*, faithful to their origins as drapers, followed advertising practices dominated by the fashion seasons (Figure 7.4). The month of June, as the annual occasion for clearance sales, was traditionally a peak period for publicity. October on the other hand, was the beginning of a new season and the principal month for sales. Less important periods for publicity occurred at the end of November with *Sinterklaas* (Santa Claus),[47] and at the end of December and the beginning of January, when Christmas and New Year were closely followed

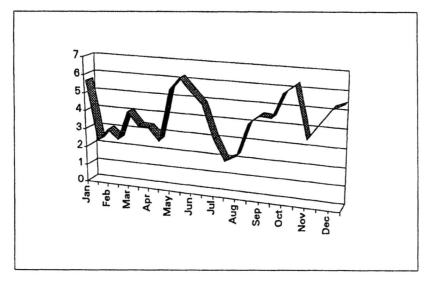

Figure 7.4 Pattern of department store advertising through the year (Ghent, 1909–59)[48]

by the *wintersolden* (winter sales). At the end of August and the beginning of September, sales of school accessories were promoted. In May, any occasion could be exploited to bring the low season to a close, including Mother's Day, First Communion, Pentecost or Easter, spring-cleaning or even the arrival of the first warm days. A typical department store advertisement therefore would be large in size and frequently would have been created for a special occasion such as seasonal sales. However, even outside the high season, advertising never ceased completely.

A specific pattern of development can be discovered through a more detailed examination of the occasions for which advertisements were published (Figure 7.5). Although sales provided the motive for almost half of the advertisements in 1909, this figure had dropped to less than 10 per cent by 1960. Advertisements for special occasions, such as First Communion, Easter, the new school year, *Sinterklaas* and Christmas, followed a similar pattern, decreasing throughout the period. In contrast, publicity for specific departments or for a limited array of articles dominated from 1929 onwards and by 1959 this type of advertisement had become the norm. This shift in the pattern of advertising illustrates the wider changes which were taking place, for as the scope of the department stores was expanding from an emphasis on fashionable articles to the whole of the retailing market, the stores were becoming less dependent on seasonal turnover, and more inclined to create an

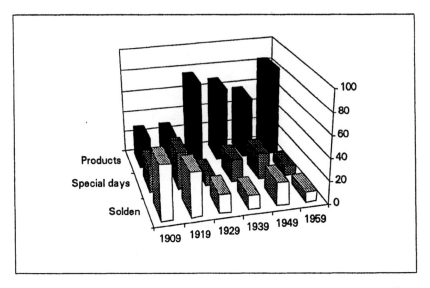

Figure 7.5   Occasions for department store advertising (Ghent, 1909–59)[49]

image through specific goods to compensate for the loss of their modernist identity.

Finally, another aspect worthy of consideration relates to the type of customers who were the targets for the advertisements published by the department stores. The advertisements themselves can not be regarded as reliable sources of information on this subject as references to customers are usually missing and the advertisements are deliberately aimed at a social level above that of the actual situation of the potential customer. However, a comparative analysis of two newspapers, published specifically to attract consumers from two different social groups gives a further insight, as the number and type of advertisements published in only one of the newspapers indicates the kind of customers the department stores were attempting to attract. Among the local newspapers in Ghent, a comparison can be made for this purpose between *La Flandre Libérale*, which was addressed to the liberal, French-speaking bourgeoisie, and *Vooruit*, a Dutch-speaking socialist workers' paper. The results as displayed in Figure 7.6 are probably exaggerated, as the French-speaking paper had become quite outdated after the Second World War, and was of much less interest to advertisers. Despite this, the pattern of development is clear, and illustrates the expansion taking place in the market.

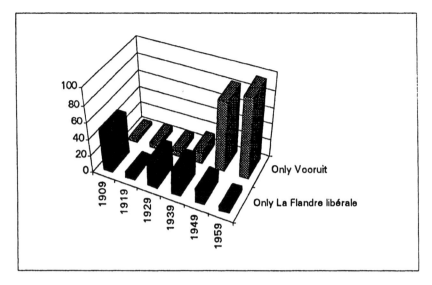

Figure 7.6 Exclusive advertising by department stores (Ghent, 1909–59)[50]

Seducing the consumer through advertisements

Following the arguments developed by Marchand in his remarkable analysis of American advertising in the 1920s and 1930s, modern advertising should be seen as having been subject to a fundamental change after the First World War.[51] Product-oriented advertisements, which rationally emphasised the utility dimension of a product, were gradually being replaced by consumer-oriented advertisements, which emotionally accentuated the pleasure dimension of an article. The most primitive example of the former type was the so-called 'brand-name' publicity, which simply depicted the brand name of the product, accompanied by a view of the factory or its owner. A somewhat more sophisticated variant of this was the 'reason-why' technique, in which a text was included summarising various arguments to justify the purchase of a product. The main disadvantage inherent in this approach was the rational character of the advertisement, which invited consumers to consider the arguments in a logical manner, thereby opening up the possibility that they would think of counter-arguments. A much more efficient approach was an appeal to the emotions, which diverted attention away from the product by emphasising the effects the article could have upon the life of the consumer, rather than on the intrinsic qualities of the product itself. The prime objective became the seduction of the customer, and the aim was therefore to market sex instead of

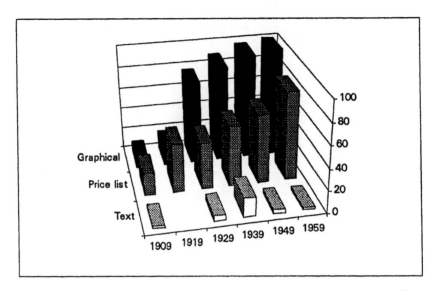

Figure 7.7   Lay-out of department store advertisements (Ghent, 1909–59)[52]

soap, personality instead of millinery, and adventure instead of lemon-ade. In this type of advertising the use of text was minimal in order to avoid a rational consideration of the product and pictures were the preferred medium through which an appeal to the consumer could be maximised.

It would not be unreasonable to suppose that with the expansion of commercial interests and the growth of the department stores, some of the changes mentioned above would be reflected in the publicity cam-paigns of the stores. Was the emphasis in the advertisements product-oriented or consumer-oriented? If it is assumed that a price list is a basic form of 'reason-why' approach, and that graphic elements are attempts to seduce the consumer, then the answer to this question would be 'both', as shown in Figure 7.7.

A change appears to have taken place during the 1920s, paralleling the evolution in American advertising described by Marchand. Graphic presentations in advertisements usually took the form of drawings of models wearing the clothing mentioned in the accompanying price list. Illustrations representing scenes from the life of an average consumer were exceptional, as the product itself was the main focus for attention until after the Second World War. The *grands magasins*, in contrast with the role they apparently fulfilled before the turn of the century,[53] were not the forerunners of modern advertising. This could be attrib-uted partly to the *prix uniques* principle: as the department stores sought to maximise the economies of scale flowing from the concentration

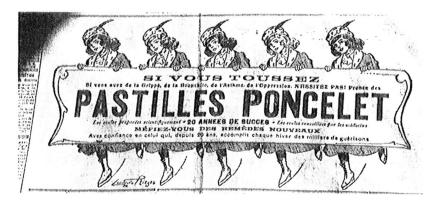

Plate 7.1 Pastilles Poncelet, 1909. (*La Flandre libérale*, 14 November 1909)

of capital, attention came to be concentrated upon the low price argument. Therefore, contrary to expectations, the price-list technique introduced by Innovation as early as 1909, did not become less important with the arrival of modern advertising in Belgium.

In 1909 the department stores could be regarded as the leaders in the field of publicity, having the largest and most frequent newspaper advertisements. However, the contents of these advertisements were certainly anything but innovative. During this period, the forerunners in the use of the latest advertising techniques were those companies publicising pills and powders for the 'quack medicine' market, introducing huge slogans, cartoons, seductive illustrations and even the first modest photographs. In general, the stores dominated the advertising market, but the brand names offered the most innovative advertisements (Plate 7.1). A modest example of graphic advertising can be seen in the *Sinterklaas* advertisement of Innovation, the title being specially drawn in calligraphy (Plate 7.2).

By 1919, Innovation appears to have developed an almost standard layout for its advertisements. A typical department store advertisement during this period consisted of a frame surrounding the prominent logo of the store with a smaller heading beneath, around which were arranged the itemised prices (Plate 7.3). A decade later, the breakthrough of graphic representations in advertising becomes apparent, as both illustrations and a variety of fonts are added to the earlier concept (Plate 7.4) thereby setting a standard which has persisted until the present day, although drawings were replaced by photographs after the Second World War and took up an ever increasing proportion of the advertisement.

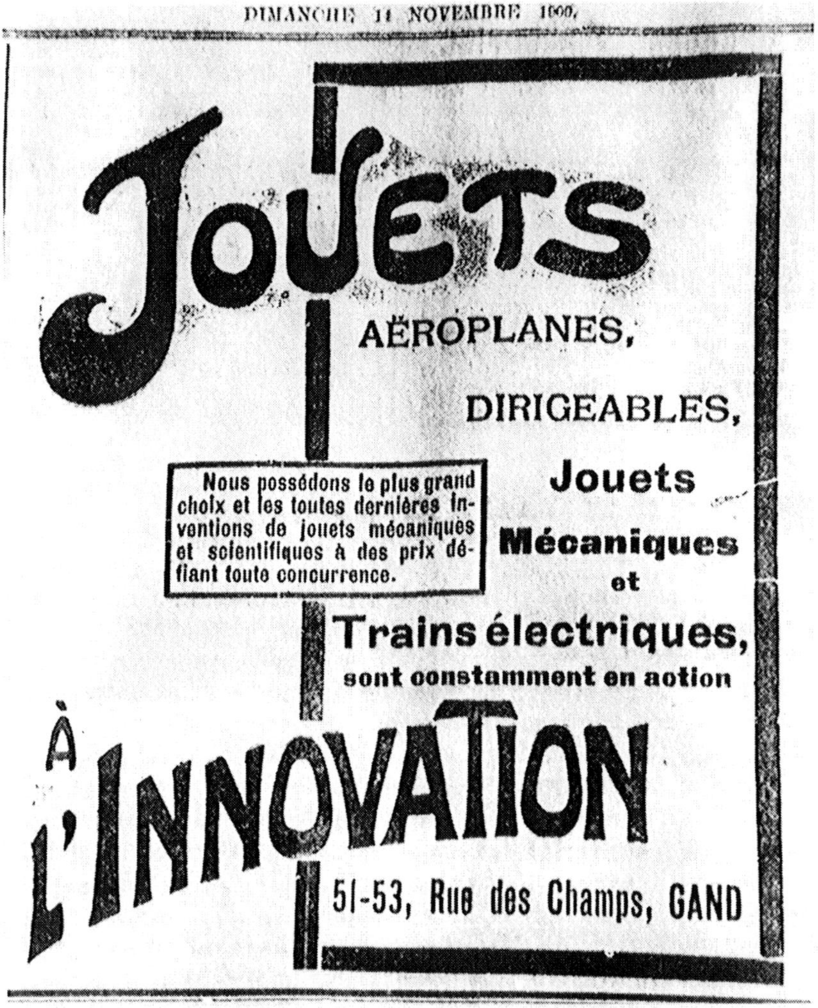

Plate 7.2 Jouets à l'Innovation, 1909. (*La Flandre libérale*, 5 January 1909)

However, Innovation was certainly not the most progressive of the department stores. Certain serious competitors, particularly Sarma and Van Goitsenhoven, were eager to integrate graphic elements in their advertisements from 1929 onwards. One of the consequences of the rapid transformation of advertising techniques during these years was the failure of the co-operative societies to maintain their position as competitors in advertising. Until then, the co-operatives had attempted

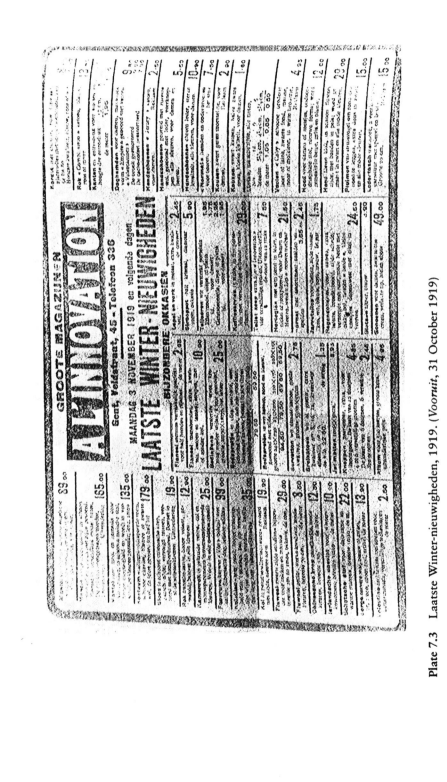

Plate 7.3   Laatste Winter-nieuwigheden, 1919. (*Vooruit*, 31 October 1919)

Plate 7.4   Blanc (A l'Innovation), 1929. (*La Flandre libérale*, 20 January 1929)

as far as possible to follow the example set by the department stores in publicity. The freethinking management of Vooruit for example, did not hesitate to advertise the celebration of the Catholic feast of First Communion, or simply to copy the more elaborate department store advertisements.

The stores were still prominent in the sales market of 1929, but were to encounter increased competition as a range of new and often technological products entered the mass-market, in particular, cigarettes, radios, kitchen-ranges and vacuum cleaners. In advertising, however, these years were dominated primarily by the automobile, which accounted for almost half of the publicity market, whilst cosmetics and toiletries had replaced the pills and powders of the 'quack' medicine market. Within this complex world of publicity, the *grands magasins* always followed the lead given by others. Several of the modern advertising techniques mentioned by Marchand were used, such as elaborated reason-why, endorsements by famous people, or scare copy, which pointed out what could happen if the consumer did *not* buy the product. Further new techniques followed in the subsequent decades, such as the use of comic strips to illustrate scenes from the consumer's daily life, beams of sacred light radiating from the sky symbolising the splendour of the advertising world, and advertisements disguised as editorial copy.

Apart from this, the *grands magasins* tried out several other strategies to gain publicity. For example, in 1927, the Bon Marché promised to cover the travelling expenses of customers from out of town, provided they spent a certain amount in the store. The Providence soon adopted the scheme, and some time later, Innovation followed suit. Innovation had also become well known for their tearoom, which made it possible for customers to enjoy a day out shopping without leaving the store. In addition to their main advertisements, this store also placed notices in the small advertisements section of the newspapers. Finally, it is interesting to note the increasing diversity which was beginning to occur in the advertising strategies of several department stores during this period, as they gradually introduced a greater variety of advertisements, each directed at a specific group of consumers. This experiment, however, was not to be continued in the years that followed.

By 1939 the Grand Bazar had become the most innovative of the department stores, regularly experimenting with illustrations, intriguing headings or slogans of striking proportions (Plate 7.5). Nevertheless, the abundant department store advertising of the 1920s was soon to disappear. Not only was there a marked decrease in newspaper publicity in Ghent after 1929, but by 1959 even cinema advertisements were insignificant. Moreover, several advertisements published during that year proved to be copies of those used a decade earlier. The only change

Plate 7.5   Voulez-vous plus de confort (Grand Bazar), 1939. (*La Flandre libérale*, 19 February 1939)

was the final breakthrough in the use of photographic images instead of drawings as the main source of illustrations. By this time, the *grands magasins* had established a dual advertising strategy, using a combination of straightforward price lists and images of genteel models to tempt

Plate 7.6 Nouveautés de printemps (Grand Bazar), 1949. (*La Flandre libérale*, 27 February 1949)

their female consumers (Plate 7.6). As such, the new-born supermarket owners had found a compromise, convincing through low prices and seducing through genteel images, thereby paying a last tribute to their modernist roots amongst the 'genteel classes' of the nineteenth century.

Conclusion

As argued above, the specific historical role of the *grands magasins* arises from their capacity to fuse modernist bourgeois culture and commercial mass production into a 'dream marriage'. The commercialisation of modernism took place in the heyday of the department store, during the last decades of the nineteenth century. From the 1920s onwards, the department stores, with a high concentration of capital in their hands, were not to remain indifferent to the major economic and social changes which were occurring as consumption rose, in parallel with the development of a welfare society. Following the *prix uniques* principle, expansion was taking place on three levels. Geographically, networks of local branches were established over a wide area; commercially, the emphasis upon fashionable goods diminished as basic products such as food were included; and finally, within the social context, the department stores were expanding beyond the limits of their bourgeois background and were attracting a much broader section of the population.

By 1960 the transformation of the former *grands magasins* had become irreversible, destroying most of the historical identity of the stores, and leading them into a confrontation with the *maisons à succursales*. However, in contrast with the situation at the end of the nineteenth century, during this second phase of the development of a consumer society from the 1920s onwards, the *grands magasins* failed to maintain their position as market leaders and became merely contestants, as generally speaking, the stores were superseded by the brand names in the field of advertising. Nevertheless, paying a last tribute to their social and cultural roots, the *grands magasins* found a compromise in an advertising style of their own, convincing the consumer through low prices and seducing them by the use of nostalgic genteel images.

Notes

1. Bill Lancaster, *The Department Store: A Social History*, London: Leicester University Press (1995), pp. 3–4.
2. Paul Glennie, 'Consumption within historical studies', in D. Miller (ed.), *Acknowledging Consumption: a Review of New Studies*, London: Routledge (1995), pp. 189–90.

3. Colin Campbell, *The Romantic Ethic and the Spirit of Modern Consumerism*, Oxford: Blackwell (1990), p. 94.
4. Neil McKendrick, John Brewer and J.H. Plumb, *The Birth of a Consumer Society: the Commercialization of Eighteenth-Century England*, London: Europa Publications (1982), p. 12.
5. Rudi Laermans, 'Learning to consume: early department stores and the shaping of the modern consumer culture', *Theory, Culture and Society*, 10, 1993, p. 82.
6. Rosalind H. Williams, *Dream Worlds: Mass Consumption in Late Nineteenth-Century France*, Berkeley: University of California Press (1982), pp. 58–106.
7. H. Pasdermadjian, *Le grand magasin: son origine, son évolution, son avenir*, Paris: Dunod (1949), pp. 1–9.
8. Gerrylynn K. Roberts, 'Food', in C. Chant (ed.), *Science, Technology and Everyday Life 1870–1950*, London: Routledge/The Open University (1990), pp. 250–56 and 258–60.
9. Fernand Simonet, *Le petit commerce de détail: sa lutte avec le grand commerce de détail*, Louvain/Paris: Ecole des sciences commerciales et économiques/Librairie d'économie commerciale (1934), pp. 25–67.
10. Peter Scholliers and Chris Vandenbroeke, 'The transition from traditional to modern patterns of demand in Belgium', in H. Baudet and H. van der Meulen (eds), *Consumer Behaviour and Economic Growth in the Modern Economy*, London: Croom Helm (1982), p. 41.
11. Siegfried Gerlach, *Das Warenhaus in Deutschland: Seine Entwicklung bis zum Ersten Weltkrieg in historisch-geographischer Sicht*, Stuttgart: Steiner Verlag (1988).
12. Typology used by the National Bank of Belgium in the 1930s, *Bulletin d'information et de documentation*, 8, 1933, p. 370.
13. Serge Jaumain, *Les petits commerçants belges face à la modernité (1880–1914)*, Brussels: Editions de l'Université de Bruxelles (1995), p. 48.
14. *Dubbele wegwijzer der Stad Gent en der Provincie Oost-Vlaanderen*, 47, 1909, p. 558.
15. Ibid., 28, 1890, p. 466.
16. *Wegwijzer der Stad Gent en der Provincie Oost-Vlaanderen*, 115, 1884, p. 468.
17. *Dubbele wegwijzer*, 47, 1909, pp. 519–20.
18. Ibid., 14, 1866, p. 429.
19. Ibid., 47, 1909, p. 513.
20. *Wegwijzer*, 114, 1883, p. 466.
21. Ibid., 94, 1863, p. 439.
22. *Dubbele wegwijzer*, 53, 1915, p. 479.
23. Ibid., 47, 1909, p. 441.
24. Jaumain, *Petits commerçants*, pp. 47–8; Jacques Roets, *La structure fonctionnelle des grands magasins*, Brussels: Ecole professionnelle de vente (1944), p. 107; Mireille Servé, 'Grands magasins et publicité à la fin du XIXe et au début du XXe siècle', *Cahiers de Clio*, 95, 1988, pp. 15–20.
25. However, Au Bon Marché initially seemed more reminiscent of a fashion shop, while Innovation seemed to show characteristics of a more modest haberdashery.
26. Jacques Lacrosse and Pierre De Bie, *Emile Bernheim: Histoire d'un grand magasin*, Brussels: Labor (1972), pp. 55–8.

27. *Recueil financier*, 37, 1930, p. 764.
28. Ibid., 37, 1930, p. 1155.
29. Ibid., 38, 1931, pp. 861–2.
30. Simonet, *Petit commerce de détail*, p. 31; Pasdermadjian, *Grand magasin*, pp. 38–39; Noël Cassé, *Etude sur les grands magasins à prix uniques*, Paris: Rousseau (1935), pp. 9–11, 21–2.
31. In addition to the American stores Woolworth, Kresge, Kress and McCrory, there were other stores such as Woolworth and Marks & Spencer (England); Woolworth, Wohlwert, EPA (*Einheitspreis AG*) and EHAPE (Germany); Unifix, Monoprix, Prisunic and Priminime (France); UPIM (*Unico Prezzo Italiano Milano*) and TAPU (*Tutto A Prezzo Unico*) (Italy); TIC (*Towary Jednolitych Cen*) (Poland); ASO (*Ander & Sohn*), JEPA and TETA (Czechoslovakia); HEMA (*Hollandse Eenheidsprijzen Maatschappij*) (Netherlands); SARMA and Uniprix-Priba (Belgium); EPA (*Enhetsprisaktielobaget*) (Sweden); and Einheitspreis and Uniprix (Switzerland). Also Takashimaya (Japan). Simonet, *Petit commerce de détail*, p. 32.
32. *Recueil des actes et documents relatifs aux sociétés commerciales (Annexes au Moniteur Belge)*, 21–22 July 1929, pp. 932–3.
33. Lacrosse and De Bie, *Emile Bernheim*, pp. 91–7; *Recueil des actes*, 5–6 March 1934, pp. 1393–4.
34. Currently known as Unic.
35. First measures introduced in Germany and Austria, 1932 and 1933. Refused by the American Congress in 1934, but accepted in France after a long debate, 1933–36. Simonet, *Petit commerce de détail*, pp. 103–9. First demands in Belgium before 1934, parliamentary proposals from 1936 onwards. *Les magasins à prix uniques: au triple point de vue du consommateur, de l'industrie et du petit commerce*, Brussels: Sarma (1934); *Rapport des Représentants des Grands Organismes de Distribution à la Commission du Commerce de Détail*, Antwerp: Chambre syndicale des Grands Magasins de Belgique (1937).
36. 'Loi interdisant l'ouverture ou l'agrandissement de certains établissements de vente en détail' of 13 January 1937, prolonged by the laws of 25 March 1937, 17 June 1937, 1 April 1938 (modified) and 26 December 1938, and by the Royal Warrant of 29 July 1939. Further prolonged during the Occupation, 1940–44. Prolongation continued by the laws of 10 September 1945, 23 December 1946, 28 February 1947 and 30 December 1947 (modified). New temporary *loi de cadenas* on 12 May 1948, and again on 3 March 1954. The latter expired March 1959 (after a law proposed on 27 November 1956 failed to get through the parliament), but Minister Paul Vanden Boeynants made an agreement with the department stores to maintain the prohibition until 1 January 1961. *Pasinomie: collection complète des lois, décrets, arrêtés et règlements généraux qui peuvent être invoqués en Belgique*, Brussels, 1936–60; René Evalenko and Marcel Michel, *La structure du commerce de détail en Belgique et la législation de cadenas*, Brussels/Louvain: Institut de sociologie Solvay/Centre de recherches en économie et gestion des entreprises (1958), pp. 16–27; Lacrosse and De Bie, *Emile Bernheim*, p. 137.
37. This led Sarma to develop another supermarket chain, Nopri.
38. Formerly the Grands Bazars Réunis Anvers-Gand, which had its name changed in 1933 to Galeries du Bon Marché and again in 1941 to Grand Bazar d'Anvers/Grote bazar van Antwerpen.

39. *Recueil financier*, 73, 1966, p. 2128.
40. Ibid., 77, 1970, pp. 2264–5.
41. Ibid., 77, 1970, pp. 2104–5.
42. Ibid., 81, 1974, p. 1241.
43. Data on advertisements taken from an investigation of *La Flandre libérale*, 1909–59 and *Vooruit*, 1909–59. All advertisements for department stores were enumerated for 1909, 1919, 1929, 1939, 1949 and 1959.
44. Figure 7.1 shows the number of advertisements published in *La Flandre Libérale* and *Vooruit*, per category of department store. Advertisements were counted for the years 1909, 1919, 1929, 1939, 1949 and 1959. Advertisements published more than once or in more than one paper were only counted once. Advertisements published by the Bon Marché, Innovation, the Grands Bazars and Sarma are to be found under the category 'Four main'; advertisements published by department stores having their main seat in Ghent under 'Locals'; and all of the other advertisements under 'Others'.
45. Figure 7.2 shows how many times a single advertisement was published on average, per category of department store. Advertisements were identified during the counting. A record was kept of how many times each advertisement was published during the year, in both *La Flandre Libérale* and *Vooruit*. The average was calculated per category of department store. Categories of department store as in Figure 7.1.
46. Figure 7.3 shows the share of advertisements considered 'large size' in the total number of advertisements, per category of department store, presented as percentages. Any advertisement with a size equal or superior to DIN A5 (half of a standard copy sheet) was considered large size. Categories of department store as in Figure 7.1
47. Santa Claus in Ghent, celebrated the 6 December.
48. Figure 7.4 shows how the advertising was distributed through the year on average between 1909 and 1959. Advertisements were counted for each half-monthly period, and the share of the number in the annual total was calculated. The left-hand numbers show the percentage of every half-monthly period in the yearly total.
49. Figure 7.5 shows the share of advertisements of three categories in the total number of advertisements, presented as percentages. The categories represent the occasions for which the advertisement was published. 'Solden' refers to seasonal sales, once or twice a year (in June and at the turn of the year); 'Special days' refers to moments throughout the year when higher sales might be expected, e.g. First Communion, Easter, the new school year, Santa Claus, Christmas, etc; 'Products' refers to publicity for specific departments or for a limited range of articles.
50. Figure 7.6 shows the share of advertisements published in only one of the two papers, *La Flandre Libérale* or *Vooruit*, in the total number of advertisements, presented as percentages.
51. Roland Marchand, *Advertising the American Dream: Making Way for Modernity, 1920–1940*, Berkeley: University of California Press (1985), pp. 1–24.
52. Figure 7.7 shows the share of advertisements containing a specific layout element in the total number of advertisements, per category, presented as percentages. The category 'Text' contains advertisements showing merely text phrases, beside the name of the product or store; 'Price list' means

the advertisement contains a price list of some articles; 'Graphical' means the advertisement contains graphical elements, such as drawings, pictures, etc.

53. Williams, *Dream Worlds*, pp. 67–70.

CHAPTER EIGHT

Acts of consumption: musical comedy and the desire of exchange[1]

Erika D. Rappaport

Between the 1890s and 1914, fierce competition between London's major department stores, furnishers, caterers, and entertainers launched the building of palatial edifices, the advent of diverse services and amenities, the introduction of new styles of display and publicity, and an increasingly feminine workforce. Never as large or as spectacular as their American and continental counterparts, several London shops had become modern department stores by 1914.[2] Whiteley's, Harrods, and Selfridges had all reached phenomenal size and diversification in the early 1900s. Competition became especially intense in 1909 after the American-born entrepreneur, Gordon Selfridge, spent enormous sums constructing and advertising a monument to mass consumption in Oxford Street. The wave of publicity that surrounded its opening and the competing celebrations and sales in established shops encouraged the perception that the stores were, as one newspaper reporter put it, 'Modernity's Creation'.[3]

Although department stores were the product of nearly a century of evolution, advertising and publicity fostered the impression that they were modern, 'feminine' pleasure centres. The West End stage took part in and profited from this development. In 1894 H.J.W. Dam, the author of the immensely popular musical comedy *The Shop Girl*, explained in an interview, 'as many thousands of people do business at the large shops and stores in London ... [I realized] the stores formed an excellent sphere to make the basis of a musical piece.'[4] The producers of commercial West End theatre believed that audiences were as happy to consume in the darkened halls of the theatre as they were in the brightly lit department stores that were but a few streets away. Department stores and similar consumer environments, thus, became especially popular 'spheres' for London's newest mass entertainment, the musical comedy.

Critics have dismissed musical comedy as nothing but pure escapism.[5] Yet this genre, like other theatrical forms of the era, reflected upon the commodification of women, sexuality, and identity in a mass culture and economy. *Fin-de-siècle* drama played a similar role to that of the early-modern period. It explored questions of identity raised by changes in market society.[6] Musical comedy in particular served both a promotional and critical role. Set within a profoundly materialistic world, the musical comedy commented upon the production of desire and new types of sociability in sites of mass consumption.[7] It stimulated and contained consumer desires by linking women's supposed lust for goods and men's lust for women to innocent flirtation, marriage and social stability.

As Joel Kaplan and Sheila Stowell have recently argued, the pre-war theatre and fashion industries were involved in a mutually satisfying relationship in which the stage advertised fashions, shops and a faith in consumerism to a middle-class audience.[8] Peter Bailey has likewise suggested that musical comedies championed a managed, rational sexuality that supported the interests of corporate capitalism and patriarchal gender relations.[9] In doing so, however, these productions also eroticised the act of exchange and altered the image of shopping promoted by department stores. If 'real' department stores cultivated a public image as feminine pleasure centres, theatrical department stores housed erotic yet socially acceptable narratives about the mingling of classes, sexes and money. The department store musical comedy enabled both producers and consumers a venue for exploring the profits, pleasures, and problems of a consumer society.

Staging consumption

For many middle-class Victorians the theatre had become a necessary ingredient during a sojourn in London. After the Great Exhibition in 1851, West End audiences were made up increasingly, but not exclusively, of middle-class suburban and provincial visitors.[10] West End managers appealed to this audience through various strategies, including pricing, architectural design and décor, and the choice of theatrical fare. The addition of restaurants and the introduction of the matinée in the 1870s also encouraged the middle classes to see theatre-going as a respectable and fashionable social experience. By the early 1900s, the expansion of suburban railways and the London Underground and the construction of new wide streets such as Charing Cross Road, Northumberland and Shaftesbury Avenues facilitated the flow of middle-class suburbia to the West End.[11] This neighbourhood never entirely shed its immoral image, however, for it also was home to a vast selection of illegal commercial pleasures, from prostitution to pornography and gambling.[12]

The theatre district was also in close proximity to London's fashionable shopping area. Department stores, hotels, restaurants and theatres collectively defined the commercial pleasures on offer, with many mass entertainments even sharing the same buildings, owners and patrons. Shopping, dining, sightseeing and play-going were engaged in and thought about together. Bourgeois women tended to visit the theatre in the midst of West End shopping trips. For example, in studying her family's diaries, Ursula Bloom discovered that in the mid-nineteenth century her great-aunt and mother travelled to London to enjoy a hectic November week of shopping, play-going, and sightseeing.[13] After the advent of the matinée, middle-class women frequently rounded off a day of West End shopping with a theatre visit. One Londoner recalled that in the first years of the twentieth century: 'Going Up West never had any connection with geography; it meant shopping in Oxford Street or visiting a theatre.'[14] The West End had become a site in which the English middle class both 'provisioned and envisioned' itself.[15]

In this neighbourhood, the large stores and the commercial stage were transforming consumption into visual pleasure and spectacle. The Victorian public acquired this taste for spectacle while reading, decorating their homes, walking along the streets, shopping, travelling, visiting museums, exhibitions, gardens, zoos and a host of other entertainments. The late-Victorian theatre had become a central facet of this larger visual culture but it had not always been so. Early nineteenth-century theatre had been primarily an aural experience which only slowly became a visual one.[16] By 1870 one critic felt this transformation had been completed. 'We go to the theatre', he wrote, 'not so much to hear as to look ... like one gigantic peep-show ... we pay the showman, and put our eyes to the glass and stare.' On stage, he sarcastically commented, 'The most complicated and familiar objects about us are ... [being] dragged upon the stage. Thus, when we take our dramatic pleasure, we have the satisfaction of not being separated from the objects of our daily life.'[17] According to this critic, the late-Victorian spectacular theatre mimetically reproduced the bourgeois material world.

The theatrical press encouraged this correspondence by directing the reader's attention to costume and set design. Victorian dramatic reviews described the costuming and *mise-en-scène* of most plays in such detail that they often served as advertisements for the retailers who supplied gowns and props. Their verbose style replicated the culture of abundance presented in store windows, catalogues, and advertising.[18] In teaching readers to watch the fashions and furnishings on stage, journalists forged a relationship with the entertainment industry and retailers. A shared view of feminine psychology sustained this tripartite alliance.

Critics, playwrights and retailers all assumed that with their acute visual sense and passion for finery, middle-class women especially enjoyed the material aspects of performances. One drapers' trade journal explained that it reported on stage fashions because 'It was not uncommon for the audience to applaud a successful toilette as they would a graceful pirouette or bit of eloquent by-play.'[19] Edwardian business viewed the stage as a promotional site in part because 'experts' felt a theatrical environment particularly conditioned the female mind for consumption. 'All women,' the famous couturière, Lucile argued, 'make pictures for themselves. They go to the theatre and see themselves as the heroine of the play.'[20] For Lucile this identification between audience and actress stimulated consumption. Whether in a shop or watching a play:

> when the lights are lowered to a rosy glow, and soft music is played and the mannequins parade, there is not a woman in the audience, though she may be fat and middle-aged, who is not seeing herself look as those slim, beautiful girls look in the clothes they are offering her. And that is the inevitable prelude to buying clothes.[21]

Lucile's picture of an intensely suggestive female consumer was shared by many Edwardian retailers. An article on 'Good Window Display' in *The Retail Trader* advised that a 'powerful note' was struck with women when 'articles of personal attire' were 'draped over lifelike figures ... [for] they represent their ideals of themselves – show themselves up as they would like to appear.'[22] Another compared the job of the window dresser to that of a stage manager:

> Just as the stage manager of a new play rehearses and tries and retries and fusses until he has exactly the right lights and shades and shadows and appeals to his audience, so the merchant goes to work, analysing his line and his audience, until he hits on a scheme that brings the public flocking to his doors.[23]

One writer scientifically concluded, 'we are beginning to see that people are influenced more through the eye than any other organ of the body.'[24]

These assumptions about female psychology and consumption facilitated a merger of stage and store. Theatre managers, store moguls and the daily press joined forces to construct a large, heterosocial consuming crowd in London's West End. They built theatres and plays that would appeal to middle-class women, while also entertaining a diverse mass audience.

'This Way, Madame'

'Hats'
Some people say success is won by dresses,
Fancy that!
But what are dresses without a Hat?

If you would set men talking when you're walking
out to shop,
You'll be all right if you're all right on top!

That's the last Parisian hat,
so buy it,
and try it!
Keep your head up steady and straight,
though your fainting under the weight!
We'll declare that you are sweet
Men will wait outside on the street
If you have that hat![25]

This ode to shopping and flirting from the production of *Our Miss Gibbs* (1909) captured the essence of Edwardian musical comedy and consumer culture. This genre staged consumption in a playful light, situating it in the realm of leisure and courtship, not economics and work. Associated with George Edwardes and the two theatres he managed, the Gaiety and Daly's, musical comedies were wildly popular with a heterosocial, middle- and lower middle-class audience.[26] Edwardes hoped that musical comedy would delight the middle-class female shoppers who by the late 1880s spent a good deal of time and money in London's West End.[27] From the late 1860s until 1886, the Gaiety had largely offered burlesque and was quite popular with 'the young men of the town.'[28] When Edwardes took over its management he transformed it into a 'ladies' theatre' by renovating the playhouse and its productions. The women's magazine, *The Lady* applauded this change, delighting in the Gaiety's new 'Moorish style' auditorium, its 'scientifically arranged and vastly improved' ventilation, and the fact that Edwardes 'boldly abandoned burlesque, and [made] a brave bid for victory with genuine English comic opera.'[29] Musical comedy still revolved around sexual themes and specialised in displaying a chorus of young working-class women, the 'Gaiety Girls,' but it banished the leg shows and overt appeals to male desire popular in burlesque. In 1909 Max Beerbohm wrote that in such comedies:

> All the classes mingle on the easiest terms. Everyone wants everyone else to have a good time and tries to make everything easy and simple all round. This good time, as I need hardly say, is of a wholly sexual order. And yet everyone from the highest to the lowest is thoroughly good ... an innocent libertinism.[30]

The backdrop for this 'innocent libertinism' was nearly always a site of exchange: shopping street, tea shop, dressmaker's, exhibition and, most popular of all, department store. These locations offered wonderful promotional possibilities for real-life retailers, seemed very 'up-to-date,' and allowed for the mixture of strangers that was central to the play's romance.

These commercial locales also emphasised the similarity between shopping and play-going and were intended to lure female shoppers into the theatre. In 1913, for example, Mark and Sydney Blow promoted the Queen's Theatre as a shoppers' rendezvous where the public could 'meet one's friends, write letters, read all the papers and magazines, use the telephones, send messages by hand, take tea and generally make themselves at home, as at Selfridge's.' To advertise the theatre as 'an anchor in the intervals between shopping and lunch and more shopping and dinner', the Blows opened with a play about shopping in a fashionable dressmakers. Mark Blow explained that when ladies 'read the title of "This Way, Madame" in the theatrical advertisements of the newspapers ... they will accept its invitation by day as well as by night.'[31] Managers like the Blows had thus been inspired by the commercial success of the new Oxford Street emporium and hoped to capture the same audience. This idea was actually quite old by 1913, however.

In the early, extremely successful musical comedy *The Shop Girl* (1894–96) the lyrics, plot, and *mise-en-scène* linked consumption and performance. The author modelled the set for the first act, the Royal Stores, after Whiteley's department store and the middle-class co-operative, the Army and Navy Stores.[32] A chorus of shoppers and shop assistants further set the scene by singing the praises of the department store:

> The noble institution of financial evolution
> Is the glory of English trade.
> It's the wonder of the nation as a mighty aggregation
> of all objects grown or made.

The following verse then compared 'the loyal, royal stores' to 'a daily dress rehearsal' and the final lines ended with the chorus of workers listing the goods for sale in the emporium: 'Dress goods/tinned food/ Bric a Brac and Parrots/Pipe racks, red wax, fishing goods galore.'[33] The lyrics thus playfully satirised the much touted but somewhat distinct images of the department store as a symbol of English economic prowess and as a site of performance and leisure.

The plot then took up the question of true love in a mass society. It opens with a solicitor coming to the Royal Stores in search of a foundling shop girl who has unknowingly inherited a great fortune. After countless twists and turns, singing and dancing, and sexual innuendo, the shop girl's identity is finally revealed. The humour is inspired by the numerous cases of mistaken identity and related scheming and flirting between everyone involved. A marriage between the heiress shop girl and the penniless but good son of the solicitor brings the play to its happy ending.

Department stores were often imagined as exclusively feminine worlds. In musical comedies like Dam's *The Shop Girl* they become sites of cross-class, heterosexual interaction, where women use commodities to become glamorous and sell themselves to men. Shop girls win the love of aristocrats, male assistants flirt with wealthy female shoppers and customers ogle each other.[34] Selling in this sexual marketplace always buys the working-class girl a successful marriage. The theme of working girl winning a wealthy husband via her fashionable style was repetitiously played out in virtually all the comedies. In Dam's production, the shop girl heroine sings:

> When I came to the shop some years ago
> I was terribly shy and simple;
> with my skirt too high and my hat too low
> and an unbecoming dimple.
> But soon I learnt with a customer's aid
> how men make up to a sweet little maid;
> and another lesson I've learnt since then
> How a dear little maid 'makes up' for men.
> A touch of rouge that is just a touch
> and black in the eye, but not too much;
> and a look that makes the Johnnies stop
> I learnt that all in the shop, shop, shop!

Once she learned to 'make up for men', this shop girl chirped, 'I think the proper thing to do/Is to watch for a wealthy Johnny! .... I won't take no less than a noble peer/with twenty-thousand a year.' Eventually, however, the millionaire shop girl marries for love. The play thus pokes fun at the newly materialistic, commercialised age of which it is also a part.

Although a new theatrical form in the 1890s, the musical comedy was a hybrid, blending aspects of British and French farce, burlesque and the comic operas of Gilbert and Sullivan. Both farce and its sibling, musical comedy, relied upon a great deal of verbal play, physical jokes, and disguise to inspire laughter and move the plot forward. Serious emotions and ideas were frequently undercut by visual and verbal gags, often added during the performance by the actor or actress, which can only be guessed at from remaining scripts. In farce a great deal of the humour is derived from physical humour but also from verbal misunderstandings amplified or created by social differences. The cast therefore included the entire social spectrum, and a few intelligent working-class characters.[35]

Musical comedy kept farce's basic structure, but placed the serving classes, particularly the favoured heroine of the day, the shop girl, in a more central role. The working girl is always intelligent but it is her knowledge of commodities and human nature that resolves the dilemmas that she and others face. The nature of identity is somewhat ambiguous, however, since the plots frequently revolved around key characters impersonating members of the 'opposite' class.

In some respects, the department store simply provided a convenient setting for the social mixture and props necessary for successful comedy. However, because they were also identified as new spectacular institutions, department stores lent a modern and novel aura to a genre that was not wholly original. The shop girl added to this sense of modernity because she was one of several common symbols of the much discussed 'New Woman' during the turn of the century. Although female workers probably did not surpass male employees in the service sector until during the First World War, they dominated certain trades and a few highly visible departments.[36] They were nearly all young and their liminal position between the upper levels of the working class and the lower reaches of the middle class made the shop girl the ideal focus of both concern and delight and sometimes both at once. A long-standing image of being sexually available and a highly public lifestyle as workers, residents and consumers in the West End also added to the shop girl's theatrical popularity.[37]

The shop girl was also a common character in contemporary melodrama, but the class and gender relations in such plays looked quite different from those portrayed in musical comedy. For example, melodrama turned musical comedy's harmless male flirt into a predatory figure out to destroy the shop girl's virtue. In the melodrama *The Shop Girl and Her Master* (1915) the emporium owner's 'wicked son' is far from harmless, for he vows to make one of the shop girls his mistress. An experienced employee warns a young, impressionable new assistant not to 'go about' with the owner's son, for she declares, 'It is that gives we shop girls a bad name and makes people think we are all for sale the same as the goods that hang around the shop.'[38] While melodramas clearly comment on the commodification of women, its stark contrasts between good and evil, vice and virtue are not present in West End musical comedies.[39]

The musical comedy working girl uses her knowledge of commodities to construct a glamorous persona and capture her upper-class prey. Male customers are seduced by consumer-aware women. Of course, this scenario could have stimulated fantasies among the male members of the audience. Indeed, Peter Bailey has argued that these plays valorised male voyeuristic pleasure and provided a reassuring response to 'contemporary challenges to male domination and sexual identity.'[40] Instead of the image of sexual anarchy represented by Oscar Wilde's trial in 1895 and the plays of Ibsen and other serious authors of the day, musical comedy offered narratives of heterosexual romance.[41] The sexually knowing shop girl was by no means a new image, but here she is presented as the model for a new feminine ideal which stressed youth, style, and performance.

The woman worker as consuming beauty also provided a stark contrast with the sick, lonely, overworked victim of long hours, low wages and poor working and living conditions developed in the works of socialists, feminists and liberal reformers. Dozens of tracts, plays and newspaper exposés invoked a melodramatic mode to cast the female shop assistant as victim of upper-class greed and vanity. In *Shop Slavery and Emancipation*, the Fabian William Paine wrote of the large draper's: 'its front doors are flung wide open to vanity, from its back doors goes forth oppression.'[42] Both store owners and their feckless customers supposedly abused service workers. The authors of *The Working Life of Shop Assistants* complained that a woman who regards shopping, 'not as a matter of business, but as a sort of recreation or pastime' selfishly ignores 'the comfort and convenience of shopworkers.'[43] In this view the shoppers' pleasure increased workers' labour. In a number of West End productions, socialist and feminist playwrights such as H.G. Wells, G.B. Shaw, Cicely Hamilton and Harley Granville Barker condemned capitalism through the portrayal of the victimised shop girl and seamstress.[44] In contrast, musical comedies avoided discussing working conditions or the strained relations between customers and shoppers. It is no wonder that in writing about musical comedy Beerbohm concluded 'all the Tory in me rejoices.'[45]

Far from being abused by capitalism, the musical comedy's shop girl manipulated capitalists through her mastery of performance and disguise. Actresses, shop girls and shoppers continually change positions in these plays. The second act of *The Shop Girl* is set in a charity bazaar in which the shop assistants, customers and a group of actresses literally change places. The actresses and shoppers tend the bazaar booths while the Royal Stores' employees act in a production of *Hamlet*. This inversion temporarily challenges the social system, but its radical impact is undermined as the plot unfolds and the working girl turns out to also be a member of the elite classes. This mass culture thus drew upon the social inversion of carnival, but then exposed its fictions as themselves fictional.

These reversals were, however, humorous and self-referential portraits of contemporary relationships between working-class 'beauties' and wealthy men. During these years, showgirls and fashion models occasionally married into money and nobility and actresses frequently sold goods for charity.[46] 'Well-known actresses' sold British perfume at Harrod's in honour of the 'all-British Shopping Week'.[47] Gordon Selfridge allowed peeresses, 'experienced in bazaars ... the sensation of selling in a real shop.'[48] Such events and relationships underscored a view of class and gender as performance. The relationship between audience and performance, 'real life' and theatre was deliberately blurred for theatrical and romantic effect.

Alongside the young and alluring shop girl, musical comedies presented the shopper as an elderly, ugly and foolish figure. The actual power relations within the shop are, for comic purposes, inverted. Instead of being lavished with attention and commodities, the shopper usually was a minor, clownish character who would not consume, would not pay for what she bought or purchased too much. Like 'Lady Dodo', a customer in *The Shop Girl*, the shopper's antics were designed to draw contempt and laughter from the audience. Numerous plays cast the shopper as a disruptive figure who literally made a mess of the stores. In *The Girl From Kay's* (1902), a satire of Jay's, the Regent Street mourning warehouse-turned-fashionable-emporium, a shop assistant lamented:

> If you'd like to know the ways of customers at Kay's,
> we observe a most remarkable variety.
> There's a lady coming there with Victoria and Pair,
> She's a duchess in the very best Society!
> And she makes us kill ourselves,
> getting velvets from the shelves.
> Till the pile of goods is big enough to bury her,
> Then she say's 'that's very nice,
> twenty guineas is the price,
> Give me half a yard of ribbon for my terrier'.[49]

The disorderly shopper was also a common character in music hall skits. In *The Toy Shop* (1915) a male assistant almost attacks a customer who looks but buys nothing. Even before she enters the shop the assistant plots against her, telling the audience:

> I've never sold a thing yet ... I hate customers and as for women if I get a woman in here I'll strangle her, they come inside and look at everything in the shop, run me up and down to fetch everything and buy nothing, the governor gets the hump, and I get the sack, and everything goes wrong ... . If I get a woman in here I'll cut her leg off.[50]

In these skits performed for working- and lower middle-class audiences buying and selling became overt expressions of class and gender antagonism. On stage this antagonism turned against the shopper making her the butt of often violent humour.

This aggression was muted but still present in West End productions. Gordon Selfridge lampooned himself and his customers when he supported the one-act farce, *Selfrich's Annual Sale* (1910). The skit presented the Oxford Street emporium as a single department selling everything: 'hats, cheese, gowns, toys, ribbons and live animals'. The walls exhibited notices which satirised Selfridge's advertising and store services.

One read, 'our prices are made to suit our customers – they are the lowest of the low.' Before a sale begins Selfrich tells his two assistants, Miss Marshall and Miss Snelgrove (a play on one of his chief rivals, Marshall and Snelgrove's), 'Never before have the public had the opportunity of buying last season's things at such vastly increased prices.'[51]

Once the doors open, however, the customers seek their revenge. One 'old lady' tries to match ribbon without the original pieces so she asks Selfrich to come to her suburban home. When he refuses, she shouts, 'you're the most impertinent and disobliging young man I've ever come across. I shall certainly report you.' An array of annoying and troublesome customers follow the performance of the 'old lady', with each trying Mr Selfrich's patience. Each customer's outlandish request intentionally satirised, but also advertised, Selfridge's services, such as his return policy, payment plans and the idea of the store as a shoppers' rendezvous. One woman wants to buy a bottle of ammonia on installment and a 'German with problem feet' removes his boots to show Selfrich that the socks he bought at the store two years before now have holes. He, of course, wants to return the socks. When asked if they 'want to buy anything?' the customers shout in unison, 'Buy anything! Why should we?' Finally, a different type of customer comes into the shop. She tells Mr Selfrich, 'say here, I want a shirtwaist – white cashmere – two dollars, my name is Sadie N. Vandergilt – Hotel Cecil – here's the bill, thank you. I won't detain you.' Selfrich asks this wonder customer, 'You are an American?' She responds quickly, 'Sure, I am! And I know what I want!' 'Thank God!' the American entrepreneur answers.[52]

English customers foolishly seem to enjoy the leisure of shopping in the large stores, but won't buy anything. The only 'rational' customer is the one who actually makes a purchase and she, of course, is American. While *Selfrich's Annual Sale* expressed popular anxieties about advertising and mass consumer culture, it also parodied English fears of economic decline and Americanization. No doubt Gordon Selfridge enjoyed being lampooned in this way because of his professed belief that all publicity is good publicity.

It is also possible that the 'shopping, but not buying' customer appeared on the West End stage to charm the large numbers of service workers who also attended performances. She was certainly a stock character in trade journals of the era. The drapers' papers constantly complained about shop rovers, shop prowlers, or the more frequently named, 'tabby'. Like the kleptomaniac, the 'tabs' or "tabby" was a customer who consumed time and space not goods. 'Shopping A La Fin Du Siecle [sic] or how Irene Worried the Drapers', published in the *Draper's Record*, is nearly identical to the assistant's song in *The Girl From Kay's*:

Irene Smith, a maid of bluest blood –
Her gens [sic] ennobled 'ere the
mighty flood ...
claimed blood with keen old 'Wealth of Nations'
Smith ...
Soon noble shop-fronts claim her willing eye,
With softest vestures, soothing as a sight,
Yet on, still on, her pretty feet must move –
But note, dear reader, how my measure drops –
She's come to Regent Street 'To see the Shops'.[53]

Often, however, the 'tab' was not a pretty 'maid' but an ugly 'shop rover and shop prowler' who 'infested' the draper's counter. The rover's 'chief delight would seem to exist in ransacking an entire stock without making a single purchase', while the 'prowler' was simply another word for kleptomaniac or thief, who goes about 'not to inspect but to lift these productions', noted one trade journal.[54] Old and ugly, often bringing her pet pug or terrier with her she was a stock source of humour in trade journals.[55] Thus, while the sets and costuming in the musical comedy were intended to please bourgeois female shoppers especially, their treatment within the drama may have found favour with the husbands and workers in the audience. This ambiguity mirrors the nature of the mass audience and a larger discomfort with buying and selling that permeated *fin-de-siècle* culture.

The 'Shopping Compendium "de luxe"'

The beautiful shop girl, troublesome shopper, and sumptuous emporium each played an important part in one of the most popular musical comedies of the era, *Our Miss Gibbs* (1909). In response to Selfridge's spectacular opening, Harrod's backed this comedy set in 'Garrod's'.[56] The play advertised this 'Shopping Compendium "de luxe"' by emphasising, the stage directions tell us, 'the sumptuousness of the architecture, decorations and general arrangements, [more] than any actual display of goods. The main feature of the scene is the luxury which makes shopping a matter of enjoyment and not a fag.' The waiting-rooms, dining-rooms, club facilities and other services that department stores now offered were readily available at Garrod's. Despite the attempt to recreate all the features of the modern store, the *mise-en-scène* was not supposed to be a 'photographic reproduction of any part of the stores, but a "composite" conveying to the audience the idea of its being "Harrod's" by certain recognizable points.'[57] Thus the authors, many of whom had worked on *The Shop Girl*, assumed that the audience would be intimately aware of department stores in general and of Harrod's in particular.

The story opens with a 'crowd of well-dressed women' engaged in 'refined enjoyment', eating dainty souffle ices, receiving an 'invigorating massage', or gossiping in 'the ladies' club'. They are soon joined by 'fashionable men about town', who are directed to sing 'something to the effect that instead of, as in the old days, shopping being a bore, it is now a joy, everything, even the opportunity for flirting being provided for.' Erotic and commercial pleasures were thus interchangeable in this marriage market.

The young Men About Town visit everyday in order to court Mary Gibbs, the shop-girl heroine. She has won the heart of the young Lord Eynsford, among others, though he is already engaged to Lady Betty. Miss Gibbs appears to be something of a new woman, singing that she wants 'to lead a single life'. On closer inspection, however, this stance allows her to play various admirers off against one another. She cares for Eynsford who has disguised his true identity and pretends to be a bank clerk. But when asked if she would love him more if he were wealthy, Mary teasingly responds, 'it must be nice to have everything you want and a little bit over.'

As Eynsford and others try to win Mary's interest, she exploits a female customer's weakness for fashions to acquire her own fripperies. Mrs Farquhar, an 'impecunious woman of fashion', finds her store credit has dried up. With no credit, no money and in need of a new Ascot gown she turns to Miss Gibbs. Mary helps her by telling the manager, Mr Toplady, that Mrs Farquhar has asked her to Ascot, 'and now she says she can't go because you won't let her have a new frock.' She begs Toplady to give both Farquhar and herself new gowns. Since she will represent 'the Girl from Garrod's' her fashionable image will be good for business. Toplady reluctantly agrees and throws in several hats as well. Both the customer and shop girl are thus played as voracious consumers who manipulate but do not challenge their roles in the economy.

Clothing became the tools for an elaborate masquerade in which numerous characters don the garb of members of a higher or lower social class. The milliner Madame Jeanne, for example, 'a step-daughter of the maid of Orleans, from the Rue de la Paix' and 'very French in appearance', confides that she is not related to French royalty. She admits, 'Aum Scotch when it's a matter of sentiment – and aum French when its a matter of business.' A master of disguise, Jeanne is also a master of attraction. It is she who sings 'Hats', the ode to consumer culture that inscribed the role of commodities in the attraction of the opposite sex. As Jeanne sings, 'If you would set men talking when you're walking out to shop/ You'll be all right if you're all right on top!' Consumption was equated with making a spectacle of oneself to attract male attention. The hats in this performance were in themselves spectacles. Designed by the famous milliner's, Maison Lewis, and costing sixty guineas each, they were carried by 'experts' from the shop each day for the performance.[58]

In comedies such as *Our Miss Gibbs* the use of commodities to purchase male attention was favorably compared to aristocratic marriages that were arranged for social and economic ends. Indeed, Lord Eynsford and Lady Betty's relationship appears vulgar when compared with the 'truer' emotions expressed between Eynsford and Mary Gibbs. Thus, the 'dream worlds of mass consumption' are presented as allowing for a freer mingling between the classes and sexes and as providing fertile ground for the growth of 'genuine' feelings. Once Mary learns Eynsford's true identity, however, she initially refuses to marry him, asserting that 'a wife should never be below a husband in station.' Class difference becomes superficial though when it is revealed that Eynsford's wealth comes from the soap industry, that the family title was itself purchased, and that Eynsford's own mother was in fact a working girl. Mary eventually gives in to her feelings for Eynsford and agrees to become his wife. This narrative does not suggest that class has no meaning, but it implies that social status is now founded on wealth and properly purchased commodities. Indeed, the older élite classes are sustained by an injection of wealth and beauty from the lower and middle classes. The department store became the venue for staging a 'modern' class and gender order that maintained difference by seeing social identities as fluid and produced by consumption.

'Wanting things' had long been seen as a natural feminine trait. On stage this desire became directly, and respectably, linked to heterosexual desire and social mobility. The 'ugly' women in these comedies are those who shop, but do not buy into this scenario. The shopper who is out for her own pleasure of looking but not buying is ridiculed and contrasted with the glamorous, youthful, consuming shop girl. Miss Gibbs who 'wants things' and uses them to capture male attention has by 1909 become a cultural heroine at home in the urban world of mass consumption.

From the treatment of the shop girl in 1894 to the independent Miss Gibbs in 1909 a noticeable shift had occurred. Both are spunky and alluring, but the open acceptance of the use of goods to stimulate sexual desire is brought to the foreground in the later production. Buying and selling are essentially interchangeable activities, both being acts in a play about heterosexual romance. Ultimately women's work in the shop becomes a means to move to the other side of the counter, to marry well, acquire money, and then lavishly spend it. Men and women were invited into theatrical department stores to look at women who had become fashionable images. Buying and selling in this erotic market-place had simply become a romantic comedy.

Notes

1. I would especially like to thank Geoffrey Crossick, Serge Jaumain, Victoria de Grazia and the other authors in this volume for their helpful comments and suggestions. Thanks also to Peter Bailey for his insights on an earlier version of this chapter. This chapter is a version of Chapter 6 in my forthcoming book, *Shopping For Pleasure: Gender, Commerce and Public Life in London's West End, 1860–1914*, to be published by Princeton University Press in 1999.

2. On French and American stores, see Michael Miller, *The Bon Marché: Bourgeois Culture and the Department Store 1869–1920*, Princeton: Princeton University Press (1981); Rosalind Williams, *Dream Worlds: Mass Consumption in Late Nineteenth-Century France*, Berkeley and Los Angeles: University of California Press (1982); William Leach, *Land of Desire: Merchants, Power, and the Rise of a New American Culture*, New York: Pantheon Books (1993); Susan Porter Benson, *Counter Cultures: Saleswomen, Managers, and Customers in American Department Stores 1890–1940*, Urbana and Chicago: University of Illinois Press (1988).

3. *European Mail*, 22 March 1909. On department store publicity, see Erika D. Rappaport, 'A new era of shopping: the promotion of women's pleasure in London's West End 1909–1914', in Leo Chaney and Vanessa R. Schwartz (eds), *Cinema and the Invention of Modern Life*, Berkeley: University of California Press (1995), pp. 130–55. For the cultural history of the department store, see Erika D. Rappaport, '"The halls of temptation": Gender, politics, and the construction of the department store in Victorian London', *Journal of British Studies*, 35, 1996, pp. 58–83; Rachel Bowlby, *Just Looking: Consumer Culture in Dreiser, Gissing and Zola*, New York: Methuen (1985); David Chaney, 'The department store as a cultural form', *Theory, Culture and Society*, 1, 1983, pp. 2–31; Rudi Laermans, 'Learning to consume: early department stores and the shaping of the modern consumer culture', *Theory, Culture and Society*, 10, 1993, pp. 79–102. For general overviews, see Bill Lancaster, *The Department Store: a Social History*, Leicester: Leicester University Press (1995); James B. Jefferys, *Retail Trading in Great Britain: 1850–1950*, Cambridge: Cambridge University Press (1954); John William Ferry, *A History of the Department Store*, New York: Macmillan (1960); H. Pasdermadjian, *The Department Store: its Origins, Evolution and Economics*, London: Newman Books (1954); Michael Moss and Alison Turton, *A Legend of Retailing: the House of Fraser*, London: Weidenfeld and Nicolson (1989); John Benson and Gareth Shaw (eds), *The Evolution of Retail Systems, c. 1800–1914*, Leicester: Leicester University Press (1992); Alison Adburgham, *Shops and Shopping, 1800–1914: Where and in What Manner the Well-Dressed Englishwoman Bought her Clothes*, 2nd edn, London: Barrie and Jenkins (1989).

4. H.J.W. Dam, 'The shop girl: at the Gaiety', *Sketch*, 28 November 1894, p. 216.

5. Max Beerbohm, 'Of musical comedy', *Saturday Review*, 15 July 1905, reprinted in Beerbohm, *Last Theatres, 1904–1910*, New York: Taplinger (1970), pp. 174–8.

6. Jean-Christophe Agnew, *World's Apart: the Market and the Theater in Anglo-American Thought, 1550–1750*, Cambridge: Cambridge University Press (1986).

7. There has been very little scholarship on musical comedy. For a brief overview, see Raymond Mander and Joe Mitchenson, *Musical Comedy: a Story in Pictures*, forward by Noel Coward, New York: Taplinger (1970) and Peter Bailey, '"Naughty but nice": musical comedy and the rhetoric of the girl, 1892–1914', in Michael R. Booth and Joel H. Kaplan (eds), *The Edwardian Theatre: Essays on Performance and the Stage*, Cambridge: Cambridge University Press (1996), pp. 36–60.

8. Joel H. Kaplan and Sheila Stowell, *Theatre and Fashion: Oscar Wilde to the Suffragettes*, Cambridge: Cambridge University Press (1994).

9. Peter Bailey, 'Parasexuality and glamour: the Victorian barmaid as cultural prototype', *Gender and History*, 2, 1990, p. 166. For a similar argument, see Tracy C. Davis, *Actresses as Working Women: Their Social Identity in Victorian Culture*, London: Routledge (1991).

10. Michael R. Booth, 'East End and West End: class and audience in Victorian London', *Theatre Research International*, 2, 1977, p. 99; Dagmar Höher, 'The composition of music hall audiences, 1850–1900', in Peter Bailey (ed.), *Music Hall: the Business of Pleasure*, Milton Keynes: Open University Press (1986), pp. 74–92. Class segregation was primarily produced by the differences in seat prices. A good seat at a West End theatre cost between 5s. and 10s. 6d., but the gallery at the Criterion for example, still only cost 1s. John Pick, *The West End: Management and Snobbery*, London: John Offard (1983); J.C. Trewin, *The Edwardian Theatre*, Oxford: Basil Blackwell (1976), p. 9.

11. Donald J. Olsen, *The Growth of Victorian London*, London: B.T. Batsford (1976), p. 16.

12. Davis, *Actresses as Working Women*, pp. 139–51.

13. Ursula Bloom, *Victorian Vinaigrette*, London: Hutchinson (1957), pp. 74–7. Unlike Faye E. Dudden's *Women in The American Theatre: Actresses and Audiences 1790–1870*, New Haven: Yale University Press (1994) and Richard Butsch, 'Bowery B'hoys and matinee ladies: the re-gendering of nineteenth-century American theatre audiences', *American Quarterly*, 46, 1994, pp. 374–405, there is no comprehensive study of gender and British audiences.

14. Michael Bonavia, *London Before I Forget*, Upton-Upon-Severn, Worcs.: Self Publishing Ltd. (1990), p. 71.

15. I am borrowing this phrase from Agnew, *World's Apart*, p. 33.

16. Martin Meisel, *Realizations: Narrative, Pictorial, and Theatrical Arts in Nineteenth-Century England*, Princeton: Princeton University Press (1983) and Michael R. Booth, *Victorian Spectacular Theatre, 1850–1914*, London: Routledge and Kegan Paul (1981). For other aspects of this visual culture, see Anne Friedberg's *Window Shopping: Cinema and the Postmodern*, Berkeley: University of California Press (1993) and Thomas Richards, *The Commodity Culture of Victorian England: Advertising and Spectacle, 1851–1914*, Stanford: Stanford University Press (1990).

17. Percy Fitzgerald, *Principles of Comedy and Dramatic Effect*, (Tinsley, 1870) cited in Booth, *Victorian Spectacular Theatre*, pp. 4, 15.
18. See, for example, *Sphere*, 9 July 1910, p. ii; *A.B.C. Amusement Guide and Record*, 7 March 1896, p. 3, and the *Era*'s review of *The Forty Thieves* produced at Drury Lane in 1887 in Booth, *Victorian Spectacular Theatre*, pp. 161–71.
19. *Warehousemen and Drapers' Trade Journal*, 30 October 1880, p. 687.
20. Lady Duff-Gordon, *Discretions and Indiscretions*, London: Jarrold's (1932), p. 76. See also, Kaplan and Stowell's analysis of Lucile's career in *Theatre and Fashion*, pp. 39–43. The film viewer/consumer relationship has been extensively analysed. See, for example, Jane Gaines and Charlotte Herzog (eds), *Fabrications: Costume and the Female Body*, New York: Routledge (1990); Charney and Schwartz (eds), *Cinema and the Invention of Modern Life*; Patrice Petro, *Joyless Streets: Women and Melodramatic Representation in Weimar Germany*, Princeton: Princeton University Press (1989); Miriam Hansen, *Babel and Babylon: Spectatorship in the American Silent Film*, Cambridge: Harvard University Press (1991); Mary Ann Doane, 'The economy of desire: the commodity form in/of the cinema', *Quarterly Review of Film and Video*, 11, 1988–89, pp. 23–34; Jane Gaines, 'The Queen Christina Tie-Ups: Convergence of Show Window and Screen', *Quarterly Review of Film and Video*, 11, 1988–89, pp. 35–60 and Jeanne Allen, 'The Film Viewer as Consumer', *Quarterly Review of Film and Video*, 5, 1980, pp. 481–99. In her 'Film and the masquerade: theorizing the female spectator', *Screen*, 23, 1982, pp. 74–87, Doane argues that the female film spectator is invited to 'buy an image of herself in so far as the female star is proposed as the ideal of feminine beauty' (p. 80). This may not have been the only position possible for this viewer, but it was the dominant understanding of the feminine audience during the turn of the century.
21. Duff-Gordon, *Discretions and Indiscretions*, pp. 74–6
22. 'Good Window Display', *Retail Trader*, 27 September 1910, p. 24.
23. 'The Show Window', *Retail Trader*, 25 October 1910, p. 18.
24. 'The Reign of the Artistic', *Success Magazine*, reprinted in *Retail Trader*, 10 May 1911, p. 16.
25. British Library, Lord Chamberlain's Plays, add. mss. 1909/3. Produced by George Edwardes, written by 'Cryptos', a team that included Adrian Ross, Percy Greenbank, Ivan Caryll and Lionel Monckton, *Our Miss Gibbs*, first performed at the Gaiety Theatre, 25 January 1909. The manuscripts for this chapter were all read at the British Library, Lord Chamberlain's Plays Collection (BL: LCP). Although, the scripts were often changed after this version was submitted for approval, these are the only surviving copy of many of the plays discussed here.
26. George Rowell, *The Victorian Theatre, 1792–1914*, Cambridge: Cambridge University Press (1978), pp. 143–45; Trewin, *The Edwardian Theatre*, pp. 160–62.
27. Charles Petrie, *The Edwardians*, New York: W.W. Norton (1965), p. 39.
28. The Gaiety had several incarnations and two distinct homes. The first Gaiety at 354 Strand was built in 1862, and was significantly altered in 1886 and finally closed down in 1903. A new Gaiety theatre was opened in Aldwych in 1903. For the Gaiety's early years, see John Hollingshead, *Gaiety Chronicles*, London: Archibald Constable (1898) and *'Good Old*

Gaiety': an Historiette and Remembrance, London: Gaiety Theatre Co. (1903). For Edwardes's management, see Stanley Naylor, *Gaiety and George Grossmith: Random Reflections on the Serious Business of Enjoyment*, London: Stanley Paul (1913) and W. Macqueen-Pope, *Gaiety: Theatre of Enchantment*, London: W.H. Allen (1949).

29. *The Lady*, 28 October 1886, p. 344
30. 'At the Gaiety', *Saturday Review*, 30 October 1909, reprinted in Max Beerbohm, *Around Theatres*, vol. II, New York: Knopf (1930), p. 722.
31. 'The Selfridge of stageland: Queen's Theatre as public rendezvous', *Daily Chronicle*, 17 September 1913.
32. Dam, 'The shop girl: at the Gaiety'.
33. BL: LCP, add. mss., 53562, written by H.J.W. Dam, music by Ivan Caryll with additional numbers by Adrian Ross and Lionel Monckton, *The Shop Girl*, first performed 22 November 1894, Gaiety Theatre.
34. On a male worker's attempt to raise his station via flirtation, see BL: LCP, add. mss., 53594u, Robert Buchanan and Charles Marlowe, *The Romance of the Shopwalker*, first performed 27 February 1896 at the Royal Colchester.
35. On Victorian farce see Jeffrey H. Huberman, *Late Victorian Farce*, Ann Arbor: UMI Research Press (1986) and Jessica Milner Davis, *Farce*, London: Methuen (1978).
36. E.B. Ashford, 'Women in the distributive trades, displacement study', *Women's Industrial News*, 20 (73), April 1916, pp. 9–14. The *Drapers' Record* believed that during the 1890s there was 'a growing tendency on the part of drapers to give more and more employment to women in the lighter trades', 6 July 1895, p. 15.
37. The best work on the female shop workers in England remains Lee Holcombe, *Victorian Ladies at Work: Middle-Class Working Women in England and Wales, 1850–1914*, Hamden: Archon Books (1973), pp. 103–40. See also Lancaster, *The Department Store*, pp. 137–42, 177–82; Wilfred B. Whitaker, *Victorian and Edwardian Shopworkers: the Struggle to Obtain Better Conditions and a Half Holiday*, Totowa: Rowman and Littlefield (1973).
38. BL: LCP, add. mss., 1915/9, Stuart Lonalti, *The Shop Girl and Her Master*, first performed 19 April 1915, Theatre Royal, Leigh, Lancaster. For a similar plot, see BL: LCP, add. mss. 1910/22., William Melville, *Shop Soiled Girl*, first performed 3 October 1910, Elephant and Castle Theatre, London.
39. Peter Brooks argues that melodrama was losing its popularity with West End audiences at the end of the century. *The Melodramatic Imagination: Balzac, Henry James, Melodrama, and the Mode of Excess*, New York: Columbia University Press (1985), pp. 11–12.
40. Bailey, 'Parasexuality and glamour', pp. 166–7.
41. Elaine Showalter, *Sexual Anarchy: Gender and Culture at the Fin De Siècle*, London: Penguin (1990); Judith R. Walkowitz, *City of Dreadful Delight: Narratives of Sexual Danger in Late-Victorian London*, Chicago, Chicago University Press (1992).
42. William Paine, *Shop Slavery and Emancipation: a Revolutionary Appeal to the Educated Young Men of the Middle-Class*, introduction by H.G. Wells, London: P.S. King (1912), p. 82.
43. Joseph Hallsworth and Rhys J. Davies, *The Working Life of Shop*

Assistants: a Study in the Conditions of Labour in the Distributive Trades, Manchester: National Labour Press (1910), pp. 77–8.

44. See Kaplan and Stowell, *Theatre and Fashion*, 82–114; Sheila Stowell, *A Stage of Their Own: Feminist Playwrights of the Suffrage Era*, Ann Arbor: University of Michigan Press (1992), pp. 71–99; Jan McDonald, *The 'New Drama', 1900–1914*, New York: Grove Press (1986), pp. 87–102; Harry M. Ritchie, 'Harley Granville Barker's *The Madras House* and the sexual revolution', *Modern Drama*, 15 (2), September 1972, pp. 150–58; Dennis Kennedy, *Granville Barker and the Dream of Theatre*, Cambridge: Cambridge University Press (1985); Heidi J. Holder, '"The Drama Discouraged": judgement and ambivalence in *The Madras House*', *University of Toronto Quarterly*, 58, 1988–89, pp. 275–94.

45. Beerbohm, *Around Theatres*, 724.

46. James Laver, *The Edwardian Promenade*, London: Edward Hulton (1958), pp. 76–7.

47. *Daily Graphic*, 27 March 1911, p.14.

48. *Standard*, 19 March 1914, n.p.

49. BL: LCP, 1902/33, Owen Hall, music by Adrian Ross and Claude Aveling, *The Girl From Kay's*, first performed 24 November 1902 at the Apollo Theatre.

50. BL: LCP, 1915/11, anonymous, *The Toy Shop*, first performed 21 July 1915, Palace Doncaster.

51. BL: LCP, 1910/26, Paul A. Rubens, *Selfrich's Annual Sale*, 24 October 1910, Savoy Theatre. A farcical Selfridge also appeared in BL, LCP, 1912/17, Fred Mailland, *Number One 'Gerrard' – or Selfridge Outdone*, 25 April 1912, Empire Liverpool.

52. Rubens, *Selfrich's Annual Sale*.

53. *Drapers' Record*, 13 September 1890, p. 353.

54. Ibid., 3 October 1899, p. 661.

55. Ibid., 20 March 1897, p. 707.

56. Macqueen-Pope, *Gaiety*, p. 422.

57. 'Cryptos', *Our Miss Gibbs*.

58. MacQueen-Pope, *Gaiety*, p. 424.

CHAPTER NINE

Department stores and middle-class consumerism in Budapest, 1896–1939

Gábor Gyáni

The transformation of small shops into department stores in Budapest can be regarded as a relatively late retail revolution in comparison with Western Europe and the USA. This delay is hardly surprising, considering the pre-industrial stage of the economy, the underdeveloped urban network, and the low income level of the middle classes in Hungary around the middle of the nineteenth century. The process of retail transformation only began to get underway during the late nineteenth century. Moreover, organisational modernisation of retailing started not in the field of drapery goods but in food, and was initiated not by private investors but by the local authorities. In 1889 the Board of Capital Public Works, a state organisation responsible for urban planning, announced its decision that, 'because of the dramatic development and sudden growth of the capital, a whole series of public works is urgently needed … . The introduction of food marketing halls to Hungary is an essential public requirement waiting to be met'.[1] The city council soon established an extended network of market halls. In 1897, five were opened in various parts of the city and another was completed five years later. The retailing of food initiated the modernisation of retailing as a whole. The example of the Central Market Hall was particularly important, because it pointed to the organisational and even the architectural future for large-scale retail institutions. The close and continuing contact between the Central Market Hall and peasant producers in order to secure supplies was an important example of organisational innovation. The hall's impressive architectural design[2] was a further example which was to serve as a model for future store proprietors.

Urban growth, embourgeoisement and the road to the department store

At the same time, in 1895, Sándor Holzer, the son of a prosperous tailor and dress warehouse owner, opened the first store-like 'fashion house' in the city centre. This began a new stage in the development of retailing, although there had been forerunners in the previous decade. The most important factor leading to the establishment of the Simon Holzer Fashion House was the extremely fast population growth which had begun in the 1870s. Between 1873, when the unification of the city took place, and 1896, the population increased by 80 per cent and reached half a million. The dynamism of this metropolitan-type demographic process continued after the turn of the century and the population of Budapest reached almost a million by 1914.

This increase in the population and rapid industrial development stimulated further immigration to the city, which by the turn of the century had resulted in the creation of a highly polarised social structure. Within that structural pattern, the prevalence of the industrial proletariat made Budapest similar to the other industrial centres of Europe, so typical of the age of early industrialisation. However, since 1867 Budapest had been a capital city which fulfilled many administrative, cultural and political functions on a national level, thereby creating an abundant need for a middle class composed mainly of public servants and professionals. These were mostly new recruits who came from the provincial cities, the countryside or even from other countries. Newcomers formed two-thirds of the population but, generally speaking, few of those working and living in Budapest were suited to urban life. These new urbanites were only partially adapted to a metropolitan environment and a burgeoning bourgeois socio-cultural domain.[3] The immature and transitional character of much of Budapest society was a factor which shaped the course of retail development as well as the character and extent of consumer behaviour. The social history of the city up to the 1890s was not particularly favourable to the democratisation of luxury embodied and facilitated by the department store. Furthermore, there was only a slow quantitative increase in the retail sector, with shops selling drapery and clothing dictating the rhythm of growth. The number of shopkeepers doubled and the increase in employees was even greater. Peddlers were increasingly replaced by permanently settled retailers with fixed outlets.[4]

The qualitative changes of the 1890s marked a new phase in the transformation of retailing. Both the high turnover of small shopkeepers and a growing tendency towards social polarisation paved the way for the appearance of the department store. On the one hand, the birth of the department store was made possible by the emergence of an entrepreneurial élite whose accumulated capital made it capable of organising the partially domestic craft industry for their business pur-poses. On the other hand, the process was aided by the internal differentiation of an expanding middle-class market whose purchasing power and bourgeois consumer taste were increasingly evident. However, the social scope of this process was broader than the size of the middle classes would suggest: Károly Vörös pointed out that the retail revolution in Budapest around the turn of the century was fuelled by an increasing embourgeoisement which embraced the petite bourgeoisie.[5] The proprietors of the first department stores were fully aware of these structural processes and tried to attract all those who aspired to middle-class lifestyle.

The distinctive pattern of the Budapest department store

Before discussing in detail each of the department stores, some of the overall characteristics of their evolution up to the late 1930s should be considered. Firstly, in addition to their relatively late emergence (which was, however, more or less parallel with the processes in Germany and Italy), department stores in Budapest rarely conformed to all the requirements of the French stores on which they were modelled. The first step in the development of department stores was taken by the owners of the dress warehouses supplying women's and children's clothing. The restrictive scope of merchandise continued into the inter-war years although the spacious and imposing sales area increased both quantitatively and qualitatively.

This limited range of merchandise supplied by the stores made the owners reluctant to adopt the term 'department store'. Sándor Holzer, for instance, opted for the old, well-established designation, 'fashion house', although his newly founded elegant store was considered by contemporaries to follow the French pattern. The next store opened in 1910 and the owner avoided the problem by naming his five-storey outlet simply Simon Fischer and Co. The first retailer to use the term, when renaming his modernised store, was the owner of the Párisi Áruház (Parisian Department Store) which opened in 1911. But even in the course of the 1920s, several of the newly founded or developing department stores either revived or simply retained the older designation, 'fashion house' or 'fashion hall'. This occurred particularly when the social image of the enterprise was ambiguous, as in the case of those stores which were less open to a middle-class clientele than to lower-class customers with less refined tastes and meagre purses. The growing importance of the latter has been suggested by Tamás Csató, who notes the surprising growth of retailing amidst the harsh conditions of the post-war years. The increase both in the number of shopkeepers and their employees, and in the size of turnover, would appear to be the result of an increasing number of low-value purchases.[6]

Other general characteristics relate to the organisational mechanisms and the selling strategy of these stores. The former is illustrated by the case of the Párisi Áruház. Despite all the formal and outer signs of a department store which characterised the new Párisi, soon after its foundation as a luxurious dream palace it had to abandon the genuinely store-like organisational structure to revive obsolete bazaar sales practices within its own walls. In the 1920s and 1930s, sales practices indicate that more than one store owner tended to depend on low mark-ups and high turnover oriented towards the lower social strata instead of towards the rich and elegant middle class.[7]

Budapest department stores: some case studies

In 1895, a year before the country celebrated with immense pomp the millennium of the Hungarian conquest of the Carpathian Basin, Sándor Holzer purchased a four-storey building on the central avenue of Budapest, Lajos Kossuth Street, in order to move to a new site the modest Ruharaktár (Dress Warehouse) he had inherited from his father. The store was named after Simon Holzer, a head tailor who had founded the firm when he established a workshop in 1869. Simon Holzer's innovation was to produce only ready-to-wear clothing, previously unknown in terms of domestic production. He achieved some prosperity by these means, but was never a major business success. On his death in 1891, his estate defined him as a member of the fairly well-to-do middle class.[8] When the buildings of the workshop and the attached warehouse were expropriated for a rebuilding project, his son, who had been trained abroad, invested the money he received from the authorities in a new store located in the city centre.

His decision led to the foundation of the first department store-like establishment in Budapest. A process of continuous extension meant that the Holzer Simon Divatház (Simon Holzer Fashion House) was by 1907 occupying four floors. In the basement there was the so called *occasio department*, devoted to lower-priced, out-of-date goods. The upper floors displayed a wide range of ready-made women's and children's clothing, but no other items. True, the Holzer store retained its restricted scope of merchandise, but in other respects it closely resembled the ideal store emporium. Other characteristics it shared with the archetypal department store included the large scale of the sales area, the high number of personnel and the division of the store into separate departments. Additional factors, such as the introduction of fixed prices and the adherence to the sale of ready-to-wear clothing, further increased the similarities. The luxury of the interior included such technical innovations as lifts and public telephones, possibly the first in the city.[9]

The next development worthy of note was the inauguration in 1910 of Simon Fischer and Co. in the heart of the old city centre. In the five-storey building, women's clothing and other textile goods could be purchased, as in the Holzer. The Fischer store imitated the Western-style department stores by employing nearly 200 saleswomen and clerks, and being divided into separate departments.[10] The major breakthrough, however, came a year later with the opening of the new building of the Párisi Nagy Áruház. The origin of the enterprise goes back to the 1890s when Sámuel Goldberger, a modest shopkeeper, set up his first retail shop outside the city centre on the Rákóczi, then Kerepesi Avenue. The enterprise rested on a high turnover and was able to expand to incorporate the neighbouring small shops. The worst store fire that had ever occurred in Budapest provided an opportunity to change it into a more ambitious emporium. Following this catastrophe of 1903, which completely destroyed the store and caused the death of 14 people, including the owner's wife, Goldberger decided to erect a new building at a new location, which was still outside the city centre but in Andrássy Avenue, Budapest's most imposing and luxurious thoroughfare. Amongst the elegant, palatial apartments of the high-income group and at a stone's throw from the magnificent Opera House, the new six-storey Párisi building, with its monumental interior and vast galleries creating theatrical effects, heralded the arrival of the real, western type department store in Budapest.[11] The entire building was the fruit of the concerted efforts of outstanding artists, including both architects and painters.[12]

This early promise, however, was at best only partially fulfilled. After this initial stage, the Párisi immediately began to lose its department store character. By 1924 the store was almost bankrupt, and this induced Goldberger to transform it into a joint stock company within which he was the majority shareholder. But, more importantly, he began to let out single departments to retailers thereby dividing the store into a series of small shops. The only common thread was the observance of basic fire regulations, the date and time of opening and closing, and the obligatory collective advertisement introduced in 1927, for which each tenant had to pay a fixed annual sum.[13]

After so many false starts (two further examples are discussed below), the first successful attempt to adapt the western European department store model occurred as late as the mid-1920s, when the

Corvin Áruház (Corvin Department Store) opened its doors. The history of the Corvin, which remained the largest store of its kind until the 1970s, can be dated back to 1922 when a joint stock company was formed to set up a new store. Two representatives of a German firm, M.J. Emden Söhne in Hamburg, bought 90 per cent of the shares. They were subsequently joined by another firm from Hamburg, M.M. Warburg and Co., and N.V. Handel Maatschappy Corvina from Amsterdam.[14] Three years later the company purchased a site along the Rákóczi Avenue, just behind the National Theatre at the junction of the Avenue and the Great Boulevard, where they constructed an entirely new building.

The Corvin, which opened on 1 March 1926, had the biggest sales area ever seen in Budapest, occupying 17 000 square metres on five floors. As a contemporary scholarly analysis argued, the Italianate palatial construction of its façade was amongst the most noteworthy public buildings, being 'one of the most successful examples of Hungarian architecture today'.[15] Presumably meeting demands from the investors, the inner arrangement of the store followed German rather than French spatial patterns. As Ervin Ybl, the art critic, wrote in 1926, 'French department stores may use almost the entire site for a single roofed hall, and are not divided into sections to the extent of the less conspicuous but much more practical German ones, which are therefore also less threatened by catastrophic large fires.'[16]

The Corvin reached its full size by the mid-1930s, with 40 departments in 1937: 34 sold clothing, three foodstuffs, and three separate departments offered mixed industrial articles. Besides these, there were the so called *ateliers*, an organisational form adopted, along with the name, from French department stores. In these, 60 saleswomen and dressmakers provided customers with tailored clothing. The sheer size of the Corvin matched the ideal of a palace of dreams: in 1937 there were 666 employees, out of whom the sales personnel numbered 584 and the remaining 59 were dressmakers and employees responsible for the technical maintenance of the building.[17] Not just the size, but the scope of services available enhanced its department store character. Firstly, the modern merchandising practices that generally went with any department store required a correspondence and mail-order service. This was an integral part of the Corvin from the very beginning. Reaching potential customers living in distant rural areas required the regular production of catalogues. Their distribution by post was a precondition of an effective mail-order store activity. In widening the range of the Corvin's clientele, the chain method was frequently applied, illustrated by the letter sent to an apothecary in a provincial town:

Respected Addressee!
In the secure supposition that you will be satisfied with the articles
ordered in our store, we ask you to inform us on the enclosed
postcard of the address of your acquaintances to whom you would
wish to have sent a catalogue free of charge.[18]

The importance of this type of service and the store turnover is shown
indirectly by the costs involved. The Corvin spent 3.2 per cent of its
revenue on advertising in 1937, a third of this expenditure being invested
in mail-order catalogues, postage and packing.[19] The services offered
included some which could be classed as non-profit-making. For example, the department store maintained a restaurant and the so-called Corvin
Buffet, which were known for their low prices. A two course meal in the
restaurant cost only 1.60 pengős.[20] The department store also operated
booking offices for the theatre and the railway, and a travel agency.

The Magyar Divatcsarnok (Hungarian Fashion Hall) also began as a
small shop, and over a period of time developed into a department
store. Márk Rosenberg began his business career as a modest shopkeeper in 1883, but before his death in the late 1910s, he was the owner
of several small drapery shops situated side by side. His son, who took
over the family firm and bore the Magyarised name, Antal Ruttkai,
decided to establish a true department store. The strategy he adopted
was one of gradual expansion, unlike Sámuel Goldberger who founded
the Párisi Nagy Áruház at a stroke. The difference between these approaches was due mainly to the changed circumstances of a later period.
The inter-war years brought economic slumps and were characterised
not only by a scarcity of entrepreneurial capital and credit facilities, but
also by a reduction in the purchasing power of the middle class. Ruttkai
moved the location of his store further from the city centre, though still
along the Rákóczi Avenue. In 1921, the new store opened near the
biggest railway terminal, looking to sell to the provincials who poured
in large numbers into the city. Many of them had prior contact with the
store through the correspondence and mail-order service: the figures for
1930 record that 3 000 letters and parcels were posted by the store
every month.[21] Within a decade, as a result of the process of gradual
enlargement, five shops occupying the street level of the neighbouring
houses were situated around the main store, employing a total of 150
sales personnel. However, due to the uninterrupted development of the
store, with investments in 1928 and particularly in 1934, there was
growth in both the sales area and the number of personnel, with 600
employees by 1934. A host of domestic tailors were also employed.[22] It
was not just the store's size but also the design and the ambience of its
building which gave Ruttkai's Magyar Divatcsarnok a department store
flavour, in spite of its spatial decentralisation.

Budapest department stores: patterns of development

How should we explain the delay and partial success of Budapest's department stores? Several factors had an impact on the process. An examination of the entrepreneurial dimensions reveals that the most striking feature is that the department stores, with the sole exception of the Corvin, were founded by domestic commercial and mercantile enterprises, in some cases evolving from a small shop or even a tailor's workshop. This points to at least two possibilities: firstly, a slow rate of capital accumulation in the sector and, secondly, that financiers were reluctant to invest in department stores. Whichever might have been the case, both signal the probable low profitability of retailing which derived directly from the immaturity of the consumer society. The relatively late emergence of the new entrepreneurial and professional middle class has already been mentioned. This delay in the evolution of the department store in Budapest reflected the retarded consumerism of the bourgeoisie. In order to understand the roots of that development, we must be aware of the trajectory of embourgeoisement in nineteenth-century Hungary.[23]

The heyday of this process of transition to a market economy and an industrialised society took place at the turn of the century, in an epoch known as the Age of Dualism, or the Austro-Hungarian Monarchy (1867–1918). During these decades an almost entirely new metropolitan bourgeoisie emerged, loosely connected to the preceding generations of urban entrepreneurs. As Vera Bácskai has demonstrated, the wealthiest wholesale merchants of Pest in the first half of the nineteenth century, the so-called forerunners of the entrepreneurs, did not survive the dramatic changes of the mid-century and disappeared well before industrialisation from the 1880s.[24] Their mentality was close to the Weberian ideal type of the classic bourgeois. They contrasted with both the aristocratic consumer lifestyle and with the profligacy of the declining – though still numerous – middling nobility, later known as the gentry. This contrast derived not just from profit-oriented behaviour, but from their non-native origins. The majority were immigrants from non-Magyar ethnic backgrounds (Germans, Jews) who, being excluded from the traditional Hungarian élites, sought through a distinct lifestyle to create an identity of their own. This took the form of a rejection of any conspicuous display of luxury and a stress on developing the cult of privacy and a close family life. The material culture around this bourgeois domesticity has been called *biedermeier*, using a term initially applied to a phase in the history of furniture styles.[25]

The succeeding generation of the new middle and upper middle class which dominated the social scene of *fin-de-siècle* Hungary tended to break away from its predecessors. In terms of domestic material culture, many bourgeois were eager to adopt an aristocratic lifestyle, focusing on excessive consumerism. Although the spreading consumerism of the upper and middle bourgeoisie of the city must not be seen merely as the imitation of aristocratic values,[26] the fact that aspects of the aristocratic and gentry style of consumption occur in the construction of this bourgeois identity is evidence of their increasing social accommodation or absorption. The model to be followed was that provided by traditional élites.

This type of commitment to the lifestyle of noble society was doubtless detrimental to the evolution of the department store. The survival of certain traditional upper- and middle-class buying habits did inhibit the development of a bourgeois consumerism organised around mass marketing in the form of the department store. Aristocratic ladies, who did not belong to the clientele of any department store and who did not even consider Budapest a preferred option for their custom, repeatedly demonstrated distinct approaches to shopping. From as remote a part of the country as Transylvania, female members of the aristocracy would visit Vienna, even in winter, to do their regular shopping. Budapest was not frequented as 'it was not interesting ... . Men made several journeys to the Hungarian capital, which was the centre of political life in the Parliament, the Lord's House. The ladies, however, preferred Vienna. They were drawn there by the ever increasing number of beautiful shops, dress salons, shoemaker's shops, hairdressers.'[27] The requirements of their superior social standing determined the choice of the shopping facilities in Vienna, 'even the selection of shops was predetermined to ensure their suitability for purchasing. The aristocracy did their regular shopping in Vienna in the establishments of the Kärtnerstrasse and the Graben. The shops alongside the Máriahilferstrasse were rated as only third-class',[28] and many among these, it might be added, were department stores.

The lower levels of the middle classes also adhered to traditional retail forms as late as the early twentieth century. There were particular advantages associated with that form of shopping, in addition to those of imitation. A discourse appeared about the supposedly permanent overspending and overconsumption of a major part of the middle classes in Budapest, or *Debt City* as a pamphleteer labelled it. Irrational consumer behaviour of this kind favoured the survival of retail establishments which retained payment by instalments and where some room remained for bargaining, both of which were unimaginable in a department store. A Budapest tailor told the author of the pamphlet, 'the customers settle their bills in most instances after the garments have been delivered: in some cases, however, I am paid annually.' The response to the question of how much middle-class ladies spent on clothing was that, 'there is one permanent rule only – more than their financial conditions allow', and, he added, this led both to bargaining and to part payment.[29] Another tailor revealed the secret of middle-class purchasing strategy: 'Every lady uses a more expensive and a cheaper dress salon, but, in addition, she employs a dress-maker who comes to her house and also a seamstress for making blouses. The concerted activity of all of these people is required to produce the wardrobe of a woman in Budapest.'[30]

Following the Great War and the fall of the Austro-Hungarian Monarchy, two contrasting processes influenced the evolution of the department store. On the one hand, the declining living standards of the salaried classes, and even of professionals and entrepreneurs, restricted the scope of a widening mass consumerism. As already seen, Sámuel Goldberger, owner of the Párisi department store, reacted by deciding to abandon several key attributes of the department store and consciously to turn towards an inferior clientele by encouraging customers from amongst the petite bourgeoisie and well-paid skilled workers. The clientele attracted to the Budapest stores was, in fact, socially far broader in the 1920s and 1930s than as it was during the pre-war period, but this was not only due to a democratisation of luxury. The store proprietors did their best to take into account both the changes in social structure and the declining income levels of the various classes to meet the obvious demand for mass consumption from a much lower social level.

The Magyar Divatcsarnok from the outset attracted a lower-class clientele by offering goods at low prices, and it is therefore not surprising to note that the Social Democrat daily newspaper, the *Népszava*, sang the praises of its low price department:

> It is beyond doubt that this will be the most popular part of the store, because with such cheap goods it immediately becomes more modern than the others ... . The Magyar Divatcsarnok is a part of life on the road to the heights ... a goal to which we aspire, but are unable to achieve on an income of a few pence.[31]

In this instance, the mass retailing achieved and symbolised by the department stores quite often amounted to no more than low prices: three categories were established in this store, all being under one pengő. Despite the fact that the Corvin was a genuine department store, its low-price department was also of great strategic importance, although the popular price in this store never fell below one pengő.[32]

The falling purchasing power of customers resulted in some cases in the revival of older buying habits, and under these circumstances the modernity of the stores came to be highly appreciated by contemporary opinion, at least in so far as it found expression in the press. The Corvin, stated a daily newspaper in 1933, only recognises fixed prices and no kind of bargaining is allowed within its walls ... . It has to be conceded that this adherence to the fixed-price system is a far-seeing and important act. The habit of bargaining is a relic from the past, and one whose renewed strength is due to the war. Today it is, of course, intolerable.[33]

These marketing techniques posed a threat to many small shopkeepers, for the stores were in direct competition with traditional retailers more than with each other. Their struggle against the stores further restricted both the scope of activity and the possible expansion of the department store. Small shopkeepers accused the stores of 'destroying price levels' and demanded state intervention to support their legitimate commercial interests. This entailed the imposition of a rigorous legal regulation aimed at department store advertising practices and, as a second step, a ban on the establishment of new stores without the prior consent of the state authorities.[34] Restaurant proprietors also complained about the competition they feared from the development of similar and cheaper services by some of the stores.[35]

The small shopkeepers, organised and represented in this campaign by their trade association, the FÖVKE, met with success in their crusade against the stores. With respect to aggressive advertising by department stores producing unfair competition, the normal method of compelling the stores to comply with *fair rules* was through the courts. The Corvin, for example, was harshly criticised for one of its advertisements which offered full repayment of the purchases of one customer, to be selected by lottery. A shopkeeper took legal action against the Corvin and the court decided against the department store, arguing that gift-giving was inconsistent with a commercial transaction.[36] The timing of seasonal sales and the form of advertisements, both before and during the sale, was another area where control was sought. The law on business competition passed in 1933, renewing and modifying the law of 1923, defined two dates for the sale, the first being on 22 January. The small shopkeepers complained that several of the stores began to advertise their January clearance sale well before that date.[37] The demands of small-scale retailers on the opening of new stores finally gained a hearing in a period when right-wing statism had become increasingly influential in government policy, particularly during the time of Gyula Gömbös's government between 1932 and 1936. According to a departmental order of 1935, the setting up of a new department store, or even the enlargement of one already in existence, required the authorisation of the Minister of Commerce.

Self-image as an emblem of identity

The nineteenth- and twentieth-century department store is usually regarded as a bourgeois institution. Miller argues that the department store 'gave shape and definition to the very meaning of the concept of a bourgeois way of life.'[38] His thesis states that 'through the department store, middle-class pretensions could find satisfaction because images and material goods were beginning to constitute life style itself.'[39] A second dimension of his approach presents the department store as mediator between bourgeois class culture and the cult of mass consumption. The stores, according to Miller, were bourgeois institutions not simply because they had a middle-class clientele, but also because they set the parameters for a culture of consumption, a status attribute of the modern bourgeoisie. As bourgeois images and values spread, and with the general increase in the income level of society, the department store made the paraphernalia of bourgeois social status available to all those who shared or were eager to share a middle-class lifestyle. Through commodification of everyday life, the department store translated middle-class values and lifestyle patterns into marketable goods and sold them to all those who aspired to respectable status. The department store, accordingly, mirrored middle-class taste as much as it fashioned it. Although Miller's view has been criticised by historians for whom it did not match the social realities of department store custom in the USA, his argument remains relevant to the case of Budapest.[40]

In attempting to answer the question of why there was such a delay in establishing department stores in Budapest, and what were the possible causes of their partial success and frequent failure, the peculiarities of their social base have already been considered. The Budapest stores nevertheless satisfied the requirements of a bourgeois public institution of that type since their architectural ambience, interior and design were all modelled on the image of the department store. The luxury displayed, the sophisticated design both of the shop windows (of which there were 33 in the Corvin), and the interior sales area, were characteristic even of the lower grade stores. One of them, the Magyar Divatcsarnok, was described by a contemporary: 'The first thing that astonishes the visitor in the rebuilt Magyar Divatcsarnok is the calm and pleasant atmosphere, indispensable for conveniently and easily meeting the demands of customers.'[41] Furthermore, the new section of the store was designed by Lajos Kozma, one of the leading artists of his day, and accordingly it

> is a marvel which excites admiration, containing many innovations
> not found elsewhere, such as a giant glass roof that can be un-
> locked, an immense elevator which is the biggest of its kind in the

country, interesting shatter-proof wire-screen window panes and tasteful mosaic pillars decorated with Hungarian ornamentation.[42]

This passage reveals another significant feature of the theme of enticement, and that is the technical advances to be found in the stores. The Corvin was particularly well-known for these innovations, such as its escalator, which was the first of its kind in the city. It soon became a sight which people wanted to visit, whether or not they had any intentions of buying. The management decided on these grounds that a fee should be charged for its use!

The department store's distinctive identity as an establishment devised to appeal to the senses through its influence on the human psyche and to entice its customers into a world of dreams, may be seen as one of the most striking expressions of the bourgeoisie's self-image. In this regard, the stores followed closely behind the much more numerous coffee houses, which have generally been seen as an authentic bourgeois public institution.[43] Direct evidence for such pretensions can be found in printed sources, although research in this area is difficult since few, if any, archival sources have survived.[44] The fact that the department store was an expression of certain bourgeois tastes and identity, and that it was their mission to disseminate these bourgeois values in a wider society, was something of which many proprietors were conscious. However, the content and the precise mode of expressing this conviction changed as time passed. The Holzer Simon Divatház was the first retail establishment to seek to identify itself as a bourgeois palace of dreams for women's clothing. The intention to create such an image can be found in every part of the store's catalogue, and the same motive can be found in the etiquette and consumption guides directed at the bourgeois market. Sándor Holzer published a book in 1909 to commemorate the fortieth anniversary of the firm's foundation, dedicated entirely to the issue of the *Hungarian Lady*.[45] The lady in this case meant specifically the middle-class woman, who needed to be instructed by experts (i.e., the authors of the book) on correct manners and consumer habits, that is to say, how to dress herself, how to have a 'bourgeois lunch', how to behave in public, etc. The norms the authors prescribed for women in the book, at least with respect to suitable dress, were best fulfilled by relying on the choice of goods available at the Holzer. This idea was advocated implicitly, but none the less effectively.

The role played by the department store, both in defining correct bourgeois taste and shaping the patterns of middle-class consumption, was to end gradually with the First World War and during the interwar years. This was not merely the result of the democratisation of luxury, because reduced prices were able to transform formerly middle-class possessions into mass consumer items. On the contrary, an ever increasing section of the middle classes was faced with serious hardships in the post-war years and during the 1930s. This, however, increased the aspirations of those who managed to maintain their incomes and for whom consumer behaviour continued to constitute a distinct status attribute. They maintained their attachment to the traditional, well-established and aristocratic exclusive fashion boutiques and salons of the city centre. These small but elegant drapers' shops, which never sold ready-to-wear clothing, remained the main destination of the middle- and upper-middle class women shoppers from as early as the 1860s and 1870s onwards.[46] Traditions were strong enough to prevent the founders of the department store from gaining a foothold in the territory of these small elegant shops. In the 1930s, when one of them toyed with the idea of opening a store in the area, the reaction was alarm on the one hand, and scepticism about its feasibility on the other.[47]

The members of once unambiguous but now declining middle-class urban families adopted a strategy of increasing self-sufficiency. A specialist in the history of fashion remarked:

> The system of domestic dressmakers was highly popular throughout the whole of society. This cheap labour force, including those in the skilled sector, worked illegally without licences. They sewed the entire wardrobe for a family during a couple of days, demanding no more than board and lodging and a small amount of pocket money as payment.[48]

Self-sufficiency was nevertheless a preferred method of resolving problems associated with the need for suitable clothing. Since the skill of dressmaking was accepted as an expertise worthy of a middle-class woman, and was even accepted as a wage-earning activity, families were able to turn to it in times of financial hardship. The ever growing availability of fashion magazines also made the practice of dressmaking easier to pursue.[49]

In fact, not even the Corvin, a genuinely high-quality department store in Budapest, was able to achieve recognition as an arbiter of bourgeois or middle-class taste. When one of the store's senior managers, Miksa Lewin, published a study on the subject, he focused merely on the organisational modernity of a department store like the Corvin, saying not a word about the method of consumption that would be necessary to gain middle-class status.[50] The contrast with Holzer's attempt to create a self-image is clear. This is further illustrated by the Four Corvin Points, the so called 'Bible' of the department store, another presentation of the store's self-image:

1. Quality is the most important special feature of the Corvin ... .
2. The range of merchandise matches that on offer in the metropolis ... . Buying at the Corvin means that purchases can be made according to personal taste.
3. The Corvin offers good value for money.
4. The Corvin's customer service.[51]

While the first two points apparently focus on the willingness to cater to the refined and costly demands of wealthy bourgeois customers, the latter two are addressed more closely at the store's lower-class clientele.

It is not possible to arrive at a simple definition of the significance of the department stores amidst the changing circumstances of a city like Budapest. Further examination of the mechanisms and operations within the city's department stores, as well as of the social dimensions of the newly emerging mass consumerism, will be needed to establish the full extent to which this particular type of retail establishment belonged to the public domain of the bourgeois middle class.

Notes

1. Mária H. Kohut, (ed.), *Források Budapest múltjából vol. II. 1873–1919* [Sources from the Past of Budapest], Budapest: Budapest Főváros Levéltára (1971), p. 185.
2. The construction, which made use of iron stanchions, was planned by one of the eminent architects of the time in neo-Gothic style. The basilica-like interior of the Central Market Hall is astonishing in size. Both the 60 metre wide façade, and the 150-metre-long main aisle put even the largest cathedrals to shame.
3. On the relationship between immigration and acculturation see Gábor Gyáni, 'Ethnicity and acculturation in Budapest at the turn of the century', in S. Zimmermann (ed.), *Urban Space and Identity in the European City 1890–1930s*, Budapest: Central European University (1995), pp. 107–15.
4. Károly Vörös, *Budapest története* [History of Budapest], Budapest: Akadémiai (1978), vol. 4. pp. 366–7.
5. Ibid., p. 540.
6. Tamás Csató, 'Middle-class shopping and the structure of domestic trade in Hungary', paper presented at the conference on Consumerism, Domesticity and Middle-Class Identity, New York, 1993.
7. Strikingly similar tendencies are to be found in England in the inter-war period: Bill Lancaster, *The Department Store: a Social History*, London: Leicester University Press (1995), p. 105.
8. Gábor Gyáni, *Hétköznapi Budapest. Nagyvárosi élet a századfordulón* [Everyday Budapest: Metropolitan Life at the Turn of the Century], Budapest: Városháza (1995), pp. 67–9.
9. István Szilágyi, *Régi boltok krónikája. A pest-budai kereskedelem történetéből* [Chronicle of Old Shops: from the History of the Commerce of Pest-Buda], Budapest: KJK (1986), pp. 118–22; Katalin F. Dózsa,

Letűnt idők, eltűnt divatok 1867–1945 [Past Times, Vanished Fashions 1867–1945], Budapest: Gondolat (1989), pp. 157–8.

10. Szilágyi, *Régi boltok*, pp. 236–9.
11. Ibid., pp. 243–5.
12. Géza Komoróczy, *A zsidó Budapest* [Jewish Budapest], Budapest: Városháza (1995), vol. 1. p. 324.
13. 'A Párisi Nagy Áruház élete egy tisztességtelen versenyper tükrében' [The life of the Parisian Great Department Store in the light of an unfair law suit], *Magyar Közgazdaság*, 22, 24 May 1934.
14. Jegyzőkönyv a Corvin Áruház Rt. alakulásáról, 1922 március 30. [Minutes of the formation of the Corvin Department Store Co.], Magyar Kereskedelmi és Vendéglátóipari Múzeum Levéltára (hereafter MKVML), áruházi iratgyűjtemény: János Kallós, (ed.), *Gazdasági, pénzügyi és tőzsdei kompasz 1927–1928. évre* [Economic, Financial and Exchange Register for the years 1927–1928], Budapest: (1927), p. 207.
15. Ervin Ybl, 'A Corvin-Áruház' [The Corvin Department Store], *Magyar Iparművészet*, 1926, p. 6.
16. Ibid., p. 7.
17. Lajos Halász, 'A Corvin Áruház 50 éve' [50 Years of the Corvin Department Store], MS, in MKVML.
18. Ibid.
19. Ibid.
20. 'Világvárosi áruház' [Metropolitan department store], *A Magyar Élet Képeskönyve*, 1928, pp. 286–7.
21. 'Magyar Divatcsarnok' [Hungarian Fashion Hall], *Pesti Hírlap Évkönyve*, 1930, p. 101.
22. For the full story see, 'Magyar Divatcsarnok: Kis ár – nagy áruház' [Low price – big store], *Népszava*, 24 November 1934.
23. The process of modernisation in every sphere (legal, social and economic) has traditionally been called *embourgeoisement*, denoting either the creation of parliamentary constitutionalism, or the birth of an urban entrepreneurial class as a result of industrialisation and urbanisation.
24. Vera Bácskai, 'Jewish wholesale merchants in Pest in the first half of the nineteenth century', in M.K. Silber, (ed.), *Jews in the Hungarian Economy 1760–1945*, Jerusalem: Magnes Press, (1992), pp. 40–50.
25. Péter Hanák, *The Garden and the Workshop. Essays on the Cultural History of Vienna and Budapest*, Princeton: Princeton University Press (1998), p. 8.
26. Gábor Gyáni, 'Bürgerliches Heim und Interieur in Budapest', in P. Hanák, (ed.), *Bürgerliche Wohnkultur des Fin de Siécle in Ungarn*, Wien: Böhlau Verlag (1994), pp. 45–89: Gábor Gyáni, 'Domestic material culture of the upper-middle class in turn-of-the-century Budapest', in A. Pető and M. Pittaway, (eds), *Women in History – Women's History: Central and Eastern European Perspectives* Budapest: CEU (1994), pp. 55–73.
27. Eugénie Odescalchi, *Egy hercegnö emlékezik* [Recollections of a Duchess], Budapest: Gondolat (1987), p. 20.
28. Ibid., p. 34.
29. Mihály Pásztor, *Az eladósodott Budapest* [Budapest in Debt], Budapest: (n.d.), p. 128.
30. Ibid., pp. 130, 132.
31. *Népszava*, 24 November 1934.

32. 'Világvárosi áruház' [Metropolitan store], *Magyar Élet Képeskönyve*, 1928, p. 287.

33. 'Corvin Áruház' [Corvin Department Store], *Tolnai Világlapja*, 13–20 December 1933.

34. 'Birói eljárás a Corvin, Divatcsarnok és Fenyves Áruház ellen a kora-januári kiárusítások miatt' [Judicial Procedure against the Corvin, the Fashion Hall and the Fenyves Store Resulting from an Early January Sale], *Magyar Közgazdaság*, 18 January 1934; 'Kudarcba fulladt az áruházak téli leltári kiárusítása' [The winter clearance sale of the department stores failed], *Pénzügyi Kurir*, 1 March 1935.

35. *Pénzügyi Kurir*, 1 March 1935.

36. 'A Corvin Áruházat tisztességtelen verseny abbahagyására kötelezte a Kúria' [The Corvin Department Store forced by the Supreme Court to abandon unfair competitive tactics], *Tőzsdei Kurir*, 1 March 1934.

37. *Magyar Közgazdaság*, 18 January 1934.

38. Michael B. Miller, *The Bon Marché: Bourgeois Culture and the Department Store, 1869–1920*, Princeton: Princeton University Press (1981), p. 182.

39. Ibid., p. 184.

40. See Susan Porter Benson, 'Consumption and its discontents: the construction of the middle class in the United States', paper presented at the conference on Consumerism, Domesticity and Middle-Class Identity, New York, 1993; Jeanne Catherine Lawrence, 'Geographical space, social space, and the realm of the department store', *Urban History*, 19, 1992, pp. 64–84; Lancaster, *The Department Store*, esp. ch. 6.

41. *Népszava*, 24 November 1934; on the Fenyves Store see *Népszava*, 8 July 1928, 'I made efforts, the proprietor says, to display the great quantity of goods in an adequate artistic milieu, therefore I commissioned Sándor Petten, the well-known domestic designer, to plan the ornamentation'.

42. *Népszava*, 24 November 1934.

43. On the coffee-house interiors of turn-of-the-century Budapest, Ilona Sármány and Gyula Juhász, 'Amit a századforduló kávéházainak berendezéséről tudunk' [What is known about café furnishings at the turn of the century], *Budapesti Negyed*, 12–13, (1996), pp. 243–61.

44. The Corvin archives were destroyed in a fire at the store in the siege of Budapest during the last months of the Second World War. See the letter sent by the store management to the Budapest Financial Directorate, 11 January 1947, in MKVML.

45. *A magyar úrinő* [The Hungarian Lady], kiadja Holzer csász. és kir. udv. és kamarai szállitó cég negyvenéves fennállásának évfordulója alkalmából 1869–1909. *Az Ujság* karácsonyi mellékletéből.

46. Gyáni, *Hétköznapi Budapest*, p. 75.

47. *Munkaügyi Közlöny*, 13–14, 1933, p. 85.

48. F. Dózsa, *Letűnt idők*, p. 159.

49. This widespread practice made it possible for the Berlin firm, the German Singer Sewing Machine Co. Ltd., to open 33 branches in Hungary in the 1930s, five of which were in Budapest.

50. Miksa Lewin, *Az áruház* [The Department Store], Budapest: (1935)

51. File of the Corvin, in MKVML.

CHAPTER TEN

Les Magasins Réunis:
from the provinces to Paris,
from art nouveau to art deco*

Catherine Coley

> One of the characteristics of today's department stores from an artistic point of view is unadorned triteness. The large companies that operate these stores generally spend as little as possible on aesthetic features, neglecting any ornamentation or reducing it to insignificant motifs. It can be said without exaggeration that the rigid art of the engineer has superseded that of the architect.[1]

The 'lack of any artistic concepts' in the commercial practice of certain department stores, caricatured here by the critic Emile Nicolas writing in 1909, contrasts with the policies pursued by the Corbin family in Nancy and in the branches of their Magasins Réunis department store between 1890 and 1939. The originality of these retailer-builders can be seen, the second generation moving within just a few decades from an interest in architecture to a genuine and lasting patronage of the arts. The ambitions of the Corbin family, and above all Eugène Corbin who was the principal creative influence in the development of the family's chain of department stores, were heterogeneous but interconnected, combining pedagogic ambitions with commercial benefits. At one level there was the determination to found a thriving commercial business. At another there were the architectural ambitions which saw distinctive design principles used to give identity and unity to department stores that were sometimes the result of an accumulation of smaller adjacent properties, but on other occasions buildings specially erected for the purpose. And at a third level, there were the family's artistic ambitions, as leading patrons of artistic and craft activity in Nancy and Lorraine, for whom their stores were a medium through which to display and diffuse what they regarded as good taste.

* Translated by Paul Lybarger.

The Magasins Réunis in Nancy: from shop to department store

The history of the Magasins Réunis is the classic story of the social rise of a small 'retailer' and of the expansion (and then the demise) of the group of businesses that he formed. In 1867, Antoine Corbin (1835–1901), a former commercial traveller, opened his first business establishment in Nancy. In the years between 1880 and 1930 Nancy was to become the most important city in north-eastern France, in terms of population (120 000 inhabitants in 1911), economic activity (as an industrial and trading centre) and culture (university, learned societies, artistic activity). It was here that Corbin's businesses were to develop. His Bazar Saint Nicolas was modest in size, but was located at the strategic site of a city gate. The name *Bazar*, which implies an extensive variety of merchandise, including the famous *nouveautés* or new lines, placed the store in a category that was relatively new in Nancy, where retail trade remained highly specialised.[2] Starting with this store, Antoine Corbin put into practice the concepts that had been applied for several years in Paris and which were being adopted by a few local traders: *entrée libre* (in effect, entry without obligation to purchase), fixed and ticketed prices, and a vast selection of goods. The success of this formula seems to have been immediate and, after a series of expansions, the shop had rapidly reached the limits within which it could grow. Corbin now sought to benefit from the new economic and political conditions of the town to establish his business on a new scale.

Commercial development was favoured by the arrival of large numbers of inhabitants of Alsace-Lorraine who refused to accept the German annexation after 1870. Businesses were established, new industries were created and developed, the number of banks increased. At the same time, in the immediate vicinity of the railway's passenger station, military and religious activities in the Saint-Jean neighbourhood were gradually replaced, and the enormous potential of this neighbourhood was quickly recognised. Antoine Corbin was one of the first to buy a site, with the aim of establishing in this strategic location premises which would adequately reflect his business ambitions.

Starting in 1880, Corbin pursued a dual acquisition policy. While availability of sites and division into lots were delayed by the hesitancy of municipal authorities,[3] he sought to purchase land or buildings in the Mazagran area being developed around the new Place Saint-Jean, but encountered problems there.[4] Antoine Corbin therefore gained his first foothold in 1885 as a lessee, taking under his own name a store which had opened four years earlier and which had already made its owner's fortune. In spite of its modest size, this new establishment, named the Maison des Magasins Réunis, seems to have embodied Antoine Corbin's plans: advertisements announced that the Corbin-Guilbert husband and wife team were seeking to enlarge their business at this site by improving the quality of services offered to customers.[5] Nevertheless, the parallel projects that Antoine Corbin was pursuing indicate that he had come to this neighbourhood to put together a 'department store', whose Parisian image was already known in the provinces. His business strategy was to be present at this site from the very start of its growth, which explains his early arrival.

At the beginning of 1888, while the adjacent site had just been purchased by an individual in order to erect an imposing commercial building, Antoine Corbin proposed to the city of Nancy that he should acquire the whole of the area previously occupied by a barracks, and which offered a frontage of approximately 60 metres on Place St Jean. His architectural plan was already specific, as is shown by a wash drawing of a monumental department store façade, entitled the 'Maison des Magasins Réunis to be erected on the former site of the St Jean Barracks'[6] (Plate 10.1). This document articulates at one and the same time the scale of Antoine Corbin's commercial ambitions and his family's credentials as builders.

The drawing was by Jean-Baptiste Corbin, known as Eugène (1867–1952), Antoine Corbin's youngest son. Although he had entered his father's business early, he seems from a very young age to have been more attracted by the artistic world. His elder brother, Louis Corbin also loved art and introduced him into the circle of young local painters. Eugène Corbin was soon enthusiastically pursuing two activities as an enlightened amateur: drawing and purchasing works of art.[7] It is therefore not surprising that the only known graphic expression of Antoine Corbin's 'commercial dream' is the work of his artistically talented son who appears to have matured in a family environment fascinated by building.

Antoine Corbin, son of a wine grower, appears as an archetype of the honest and courageous worker, one in whom solid business acumen was combined with a peasant's common sense. To this we can add artistic inclinations, because before entering commerce he had earned his living as a musician. His social ascent shows the soul of a builder: he built endlessly, not only to house or to improve his stores and their branches, but also for his own satisfaction. His choice of sites and architects is revealing: commencing in 1889, in co-operation with an architect from Nancy who worked in the 'troubadour' style,[8] he reinvented in a romantic style the medieval remains of a fortified castle to use as his country dwelling. Later, he regularly called upon Lucien Weissenburger, the Magasins Réunis 'house architect', for his personal residences, including his villa 'La Garenne' built in the purest art nouveau style at Liverdun (1900).

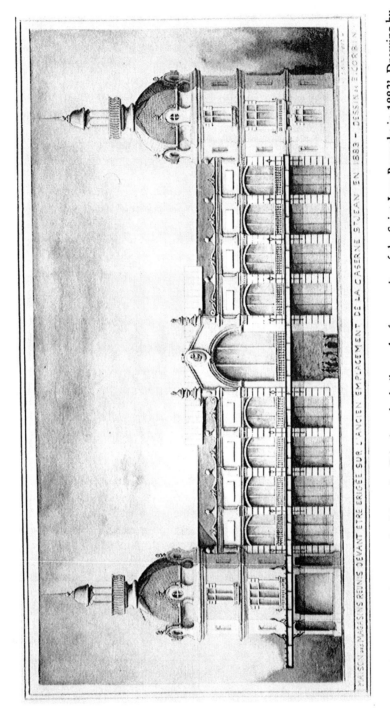

MAISON des MAGASINS RÉUNIS DEVANT ETRE ERIGÉE SUR L'ANCIEN EMPLACEMENT DE LA CASERNE ST-JEAN EN 1883 — DESSIN d'E CORBIN

Plate 10.1 'Front of Maison des Magasins Réunis to be built on the former site of the Saint Jean Barracks in 1883'. Drawing by E. Corbin. The project was never realised. (Musée de l'Ecole de Nancy: Inventaire Général de Lorraine, all rights reserved)

There is no doubt that Antoine Corbin influenced this plan for a department store. The building designed by Eugène Corbin showed elegant craftsmanship and a simple arrangement on three storeys of different sizes: a central entrance flanked on each side by four bays with two extending corner wings forming canted walls. There was no ostentatious luxury, and hardly any signs of sculpted ornamentation, apart from details; it is possible that a metal or semi-metal frame was intended, given the vast openings of the two lower levels. The strong points of its rigorous composition were the corner turrets and the treatment of the monumental porch at the entrance, extending through the three storeys. It was entirely covered with glass like a railway station, and it ended with a pediment bearing the Corbin-Guilbert monogram, flanked by two high pinnacles. Although the execution was skilful, the model was a conventional one, and may have been taken from the national press; the skylights surrounded by a walkway show a certain similarity to those at Printemps in Paris (built 1881–83). Its image was widely reproduced at the time, and one is struck by the close similarity between this version and drawings by students at the Ecole des Beaux-Arts published in 1889.[9]

Notwithstanding the quality of this project, Antoine Corbin's offer to buy the site[10] was rejected, and the real reasons remain unclear: pressures from competitors, the unfavorable image of a department store which would be detrimental to the neighbourhood's fashionable destiny, or the desire to diversify the façades facing on to the square. Antoine Corbin abandoned the idea of a separate large building such as those being constructed nearby at the time, and decided to concentrate on the site of his principal place of business. This venture lasted for over 20 years and commenced in 1890 with the erection of a 'doorstep' that united two large parcels of land and permitted the two stores to be connected at the rear. In sharp contrast to Eugène Corbin's extremely conventional department store design, the façade revealed nothing about the internal sales area or its layout. With restrained ornamentation and an elegant arrangement of elements, nothing apart from the window openings on the ground floor distinguished this building from the bourgeois dwellings on the street, whose academic style had been determined by the Salle Poirel nearby.[11] Ferdinand Genay (1846–1909), the architect who was chosen, had designed opulent mansions and large industrial and commercial buildings in Nancy. As an inspector of diocesan buildings and a member of learned societies, Genay combined all the qualifications of a 'bourgeois' architect needed by Antoine Corbin, for he now had a social standing in the town which signified his admission into the world of the local élite of 'notables'.[12]

The expansion of Magasins Réunis accelerated, marked by the purchase of parcels of land and buildings.[13] An initial section was quickly completed, occupying half the site and giving direct access opposite the railway station. The disparate façades of the restored buildings were left in their original form and concealed the interior layout which revealed the real scale of this department store. In 1894 a vast hall was built, with a width of 18 metres, and it was completely covered with glass extending from one end of the site to the other at a height of some 10 metres.

For Antoine Corbin, this project marked the start of his creation of a cathedral of commerce, that iron and glass construction whose image had haunted him ever since his visit to the Paris World Exhibition of 1889. Lucien Weissenburger, the architect to whom this project was entrusted, was well known in Nancy for the construction of both bourgeois residences and industrial buildings, in which he later specialised.[14] This choice of architect leads us into new architectural trends towards the end of the nineteenth century.

The first architect from Nancy to receive a diploma from the Ecole des Beaux-Arts in Paris, Weissenburger already possessed sound credentials when Antoine Corbin asked him to take responsibility for the extension of his stores (Plate 10.2). He initially worked within the classical tradition before promoting the application of the principles of art nouveau within architecture, while never departing from the strict building principles in which he had been trained.[15] In 1894, while the first section of improvement and extension work at the Magasins Réunis was being completed, Antoine Corbin asked Weissenburger to erect a corner building across from it. Although this building was only partially intended for sales,[16] the architect realised the classic although truncated form of a 'department store' with a metal frame mounted upon cast-iron poles. The canted walls imposed by urban planning regulations were extensively covered with glass and treated in an 'industrial' manner which differed from the more residential façades with their ornaments and balconies of sculpted stone.

At the same time, Weissenburger gave a new stylistic dimension to the expansion of the Magasins Réunis by harmonising the façades of the remodelled buildings, a considerable technical, commercial and stylistic achievement. The unification required major construction works, with the first of these projects, begun in 1895 under the direction of Antoine Corbin, setting the tone: two then six bays, arranged in four levels ending in a terrace. The 'industrial' character of the building was emphasised: beneath the façades, the new glass hall stood out, and it was significantly higher than the earlier hall, while being arranged perpendicular to it. The metal frame was readily observable, and permitted the wide opening at the two lower levels. The external upper portions were particularly well designed, with the freestone facing providing for the

Plate 10.2 Headed notepaper for Maison des Magasins Réunis, Nancy, c. 1894. View of various buildings and of the main glazed hall. (Musée Historique Lorrain: Inventaire Général de Lorraine, all rights reserved)

building as a whole an imposing but elegant effect of solidity. Each bay was marked at the level of the terrace with an escutcheon motif topped by a cowl which accentuated its vertical quality and introduced a neo-Gothic note which was to become one of the reference points for art nouveau architecture in Nancy. A monumental entrance was supported by a large wrought-iron canopy vaulted in a circular arc.[17] This provided the opportunity for the architect to erect the first 'sign' of the intense business going on within these walls: a corner turret with a proudly raised dome and its skylight adorned with a bronze representation of Mercury, the god of commerce.

The final phase (1905–10) finally gave the Magasins Réunis their actual architectural identity with an imposing principal façade opposite the railway station. The work was carried out efficiently and in a spectacular fashion. The France-Lanord et Bichaton Company made the project a showcase for its technical expertise and placed in the centre of the new area cleared by demolition an enormous steam derrick crane specially imported from the USA. Nine new bays soon rose as the modernisation process continued. The repetitive element made sublime this elegant but sober framework. The entire complex thus formed, interrupted by a new corner turret, saw an additional floor erected upon the final terrace (Plate 10.3). The supple lines of the bays added at this level constituted the only outward architectural sign of an art nouveau presence in this vast building.

From 1908 publicity boasted of the 'amazing additions to the Magasins Réunis' and used the architectural shell of the establishment as an advertising medium. The most spectacular were night views in which the vast building was entirely illuminated from the inside, symbolising the exuberance of this 'beehive' or even its radiant effect on the city.[18] This use of the building as a mode of communication primarily applied to its external image. The monumental proportions of the building, often exaggerated by a false perspective, were exaggerated by signs, banners and standards, which enlivened the sober façades and gave a festive atmosphere to the structure as a whole.

Only two limited portrayals of the interior of the largest hall are known to exist: one photograph taken around 1909 shows a pile of merchandise, while the other taken at around the same time has this profusion of goods displayed upon carefully arranged shelves. A contemporary article identified the different contributions to the interior décor of the building, and its harmony was universally praised by journalists[19] (Plate 10.4). This was the largest collective project entrusted by Eugène Corbin to local artists, and provided the Nancy School (which will be discussed in more detail later) with a setting in which to express itself that was large in terms of both size and

Plate 10.3 Publicity drawing for Les Magasins Réunis, Nancy, in *Annuaire de la Meurthe*, 1914. (Original in Musée de l'Ecole de Nancy: Inventaire Général de Lorraine, all rights reserved)

Plate 10.4 Les Magasins Réunis, Nancy: interior view, *c*. 1908. (Photograph published in L. Lafitte, *L'Exposition Internationale de l'Est de la France*, Nancy: Berger-Levraut, 1912: Inventaire Général de Lorraine, all rights reserved)

Plate 10.5   Les Magasins Réunis, monumental iron entrance by L.
Weissenburger, architect, and F. Schertzer, manufacturer, 1907.
(Postcard: Inventaire Général de Lorraine, all rights reserved)

finance.[20] Along with the internal improvement of the main building,
the interior of the annexe opposite was enlarged and redecorated by the
same artists, to provide an elegant setting for the new department of
Jewellery and Objets d'Art.

   Art nouveau was even more prominent in the final external improvements, as if it had finally gained acceptance. The canted wall of the

Jewellery department contained two bronze caryatids by Victor Prouvé, flower-women with gracefully flowing long hair. Likewise, the large new entrance to the main building contained on the outside an extraordinary metal facing in the form of a butterfly wing,[21] which was set in front of an inner door whose free-flowing frame was executed in enamelled sandstone from Rambervillers (Plate 10.5).

This department store, dreamed of by Antoine Corbin some 25 years before, was almost finished. It was a success as a feat of construction, taking almost a whole building block on which was erected an architecturally coherent and commercially competitive ensemble. The achievement followed a classic pattern in the history of department stores,[22] but the building also stands to provoke thought, hopes, common endeavours, which went well beyond the built structure. What made the Magasins Réunis original was its prominent place in the great artistic adventure of the years 1894–1914 in Nancy, an adventure which reached Paris.

An architectural policy of unification

The owner of this vast project was also the principal contractor. We have seen the decisive role played by Antoine Corbin in establishing an architectural policy associated with the Maison des Magasins Réunis, both through his choice of architects of contemporary significance and through the image that he himself sought to attach to his stores. The architects were Ferdinand Genay, a bourgeois academic, and then Lucien Weissenburger, an innovative technician. Eugène Corbin continued the programme while seeking the collaboration of others. This establishment of a 'house-architectural style' may be detected in the buildings of branches and affiliated establishments for here the unifying influence of the Corbins is undeniable.

The policy of commercial development launched by Antoine was not limited to Nancy itself: branches were created from the Meuse to the Vosges and the Ardennes in the period after 1885.[23] Stores were initially opened in existing buildings, their bric-à-brac spilling on to the pavements. In Paris in 1894, the creation of a central purchasing office[24] allowed branches and associated companies, such as the Marlin-Viard-Magu family group which originated in the Vosges region, to come together. This development was to have visible repercussions for the architecture of the buildings concerned.

One cannot truly speak of a 'style' *per se*, because although each structure was the result of a plan, no models as such existed. Nevertheless, a case by case examination of the main branches and affiliates reveals certain technical and stylistic features that were constant. It was more a question of common sources of inspiration and reference. Certain characteristics arose from the style of the European department store, such as industrial building techniques to provide iron and glass structures, while other characteristics, such as use of the principles of art nouveau (especially from the Nancy School), seem to follow the wishes or the suggestions of the chain's directors. This stylistic current, more or less evident according to the type of building, its size or even its administrative status, is a recurrent presence in the architecture of various Magasins Réunis between 1897 and 1910. Formal evidence of directives may be difficult to find, but the continuity and choice of architects attached to the company none the less confirms this intention.

Weissenburger had been chosen by the Corbin family to co-ordinate the extension of the Magasins Réunis in Nancy on account of his experience in industrial construction techniques and art nouveau, and he built, remodelled, or rebuilt eight branches of the Magasins Réunis between 1895 and 1910. The construction of the branch in Troyes, which began in 1895, reflects the architect's and the owner's hesitations, going beyond the academic model of the Parisian department store. Beneath a reassuring and opulent stone exterior, the classic composition of the façades concealed the metal structure, which could be more readily detected from the inside. This caution can be partially explained in terms of the collaboration of a local architect, Louis Mony, who was also the mayor of the town, or more confidently in terms of the early date of this structure within Weissenburger's work.

A few years later, two other branches provide evidence of the architect's adaptability, as well as of his genuine virtuosity in using 'modern' materials and daring construction methods, often working with Frédéric Schertzer, an engineer and builder from Nancy. Construction of the Toul branch in 1904 was the most successful and boldest expression of art nouveau commercial architecture in the region. Abandoning the traditional composition with corner turrets, this building combined purity of décor, boldness in composition, and technical prowess, with the energetic expression of modern elements highlighting the lightness of the metal. At Pont à Mousson (1910), the original façade which was lightened by a metal structure with superimposed cast-iron columns, became entirely glass on two levels. In contrast, the sculpted décor of the stone side jambs hurtles toward a sculpted crown rendered in a fast-flowing art nouveau style, in a real sense a production, which gave the sign an urban role that was almost theatrical.

At a later date, for the Grand Bazar de la Marne in Châlons,[25] Weissenburger proposed an ambitious expansion plan upon an architectural frame with wide, open bays, and domed corner turrets. This

Plate 10.6 Maison des Magasins Réunis, Grand Bazar des Vosges Viard-Gardin, Epinal. Watercoloured drawing of the façade by J. Hornecker, architect, c. 1907. (Musée d'Orsay, Paris: Inventaire Général de Lorraine, all rights reserved)

project, which was closely related to the completed Magasins Réunis in Nancy, allows the link between two groups which had combined to their mutual advantage. The influence exercised by the Corbin family upon the architecture of buildings for affiliated establishments can on this occasion be readily detected, although it is not possible to say whether the establishments had requested this type of architecture, or whether the very fact of expanding the buildings dictated a search for architectural quality.

Confirmation of these architectural relationships among affiliated commercial groups, is provided by the spectacular example of the Grand Bazar des Vosges in Epinal (Plate 10.6). Joseph Hornecker (1873–1942),[26] an associate of the Gutton group of architects involved in building other branches for Magasins Réunis, was given responsibility for rebuilding the structure. The programme given to the architect required creating a uniformity of façades corresponding to the store's various stages of expansion, proudly emphasising that it belonged to the Magasins Réunis chain.[27] Use of a metal outer frame studded with iron crests, and highlighted by mosaic panels, allowed the silhouette of the building to be remodelled, while providing an obvious reference to the art of the School of Nancy.

There is an obvious plastic relationship between this building and the Grand Bazar building on the Rue de Rennes in Paris. Construction of the latter building had been assigned to Henry-Barthélemy Gutton (1874–1963), an architect from Nancy who acquired an individual status within the company, leaving Nancy in 1905 to devote himself to the company's affairs and later becoming one of its directors. In the same way, the choice of this architect by the directors of the Société des Magasins Réunis was not fortuitous, for it was evidence of a desire to place their buildings within the current represented by the School of Nancy, in which Gutton was himself an active participant. Combining plastic qualities and technical resources, the Grand Bazar, which opened in 1907, is the archetype of the direct relationship between architecture and commercial function, one which eschewed useless artifice. It was also the 'manifesto in Paris of art nouveau from Lorraine'[28] and was hailed as such by the national press.

It is important to bear in mind the originality of the School of Nancy, genuinely 'anchored in the city',[29] and the Magasins Réunis of Nancy were undoubtedly the only permanent location for expressing this originality, albeit during a brief yet brilliant period. This role extended far beyond the multiple contributions of local artists, members of the parent company's Alliance Provinciale des Industries d'Art. Their contributions are no more than the tip of the iceberg of the immeasurable part played by Eugène Corbin in the brilliance and influence of the School of Nancy.

The School of Nancy: enlightened patronage

Eugène Corbin was an unusual personality who left a permanent mark on the economic and artistic life of Nancy at the beginning of the twentieth century. As a young man Eugène was less involved in the family business than were his brother and brothers-in-law, appearing as a member of the city's 'gilded youth', and displaying a fascination with the latest trends of contemporary ideas. A keen sportsman, he was both oarsman and fencer, passionately interested in automobiles, aviation and hot air balloons. Eugène was a great traveller, visiting Egypt and Abyssinia at the turn of the century. His outlook was that of the artists and writers of his generation, and he bought everything associated with art in Lorraine, from engravings by Callot to paintings by Victor Prouvé, whom he got to know in 1890. By then one can speak of a 'collection' being established, one which might appear slightly eclectic, but which 'encompasses everything interesting that modern Lorraine was able to produce.'[30]

It was his participation in the development of the School of Nancy, however, that gave this collection its real significance and marked it out as an example of real artistic patronage. The creation in 1901 of the School of Nancy – the Alliance Provinciale des Industries d'Art – under the aegis of the glassmaker Emile Gallé gave formal existence to a current of original ideas. It grew out of Gallé's personal efforts over more than a decade and from the active participation of local artists and craftsmen, amongst them Prouvé, Gruber, Majorelle, Vallin, Daum and the architects Weissenburger and André. This group of artists and master craftsmen, acting out of a shared outlook and shared ideas, sought to put an end to the damaging influence of imitation by renewing their sources of artistic inspiration in order to achieve an originality of expression which would be diffused as widely as possible to the public as a whole.

Eugène Corbin, described by Victor Prouvé as 'an intuitive person shining with a spirit of frenetic and tireless enthusiasm, fascinated by new ideas', was invited by Gallé to join the movement of which he was to become the principal pillar: 'his support for artists is so great that it cannot be encompassed within the term patronage.'[31] Eugène Corbin not only purchased many works, he also provided artists with the emotional and financial support which allowed them to move their projects forward. He planned 'invitational' artists' studios and even employed artists in his enterprise, amongst them the poet Léon Tonnelier and the jeweller Déon. Overall, his relations with these artists were extremely close.[32] His role in the School of Nancy, however, was not merely that of a 'financial backer'.

Eugène Corbin was, above all, a retailer and in this role, too, he became interested in the School of Nancy, this time as an industrial and commercial medium. The Magasins Réunis were for him to become the showcase for the values proclaimed by the School of Nancy: a new aesthetic, adapted to the requirements of modern life and applied to the objects of daily existence, and made accessible to all. The School of Nancy's emphasis on the importance of 'fine craftsmanship' to the preservation of artisanal skill, was carried further, into the vision of industry properly constituted to diffuse as widely as possible mass-produced goods of real quality.

'Art and industry', 'art for all', 'useful and beautiful', these concepts were clearly expressed in 1901 in the Statutes which constituted the manifesto of the School of Nancy. 'Art and industry', 'art and commerce' 'commerce and culture': this duality which ran through artistic movements of the late nineteenth and early twentieth centuries was embodied in Eugène Corbin's activities. His mind was imbued as much with culture as with commercial intuition, and for him everything was connected: 'Eugène Corbin's genuine taste for artistic activity turned out to be a great asset in terms of expanding sales.'[33]

Eugène Corbin thus put in place a genuine 'commercial culture' associated with the School of Nancy. The logical next step was to disseminate this culture and render it accessible to his customers. In 1903, Eugène Corbin asked Gallé for the sales concession for his works, so that certain models might be distributed in his stores. Gallé refused, anxious to retain control of the distribution of his work. Undaunted, Corbin seized the initiative and began to publish, produce and diffuse ordinary objects created by the city's artists. The main development of this organisation took place after the war, under the influence of the Paris department stores and their brand names. The embroidery patterns of Jacques Gruber were published by Magasins Réunis, while they distributed exclusively the furniture designed by Lucien Weissenburger for Majorelle. The competitions which Corbin organised with the School of Nancy after 1908 seemed to be as much an attempt to spread the school's ideas as to encourage local artists, craftsmen, and manufacturers. Unfortunately, we know little about the extent to which the prize-winning designs were subsequently distributed.[34]

The commitment to art for all found more direct expression in the everyday public spaces within the store: the tearoom where concerts took place, the reading-room whose décor was entrusted to Louis Majorelle, the puppet theatre, the book shop where a special counter was devoted to authors from Lorraine, and above all the art gallery where paintings and other works of art were on continuous display: 'The Magasins Réunis was not only an important retail enterprise. It was, above all for art lovers, a sort of temple where one went simply to appreciate the delights of good taste.'[35]

Eugène Corbin's calling drew him on, and in 1909 he established the luxurious journal, *Art et Industrie* which achieved a national distribution. In its columns an entire philosophy was presented with the goal of ensuring that 'the future of decorative art would be wedded to that of industry', not only through the enterprise of leading manufacturers, but also through once again valuing the work of the producer, whether artistic worker, contractors, or craftsmen. Victor Prouvé was responsible for co-ordinating this educational project, by attempting to get more importance attached to apprenticeship, and by shaping the role of each participant in order to redefine the relationship between the artist as creator of models, the craftsman as executor of these models, and the potential manufacturer-distributor. The publication of *Art et Industrie* ended with the war, but it represented the final attempt to put into practical (and business) effect the theoretical principles which had been enunciated by Gallé in 1901 with respect to the diffusion of art nouveau. Through Eugène Corbin, the Magasins Réunis emerged as the medium for this artistic movement, a role which went far beyond the luxurious creations which various artists from the School of Nancy had attached to the buildings of different establishments within the chain.

The war put a permanent end to this fine adventure, especially as many artists never returned from it. Almost as a testament to the fading School of Nancy, Weissenburger's Magasins Réunis disappeared in smoke during bombing raids on the night of 16 January 1916, as did the branches in Toul, Pont à Mousson, and Epinal. This event symbolised the end of an era, but it equally marked the beginning of what was a logical continuation of the work initiated by Eugène Corbin, the development of whose artistic taste had been clearly evident in the pre-war years. Always alert to new forms of expression, he befriended Victor Guillaume, a Nancy painter who was a follower of Cezanne. A subscriber to many art periodicals, Guillaume belonged to the small group in Nancy familiar with the Cubists' adventures. Corbin had become acquainted during the war with young Parisian painters recruited into his regiment, and he bought paintings from them and from their friends, including Dunoyer de Segonzac, Dufresne, Laprade and Luc-Albert Moreau. His inquisitive mind was always drawn to the new and the innovative, and each new artistic current attracted his interest.

A symbolic moment arrived in 1917, when Eugène Corbin rejected a plan for the reconstruction of the Magasins Réunis in Nancy, perhaps acting on Weissenburger's advice. It can only be assumed that the plan no longer corresponded to the owner's new aesthetic preferences. 'Corbin's change of direction dealt a mortal blow to the work of the

School of Nancy.'[36] At the end of the war, he founded the Cercle Artistique de l'Est and loaned his new acquisitions for exhibitions. In 1923, he played a part in the formation of the Comité Nancy–Paris, which shook off the yoke of the local artistic tradition. The first exhibitions and lectures, such as those given by the Lurçat brothers, caused a scandal among the relatively uninformed public of Nancy.[37] Corbin actively supported these initiatives and the projects to educate the public. A local critic emphasised that 'since before the war, Nancy had been kept aware of this modern movement through the eclecticism of Monsieur E. Corbin.' Although certain harsh critics denigrated Corbin's choices in modern painting, arguing that 'exhibiting such unrepresentative works serves only to warp public taste', Eugène Corbin contributed significantly to familiarising the local public with 'modern art', even if the term was far from embracing avant-garde painters. Corbin's support was both practical and financial: in 1924, he bought a painting by Guillaume for the Comité Nancy–Paris. As in the past, he was prepared to help all artists at the start of their career or faced with material difficulties which might affect their creative work, such as Victor Guillaume, Paul Colin before his overnight success in Paris, Michel Colle or the Ventrillon brothers.

Large-scale retailing and the dissemination of modern taste

Corbin continued his pre-war activities, combining a role as driving force in the artistic life of Nancy with preoccupations which linked closely to his business: the new headquarters in Nancy for Magasins Réunis was to be both a showcase for his artistic convictions and a base for commercial distribution and a developing consumer culture.

At the beginning of the 1920s, Eugène Corbin created the Arts Réunis, a body set up to distribute regional applied art through the Magasins Réunis chain; Ernest Ventrillon, a painter-decorator from Nancy who had settled in Paris, was made director of the new project, which was to function at two levels: firstly, selecting and selling mass-produced items manufactured by Lorraine industries, such as Baccarat crystal, Vallerystahl and Portieux glasswares, and Longwy earthenware; and, secondly, by setting up a creative studio modelled on those in all the main Parisian department stores, and committed to encouraging original creativity with a view to 'encouraging the contemporary arts'.[38] In furniture, tableware, vases, fabrics and wallpaper, Arts Réunis creations were sold in a special department in each store and branch of the chain: in the Magasins Réunis-Republique in Paris this occupied an entire floor. Although these products lacked the sheer diversity of those in the

Paris department stores, they did possess the advantage of existing and being distributed to customers at reasonable prices while continuing to stimulate regional artistic industries.

In 1925, when Eugène Corbin decided to rebuild the headquarters of the Magasins Réunis in Nancy 'according to the most modern principles and in accordance with modern taste', he was equally concerned to demonstrate his own artistic development, one which he sought to share with his customers. He wanted to make a definitive break with the ghost of the School of Nancy, something still close to the hearts of the city's inhabitants. The architect Pierre Le Bourgeois (1879–1971) was given the task, appearing to be very much the man for this job, because the project was one which coincided with his own preoccupations.

Whereas in his early projects Le Bourgeois had expressed the tension between his desire to innovate and to renew in architectural vocabulary on the one hand, and on the other a certain 'moral obligation' to respect the themes of art nouveau, his post-war work represents a complete break.[39] As an admirer of concrete, for which the *Hennebique* process had been developed in Nancy by the France-Lanord et Bichaton Company, Pierre Le Bourgeois proposed a reinforced concrete supporting structure, whose façade would be closed by metal panels (Plate 10.7). This 'rationalist model' immediately provoked an outcry among local inhabitants. Adapting the project in order to please his customers was not the issue for Corbin. On the contrary, the initial sketches for façades which still contained art deco ornamentation rapidly evolved towards a much greater sobriety. This may have appalled Nancy's citizens, but it reflected the development of the architect and the owner themselves. They were familiar with the new trends of the 'International Style' that they had found in several pavilions at the 1925 Paris Exhibition, and which they encountered again on their home territory during a large exhibition organised in Nancy in March 1926 by the Comité Nancy–Paris, the selection of items for whose modern architecture section had been the responsibility of André Lurçat.

By 1925 the principles of construction and the interior layout had been established: the new store, described as 'a commercial factory',[40] occupied the entire area (*c.* 4 000 m²) and was organised around two large halls under glass which extended across the entire height of the building. The façades were deliberately plain, and their bays were simply spaced by fluted pillars which employed young artists closely associated with Corbin, such as Jean Prouvé, the wrought-iron craftsman who seemed destined for a brilliant career, the decorator Jean-Louis Burtin, and Emile Bachelet, a sculptor whose bas reliefs provided harmony for the ground floor external bays and whose work was already in Eugène Corbin's collection. In addition to its own intrinsic

Plate 10.7 Les Magasins Réunis, Nancy: projected new building *c.* 1925. Ink drawing by P. Le Bourgeois, architect. (Musée de l'Ecole de Nancy: Inventaire Général de Lorraine,)

architectural value, the new building allowed Eugène Corbin to sustain his dream of a popular artistic culture. He established on the third floor an art gallery open to the public, where displays of the works of young artists alternated with those drawn from his own collections. This building was Eugène Corbin's true legacy. It demonstrated the strength of his artistic spirit, which may not have always been very critical, but which was always drawn to the innovative and fascinated by all kinds of art. It is also the symbol of a determination to impose a consumer culture, which found its most complete expression in architecture, and its most definitive expression in its transformation of the urban space and the urban landscape.

The pedagogical dimensions of Eugène Corbin's work both before and after the First World War are particularly instructive, being applied to wholly different modes of artistic expression over two distinct periods. His concern between 1890 and 1910 was with the dissemination of a regional and very specific form of artistic expression: the School of Nancy. This support was reflected in very specific forms of patronage. In addition to his personal collection and the commissioning of artistic works for his own use, Corbin financed the output of individual painters and artists. By this means he became a full participant in the School of Nancy, for its development would have been far less exceptional without patronage. As a mediocre but conscientious painter, it provided him with the means to situate himself within an artistic milieu which he had frequented since his youth, while identifying himself with the artists whom he supported and from whom he received advice, such as Victor Prouvé whom he invoked as his mentor.

The transition to commercial dissemination in his stores also originated in this policy of providing material support for artistic expression. Corbin's role was decisive here too, because even modest practical application of the principles about the popularization of art laid down by Gallé and repeated by members of the School of Nancy had no other means of expression than that provided by Corbin initially through his Magasins Réunis and then Arts Réunis. The experiment was relatively unique on this scale, for it was not closely comparable to groups such as the *Werkbund*.

Whereas it is difficult to assess the contributions of Corbin's personal convictions and his commercial motivations in this policy of diffusion directed at his customers, one can find evidence that relates to the image of the department store held by consumers, in so far as this image can be discerned through advertising, sales catalogues, and glimpses in the local press. The Magasins Réunis in Nancy acquired a precise status between 1890 and 1914, one which directly resulted from the architectural pattern which emerged from its transformations: vast halls side by

Plate 10.8   Corbin Bequest in the Galeries Poirel, Nancy, c. 1936. (Photograph: Inventaire Général de Lorraine,)

side with points of sale or with quiet, more intimate corners. The clientele was vaguely composed of all social classes, with an accent being placed upon the elegance, comfort, and 'good tone' of the store, which created a very particular character, especially with respect to female customers. The establishment became a reference point for 'good taste', even though surviving sales catalogues indicate that the term may not have always been justified. This reveals the commercial limits of the 'consumer culture' that Corbin sought to create and the concessions that were needed to satisfy a larger clientele.

On the other hand – and this holds true for subsequent construction – the building itself and its decorative aspects were an incarnation of the owner's tastes and, by extension, may be regarded as a high-quality artistic expression that might be seen as a model. Weissenburger's architecture, along with the decorations of Victor Prouvé, Gruber and Majorelle, were completed too late for one to believe that they could truly have influenced the citizens of Nancy, who were already adherents of art nouveau. On the other hand, it is far more plausible to conclude that the controversial architecture of Le Bourgeois and the bold projects of Jean Prouvé, as well as regular presentation of avant-garde exhibits within or outside the Magasins Réunis, contributed to the formation of the tastes of the citizens of Nancy, who still were not accustomed to such forms of expression.

Eugene Corbin's last and most lasting act on behalf of art, and the one which confirms his essentially educational orientation, was to leave his decorative art collection to the city. In 1935, Corbin 'imposed' on the City of Nancy the gift of a large portion of his treasures from the School of Nancy, intending thus to create a permanent testimony to the movement and to leave the image of a period of creativity underpinned by authentic moral values (Plate 10.8). This bequest was accompanied by clear provisions concerning its being permanently exhibited to the public, something which would be only be achieved 30 years later.[41] The only obvious trace of this extraordinary adventure of the Magasins Réunis, the prestige which is now attached to the museum built around this collection, is the most complete expression of the osmosis of the artistic and commercial ambitions of the Corbin family between 1890 and 1939.

Notes

1. Emile Nicolas, 'Un grand magasin moderne', *L'Art Décoratif*, 1909.
2. Odette Voillard, *Nancy, une bourgeoisie urbaine au XIX siècle*, Nancy: Presses Universitaires de Nancy (1978).

3. Catherine Coley, 'Un quartier en mutation', in *La Salle Poirel*, Nancy: Archives Modernes de l'Architecture Lorraine/Presses Universitaires de Nancy (1989). The site for this building would change no fewer than four times between 1885 and 1888.
4. In 1880, Corbin acquired in the Mazagran area a corner house that was 'half wood and half stone' which he let out on lease. In 1883, the architect F. Genay tried to acquire land for a client who could well have been Corbin.
5. 'The system of selling at low margins and in total confidence is the rule in the Maison des Magasins Réunis, with merchandise on a hitherto unknown scale concentrated in 70 departments', *Le Patriote de l'Est*, 10 April 1885.
6. A drawing in the Musée de l'Ecole de Nancy, entitled 'Drawing of E. Corbin' and signed 'JBC 1883'.
7. From when he was 16 years old, he bought drawings from Charles Sellier, the recipient of the Prix de Rome in Lorraine, when his studio was being sold.
8. 'Une maison Renaissance, la maison Lanternier', *Nancy-Artiste*, 2 June 1887.
9. 'Ecole des Beaux-Arts, concours de 1° classe: un bazar ou grand magasin', *La Construction Moderne*, 13 April 1889, pp. 314–15.
10. On 6 January 1888, he offered the city two alternatives, one of which included the possibility of an exchange (with compensation) of a parcel of the Mazagran area which was to be aligned; the other alternative was the purchase of a part of the St Jean barracks. These proposals were reiterated in February, then in July, 1888, accompanied by higher financial offers. Archives de la Ville de Nancy, ND (10), Caserne Saint Jean.
11. Starting in 1874, the date of the quarter's first buildings, the city had laid down clear prescriptions which required quality architecture, 'elegant and with a certain luxury'. Coley, 'Un quartier en mutation'.
12. In 1889, he joined with prominent manufacturers such as Vilgrain, Tourtel, Gallé or Daum in establishing *L'Est Républicain*, an anti-Boulangist political paper.
13. In Nancy in 1896, the first issue appeared of the paper *La Défense du commerce qui défend les petits et moyens commerçants et industriels* 'against the monopolistic stores and co-operative societies which sow ruin around them to no-one's advantage, for the cheap price of the articles they offer to buyers is only an illusion'.
14. In 1888, at the end of his studies, he displayed at the Paris Exhibition a plan for a 'covered market' with a metal frame for which he received an 'honorable mention'.
15. Weissenburger was a founding member of the School of Nancy and would be chosen by Henri Sauvage in 1901 to be the executing architect of the Maison Majorelle in Nancy.
16. Antoine Corbin occupied the upper floors with his family. He reserved the second floor for himself and direct access by elevator to the landscaped terrace, where he himself made the decisions about the beds of rosebushes. The ground floor was occupied by the hardware section, an annexe to the neighbouring Magasins Réunis to which it was connected by an underground passage.
17. 'A colossal door formed by an arc without jambs, fairly analogous to the

great arcs of the Eiffel Tower, indicated the rushing of the crowds which on certain days occurred in these stores': *La Construction Moderne*, 13 April 1889. The model was not new, and had been used in Paris in 1883 by Paul Sedille for the porch of Printemps. The advantage of these wrought-iron works was that they required no ground-level attachment, while opening broadly on to the street.

18. Paul Colin poster, *c*.1909: the skylight projecting its beam of light (Musée Lorrain, Nancy).

19. Nicolas, 'Un grand magasin moderne'.

20. Jacques Gruber, the Daum brothers, Louis Majorelle, Victor Prouvé and Louis Guingot.

21. Lucien Weissenburger designed the model for execution by Frederic Schertzer, the largest local contractor in metal construction.

22. As Bernard Marrey points out in *Les Grands Magasins des origines à 1939*, Paris: Picard (1979), many Parisian stores were created in this form. In the words of Emile Zola

> although the architect used existing structures, he opened them on all sides to furnish them and, in the middle, in the opening from the courtyards, he built a central gallery, which was as vast as a church, which was to open onto the street through a main doorway in the center of the façade.

Emile Zola, *Au Bonheur des Dames*, [1883], Paris: Folio Classique edition (1980), p. 279.

23. Pont à Mousson, Lunéville, Pont St Vincent, St Mihiel, Toul, Neufchateau, Charmes, Longwy-haut and Vaucouleurs.

24. ' ... marvellous organization whose role was to provide all the member houses as needed with merchandise purchased at a good price.' 'Les Magasins Réunis', a commemorative plaque published on the occasion of the centennial of the company. Nancy, 1967.

25. Founded in 1902 by Jules Marlin, affiliated with the Maison des Magasins Réunis through a supply agreement in June, 1913.

26. See Vincent Bradel, *Joseph Hornecker, architecte à Nancy 1873–1942*, Nancy: Archives Modernes de l'Architecture Lorraine/Presses Universitaires de Nancy (1989).

27. Founded in 1878 by Adolphe Marlin and taken over by his brother-in-law Jules Viard, the Grand Bazar des Vosges in Epinal became Magasins Réunis in 1902.

28. Francis Roussel, *Nancy architecture 1900*, Metz: Editions Serpenoise (1993), vol. 1, p. 40.

29. 'The relations between the Nancy creators and the city show a real originality, which may explain the consistency and the relative longevity of the movement', Henri Claude, Preface to *Nancy 1900, rayonnement de l'art nouveau*, Thionville: G. Klopp (1989), p. 25.

30. Nicolas, 'Un grand magasin moderne', n.p.

31. Speech by Prouvé at the opening ceremony of the Corbin Bequest in 1936: *L'Est Républicain*, 16 March 1936.

32. Victor Prouvé put it this way,

> you love artists, you are allied with them. Having learned to know them, they interested you in their work, their research.

Becoming their confident, you know their torments, their joys and also their disillusionments and troubles. You knew how to stimulate their enthusiasm and strengthen their courage by making the road, which is often so hard, easier for them. You knew how to make them come to you. (*Le Pays Lorrain*, February 1936, p. 69)

33. F.T. Charpentier, 'Hommage à Jacqueline Corbin', *Bulletin de l'Association des Amis du Musée de l'Ecole de Nancy*, 1989, p. 13.
34. Competition for inexpensive furnishings, jewellery models, tapestries, table linens, needlework, etc.
35. Nicolas, in *L'Etoile de l'Est*, 2 January 1926.
36. André Thirion, *Revolutionnaires sans révolution*, Paris: R. Laffont (1973), p. 66.
37. Catherine Coley, 'L'effort moderne à Nancy dans les années vingt. Chronique du comité Nancy–Paris', *Le Pays Lorrain*, 1, 1986, p. 14.
38. 'Le Goût moderne', *Agenda des Magasins Réunis*, 1924.
39. Patrick Dieudonné, 'Pierre Le Bourgeois, de l'art nouveau à l'art déco', *Cahiers de la Recherche Architecturale*, 24/25, 1989, pp. 24–9.
40. Emile Badel, 'La reconstruction des Magasins Réunis', *L'Immeuble et la Construction dans l'Est*, 28 February 1926, p. 1.
41. Presented to the public provisionally during Corbin's lifetime, it was only at the end of the 1960s, and after a series of remarkable episodes, that this collection, along with other contributions from the family, would be brought together in a Musée de l'Ecole de Nancy in the former Corbin property in Nancy. On the other hand, nothing or almost nothing remains of the records of the powerful commercial group built by Antoine Corbin and his children, whose centennial also marked the beginning of its decline.

CHAPTER ELEVEN

From Messel to Mendelsohn: German department store architecture in defence of urban and economic change

Kathleen James

From their appearance at the end of the nineteenth century until the outbreak of the Second World War, German department stores were among the most successful in Europe, quickly seizing an impressive percentage of retail trade. They were also extremely controversial. Prominent evidence of the country's new consumer culture, they were castigated by conservative and often anti-Semitic opponents for decimating the country's legions of small shopkeepers. The architects of prominent department stores responded directly to these attacks. The linchpins of Germany's new city centres, preceding the emergence within these districts of purpose-built office blocks on the same scale, department store buildings were not shaped merely by function and construction. Instead two generations of influential German architects designed their most celebrated stores to defuse criticism of the new buildings by integrating art and commerce in ways that were not called for in countries like France and the USA, where the giant stores were less often attacked by politicians and cultural critics.

For a century after its emergence in the 1850s in Paris and New York, the department store was the building type which most completely embodied the fashionable urban face of the new industrial economy. Their architecture paired ornamental splendour with technical innovation. The enormous glazed openings of such celebrated turn-of-the century stores as Franz Jourdain's the Samaritaine in Paris (1891–1907), Victor Horta's Innovation in Brussels (1901), and Louis Sullivan's Carson, Pirie, Scott in Chicago (1899–1904) served not only as daring examples of metal and glass construction, but as richly embellished frames for carefully arranged displays of goods (Plate 11.1). In Germany however, Alfred Messel, the architect of the Wertheim Department Store on Berlin's Leipziger Straße (1896–1905), and Erich Mendelsohn, in his Schocken store in Stuttgart (1926–28),

Plate 11.1   Franz Jourdain, La Samaritaine department store, Paris, 1907.
(Alfred Wiener, *Das Warenhaus: Kauf-, Geschäfts-, Büro-Haus*,
Berlin: Ernst Wasmuth (1912), p. 195)

attempted to move beyond the mere goal of selling to impose order
upon the urban chaos spawned by modern retailing (Plates 11.2 and
11.3).[1]

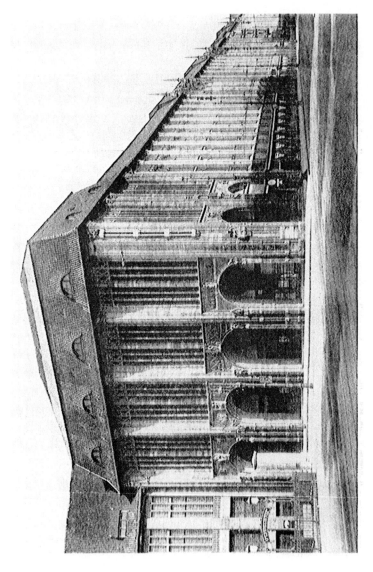

Plate 11.2 Alfred Messel, Wertheim department store, Berlin, Leipziger Platz, 1904–05 (left) and Leipziger Straße, 1896–97 (right) façades. (Walter Müller-Wulkow (ed.), *Deutsche Baukunst der Gegenwart*, 3, *Bauten der Arbeit und des Verkehrs*, Königstein im Taunus: Karl Robert Langewiesche Verlag (1929), p. 84)

Plate 11.3 Erich Mendelsohn, Schocken Department Store, Stuttgart, 1926–28. (*Erich Mendelsohn: Das Gesamtschaffen des Architekten*, Berlin: Rudolf Mosse Verlag (1930), p. 151)

For Messel and his generation, the main problem posed by Germany's rapid industrialisation and the urbanisation which accompanied it was the redevelopment of small-scale, mixed use urban centres triggered by the abandonment of small, family-owned shops and the guild-sponsored craftsmanship they fostered. In the Wertheim store, Messel crafted an image of cultural continuity that belied the role of department stores in these disruptions. Seeking to create a specifically German solution to what was perceived as one of the most frankly modern – and thus to many Germans dangerously international – of all turn-of-the-century building types, he neutralised the impermanence of fashion by establishing a 'timeless architecture' securely tied to the country's medieval cultural and commercial traditions. Shorn of most of the effusive ornament and advertising that Germans criticised in earlier department stores, and structured by the repetitive rhythm of stone-clad steel columns, the dignified Wertheim store was lauded by contemporaries as the harbinger of a new architecture which would integrate patriotic references with modern functions and building materials. At the same time the building's palatial interior encouraged the sense, crucial to the success of other early department stores, that consumption offered the bourgeois consumer the key to aristocratic splendours.

While the Wertheim store created a reassuring image of historical and social continuity, Mendelsohn in his Schocken store rejected patriotism and conventional luxury in favour of the industrial imagery favoured by the inter-war avant-garde. Turning away from history, he chose instead – in what was understood at the time as a highly democratic gesture – to expose the connection between the sites of mass production and consumption and equate the department store with the factory rather than the palace. Introducing the factory into the commercial core of Stuttgart was insufficient, however, to the challenge of luring shoppers into a building stripped of ornament. Displacing the drama of Messel's atria on to the exterior of his store, Mendelsohn unleashed dynamic curves and bold night lighting to draw attention to the mass-produced merchandise behind the vast shop windows. With historicism's illusion of social status rather than advertising now perceived as the major threat posed by consumerism, he embraced abstract art's new strategies for reaching a mass audience. In a final departure from Messel's emphasis upon stability, Mendelsohn embraced the automobile-charged pace of urban life, which he claimed as the inspiration for his floating cantilevers.

Although conditioned in part by the individual taste of their architects and the different character of the department store chains who employed them, many of the differences between the Wertheim and Schocken stores are mirrored in the writings of two generations of

German architectural critics, whose attitudes toward consumerism changed dramatically after the First World War. Right-wing criticism of department stores continued unabated into the 1920s and 1930s, becoming a prominent part of Nazi propaganda. During the same years, however, many younger intellectuals embraced mass culture's potential for sponsoring a genuinely popular art. For them Mendelsohn's fusion of abstraction and commerce was enormously exciting.

Although Mendelsohn's approach to department store architecture was in many ways a bold critique of the model established by Messel, in other ways the two architects were very much alike. Both excelled at taming urban building types (office and apartment buildings, as well as department stores) more typically associated with the most chaotic aspects of contemporary real estate speculation. Many of their patrons, including the Wertheim and Schocken families, were Jewish, as they were themselves. Each also managed to play down the aspects of commercialism that most distressed him and his contemporaries while satisfying his patron's need for environments suitable to selling. Finally, each set the tone for German commercial architecture of his day: Mendelsohnian stores were also built around the world during the 1930s.

The diffusion of department stores: economic success and cultural controversy

Because the new emporia first emerged in Paris and New York most historians of department stores and their architecture have focused on French and American examples.[2] In their accounts the building type is a locus of technical and stylistic innovation until only the first years of the century, its inevitable connections to fantasy and luxury hindering the interest of store builders in experimenting with more austere architectural forms. Stores built since the early years of the century have proven more important to social historians and geographers interested in understanding the expanding consumer culture and tracking the continued vitality or collapse (depending on the city) of specialised city-centre shopping districts than to historians of twentieth-century architecture.[3] Still more concerned with stylistic and political purity than those who in recent years have rewritten the story of nineteenth-century architecture, finding beneath a veneer of eclecticism important evidence of social, economic and urban change, these scholars have largely ignored the degree to which German commercial architecture differed between 1900 and 1930 from its more decorative counterparts elsewhere.

Germany industrialised later than Britain, France, or the USA, but between 1880 and the outbreak of the First World War, the economy of the newly unified nation grew at a furious pace, as did its cities. Nothing symbolised the impact of these changes upon consumers or city centres better than the new department stores. Whether branches of multi-city chains such as Karstadt, Tietz and Wertheim, or among the countless smaller businesses still limited to a single store, German department stores flourished, like their counterparts elsewhere, by offering shoppers lower prices on a wider selection of goods. Although the department store arrived in Germany a generation later than in France and the USA, by 1914 German store buildings were larger than their counterparts elsewhere and more likely to be organised into chains.[4]

The enormous success of German department stores was an important indicator of the economic integration spurred by the country's successful industrialisation. It also made the stores lightening rods for criticism of the new consumer culture. Political and economic as well as cultural, this opposition was often also inspired by religious prejudice.[5] By the end of the century department store owners in many parts of the country faced extra taxes designed to diminish their competitiveness vis-à-vis established shops.[6] That the owners of many department stores were Jewish contributed to right-wing demonisation of the new form of retailing. Criticism of department stores, however, also encompassed legitimate critiques of modernisation.

For many, the department store's role in the spatial transformation of the country's rapidly expanding cities was emblematic of the cultural cost of rapid economic transformation. In Germany changes in retailing rather than the emergence of office buildings sparked the initial redevelopment of commercial districts during the Wilhelmine period and dominated the debate over the appearance of the modern city. No longer could middle-class families afford to live literally above the store in centrally located high-rent districts as German merchants had done on and around market squares since the Middle Ages. Furthermore many almost exclusively residential areas like Berlin's Leipziger Straße were quickly converted to commercial uses. On Leipziger Straße houses that dated from only the early decades of the nineteenth century were by 1900 being converted into elegant shops or even torn down in bunches, to be supplanted by the new scale of the vast glass shopfront of Bruno Sehring's Tietz department store (1899–1900) as the street became the city's most elegant shopping district (Plate 11.4).[7]

Cultural critics from the left and the right condemned this commercialisation of public life, which threatened the social patterns and architectural heritage integral to definitions of Germany's fragile new nationhood. Sociologists like Georg Simmel portrayed the turn-of-the-century metropolis as a frenetic environment in which the nerves of inhabitants were overstimulated by the pace of traffic and the stress of

Plate 11.4   Bruno Sehring, Tietz department store, Berlin, 1899–1900. (Alfred Wiener, *Das Warenhaus: Kauf-, Geschäfts-, Büro-Haus*, Berlin: Ernst Wasmuth (1912), p. 185)

competition.[8] Simmel noted the dependence of modern urban life upon money and the clock, in place of what he saw as the more organic quality of pre-industrial communities. Department stores, environments in which impersonal cash transactions replaced the ties of friendship (and often credit) which had supposedly once linked customer to small town retailer, served as emblems of this transformation. Critics were also often troubled by the low quality of the goods for sale, as the craftsmanship for which the guilds of Nuremberg and Augsburg had once been famous was superseded by industrial production. The subject which attracted the most attention, however, in the pages of the country's many architectural journals was the artistic integration of architecture and advertising, especially but not exclusively in the design of shop windows and their displays.[9]

The German discomfort with department stores made art nouveau (*Jugendstil* in German) a much less appealing architectural style there than it was in Western Europe and the USA. The brief flowering of this style encompassed Frantz Jourdain's the Samaritaine, Victor Horta's Innovation, and Louis Sullivan's Carson, Pirie, Scott. Patently modern, these buildings married both technological and stylistic innovation. Iron and steel framing made possible almost unprecedented expanses of window fronts, while sinuous ornament constituted a radical break from nineteenth-century historicism. In Germany, this effort to reknit art and craft, industrial production and nature through the invention of a new decorative style made relatively few inroads into commercial architecture. Indeed the style's association with ephemeral fashion limited its appeal.[10] In the last years before the outbreak of the First World War, Germans sought to tame the most threatening visual manifestations of industrial capitalism through a very different kind of architecture, one in which much of the opulence of foreign department stores would be drastically curtailed.

The Wertheim store: balancing culture and consumerism

Department stores may have been a foreign import, but that did not prevent Messel from transforming his commission to design the Wertheim store into a vehicle for addressing German concerns about the impact upon the tenuous national culture of the country's new wealth. Built in stages, three of them the work of Messel, this was Germany's largest and most elegant department store, the flagship of the capital city's leading chain.[11] Although the differences between the first phase of the building and the nearby Tietz store were subtle, Messel's final block, which turned the corner from Leipziger Straße on to Leipziger Platz, lined with mansions and embassies, contained in the eyes of its contemporaries the key to a new architecture, one that was patriotic rather than international in outlook and distinguished as much by its historicism as its forthright expression of skeletal frame construction.

For Sehring, as for most architects of the commercial and civic buildings erected in Western Europe and America from the middle of the nineteenth century through the 1920s, there was little conflict between modern construction and lavish ornament. Art nouveau architects attempted to invent new ornamental forms more in keeping with new materials such as iron and glass, but did little to diminish the cacophony of decoration and advertising assaulting those who walked or rode through city streets. Already in his initial Leipziger Straße façade for the Wertheim store, Messel focused on rational organisation, downplaying decoration and advertising. In the Leipziger Platz addition, he overtly equated this understated simplicity with a specifically German past. Prohibited by the city's strict fire code from exposing the store's steel frame, this part of the building's rhythmic procession of stone-clad piers now explicitly recalled late medieval north German architecture, an association communicated through structure and massing more than ornamental detail. The result was a building that presented contemporary commerce as part of a long and distinguished national tradition and largely ignored the development of a new consumer culture dependent upon constant novelty.

The dignity Messel's sedate Leipziger Platz façade bestowed upon the nearly riotous burgeoning of Berlin's commercial district won him the almost unanimous admiration of his contemporaries.[12] Noting the absence of signs, banners, colour or illumination, Paul Göhre praised the understated way in which Messel addressed the advertising functions implicit within the building type, agreeing with Alfred Weiner that the entire addition served as an advertisement of the firm's good taste, rather than of specific merchandise.[13] Although the façade of the first Leipziger Straße stage of the building had been little more than a giant shop window regularly interrupted only by the structural grid of columns and floor slabs, on Leipziger Platz Messel tucked the show windows behind a generous arcade. Offering window-shoppers protection from the elements, from a distance this arcade further muted the building's commercial function.

Inside the story was slightly different. Here Messel retained the atria around which most French and American department store interiors were organised. Developed originally to provide adequate illumination to block-long enclosures and to announce to inexperienced customers the existence of multiple floors of goods, atria became a key component of seductive marketing strategies, their imposing scale bestowing upon

Plate 11.5   Messel, Wertheim department store, atrium, 1904–05. (Gustav Adolf
Platz, *Die Baukunst der Neuesten Zeit*, Berlin: Propyläen-Verlag
(1927), p. 232)

bourgeois shoppers a sense of vicarious aristocracy, especially when
descending their grand staircases. Messel did not challenge this arrangement but almost overwhelmed its purpose. In the larger of the two atria
which punctuated the Wertheim interior rich materials and bold technical effects were almost dwarfed by the spatial drama: barrel-vaulted
skylights and two precariously perched bridges eclipsed marble facing

and chains of electric lights, still a novelty (Plate 11.5). Almost lost amidst the magnificence of a space which awe-struck contemporaries equated with princely palaces was the mundane goal of selling.[14] Simultaneously Berlin's grandest publicly accessible space and Germany's largest display of merchandise, it transcended without precluding its obvious commercial purpose.

Messel's Leipziger Platz façade offered Berliners a patriotic stateliness that belied the building's commercial rather than civic purpose. Although more historicist than its art nouveau contemporaries, the Wertheim store's coherent relationship between form and construction, largely devoid of extraneous ornament, comprised an unusual and welcome departure from the language of turn-of-the-century consumerism. On the interior, however, the atrium added to the building in the same phase of construction as the Leipzigerplatz façade offered a lavishness unimaginable from without and ensured the store's reputation as the country's most luxurious emporium.

Democracy and mass culture

Critical praise in the architectural press offers only one measure of the Wertheim store's success. Until construction of new store buildings came to a halt with the outbreak of the First World War, the architect of almost every new department store in Germany owed Messel an obvious debt, while his rational historicism influenced the design of everything from office buildings and factories to garden suburbs. A decade later, however, when the construction of new store buildings finally resumed, Messel's patriotism had been discredited, if not with the public at large, then among a new generation of architects, many of whom had served at the front during the war. And with nationalism increasingly the exclusive property of the racist right, some store owners were ready to join the intellectuals, feminists and socialists who embraced a new image for modern consumerism, one which celebrated mass production rather than German cultural traditions.

During the Weimar Republic opposition to department stores was increasingly associated, not with thoughtful critics of unchecked urban growth, but with those, including the Nazis, who sought scapegoats for Germany's disastrous defeat.[15] Meanwhile, many intellectuals turned away from the assumptions that had shaped Messel's architectural reforms. Eager to invent a new architecture and urbanism appropriate to Germany's changed political circumstances, they equated mass culture and democracy. Urban sprawl still needed to be carefully controlled, but technology now appeared to offer an almost immaterial alternative to Messel's skilful appeals to history and social snobbery. For this generation the greatest problem posed by the consumer face of the mass production they lauded was its betrayal of its roots in the factory. Championing industry as a rational force with the potential to create a more equitable society free of the outmoded social constraints, including historicist ornament, that they associated with the Wilhelmine empire, they welcomed many of the developments that had made Messel and Simmel uncomfortable.[16] Nor were intellectuals alone in their support of a rationalised consumer culture. Home economics experts argued for the standardisation of household equipment, while Social Democrats numbered among the greatest enthusiasts for the American model of high wages and mass consumption.[17]

Although almost inseparable from the post-war vogue for American mass production, whose fans included businessmen as well as architects, important aspects of this approach had been anticipated in the last years before the war by one of Germany's most astute department store owners, Salman Schocken.[18] With his brother, Schocken had founded a chain which by the outbreak of the war numbered ten stores. While other pre-war chains competed to awe the consumer through imposing architecture and splendid displays of merchandise, Schocken focused on the efficient marketing of inexpensive staples. He was also a Zionist and an intellectual; after emigrating from Germany to first Jerusalem and then New York he founded the Schocken press and supported a number of prominent writers, including the poet Else Lasker-Schuler.

Already in the last years before the war Schocken had criticised the Wertheim store's luxurious architecture, which he felt betrayed the disciplined organisation that gave department stores their economic edge.[19] Although he advocated standardisation of manufactured products, Schocken never attempted, however, to impose a prototypical architectural solution on his store buildings. Instead he favoured designs which were carefully integrated into their specific urban settings. Unique designs also attracted more publicity.[20] In the seven new stores he built during the 1920s, three of them designed by Erich Mendelsohn, he sponsored the most compelling alternative to Messel's Wertheim prototype.[21]

The Schocken store in Stuttgart: advertising mass production

During the brief German building boom (which consisted largely of renovations and expansions of existing structures) between 1924 and 1929, Mendelsohn created a new department store architecture in a series of stores whose influence, unlike that of his predecessor, eventually stretched far beyond Germany's borders. In his first entirely new store, built for Schocken in Stuttgart, he confronted not the integration of the department store into pre-industrial culture but the invention of an appropriately technological and yet commercially effective version of this crucial building type. Accepting rather than disguising the place of advertising within urban life, he integrated industrial imagery with Utopian elements to enliven inexpensively his otherwise austere architecture. Substituting the factory for the palace, favouring horizontals over Messel's verticals, and shifting the store's show-stopping spatial exclamation point onto the street front, Mendelsohn explicitly offered a critique of the Wertheim store, proposing in its place a quite different vision of urban order.

Mendelsohn's generation of German architects were fascinated with American cities and factories.[22] Having toured the USA in 1924, he was aware, however, of the dichotomy between the architecture of American daylight factories, whose rational concrete frames he and his contemporaries greatly admired, and the city-centre commercial buildings whose lavish ornament, he believed, did not honestly reflect their modern scale and construction.[23] For Schocken Mendelsohn reworked influences from his recent trip to the USA and from innovative German industrial architecture (most notably Sullivan's Carson, Pirie, Scott store, Albert Kahn's automobile plants, and Gropius and Meyer's Werkbund Factory) to suit the store's prominent central site. This frank acceptance of industry in buildings located within blocks of the city's major civic structures rather than in outlying factory districts broke dramatically with Messel's genteel effort at recalling the traditional market square.

Like Messel, Mendelsohn remained attentive, however, to the intrusive scale of his new building. In Stuttgart he fused a bold new architectural vocabulary to plans and massing which respectfully clarified an urban order that had often been difficult to discern. Mendelsohn developed his designs in terms of mass seen in perspective, a method which stressed urban context over the details of interior arrangement. Schocken's site comprised an entire square block, and Mendelsohn adjusted each of the building's façades to the width and importance of the street it faced. In place of Messel's emphasis upon permanence, however, Mendelsohn substituted his excitement about the rapid pace of modern urban life. This in turn generated a series of design decisions which animated his stark industrial imagery.

Mendelsohn interpreted Messel's adaptation of the regular rhythms of Gothic piers as betraying the spirit of the age, which was instead the product of speeding traffic and the only slightly slower bustle of pedestrians. Inspired above all by the roar of traffic and what he saw as the dynamic qualities of steel and concrete frame construction, he tailored his sleek horizontally-oriented façades to participate in, rather than dam, the frenetic movement that surrounded them.[24] From almost the beginning of the design process he planned to juxtapose two towers situated on opposite ends of the main Eberhard Straße façade.[25] That each façade treatment wrapped around a corner further energised the final design. Apparently poised on the verge of kineticism, the building seemed almost alive, ready to step down into the rushing avenues it framed.

Inserting the image of the factory into central Stuttgart challenged the social pretensions of the Wertheim store and its successors and exposed the source of the goods for sale within. Industrial austerity was inadequate, however, to the task of attracting shoppers. Manipulating light and glass – the almost immaterial ingredients widely associated with the visions of Expressionist Utopias that had briefly flourished after the war – Mendelsohn created an architecture that advertised the Schocken chain's efficiency as well as the actual goods for sale.[26]

Mendelsohn's acceptance of Schocken's advertising needs was inseparable from his own interest in exploiting the dynamic possibilities of modern materials and effects. Skeletal frame construction, ample glazing and electric lighting enabled him to substitute spacious display windows and dramatic night lighting for the circumspect ornament of Messel's façades (Plate 11.6). Cantilevering his façades several metres forward of the last line of columns, for instance, he floated the upper storeys above an uninterrupted band of shop windows in which only a thin glass membrane separated pedestrians from the tempting displays. He also carefully calculated the balance between solid and void in the façades, ensuring that the store would be as compelling by night as during the day, with enormous illuminated letters providing a sober alternative to ornament.[27] The composition climaxed in the completely glazed corner tower, in which he relentlessly exposed the building's steel skeleton. Here Mendelsohn turned Messel's Wertheim model inside out, moving the technical prowess of its atria to the exterior where, he declared, 'out of the staircase tower [I made] a mountain of glass-rings, an advertisement which requires to be paid for only once and *works* for *always*.'[28]

Little of this drama penetrated the interior. Most shoppers used elevators rather than make the dizzying climb up the corner stair. The almost puritanical sales floors were embellished with little more than lettering spelling out Schocken's business principles (Plate 11.7). They were organised around an open light court, not a covered atrium. Here Mendelsohn placed a loading dock rather than a grand central stair. Nowhere did Mendelsohn or Schocken depart from their belief that, once inside, shoppers would be satisfied by the straightforward exhibition of inexpensive, well-made goods.

Plate 11.6   Schocken department store, night view. (*Erich Mendelsohn: Das Gesamtschaffen des Architekten*, Berlin: Rudolf Mosse Verlag (1930), p. 156)

Mendelsohn and Schocken were explicit about the functional and technical orientation of the New Building, the term Germans most often used to describe the industrially-oriented architecture of the 1920s. At the opening of an earlier Schocken store in Nuremberg, housed in a

Plate 11.7   Schocken department store, interior. (*Erich Mendelsohn: Das Gesamtschaffen des Architekten*, Berlin: Rudolf Mosse Verlag (1930), p. 165)

renovated factory, Mendelsohn defended his choice of architectural style with the argument that it fit the new spirit of the times, a spirit of 'Bare knees and short haircuts/Radio and film/Car and airplane/Banana wholesalers and combines that run department stores.' He justified its style in terms of the design of the goods it sold. 'Do you want to be deceived by the things that surround you, by your house, the shops you buy from?' he asked. 'Are they, then, things that do not belong to you, your electric cooker, your safety razor – so functional, so simple and so natural?'[29] At dedication ceremonies held two years later in Stuttgart, Schocken explained his adherence to the tenants of the New Building. 'Architecture is a purely economic affair,' he explained, in which 'all technical perfections are exploited; examination of the beauty of the whole results technically from the new means [of production].'[30]

Mendelsohn and Schocken's enthusiasm for advertising and technology coincided with their rejection of the bourgeois nationalism embodied by Messel's store. Zionists at a time of revived prejudice, they did not share in an earlier generation's patriotism or its imitation of aristocratic taste.[31] Instead they tended to ally themselves with the working class with whose internationally-oriented socialism they sympathised, although neither man ever actually joined or perhaps even voted for the Social Democratic Party. After the opening in 1929 of the Schocken store in Waldenburg (not designed by Mendelsohn) the local socialist newspaper credited it with increasing the purchasing power of the town's workers.[32] Two months after the Stuttgart store's opening its architect commented on the relationship between architectural change and its social and political equivalents in a response to a questionnaire from the *Frankfurter Zeitung*, 'There is just as logical a connection between clinging to traditional forms and looking backwards politically as between supporting the new architectural purpose of our age and its revolutionary political ideas.'[33]

Although the New Building is often assumed to have been, like Messel's earlier stores, a bulwark against the whims of fashion, for many the problem was not fashion or advertising, but the need to integrate both into an abstract industrial aesthetic.[34] Mendelsohn's dynamic functionalism created an up-to-date image for the post-war department store and corresponded with the belief – shared during the Weimar Republic by artists, architects and businessmen – that the best advertisement was a straightforward, but lively, display of available goods, tinted with the implication that they were the products of modern, technological production, and aimed at the masses to whom their widespread availability would bring a higher standard of living.[35] Advocates of the New Building such as Adolf Behne, Hugo Häring, Ludwig Hilberseimer and Ernst May, attempted to make the commercialisation of new aspects of daily life palatable through integrating advertising, structure and industrial imagery, a combination which, they believed, would sell goods more effectively than 'badly' designed (ornamental or psychologically-driven) advertisements, while making an invaluable contribution to visual culture.[36] Adolf Behne, for instance, once defended the different forms of advertising adorning Berlin's stores and cinemas as the city's least expensive and most beautiful art exhibition.[37]

The New Building was an important expression of the shift away from the climate of pre-war architectural reform, grounded above all in questions of national identity, to the identification Mendelsohn's generation gained after the war with an international community.[38] Mendelsohn, like his colleagues, cultivated ties with architects abroad, especially in France, The Netherlands and the Soviet Union. This attitude encouraged the dissemination of their architecture, even to countries which had opposed Germany in the recent war. Thus whereas the considerable influence of the Wertheim store had been almost entirely limited to Germany, Mendelsohn's commercial architecture quickly set the tone of store architecture across Europe and even influenced the direction of the modern movement in the USA.[39]

During the 1930s Americans, Britons and Swedes embraced the New Building, which offered businesses threatened by the Depression a less expensive and more democratic modernism than the discrete ornamentalism of art deco. In an interview given in 1990, William Crabtree, the architect of the Peter Jones store (1935–39), London's first department store designed in the German manner, acknowledged his admiration for Mendelsohn. Crabtree had travelled to Berlin and Breslau (but not apparently Stuttgart). He declared, '[Mendelsohn's] later work I thought was excellent. And his latest building in Berlin, Columbus House, was really outstanding. [Mendelsohn's architecture] had a delicacy and a general pattern. He always had a big idea, he was a strong architect'.[40]

Aftermath

Neglected in accounts of the department store which focus on its birth rather than later development, two generations of twentieth-century German department stores designed by Alfred Messel and Erich Mendelsohn and their many imitators indicate the continued importance of the building type as the locus of innovative architecture. While French and American stores are most interesting as the fulfilment of complex marketing requirements balancing efficient organisation with enticingly palatial surroundings, their German counterparts effectively responded to, indeed encompassed aspects of, contemporary critiques of precisely these aspects of the giant stores. Messel compensated for what many German critics understood to be the overly mechanistic and ephemeral nature of modern economic life by investing the steel-framed Wertheim store with monumentalised references to the tradition of grand merchant houses circling the market square that it superseded. A generation later Mendelsohn embraced technological imagery as part of his generation's rejection of the class-based fantasies which continued to be an essential component of the marketing strategies of store owners in most of the rest of Europe and in the USA, instead choosing to expose, even to exploit, the connection between the places in which mass-produced goods were produced and sold.

Messel and Mendelsohn's departments stores need to be more thoroughly integrated into the history of modern architecture. Accounts of modern architecture that marginalise the degree to which early twentieth-century commercial architecture both served and offered a critique of consumer culture conceal the realities of the modern movement in several important ways. Firstly, since neither the Bauhaus nor most German factories needed to be sited with the same sensitivity, privileging the image of production over the realities of consumption favours an understanding of buildings as abstract objects, rather than rooted in complex urban contexts. Secondly, it ignores the degree to which few buildings exist as diagrams of architectural theories conceived independently of function. The design of the Wertheim and Schocken stores cannot be detached from their purpose as department stores. Rather than distorting some abstract notion of stylistic purity, Messel and Mendelsohn's understanding of their patron's needs was integral to their architectural solutions. These Wertheim and Schocken stores testify to the existence of an often complicated terrain situated between the intellectual heights of cultural criticism and the often mundane specifics of individual building types. The original goals of the modern movement were not betrayed as it spread from origins in factory design and social housing to encompass the realities of commercial commissions for department stores and cinemas. Instead these two store buildings remind us that many of the movement's pioneering monuments dealt directly with the place of consumerism in the modern city.

In the Wertheim store on Berlin's Leipziger Straße and the Schocken store in Stuttgart, Messel and Mendelsohn adroitly balanced the competing interests of merchants and their critics, creating buildings that muted as well as served the intrusiveness of modern commercialism. The fissures which modernisation opened up within German society could not be healed, however, through architecture. Following Hitler's seizure of power in 1933, those department stores owned by Jews became major Nazi targets, even as retail sales soared after the country's depression-ravaged economy was primed by rearmament.[41] Badly damaged by aerial bombardment, the wreckage of the Wertheim store was pulled down by the East Germans following the eruption of an anti-Communist uprising in 1953. Located just to the east of the path of the infamous Wall, the long abandoned site is finally being rebuilt.[42] The Schocken store survived the Second World War almost intact only to be demolished in 1960, despite international protests, as part of a street-widening scheme.[43]

Architecture cannot solve the dilemmas which shape the designs of its most thoughtful practitioners, but it continues to be an important arena for confrontations over modern commercial culture. Ironically, the reconstruction of Leipziger Platz, the adjacent Potsdamer Platz, and nearby Friedrich Straße has been dogged by updated versions of familiar controversies. Opposition to the Berlin Senate's sale almost immediately after reunification of prominent sites to multinational corporations and developers focused upon whether the city should suddenly rival Frankfurt, London and Paris as a financial centre and, if it should, whether the precedents established by Messel or Mendelsohn's rebellion against them should guide development. The threat of a unifying and rather faceless global capitalism replacing the city's post-war tradition of showcase architecture coupled with the one time paucity of development pressures that had preserved much of its modest pre-war scale was quite real, but many found the specific character of the reaction against this real estate boom equally troubling. While locals often advocated a higher proportion of housing to maintain the neighbourhood's mixed use character, many architects were appalled to watch city building authorities redefine Berlin's architectural tradition to exclude many of the innovations pioneered in Germany during the 1920s, the only other period when the eastern sector of the city had experienced democracy.[44]

Two architects dominated the debate. Hans Stimmann, the city's building director from 1991 until January 1996, advocated a Prussian regionalism in which Messel figures as an important exemplar. Daniel Libeskind, who in 1989 won the competition to design a Jewish Museum extension to the Berlin Museum, instead offered Mendelsohn as the point of departure for an architectural vocabulary complex enough to acknowledge democracy's inherent tolerance of competing voices. The disagreement focused upon the appropriate imagery and symbolism for the capital of a reunited Germany, and the degree of variety and individuality versus apparent continuity and order that should be present in the contemporary city. On the one hand, this was a conflict between postmodern historicists and those who supported a revival of the high-technology designs first pioneered during the 1920s. On the other, it was a battle over which image of the German past deserved to be revived, the prosperous but undemocratic Wilhelmine empire, or the economically and politically fragile yet democratic Weimar Republic. For Stimmann, 'Critical Reconstruction' along regionalist lines represented an intelligent, orderly, attempt to address the completely unproblematic reintegration of commerce and the new national government into a desolate and disturbing reminder of Germany's horrific past. Libeskind on the other hand defended height and transparency as among the Weimar Republic's most important contributions to twentieth-century architecture, symbols of urban and democratic vitality that should be cherished and revived.

And once again a bold new department store, one which redefines the type, has risen in response to a larger debate over the role consumer culture should play in the central city. Designed by the French architect Jean Nouvel, the Berlin outpost of the Paris-based Galeries Lafayette opened in 1996 on Friedrichstraße, just a short distance from the Potsdamer Platz site for which in 1928 Mendelsohn designed a never realised store for the same chain (Plate 11.8).[45] In one the last designs to be accepted before Stimmann gained almost total control of the

Plate 11.8 Jean Nouvel, Galeries Lafayette, Berlin, 1992–96. (John Maciuika)

approval process, Nouvel, without in any way acknowledging the complicated past emphasized by Libeskind, affiliated himself with Mendelsohn's penchant for dynamic curves, bold glazing and jazzy electronic signage, rejecting the windowless box characteristic of department stores for half a century in favour of a more active engagement with the street.

Notes

1. I would like to acknowledge the impact upon my thinking about the Wertheim store of an unpublished paper by my former student Kai Gutschow.

2. Meredith Clausen, *Frantz Jourdain and the Samaritaine: Art Nouveau Theory and Criticism*, Leiden: E. J. Brill (1987); William Leach, *Land of Desire: Merchants, Power and the Rise of a New American Culture*, New York: Pantheon (1993); Michael B. Miller, *The Bon Marché: Bourgeois Culture and the Department Store, 1869–1920*, Princeton: Princeton University Press (1981); Joseph Siry, *Carson, Pirie Scott, Louis Sullivan and the Chicago Department Store*, Chicago: University of Chicago Press (1988); and Rosalind Williams, *Dream Worlds: Mass Consumption in Late Nineteenth-Century France*, Berkeley: University of California Press (1982).

3. Susan Porter Benson, *Counter Cultures: Saleswomen, Managers, and Customers in American Department Stores, 1890–1940*, Urbana: University of Illinois (1986), and Neil Harris, 'The City that Shops', in John Zukowsky (ed.), *Chicago Architecture and Design, 1923–1993: Reconfiguration of an American Metropolis*, Munich: Prestel (1993), pp. 179–200.

4. Siegfried Gerlach, *Das Warenhaus in Deutschland: Seine Entwicklung bis zum Ersten Weltkrieg in Historischer-Geographischer Sicht*, Stuttgart: Franz Steiner Verlag (1988), pp. 38–64.

5. Margarete Böhme, *The Department Store: a Novel of Today*, trans. Ethel Coburn Mayne, New York: Appleton (1912), repeats many of the standard criticisms.

6. Gerlach, *Warenhaus*, pp. 48–9, and Peter Stürzebecher, *Das Berliner Warenhaus: Bautypus, Element der Stadtorganisation, Raumsphäre der Warenwelt*, Berlin: Archibook (1979), pp. 22–3.

7. Gerlach, *Warenhaus*, pp. 65–96.

8. Georg Simmel, 'The metropolis and modern life', in Richard Sennett (ed.), *Classic Essays on the Culture of Cities*, New York: Appleton-Century-Croft (1966), pp. 47–60.

9. Franz Behring, 'Moderne Schaufensterauslagen', *Baumeister*, 4, 1905, p. 91; Cüddow, 'Architektur und Reklame', *Bauwelt*, 1.76, 1910, pp. 5–7; Hans Haupmann, 'Das Haus als Reklame', *Bauwelt*, 3.2, 1912, pp. 35–6; Leo Nachtlicht, 'Das Schaufenster', *Bauwelt*, 1.11, 1910, pp. 1–2; Karl-Ernst Osthaus, 'Das Schaufenster', *Jahrbuch des Deutschen Werkbundes*, 1913, pp. 59–69; Hans Schliepmann, 'Das Geschäftshaus als Architekturproblem', *Bauwelt*, 3.12, 1912, pp. 10–12; and Ernst Schur, 'Das Schaufenster', *Bauwelt*, 1.51, 1910, pp. 3–4.

10. Jost Hermand, 'The commercialization of the avant-garde', *New German Critique*, 29, 1983, pp. 71–83.

11. Messel's original block dates to 1896–97, the additions along Leipziger-
     and Voßstrasse to 1899–1900, and the Leipzigerplatz extension to 1904–
     06. The final phase was built on Leipzigerplatz during the Weimar Republic
     by Ludwig Hoffmann. See Julius Posener, *Berlin auf dem Wege zu einer
     neuen Architektur, Das Zeitalter Wilhelms II*, München: Prestel (1979),
     pp. 353–85, 475–81; Stürzebecher, *Das Berliner Warenhaus*, pp. 27–31;
     and Klaus Konrad Weber and Peter Gürttler, 'Die Architektur der
     Warenhäuser', in Architekten- und Ingenieur-Verein zu Berlin (ed.), *Berlin
     und seine Bauten. Teil VIII. Bauten für Handel and Gewerbe. Band A.
     Handel*, Berlin: Ernst (1978), pp. 28–39.
12. Walter Curt Behrendt, *Alfred Messel*, Berlin: Bruno Cassirer (1911),
     pp. 62–87; Paul Göhre, *Das Warenhaus*, Frankfurt am Main: Rütten and
     Loening (1907), pp. 7–35; Karl Scheffler, 'Alfred Messel', *Moderne
     Bauformen*, 4, 1906, pp. 38–40; Alfred Wiener, *Das Warenhaus: Kauf-,
     Geschäft-, Büro-Haus*, Berlin: Ernst Wasmuth (1912), pp. 174–82; and
     Alfred Wiener, 'Das Warenhaus', *Jahrbuch des Deutschen Werkbundes*,
     1913, pp. 49–50.
13. Göhre, *Warenhaus*, p. 7, and Weiner, 'Warenhaus', p. 45.
14. Göhre, *Warenhaus*, p. 21, and Behrendt, *Messel*, p. 86.
15. Hans Bucher, *Warenhauspolitik und Nationalsozialismus*, Munich: F. Eher
     (1931); Klaus Strohmeyer, *Warenhäuser, Geschichte, Blüte und Untergang
     im Warenmeer*, Berlin: Wagenbach (1980), pp. 151–8; and Stürzebecher,
     Das Berliner Warenhaus, pp. 43–4.
16. Miles David Samson, 'German-American dialogues and the Modern Move-
     ment before the "Design Migration", 1910–1933', dissertation, Harvard
     University, 1988, pp. 93–155.
17. Mary Nolan, *Visions of Modernity: American Business and the Moderni-
     zation of Germany*, New York: Oxford University Press (1994), pp. 118–20,
     214.
18. Evidence of German interest in American department stores, which en-
     compassed business practices and advertising, but not architecture, includes
     the translation into German of Paul Mazur, *Principles of Organization
     Applied to Modern Retailing*, New York: Harper (1927), published as
     Moderne Warenhaus-Organisation, Berlin (1928). H.G. Reissner, 'The
     Histories of "Kaufhaus N. Israel" and of Wilfried Israel', *Leo Baeck
     Institute Yearbook*, 3, 1958, p. 241, documents one of the many study
     trips made by members of German department store families to the USA.
19. Siegfried Moses, 'Salman Schocken: his economic and Zionist activities',
     Leo Baeck Institute Yearbook, 5, 1960, pp. 73–104, and Konrad Fuchs,
     *Ein Konzern aus Sachsen: Das Kaufhaus Schocken als Spiegelbild deutscher
     Wirtschaft und Politik, 1900 bis 1953*, Stuttgart: Deutsche Verlags-Anstalt
     (1992). See also Stephen M. Poppel, 'Salman Schocken and the Schocken
     Verlag', *Leo Baeck Institute Yearbook*, 17, 1972, pp. 93–113, and Else
     Lasker Schüler, '*Was soll ich hier tun?*': *Exilbriefe an Salman Schocken:
     dokumentarische Erstausgabe mit vier Briefen Schockens im Anhang*,
     Heidelberg: Schneider (1986). For his familiarity with advanced architec-
     tural theory see Salman Schocken, 'Zeitlupe', *Das Kunstblatt*, 14, 1930,
     p. 219, which cites his reading of Adolf Loos. His writings about the
     department store business include *Die Entwicklung der Warenhäuser in
     Deutschland*, Leipzig: C.E. Poeschel (n.d.), which includes his critique of
     the Messel model; 'Warenhausbauten', *Der Kaufmann und das Leben*,

1913, pp. 1–6, 33–9; and 'Zwischen Produktion und Konsum', in *Vier Vorträge über den gegenwärtigen Stand und die Aufgaben des Grosseinhandels: Gehalten anlässlich der 29. General-Versammlung des Verbandes Deutscher Waren- und Kaufhausen E.V.*, Berlin: L. Borchardt (1931).

20. Such as Karl Konrad Düssel, 'Drei Kaufhäuser Schocken in Nürnberg, Stuttgart und Chemnitz von Erich Mendelsohn', *Moderne Bauformen*, 11, 1930, pp. 480–82.

21. For Mendelsohn's other stores, including the renovation of a Nuremburg factory for Schocken (1925–26) and the entirely new Schocken Store in Chemnitz (1928–30), see Kathleen James, *Erich Mendelsohn and the Architecture of German Modernism*, Cambridge: Cambridge University Press (1997), and Regina Stephan, *Studien zu Waren- und Geschäftshäusern Erich Mendelsohns in Deutschland*, München: Tudev (1992).

22. Reyner Banham, *A Concrete Atlantis: U. S. Industrial Building and European Modern Architecture*, Cambridge: MIT Press, (1986); Jean-Louis Cohen, *Scenes of the World to Come: European Architecture and the American Challenge, 1893–1960*, Montreal: Flammarion (1996), pp. 63–84; and Winfried Nerdinger, *Walter Gropius*, Berlin: Gebr. Mann Verlag (1985), pp. 9–28.

23. *Erich Mendelsohn's 'Amerika'*, New York: Dover (1993), a translation of Erich Mendelsohn, *Amerika: Bilderbuch eines Architekten*, Berlin: Rudolf Mosse (1926), and Erich Mendelsohn, 'Der moderne Industriebau auf dem Kontinent', *Europäische Revue*, 5, 1929, pp. 473–9.

24. Erich Mendelsohn, 'The international consensus of the new architectural concept, or dynamics and function', *Erich Mendelsohn: the Complete Works*, Antje Frisch (trans.), New York: Princeton Architectural Press (1992), pp. 22–34 and Erich Mendelsohn, 'Das neuzeitliche Geschäftshaus', an undated manuscript in the Mendelsohn Archive, Kunstbibliothek, Staatliche Museen Preußischer Kulturbesitz, Berlin, quoted in Stephan, *Studien*, pp. 199–201.

25. Bruno Zevi, *Erich Mendelsohn, Opera Completa*, Milano: ETAS Kompass (1970), pp. 142–5.

26. Iain Boyd Whyte (ed.), *The Crystal Chain Letters: Architectural Fantasies by Bruno Taut and his Circle*, Cambridge: MIT Press (1985).

27. Ernst Reinhardt, 'Gestaltung der Lichtreklame', *Die Form*, 4, 1929, p. 74, and Wilhelm Schnarrenberger, 'Reklamearchitektur bildend', *Die Form*, 3, 1928, pp. 268–72, advocated such substitutions of lettering and signage for ornament.

28. Erich Mendelsohn, 'Own Work', unpublished typescript in the Mendelsohn Archive, p. 7.

29. Erich Mendelsohn, speech delivered at the opening of the Nuremberg Schocken store, 11 October 1926, *Erich Mendelsohn: Letters of an Architect*, Oskar Beyer (ed.), Geoffrey Strachem (trans.), London: Abelard-Schuman (1967), pp. 93–4.

30. Schocken, 4 October 1928 speech, typescript, Salman Schocken archive, Schocken Institute for Jewish Research of the Jewish Theological Seminary of America, Jerusalem, pp. 2, 7.

31. For their Zionism see Moses, 'Schocken', and Kurt Blumenfeld, *Im Kampf um den Zionismus, Briefe aus fünf Jarhzehnten*, Miriam Sambursky and Jochanan Ginat (eds), Stuttgart: Deutsche (1976), p. 86.

32. Moses, 'Schocken', p. 79.
33. Erich Mendelsohn, response to a questionnaire in the *Frankfurter Zeitung*, December 1928, *Mendelsohn: Letters*, p. 102.
34. Mary McLeod, 'Undressing architecture: fashion, gender, and modernity', in Deborah Fausch, Paulette Singley, Rodolphe El-Khoury and Zvi Efrat (eds.), *Architecture: in Fashion*, New York: Princeton Architectural Press (1994), pp. 38–123; and Mark Wigley, *White Walls, Designer Dresses: The Fashioning of Modern Architecture*, Cambridge: MIT Press (1995).
35. 'Werbedrucksache', *Die Form*, 3, 1928, pp. 372–3, which praises the advertising campaign that accompanied the opening of the Stuttgart store; Maud Lavin, 'Advertising Utopia: Schwitters as commercial designer', *Art in America*, 73.10, 1985, pp. 134–9; and Maud Lavin, 'Photomontage, mass culture, and modernity: utopianism in the circle of new advertising designers', in Matthew Teitelbaum (ed.), *Montage and Modern Life 1919–1942*, Cambridge: MIT Press (1992), pp. 36–59.
36. Adolf Behne, 'Kultur, Kunst und Reklame', in Heinz Hirdina (ed.), *Neues Bauen, neues Gestalten: Das neue Frankfurt; Die neue Stadt: eine Zeitschrift zwischen 1926 und 1933*, Dresden : VEB Verlag der Kunste (1984), pp. 229–32; Adolf Behne, 'Kunstausstellung Berlin', *Das neue Berlin*, 1, 1929, pp. 150–52; Walter Dexel, 'Reklame in Stadtbild', *Das Neue Frankfurt*, 1, 1926, pp. 45–9; Hugo Häring, 'Probleme um der Lichtreklame', *Bauhaus: Zeitschrift für Gestaltung*, 2, 1928, p. 7; Ludwig Hilberseimer, 'Die neue Geschäftstraße', H. Hirdina (ed.), *Neues Bauen, neues Gestalten: Das neue Frankfurt: Die neue Stadt: eine Zeitschrift zurischen 1926 und 1933*, Dresden: VEB Verlag der Kunste (1984), pp. 235–40; and Ernst May, 'Städtebau und Lichtreklame', in Wilhelm Lotz (ed.), *Licht und Beleuchtung*, Berlin: Reckendorf (1928), p. 45, republished in translation as 'Town planning and illuminated advertisements', in Tim Benton and Charlotte Benton (eds) with Dennis Sharp, *Form and Function: a Source Book for the History of Architecture and Design 1890–1939*, London: Crosby Lockwood Staples (1975), pp. 238–40.
37. Behne, 'Kunstausstellung Berlin', 150–52.
38. As demonstrated by Walter Gropius, *Internationale Architektur*, Munich: Albert Lagen Verlag (1925).
39. For Mendelsohn's influence, for instance, upon Howe and Lescaze's PSFS tower in Philadelphia, America's first International Style-style skyscraper see William Jordy, *The Impact of European Modernism in the Mid-Twentieth Century*, vol. 4 of *American Buildings and Their Architects*, Garden City: Doubleday (1976), pp. 140–43, 434, and Lorraine Welling Lanman, *William Lescaze, Architect*, Philadelphia: Art Alliance Press (1987), pp. 55–6.
40. William Crabtree to Edwin Johnston, 'Sloan Leader', *Architectural Review*, 187.1, 1990, p. 79.
41. Fuchs, *Konzern*, 189–257, outlines Nazi opposition to the Schocken chain.
42. Horst Mauter, Lázló F. Földényi, Ulrich Pfeiffer and Alfred Kernd'l, *Der Potsdamer Platz: Eine Geschichte in Wort und Bild*, Berlin: Nischen (1991), pp. 103–4.
43. 'Modern Monument Destroyed', *Architectural Review*, 129, 1961, pp. 293–4. See also Ignaz F. Hollay, 'Schocken ... Merkur ... Horten: die 60 Jahre eines Stuttgarter Kaufhauses', *Deutsche Bauzeitung*, 122.9, 1988, pp. 102–12, and Stephan, *Studien*, pp. 235–47.

44. Alan Balfour (ed.), *World Cities: Berlin*, London: Academy Editions (1995); Annegret Berg (ed.), *Berlin-Mitte*, Berlin: Birkhauser Verlag (1995); and Don Cruikshank, 'Cross roads Berlin' and 'Friedrichstrasse', *Architectural Review*, **192.1**, 1993, pp. 20–29 offer an introduction to this acrimonious debate.

45. Berg, *Berlin-Mitte*, pp. 106–11, and Don Cruikshank, 'Nouvel', *Architectural Review*, **192.1**, 1993, pp. 30–31.

CHAPTER TWELVE

Training sales personnel
in France between the wars*

Marie-Emmanuelle Chessel

The inter-war period was a fruitful time for the development of rational
methods of production, sales and advertising.[1] Teaching courses, as well
as specialised journals, manuals and associations, facilitated the spread
of these new methods. The leading French business schools, as is well
known, concentrated on management techniques and organising teams
of sales representatives, but it is not so clear what sort of instruction
was given to retail staff. An important question remains unanswered:
were salesmen and women specially trained? If they were, we must ask
in which institutions and when this started to take place, as well as
what one needed to know to be a good salesperson.

This investigation fits in with the recent renewal of interest in general
technical instruction and more particularly in commercial training. Business and management historians have sought to understand the role
played by engineers' training in the spread of techniques and the rationalisation of industry. As a result, studies have tended to focus on the
main engineering colleges, such as the *École centrale*, while the trades
colleges (*Écoles d'arts et metiers*) and business schools have been com-
paratively neglected. More recently, re-evaluations of the role of the
market and of marketing methods have encouraged historians to take
more interest in commercial education. Yet here, too, most attention
has been paid to the training of executives and entrepreneurs in the
leading (all-male) business schools.[2]

Investigating the instruction given to sales personnel allows us to
analyse the transmission of sales methods between different countries as
well as between executives and their employees, and also the application of these techniques.[3] Privately organised training courses abounded
in inter-war France; the private nature of these courses and their great
number, together with the scarcity of surviving documentation, create
difficulties for anyone studying this subject.[4] As far as sales instruction
in Parisian department stores is concerned, neither Printemps nor the
Galeries Lafayette, nor for that matter, the department stores' own

---

*   Translated by Patricia Allerston.

study group, the *Groupement d'étude des grands magasins*, have kept many records. A number of unpublished sources, such as the archives of the Paris Chamber of Commerce (CCP) and eyewitness accounts do, however, allow us to explore this subject.

Specialised training for sales personnel was developed by a number of institutions in the 1920s. This prompts intriguing questions about the kind of staff training given by department stores: did the stores team up with business schools in the inter-war period or did they refuse to deal with them? If they did not engage with the schools, their limited involvement needs to be explained.

The emergence of specialised sales training

New schools for sales personnel developed during the inter-war period within the general sphere of technical and commercial education which had, since the nineteenth century, involved many different types of institutions located mainly in the private sector. Technical education was offered on three different levels: the upper level was dominated by the engineering colleges; schools on the second level catered for trainee foremen and 'middle management' (the *Écoles d'art et métiers*); and lower-level institutions provided training for manual workers (the *Écoles pratiques de commerce et d'industrie* and the *Écoles nationales professionnelles*).[5] Commercial education in France, which also developed privately but was subject to increasing state involvement, was similarly organised. It was divided among higher-level business schools catering for advanced and intermediate students; sales schools and practical business colleges training sales personnel; as well as specialised apprenticeships and in-house training, offered, for example, by department stores. Commercial education in France took longer than other forms of training to identify its market: it catered for future employees as well as future bosses. The Paris Chamber of Commerce resolved this ambiguity by creating different types of institutions, ranging from training schools for apprentices to the *Centre de préparation aux affaires* (CPA) destined for future chief executives. The distinction was not so clear at the *École supérieure de commerce* in Lyon (ESCL) which trained employees and managers on the same premises.[6]

Chambers of commerce were the principal founders of business schools[7] and it was some of these institutions which trained sales personnel.[8] For example, from 1860 onwards the Paris Chamber of Commerce became involved in training employees for banks, business and industry. It created its first business school for men in 1863,[9] set up night classes in 1873, and it also founded a business school for young women in 1916. To ensure that the latter institution enjoyed 'a good reputation from the start', it was intended solely for young women from respectable backgrounds, that is to say from the families of shop-keepers, industrialists and local civil servants.[10] In 1917 this school accepted 160 students, between 12 and 15 years of age. Its curriculum included courses on moral conduct, household management, hygiene and childcare which were evidently designed to prepare the students for their future family role.

Two trends favoured the development of specialised sales training in the 1920s. First, the State had been seeking to regulate private training institutions since the start of the century. It did not try to replace the assortment of individuals, commercial organisations and local authori-ties involved in this field. However, starting with the Astier Law of 1919, the Minister of Trade took overall control of what was then known as technical and business training, directed at engineers, factory bosses, foremen, travelling sales representatives, traders and business employees (training of professionals came under another government department). This law had a catalytic effect on technical education, launching obligatory training courses for apprentices, as well as op-tional courses for other types of employees. A finance law of 1925 extended the State's role by introducing an apprenticeship tax. The Under-Secretary for Technical Education introduced a number of addi-tional measures. He helped to create training programmes and promoted the first sales courses offered in state-run schools (the *Écoles pratiques de commerce et d'industrie*). He also standardised qualifications within the field, creating, by a decree of 23 March 1928, general vocational certificates – the *Brevets Professionnels*. The Under-Secretary also for-mally endorsed a number of colleges, allowing him an even greater measure of control.[11]

After the Astier Law, the Paris Chamber of Commerce set up voca-tional courses and training schools with the aim of creating, as they put it, 'a qualified workforce, required by industry and trade in the Paris area'.[12] Pupil numbers in these institutions increased from 318 students in 1922 to 760 in 1924 and from 1 826 in 1927 to 2 000 in 1932. By 1935 they had reached 2 445, and in 1938, 2 961. The majority of boys learnt trades such as metalworking, woodworking and food provisioning, whereas girls learnt 'feminine' trades such as dressmaking, hairdressing and ironing. One training school, which specialised in stationary, pack-aging, bookbinding, gilding, leatherwork, fancy coverings and travel items, accepted boys and girls alike.[13]

In addition to growing state involvement, sales training was increas-ingly distinguished from other forms of commercial education.[14] 'Active sales', the direct act of selling, broke away from 'passive sales', support services such as bookkeeping, secretarial activities and other types of office work. International conferences of technical and commercial education promoted this development: office workers were specially trained and it was considered right that sales personnel – window-dressers, shop assistants, travelling sales representatives and delivery men – should follow.[15] Specialised training for sales staff developed later than training for clerical employees, because of the distinctive nature of sales techniques. The 'gift' or the natural ability to sell is often cited in contemporary sources and it was hard to simulate real conditions in training sessions.[16]

In this context of increasing state involvement and the differentiation of sales training, the Paris Chamber of Commerce founded, in 1924, the first training school for shop assistants and other retail personnel.[17] In 1925, it established a college (*École technique de vente*) for top sales assistants and teachers of sales techniques. The Paris Chamber of Commerce also joined forces with federations of traders and the city council: when the first sales school was set up, a vocational college for sales staff, financed by employers' federations from the clothing trades, the Paris Chamber of Commerce, the city authorities, and the Under-Secretary of State for Technical Education, was established on the same premises.

Similar vocational courses were offered in other cities, such as Toulouse, where, in 1928, the employers' federation of clothiers, together with the local chamber of commerce, set up a sales school.[18] In other places, initiatives were taken by existing institutions. When a new department store opened in Lille, the local business school was asked to supply young, female sales assistants; being unable to meet this request, the school organised its own sales courses.[19]

Struck by the great variety of private initiatives, the General Inspectorate of Technical Education, encouraged by its current head, Émile Paris[20] (former principal of the *École supérieure pratique de commerce et d'industrie* in Paris), also became involved in sales training. The *Écoles pratiques de commerce et d'industrie* (EPCI) were state-run trades schools which were originally set up to train skilled manual workers and had increasingly centred on bank employees and office workers, as well as sales staff and commercial travellers. Administered by the Director-General of Technical Education, they were organised on a regional level and were tailored to suit the needs of the local economy. Thus, at Grenoble, the Vaucanson college specialised in training glove-makers for the local industry.[21] From 1922 onwards, the EPCI curricula were revised and sales courses were introduced throughout France.[22] It was, then, in the 1920s, a period marked by economic growth, the spread of American ideas and the introduction of rational production methods, as well as by the French State's increasing interest in technical training, that specialised educational institutions catering for sales personnel developed in France.[23]

Parisian schools: sales trainees in luxury goods

It is impossible, within the constraints of a short chapter, to discuss the majority of sales training institutions established in France in the inter-war period. The schools set up by the Paris Chamber of Commerce can serve as a pertinent example, as they allow us to explore the relationship between the new sales schools and the capital's department stores. Young people of pre-apprenticeship age were accommodated in the training schools run by the Paris Chamber of Commerce, whereas more experienced saleswomen were trained at the *École technique de vente.*

The sales school for boys catered for about 50 students split into two years and several retailing specialisations: fabrics, clothing, shirts, hats, shoes and hardware.[24] Courses were designed for pre-apprenticeship-age students intending to become general shop assistants and then specialised sales personnel. The school's official title was 'Preparatory school for apprenticeship in the professions of retail sales personnel and shop assistants'. Initially focusing on the fashion trade and on department stores, the school quickly diversified into other spheres such as food and hardware sales. Indeed, when the first schools were set up, the Seine region's inspector of technical training noted that 'the importance given to the fashion trade does not unduly limit the choice of young students to the detriment of other sectors'.[25] More girls were trained than boys and they had their own training establishment in the Rue de l'Arbre Sec. The first shop assistants' school was devoted to clothing and contained mannequins and shop windows for use in training. In 1930, the federation of grocers and confectioners contributed towards another training school in their own field.[26]

As well as creating these institutions, the Paris Chamber of Commerce also benefited from initiatives taken by Louli Sanua, a former primary school teacher in the private sector and a member of the *Conseil national des femmes françaises.* Having set up an association to promote the interests of other female primary school teachers, she looked for ways of retraining these women in commerce. Prevented from enrolling women in the commercial colleges, Sanua decided to set up her own institutions. She founded several business schools in the period from 1909 to 1920: the best known of these institutions is the *École de haut enseignement commercial pour les jeunes filles* (HECJF) which she established in 1916.[27] In 1925, at the same time that training for women entering the professions was beginning to develop (the women's *École polytechnique* was established in the same year), Sanua founded a specialised sales school, the *École technique de vente*.[28]

Sanua's actions were intended to get women into enterprises. It was not the case, as is often thought of the HECJF, that women were trained exclusively as secretaries or shop assistants. The training was designed to allow women to enter a traditionally unwelcoming environment; once inside, they would be promoted to more important positions thanks to their natural abilities. The demanding training programme was shaped by Sanua's personality and by her concept of 'bourgeois feminism' which asserted 'equality in dissimilarity'. Sanua believed that women needed to be 'more' trained than men, to be better prepared for contingencies and that this would make them essential in business.[29]

The establishment of this sales school was closely linked to American developments, while Swedish and British examples served to show that 'the trade of a salesperson had to be learnt'.[30] Recent research on commercial education seeks to play down the influence of America on Europe in the post-1945 period, however, the role of American ideas in the development of commercial training between the wars needs to be re-evaluated. As far as the Paris Chamber of Commerce is concerned, this influence can be seen in fact-finding missions made by its members to the USA and the assimilation of American teaching methods. The transatlantic example affected the sales school set up by Sanua as well as the *Centre de préparation aux affaires* (CPA) founded by the Paris Chamber of Commerce and inspired by the Harvard Business School. In both these cases, though, the means of transfer and of appropriation of American teaching methods are complicated.[31]

In 1925, at the behest of the Minister of Public Instruction and financed by the Paris Chamber of Commerce, Sanua made a trip to the USA. She visited the Prince School in Boston, founded 20 years earlier to teach young saleswomen, which emphasised psychological aspects of sales techniques. Sanua attended classes, collected documentation, studied the school's procedures and made a great many useful contacts.[32] In 1926, Isabel Craig Bacon, General Inspector of American sales schools, was given leave by the Federal Board for Vocational Education to help run the new *École technique de vente* in Paris. She attended the last week of classes in the first teaching session, invigilated at the examinations and started off the second session in the spring. Craig Bacon emphasised the need for simple and practical training methods and she also advocated working with shop managers to get to know their requirements.[33] Subsequently, one of the French sales teachers, Madame de Nanteuil, received a grant from the head of the Boston school, and spent a short period there.[34] The Paris Chamber of Commerce was supported in this initiative by A. Lincoln Filene, brother of Edward Filene, who had been a champion of the Prince School for 20 years. Filene highlighted the difficulties encountered in the USA, saying 'it was a good seven years before anyone realised the worth of the school in Boston.'[35] In 1932, Prince came to France to see the new undertaking for herself and to visit the major Parisian department stores. During her visit, she promoted the new school, reminding everyone that having been dismissed at first – she explained that her 'school made little progress for ten years' – it had become the 'nursery where retailers came to find sales teachers to train their own staff.'[36]

Like the school in Boston, the *École technique de vente* (ETV) was split into two sections. The syllabus and the examination papers were also based on the Prince School model, though certain elements of the syllabus, such as 'types of sales', were difficult to apply in the French context.[37] 'Practical courses' were designed for saleswomen aged from 18 to 20 who wished to 'fill the gaps in their general and vocational education'. 'Teacher-training courses' were aimed at young women who had been educated up to the age of 18. They were taught to 'organise the supervision, management and teaching of retail sales in commercial firms.' These students followed the same courses as the others, but they took an additional exam which covered political economy, law and teaching methods. It was in this section that sales-school teachers and supervisors organising sales training in department stores, were intended to be recruited.[38]

It is clear, then, that the *École technique de vente* had a different purpose from the CCP's other school in the Rue l'Arbre Sec since it did not aim to train 'good little employees', but women who were over 18 years of age or had completed secondary education. These students belonged, it was specified, to 'the French bourgeoisie', the 'petite bourgeoisie' and the 'civil-servant milieu', or they were '"ladies" who had fallen on hard times'.[39]

Recruitment was the main problem facing the ETV since it was halfway between sales training school and HECJF. Sanua stepped up her visits to firms and mounted publicity campaigns in the hope of recruiting more students. She made use of her network of contacts and took advantage of every conceivable opportunity to make her school better known among the business community.[40] When Printemps set up sales courses in 1925, she wrote to the store's director, M. Vigneras, to congratulate him. Armed with letters of introduction, she arranged meetings with department store managers, several of whom organised their own courses.[41] When members of the federation of food chain stores visited the USA in 1930, Sanua wrote to its president about the training of sales personnel in America.[42] She also contacted schools likely to send students her way. The ETV had an active advertising policy aimed at these schools; it included posters in the underground and newspaper and radio advertisements.[43] In 1931, Sanua took part in an international conference of chain stores and proposed a motion on the training of sales personnel.[44]

The first sessions of the ETV attracted about 15 students, who were sent either by department stores (two students came from the Bon Marché and Printemps) or by retail stores.[45] In 1926, three students came from the Louvre and the Nouvelles Galeries.[46] A detailed list citing pupils' names and their provenance, which starts in 1927, reveals the heterogeneous nature of the student intake: a number had links to former students or were former students of the HECJF; others came from local authority schools; there were ex-primary school teachers wanting to enter retail trade; and others who were sent by department stores.[47] Student numbers did not, though, ever exceed 20 per session.

Sanua's activities were not limited to recruitment: she was also concerned with students' employment and their subsequent careers. Her files contain details on work experience and jobs undertaken by students from the school, enabling her to keep account of their progress. M. Machard, a member of the Paris Chamber of Commerce and General Administrator of the Société du Louvre, acknowledged in 1926 that the two saleswomen recruited by him had settled in well.[48] That same year, students had work placements in a fashion house, a bookstore, and a shop selling artificial flowers. Others were employed – usually in jobs found by the school – in establishments selling corsets, lingerie and fancy goods.[49] In 1932 and 1933, ten or so students were found jobs by the school, half of them in the main department stores – Printemps, the Trois Quartiers, the Bon Marché and the Galeries Lafayette – the others in smaller shops.[50] In 1934 more than 40 students found work, but only eight of them entered department stores compared to 28 going to specialist shops.[51] .

The reluctance of department stores?

Do these low numbers signal a setback in this initiative? The answer is qualified. On the one hand the *École technique de vente* remained active and sister institutions sprung up elsewhere in France and in Belgium.[52] A former student from Paris was chosen to run the new school in Toulouse in 1928.[53] The Vice-President of the Caen Chamber of Commerce together with the head of the federation of fashion trades and specialities of the same city decided to start up sales courses and consulted Sanua. Requests for information came from other parts of

France and from abroad, including Poland and Sweden.[54] On the other hand, some of the department stores took on former students from the school to start up their own in-house training. This was the case with M. Decré, of the Decré stores in Nantes, who had links with the Paris Chamber of Commerce. He asked Sanua to train a young Parisian woman who had studied drawing and wanted to go to Nantes to become a window-dresser.[55] He then hired a former student of the school along with an assistant, to look after the recruitment, teaching, supervision and general welfare of his sales staff.[56] A Parisian florist, M. Bauman, hired the head of the Toulouse sales school, to start up a sales course in his shop.[57] In 1931, following discussions with various traders, Sanua organised classes in two Parisian shops selling clothes and fine leather goods.[58] These classes, which covered window-dressing, advertising, drawing and history of art, were intended for former students of the school, but half of the participants came from outside.[59]

These initiatives are proof of Sanua's energetic attempts to counter the problem of student recruitment as well as the general lack of cooperation shown by department stores, for whose benefit, ironically, the school had in part been founded.[60] However, the diversifiction of activities, in addition to the professional nature of the sales courses offered by Sanua, failed to win over the management of department stores.[61] Although they did employ sales assistants from the school, it was usually only for work experience or on a temporary basis for seasonal sales promotions.[62] In 1933, the assistant director of the school, Madame de Nanteuil, had a meeting with the management at Le Louvre. They emphasised the staffing problems and other disruptions caused by the temporary absence of sales personnel as well as the difficulties faced by saleswomen who sacrificed their sales commission while on training courses. They also remarked that 'notions of general order would be more useful for young women who had not yet acquired sales experience.' The stores organised their own in-house lectures for sales staff and employees were 'taught to conform to the firm's procedures'. One of the reasons given for the specificity of French business organisation is the absence of slack periods due to the practice of mounting regular seasonal displays such as the annual promotion of household linen (*Exposition de Blanc*) after Christmas; another is the low salaries paid to employees which made sales commission so important.[63] The department stores' reluctance to release their saleswomen forced Sanua to consider other options, such as, in 1930, organising part-time courses.[64]

The Parisian department stores formed their own study group and, in the 1920s, awarded a number of grants to the sales schools. They also accepted students on full-time work placements for short periods, and sometimes supplied merchandise for use in courses and as end of year prizes.[65] They refused, though, to take students one day a week and they failed to take action on an exchange project involving sales assistants from stores in Berlin. Their grants were also reduced in the 1930s.[66] Sending sales staff to the schools did require a financial commitment, not to mention the loss of earnings incurred during their absence. Yet, it is also possible that the department stores were reluctant to send young sales assistants on training programmes which might make them more independent or demanding, as was the case with trainees sent to the Louvre by Sanua who expressed their contempt for that store.[67]

Many department stores simply preferred to organise their own sales training. Although little evidence survives of this in-house instruction, Printemps and the Galeries Lafayette are known to have initiated programmes, and the employees' federation at the Louvre organised classes at lunchtimes.[68] Vocational courses, similar to ones offered by American and German institutions (such as the Hermann Tietz department stores of Berlin), were introduced at the Printemps department stores in 1927 and were placed under the direction of E. Rachinel, head of personnel. Optional and obligatory day classes were provided for clerical staff, workshop apprentices, bellboys and sales assistants alike. The latter were taught to do rapid calculations, record customers' addresses correctly and do paperwork. They learnt about the firm's organisation and their expected role within it.[69] The Galeries Lafayette even sent a young woman to spend a year at the Prince School in Boston, so that she could teach a course on sales techniques on her return. M. Laguionie, manager of Printemps, made his own feelings clear when he said that the ETV 'should concern itself solely with training teachers in sales techniques.'[70]

One of the aims of this in-house training was to enable new employees to get used to a department store's mode of conducting business: the firm's *esprit-maison*. For this reason apprenticeship training was usually undertaken within the stores, giving apprentices experience of a number of different jobs, such as labelling stock, wrapping purchases, replenishing goods and helping with displays, before working at the sales counter.[71] In addition, the use of mentors, an informal training method whereby one sales assistant instructed another, allowed the new employee to integrate more quickly.[72] The familial ethos of the department stores and their penchant for combining social paternalism with modern management methods may have discouraged the use of external sales schools and benefited in-house training instead.[73] Moreover, it was probably not commercially viable for the stores to invest too much in training young workers as there was a rapid turnover of staff in those establishments; a better training would, though, have reduced the number of sackings due to errors made at work.[74]

Since the department stores did not have recourse to the school for instructors and sales personnel, the dual nature of the ETV – a mixture of sales training school and HECJF – became difficult to justify. The school had been criticised from the start for unnecessarily duplicating the Chamber of Commerce's other sales school for women in the Rue de l'Arbre Sec. Closure of the school was therefore planned with some members of the board of governors doubting the need for specialist sales training at all. The school was saved, though, by its secondary activities as well as by its success outside Paris and abroad. It was transformed into a study centre for retail trade designed to help 'young girls who wished to set up on their own' instead of sales assistants.[75] As a result the ETV was renamed *Cours féminin de préparation au commerce de détail* (Women's preparatory school for the retail trade). It was no longer administered by the board for training schools. Sanua's resignation was, however, refused.[76] The change in name is in fact indicative of Sanua's changing role in the sphere of retail training. Being unable to find allies within the department stores, she directed her attention towards smaller traders, especially dealers in luxury goods. M. Laguionie, manager of Printemps (a member of the Paris Chamber of Commerce and a promoter of modern management methods) did not support the school in its initial form, but he did encourage it to train shopkeepers. This was in order to reduce the rapid turnover of small retail businesses due to poor bookkeeping and inadequate management skills: department store employees who set up in business on their own failed eight times out of ten, he explained, 'through not having the necessary knowledge of practical management methods.'[77]

In other words, the department stores did not seek to train their sales personnel thoroughly, before or during their employees' (short) careers with them. It was more important for those organisations to find teachers who could inform new sales staff about in-house procedures, although they were interested in helping their best employees to set up small businesses of their own. In effect, as Laguionie of Printemps explained, 'above all else, a manager needs to know how to deal with suppliers, public authorities and owners; these are things which the majority of employees who are with the firm for only a short period of time do not (need to) know.'[78]

The development of training programmes in France between the wars is evidence of the formal, though limited, admission of sales methods into the canon of acceptable teaching subjects. It says nothing about the reality of the training courses.

Merchandise and customer psychology

Sales training in all the schools dealt first and foremost with merchandise. This ties in with the rising number of industrial products and increasingly complicated methods of production in the inter-war period, which gave the salesperson a vital educational role.[79] Courses on merchandise were related to regional specialisations; for example, at Roubaix, they were devoted exclusively to textiles.[80] In the technical colleges of Romans, a shoe-manufacturing town, traders were called upon to act as teachers. At Grenoble, heads of department from three regional firms – a chocolate manufacturer, a coffee firm and a producer of pasta – ran courses. At Vienne, training centred on drapery, whereas at Reims it focused on champagne.[81] In the Parisian training schools, the processes involved in making shoes, lingerie and foodstuffs were explained. These courses were based on samples of products, together with occasional factory visits. On a more practical level, trainee sales assistants were taught how to fold and display cloth and how to recommend goods, as well as how to discuss the quality of a particular product with clients.[82]

Lessons in sales psychology were the second important element in the teaching programme. These courses fit in with the development of applied psychology in advertising and sales in the inter-war period, which is less well known than the application of psychology to factory organisation, but is just as important.[83] Trainee sales assistants learnt to 'recognise customers' characters in order to be able to influence them'. They had to know the correct answers to questions such as: 'how can you recognise an indecisive customer before speaking to them?'; 'what must you do as soon as you engage in conversation?'; 'what are the different ways of discovering exactly what a client wants?'; 'how can you satisfy a mother and a daughter when they disagree?'; 'how should you persuade a customer who says that a hat does not suit him?'.[84] These courses analysed the different stages of sales, focusing on the arrival of a customer, the conclusion of the sale and the customer's departure.[85]

Differences between sales schools arose mainly from the teaching methods and the teachers employed. The weekly teaching programme comprised 15 hours of general instruction, 12 hours of practical work and a further 12 hours of technical education. Compared to similar institutions teaching industrial trades, the sales training schools did not need much in terms of equipment and materials. The classroom resembled a shop, complete with sales counter. The raw materials – sales goods – were displayed in shop windows which the students cleaned and arranged just as they would in a real shop.[86]

The general classes at the ETV taught shop management, sales techniques, theory of presentation, rapid calculation and hygiene, as well as language courses in French, and business English and Spanish. A distinctive feature of this training was the use of class discussions with the students actively participating instead of learning by rote. In this way, the students tackled paperwork, drew up plans for sales catalogues, and practised writing letters to suppliers. They also considered the finer points of shop location. As mentioned above, the teacher-training section of the schools featured a more advanced psychology course, together with law, political economy and teaching methods. There were also additional courses in window display.[87]

Questions arise about the recruitment of specialised sales teachers. In this respect, apart from the lectures delivered by professionals, the schools functioned in many different ways. Teachers from the state-run *Écoles pratiques de commerce* were confused by the new syllabi which introduced sales and advertising without explaining how to teach these subjects. A few teachers went to Sanua for advice and André J. Connord is a good example.[88] Originally a journalist, Connord had the standard training. He followed courses in law and political economy at the Bordeaux Chamber of Commerce, then studied at the two private sales schools in Paris. Connord found himself arranging night classes in sales and advertising for the Federation of commercial employees, which were intended, as he put it, for 'young people with little training'. He realised that there was a severe lack of such training programmes, especially in sales which was, in his opinion, 'based on straightforward experimental psychology'. He taught courses called 'the art of decisive action' and 'the art of speaking in public' and, in the third year, he lectured on basic customer types: men, women and children.[89]

The Paris Chamber of Commerce benefited from more experience. It encouraged professionals from the business world to join forces with teaching specialists. The professionals were required to do regular stints in shops to keep in touch with trading practices.[90] Sanua was keen to train the sales teachers in her teacher-training section. When Sanua began to find jobs for her students, she encouraged one of her best pupils, Anne Catala, a graduate of the HECJF, to gain an extra qualification in psychology and to take control of the new sales school set up in Toulouse.

As a young woman in the 1930s, Anne Catala taught most of the sales courses at that school. She based her lessons on notebooks entrusted to her by Sanua; literature on sales merchandise bought from a specialist institute; and experience gained during a summer spent visiting factories throughout France. From 1937 onwards, she made use of a book on sales pyschology brought back from Germany. This was a technical manual published by a retail trade institute set up in 1929, specialising in training sales personnel.[91] With the aid of this material,

Catala offered additional lessons on sales psychology in which she discussed character profiles of clients and the means of adapting to them.

Sales techniques, she explained, had to be altered to suit particular clients, whether man or woman, adult or child, young or old, a regular customer or a new one. They also varied according to the state of mind of each customer. For example, when faced with an indecisive customer, a saleswoman was advised to remove items systematically from show which did not suit the customer's specifications, thus reducing the number of objects on display and influencing the customer's choice. Although she limited her demands with regard to dress since her students were often hard up, Catala did instruct in bearing and elocution and emphasised the importance of professional courtesy.[92]

Male students at the sales training schools run by the CCP wore white smocks and they were obliged to wear detachable collars and ties.[93] These aspiring salesmen were taught to behave in a respectable manner according to the mores of their middle-class clientele: they had to speak well, impart confidence and exhibit good taste, refinement and tact.[94] This evidence serves to show that sales teachers sought to instil in their students knowledge of how to present themselves rather than how to act, that is to say, *savoir-être* instead of *savoir-faire*.[95] As good employees, sales assistants had to know how to read, write and add up quickly but, above all else, they needed to obey both the boss and the customer, having understood, without it needing to be spelt out, what was expected of them.[96]

Conclusion

The training of sales personnel in France began in the inter-war period, as it did in other countries. The vigour shown by the founders of the first French training schools and their openness to foreign methods are both significant. Contact with the USA and with Germany encouraged the spread of new ideas, especially on sales psychology which the French schools embraced wholeheartedly. Initiatives taken in the period show that there was a real need for good sales staff among industrialists and traders.[97] It could just as easily be argued, though, that specialists who were keen to promote the new sales methods created the demand for such employees. The survival and achievements of the schools suggest that the phenomenon was produced by supply as well as demand.

The existence of these institutions is proof that, however limited in scope, ideas did circulate in the inter-war period. This does not mean, though, that sales techniques were widely dispersed at that time. This is compatible with the fact that the agents involved were usually self-taught and that a number of them sought to formalise their experience. Other forms of vocational training, such as exchanges of knowledge within the workplace[98] and by means of the media or books, cannot be excluded. These transfers of information are, however, much more difficult to define.

The sales schools set up in the inter-war period did not replace in-house training offered to sales staff by department stores. It might have been expected that the big stores would have sought to train their personnel in the latest sales methods, such as sales psychology, complementing their advanced policies in other areas such as advertising. One might also have anticipated a closer relationship with the sales schools. Yet, there was a clash of interests between, on the one hand, the need to influence consumers and giving sales assistants the means of doing this and, on the other, the need to regulate sales personnel and integrate them into the firm. The reasons for the department stores' reluctance to engage with the sales schools need further investigation, as do the alternative forms of sales training. It remains to be clarified whether this was a purely French phenomenon caused by the training and management structures in place in France. The problems faced by the Prince School in the USA do suggest that the reticence of the department stores was shared on both sides of the Atlantic.

Notes

1. Marie-Emmanuelle Chessel, 'L'émergence de la publicité: publicitaires, annonceurs et affichistes dans la France de l'entre-deux-guerres', PhD thesis, European University Institute, Florence (1996) and *La publicité. Naissance d'une profession (1900–1940)*, Paris: CNRS-Éditions (1998). Thanks go to Patricia Allerston, to Anne Catala, to Anne Goulet and Olivier Cottarel at the archives of the *Chambre de Commerce de Paris*, and to Geoffrey Crossick, for their help.
2. Henri Le More, 'L'invention du cadre commercial: 1881–1914', *Sociologie du Travail*, 4, 1982, pp. 443–50; Philippe Maffre, 'Les origines de l'enseignement commercial supérieur au XIXè siècle, 1820–1914', doctoral thesis, Université Paris I (1983); Marc Meuleau, 'Les HEC et l'introduction du management en France', doctoral thesis (Thèse d'Etat), Université Paris X-Nanterre (1992).
3. Patrick Fridenson, 'La circulation internationale des modes managériales', in Jean-Philippe Bouilloud and Bernard-Pierre Lécuyer (eds.), *L'invention de la gestion: histoire et pratiques*, Paris: L'Harmattan (1994), pp. 81–9.
4. Thérèse Charmasson (ed.), *L'enseignement technique de la Révolution à nos jours*, vol. 1, Paris: Économica (1991); Alain Prost, *L'enseignement et l'éducation en France, l'école et la famille dans une société en mutation, Histoire générale de l'enseignement et de l'éducation en France,*

L.-H. Parias (ed.), vol. 4, Paris: Nouvelle Librairie de France (1981); François Simiand, 'L'enseignement commercial et la formation des professeurs', *Revue politique et parlementaire*, July 1914, p. 5.

5. Pierre Quef, *Histoire de l'apprentissage: aspects de la formation technique et commerciale*, Paris: Librairie Générale de Droit et de Jurisprudence (1964), pp. 161–83.

6. Pierre-Henri Haas, 'Histoire de l'École supérieure de commerce de Lyon: 1872–1972', DEA d'Histoire, Paris IV-Sorbonne (1993), pp. 27, 62–3.

7. Archives de la Chambre de commerce de Paris (CCIP)-3J, 'Notes sur les ateliers-écoles de la Chambre de Commerce de Paris', *Bulletin du Centre de préparation aux affaires*, 1 January 1936, p. 1.; CCIP-II-5.45(2), Les ateliers-écoles depuis l'origine (1920) jusqu'au 31 December 1934, pp. 1–2.

8. CCIP-I-273(28), Recrutement du personnel commercial et industriel (1935), p. 6.

9. Chambre de commerce de Paris, *Notice sur la fondation, le développement de l'École commerciale de Paris (rive droite) et des cours gratuits du soir de l'Avenue Trudaine* (1931).

10. CCIP-I-274(67), École commerçiale de jeunes filles, 11 October 1916, p. 18.

11. On the state's role, see CCIP-II-525(1), M. Bayle, 'Formation complémentaire des commerçants après la sortie de l'École de commerce ou à la fin de l'apprentissage', *Congrès international de l'enseignement commercial*, Amsterdam (1929), pp. 1, 12–14; CCIP-II-545(4).

12. CCIP-EDV-BA-56, article 1 of the law.

13. Ibid.

14. On office-workers, see Delphine Gardey, 'Un monde en mutation: les employés de bureau en France 1890–1930: féminisation, mécanisation, rationalisation', doctoral thesis, Université Paris VII (1995), pp. 111–18.

15. CCIP-II-525(1), M. Turotte, 'Formation des futurs employés de magasins', *Congrès international de l'enseignement commercial*, Amsterdam (1929), p. 5; Daniel Briod, *La science de la vente et sa place dans l'enseignement commercial*, Lausanne: Payot (1929).

16. Charlotte Billard, *Les tendances de l'enseignement du commerce*, Paris: CCI, pp. 8, 29; CCIP-II-525(1), E. Von Rossing, 'La formation des vendeuses', pp. 1–3; M. Lomont, 'Initiation et préparation à l'apprentissage', *Congrès international de l'enseignement commercial*, Amsterdam (1929), pp. 1–2.

17. CCIP-3J, 'Notes sur les ateliers écoles'; CCIP-EDV, 'Ecole de vente', Note préparatoire à la constitution de l'inventaire.

18. CCIP-EDV-BA-56, G. Lamoril, 'Quelques "moyens" et quelques "fins" de l'enseignement commercial', in *Congrès de l'enseignement technique, agricole et ménager*, Charleroi (Belgium) (1925), p. 11; CCIP-II-525(1), E. Rachinel, M. Contenot, 'Liaison entre l'enseignement commercial et la pratique', *Congrès international de l'enseignement commercial*, Amsterdam (1929), p. 9; conversation with Anne Catala (Paris, June 1995), drawn upon more extensively below.

19. Briod, *La science*, p. 190.

20. Émile Paris, *Pour devenir commerçant*, Paris: A. Colin (1918).

21. J. Roumajon, 'L'organisation actuelle de l'enseignement technique: initiatives officielles, initiatives privées', *Bulletin de la société scientifique du Dauphiné*, 48, Grenoble, 1928.

22. Association française pour le développement de l'enseignement technique, *Travaux du congrès de la formation commerciale*, 1922; L. Chambonnaud, 'L'état de l'enseignement commercial en France', *Congrès international de l'enseignement commercial*, Charleroi (1925), p. 272.

23. Development was similar in Germany, see CCIP-II-525(1), Von Rossing, 'La formation', pp. 4–6; Julien Fontègne, 'La formation professionnelle du vendeur: ce qu'on fait en Allemagne et en Amérique', *Vendre*, 64, 1929, pp. 195–7; Léone Bourdel, 'La psychologie de la vente et la psychotechnique du vendeur', *Cours de l'école d'organisation scientifique du travail du CNOF*, 88, 1942, pp. 24–5.

24. CCIP-EDV-BA-56, Effectifs, 1933.

25. CCIP-EDV-BA-56, Lamoril, 'Quelques "moyens"', p. 6.

26. CCIP-II-545(9).

27. CCIP-I-274(30).

28. Before the women's École polytechnique was created, the HECJF was located at CNAM, see André Grelon, 'Marie-Louise Paris et les débuts de l'École polytechnique féminine (1925–1945)', *Bulletin d'histoire de l'électricité*, 19–20, 1992, pp. 133–55. In 1934, the *École technique de vente* was renamed the *École supérieure de vente*; here, the original name is maintained.

29. Frédérique Pigeyre, 'Socialisation différentielle des sexes, le cas des futures cadres dans les Grandes Écoles d'ingénieurs et de gestion', doctoral thesis, Université Paris VII (1986), p. 93; Marielle Delorme-Hoechstetter, 'Louli Sanua et l'École de haut enseignement pour jeunes filles (HECJF): Génèse d'une grande école féminine (1916–1941)', DEA d'histoire, Paris: EHESS (1995).

30. CCIP-I-274(72), École de vendeuses rue Daunou. *Rapport sur les résultats des deux premières sessions*, 1926, pp. 3–4.

31. Giuliana Gemelli, 'Pour une analyse comparée du développement des Écoles de gestion en Europe: le rôle de la Fondation Ford', in Bouilloud and Lécuyer, *L'invention*, pp. 285–7.

32. CCIP-I-274(72), 'L'École de vendeuses à Boston en Amérique', 1925; Helen Norton, 'Department-store education: an account of the training methods developed at the Boston School of Salesmanship under the direction of Lucinda Wyman Prince', *Bulletin of the Bureau of Education*, 9, 1917, p. 79.

33. CCIP-I-274(72), M. Baudet, report on the creation of an *École technique de vente*, 21 October 1925; Sous-commission administrative de l'ETV, 27 April 1926. Except when otherwise indicated, information on the ETV comes from this file.

34. Sous-commission de l'ETV, 30 June 1926, 8 July 1926.

35. Ibid., 30 June 1926.

36. Ibid., 19 October 1932 and report made in June 1936.

37. On the Boston syllabus, see Norton, 'Department-store education', p. 13; CCIP-I-274(72), Organisation des cours à l'ETV (practical courses); Commission administrative des ateliers-écoles, 25 February 1925.

38. CCIP-I-274(72), École de vendeuses, Rue Daunou; École supérieure de vente. Sanua recorded that the same syllabus and organisational division existed in Boston, see the meeting of 7 November 1925.

39. CCIP-I-273(7), 'Rapport présenté par M. Perron sur les écoles et ateliers de la Chambre de commerce à la commission d'étude des services de la

chambre' (1936); CCIP-I-274(72), letter from Paul Templier to Louli Sanua, 9 August 1928.

40.   CCIP-I-274(72), Sous-commission administrative de l'ETV, 8 February 1927.

41.   Letter from Sanua to M. Vigneras, manager of Le Printemps, 3 August 1925; Letter from the Director-General of the Paris Chamber of Commerce to Sanua, 28 October 1925; letters of introduction to Messrs Bader (Galeries Lafayettes), Renaudin, Laguionie (Printemps), Laporte and Cognacq.

42.   Letter from Sanua to M. François, President of the Syndicat général des maisons d'alimentation à succursales, 28 November 1930.

43.   Letter, 2 June 1927; visit of Sanua to the Vaucanson school; and report by M. Templier on behalf of the Sous-commission administrative de l'ETV, 'Activité de l'ETV', 26 April 1929.

44.   Letter from Sanua to the President, 3 July 1931.

45.   'École de vendeuses rue Daunou', p. 2.

46.   Commission administrative de l'ETV, 30 June 1926.

47.   Note of 29 November 1927. Following a visit made by Sanua to the head of personnel, Les Trois Quartiers sent three saleswomen in 1927: letter from Sanua to M. Gaillard, 4 March 1927.

48.   Letter from M. Machard, Administrateur général de la Société du Louvre to Émile Paris, Inspecteur général de l'enseignement technique, 27 July 1926.

49.   Letter from Sanua to P. Templier, 9 October 1928.

50.   Commission administrative de l'ETV, 15 June 1932; 5 April 1933; 12 July 1933.

51.   Ibid., 7 February 1934.

52.   Ibid, 14 January 1929.

53.   Note of 29 November 1927.

54.   Letter from the Président of the Paris Chamber of Commerce to Sanua, 27 January 1931.

55.   M. Decré made a presentation on his firm to the *Centre de préparation aux affaires* (CPA) where training was based on case studies of firms: CCIP-CPA, Cas n° 695, 1931–32. On his links with Sanua, see CCIP-I-274(72). M. Bauman also had contacts with the CCP and CPA: CCIP-CPA, Cas n° 1688, 5–11 May 1942.

56.   CCIP-I-274(72), Commission administrative de l'ETV, 17 February 1932.

57.   Ibid., 5 April 1933.

58.   CCIP-I-274(72), letter from Sanua to the president of the CCP, 12 December 1931 and Commission administrative de l'ETV, 17 February 1932.

59.   Commission administrative de l'ETV, 13 April 1932 and 6 February 1935.

60.   Report on the ETV adopted in June 1936.

61.   Letter from Templier to Sanua, 14 November 1925: 'we will set up the school all the same ... if the department stores don't follow us, others will, we only need to know where to strike.'

62.   Commission administrative de l'ETV, 8 February 1933.

63.   Report on the ETV adopted in June 1936.

64.   Letter from Sanua to Templier, 4 December 1930. A few stores then announced their intention to send sales assistants to Sanua's school:

Archives du Groupement d'étude des grands magasins (GEGM), meeting of 28 July 1932.

65. GEGM, 23 October 1924, 13 November 1924, 8 January 1925, 19 March 1925, 24 July 1925, 4 March 1926, 3 June 1926, 9 September 1926, 18 November 1926, 7 April 1927, 13 October 1927, 5 April 1928, 7 November 1929, 19 December 1929.

66. Ibid., 5 April 1928, 12 September and 7 November 1929, 6 March 1930, 5 November 1931, 17 January 1935.

67. CCIP-I-274(72), letter from Madame de Nanteuil, 17 December 1929.

68. Commission administrative de l'ETV, 8 February 1927. During a visit of the Society of Cash Registrars, Sanua learnt of a sales school based at the Galeries Lafayettes who also planned a visit. See the letter from Sanua to Vigneras, Director of Printemps, 3 August 1925; and Commission administrative de l'ETV, 5 April 1933.

69. Ibid., 5 April 1933; Briod, La Science, p. 185; Francis Ambrière, La vie secrète des grands magasins, Paris: Flammarion (1938), pp. 151–2.

70. CCIP-I-274(72), Commission administrative de l'ETV, 8 December 1934.

71. Jeanne Guénot, La vendeuse, le livre de la profession, Paris: Léon Eyrolles, Paris (1930), pp. 19–20.

72. Interview with Max Helbronn, son-in-law of M. Bader, Director of the Galeries Lafayette, May 1995.

73. Philippe Verheyde, 'Les Galeries Lafayette, 1899–1955. 'Histoire économique d'un grand magasin', in Comité pour l'histoire économique et financière de la France, études et documents, vol. 5, Paris: Ministère de l'Economie (1993), pp. 201–35; Michael B. Miller, The Bon Marché. Bourgeois Culture and the Department Store, 1869–1920, Princeton: Princeton University Press (1981); Marc Meuleau, 'Le Printemps – Prisunic: années 1920 années 1970', in Les HEC, pp. 1087–154.

74. Miller, Bon Marché, pp. 90–91.

75. CCIP-I-274(72), M. Templier, 'Activité de l'ETV', 26 April 1929; Commission administrative de l'ETV, 7 February 1936, 12 October 1936 and 2 December 1936; CCP, minutes, 24 February 1937. Reasons given for saving the school included the provincial schools' success, foreign nations' support, and the need to help retail trade in a time of crisis: report on the ETV, June 1936.

76. CCP, minutes, 24 February, 7 July 1937; Cours féminin de préparation au commerce de détail, minutes, 24 May 1937; Note sur la réunion de la commission administrative du cours féminin de préparation au commerce de détail, 24 May 1937.

77. Commission administrative de l'ETV, 2 December 1936. Pierre Laguionie graduated from the École supérieure de commerce de Lyon and was first president of the Association internationale des grands magasins, 1928 to 1930. He introduced new management methods at Printemps and registered the store with the CNOF: Meuleau, 'Le Printemps-Prisunic', p. 1096.

78. CCP, minutes, 24 February 1937.

79. Bourdel, 'La psychologie', p. 7.

80. CCIP-II-525(1), Turotte, 'Formation', pp. 9–10.

81. Chambonnaud, 'L'état de l'enseignement', p. 289.

82. EDV-BA-56.

83. Marjorie Beale, 'Advertising and the Politics of Public Persuasion in France,

1900–1939', PhD thesis, University of California, Berkeley, 1991; Chessel, 'L'Émergence', pp. 91–103.

84. CCIP-I-273(72), École supérieure de vente, examination questions.

85. CCIP-EDV-BA-56, Syllabus of sales theory course; CCIP-I-273(72); interview with Anne Catala.

86. CCIP-EDV-BA-56.

87. CCIP-II-525(1), 'Carrières commerciales', report presented by Madame de Nanteuil, p. 5; and more generally: CCIP-I-274(72), Brochures diverses.

88. Chambonnaud, 'L'état de l'enseignement', pp. 286–7; CCIP-I-274(72), Commission administrative de l'ETV, 5 April 1933.

89. A. J. Connord, *Congrès international de l'enseignement commercial*, Paris (1931), pp. 586–620.

90. CCIP-EDV-BA-56, M. Lomont, 'Les professeurs d'enseignement commercial: recrutement, éducation: méthodes propres à maintenir les professeurs en contact avec la pratique commerciale', *Congrès international de l'enseignement commercial*, London, July 1932.

91. Literature bought from 'Documentation Unique'. The German book covered the different stages of sales, sales dialogues and psychological profiles of clients: Professor Dr R. Seÿffert, 'Lehrmittel für die Einzelhandelsschulung', in *Schriften zur Einzelhandels- und Konsumtionsforschung*, 19, Herausgegeben vom Einzelhandelsinstitut der Universität Köln, Lehrmittelgruppe Das Verkaufsgespräch, Stuttgart: C.E. Poeschel (1936). As well as the courses at Toulouse, in the 1940s, Catala based courses at the *Centre de perfectionnement des magasins populaires* in Paris on this book: Private archives, A. Catala.

92. Interview with Catala, Paris, 1995.

93. CCIP-EDV-BA-56, note for M. Glomon, Directeur Général des ateliers-écoles, 3 October 1932; Order for white smocks chez Braillon, Vêtements de travail, 7 October 1932.

94. On taste, see especially CCIP-II-525(1), Von Rossing, 'La Formation', pp. 14–17; Lomont, 'Initiation', p. 4; and Norton, 'Department-store education', p. 13. Elocution lessons were organised by EPC de Roubaix (CCIP-II-525(1), Turotte, 'Formation', p. 10.

95. Gardey, 'Un monde', p. 112.

96. Lomont, 'Initiation', pp. 7–9; Edmond Rachinel, *Le livret de l'employé de commerce*, Paris: Léon Eyrolle, (1924), p. 33.

97. Briod, *La science*, p. 109.

98. Renaud Cayla, 'Histoire comparée de la formation professionnelle des ouvriers en France et en Allemagne (1914–1945): Projet de Recherche', DEA d'histoire, University of Lyon 2, 1993, pp. 9, 15.

CHAPTER THIRTEEN

Employers' organisations in French department stores during the inter-war period: between conservatism and innovation*

Laurence Badel

Historians of employers' organisations in France have shown little interest in large-scale retailing, while surveys of the field have but rarely included this important sector of the economy in their analyses. It is the organisation and representation of industrial employers which have dominated the field.[1] Large-scale retail trade has prompted specific studies of department stores, popular stores and hypermarkets, but has not yet provoked a single work bringing together all three of these subjects. The approach has been essentially in the form of monographs. The inter-war period and the war period itself have been particularly neglected. Entire periods of its history remain ignored: one sees little of its interventions on the political scene, its demands are little understood, its pressures on the government have been ignored. One can nevertheless suppose that, following the example of the industrial and banking sectors, large-scale retail trade forged links with the political world. In the sphere of international relations, what was its position on those important questions of the day which touched it directly, such as commercial policy (tariffs, quotas, etc.), or the first attempts at European economic organisation in the inter-war period?

In defence of historians, two remarks need making. The first is that the commercial world was a very particular one, both unpredictable and demanding, which has kept it consistently independent of the larger world of employers. A refusal to accept full integration led to the formation of a *Conseil national du commerce*, to represent commercial interests, as an autonomous force within the larger *Conseil national du patronat français*, which was established in 1946. In addition, the interests of industrialists and retailers were for a long time confused within France's first employers' organisations, and it was several decades before

* Translated by Barbara Thanni and Geoffrey Crossick.

the distinctive interests of the French distribution sector were recognised. Amongst French employers, organisation amongst those in
large-scale retailing was particularly late. As a result they long lacked
an organised framework through which to represent their interests to
government, which was consequently far more sensitive to the demands
of the better organised small shopkeepers. Although it would be a
mistake to assume too readily some correlation between the weak presence of large-scale retailing in public affairs and the lack of interest
shown by historians, it is none the less true that in its disorganised state,
large-scale retailing was not easy to encompass as an object of analysis.
The establishment of employers' organisations amongst department store
owners during the inter-war period seems to provide a useful approach
to the world of large-scale retail trade, which is the object of our
current research.[2] After describing the main chronological stages of
employers organisation, this article will explore how it helped to defend
before governments an essentially conservative social vision while at the
same time putting into action commercial practices which were both
dynamic and open to modernity.

   The first commercial organisations defended their interests as small
specialised shopkeepers rather than their general character as retailers.
These first appeared within the framework of mixed organisations: an
example is the creation in 1858 of the *Union générale du commerce et
de l'industrie*, which grouped different types of retailers – leather and
skins, lighting, furnishing and so on. The end of the 1880s saw the first
attempts more specifically to defend the interests of small retailers.
Early commercial associations appeared as the union of small shopkeepers, leading the campaign against 'monopolistic' department stores.[3]
At the end of the nineteenth century political authorities were coming
to acknowledge the pivotal role of small shopkeepers in French society:
occupying a privileged position as the *juste milieu* between the world of
business and the world of labour, they came to be seen as one of the
foundations of the social consensus upon which the Third Republic was
constructed.[4] Large-scale retail trade did not acquire a national status
until the end of the 1930s. During this time it was to a large extent
indebted to the attention of an important but little known personality
from the world of business, Jacques Lacour-Gayet. He was born into a
family of *Ecole normale supérieure* alumni, also members of the *Institut*.
Son of a historian and brother of the Inspector-General of Finances,
Robert Lacour-Gayet, he abandoned his study of the classics and changed
profession immediately upon leaving the *Ecole normale supérieure*. In
1907 he became Secretary-General of the *Conseil d'administration des
chemins de fer* for Bône-Guelma which ran a railway network in North
Africa. He worked in the *Intendance* after the outbreak of war in 1914,

he made the acquaintance of Gabriel Cognacq, nephew of the founder of La Samaritaine, and also of Pierre Laguionie, director of Printemps since 1907. From these encounters emerged the idea for an organisation of department stores which came into being soon after the war during the social crisis of 1919–20.

Reading the minutes of this organisation, the *Groupement d'études des grands magasins*, suggests that tension between employers and the working world was the factor determining the creation of the first employers' organisation in the world of large-scale retailing. The social policy of department store directors before 1914 left little scope for employee unionisation, which involved only a small selection of staff. Nevertheless, from 1869 these staff organised themselves into a *Chambre syndicale des employés*, whose membership saw new growth towards the end of the 1880s, but this generally low level of employee unionisation may perhaps have delayed the appearance amongst employers of a desire to organise. But demands which were hardening at the beginning of the twentieth century, were reinforced by the war. Workers in the clothing trades were amongst those particularly affected by the conflict, and large-scale strikes amongst clothing workers in Paris in May 1917 were part of that year's increasing strike action. In an attempt to end this agitation, the Government legislated to establish the eight-hour working day on 23 April 1919.

The case of the Belle Jardinière store reveals the extent of employer hostility: by May 1919 the directors were raising doubts about the application of the eight-hour day legislation and proclaiming a 'labour supply crisis', linked in particular to a reduction of outwork and a shift of workers to the factory.[5] Belle Jardinière was on 6 June 1919 the location for a meeting which assembled the directors of the Belle Jardinière itself, together with those of the Bazar de l'Hôtel de Ville, the Bon Marché, the Galeries Lafayette, the Louvre, Printemps and the Samaritaine. The debates concentrated on social questions and the repercussions of the law of 23 April. A press release was prepared. This first joint initiative was followed in the next few days by the formation of an autonomous organisation of department stores, whose goals would be both the diffusion of information and 'action over economic, commercial, fiscal and social questions'.[6] The *Groupement d'études des grands magasins* was constituted on 6 July 1919 by eight different department stores: the Trois Quartiers joined the seven department stores who had been represented at the 6 June meeting. All the leading directors were there: Lillaz for BHV; Bessand for the Belle Jardinière; Bader, Meyer and Lévy for the Galeries Lafayette; Laguionie, Poulet and Vigneras for Printemps; Ernest and Gabriel Cognacq for the Samaritaine.[7] The different establishments agreed upon a rotating presidency, a membership fee of 10 000 francs and a sharing out of general costs (personnel, buildings, offices). They were to be joined during the inter-war period by the Pygmalion, A Réaumur, Madélios, and others. The Paris–France company joined in 1930, a significant addition which brought with it 22 provincial establishments, notably the Aux Dames de France stores.

The birth of the *Groupement* in the context of social crisis ensured that the member establishments acted together when faced with union problems 'presenting an essential interest for all the establishments in the group, and maintaining their willingness to resist.'[8] This led them to propose employers' mutual insurance in the event of a strike resulting in the total or partial closing down of one of the member stores. The *Groupement d'études des grands magasins* had by 1920–21 already been confronted by practically all the big questions which would be at the heart of its conflict during the inter-war period: the general costs of department stores, fiscal and commercial legislation, links with manufacturers, and relations with white-collar employees and manual workers. From 15 May 1919, Jacques Lacour-Gayet held the post of Secretary-General.[9] He worked to make the *Groupement* the representative in the eyes of state authorities, sending delegations to Ministers from the outset.

At the same time, following the explosion of the tariff question in French economic affairs, Jacques Lacour-Gayet, with the support of the *Groupement d'études des grands magasins*, established a second organisation in 1925, the *Comité d'action économique et douanière* (CAED).[10] CAED's involvement in the debate on tariff policy in the 1920s concealed the fact that it was acting in the defence of department store interests.[11] This became evident once again at the beginning of the 1930s, when the number of parliamentary bills seeking to regulate *prix uniques* was on the increase. These outgrowths of department stores first appeared in France in 1928; the Uniprix company was launched under the aegis of the Nouvelles Galeries with the financial support of the German company Karstadt. CAED tried unsuccessfully to defend *prix uniques* against the restrictive parliamentary bills which multiplied from July 1933: the law of 22 March 1936 banned the opening or development of *prix uniques* stores for one year; the law was extended annually up until the war. The appearance of these stores had led to the setting up in June 1933 of a *Groupement d'études des magasins à prix uniques*, born out of the *Groupement des grands magasins* and then transformed in June 1934 into a *Chambre syndicale des magasins et bazars populaires*, led by Camille Lafarge, then Lucien Dufourcq-Lagelouse, of the Monoprix group. Lacour-Gayet subsequently regrouped these commercial organisations into one *Fédération nationale des entreprises à commerces multiples*, following the restructuring of employers' organisations brought about by the Popular Front. The Federation was born on 9 July 1937, joining the *Groupement d'études des grands magasins*, the *Chambre syndicale du commerce de la nouveauté*, the *Chambre syndicale des magasins et bazars populaires* and the *Chambre syndicale des magasins et galeries*.[12] Based on a solid administrative structure benefiting from the experience acquired by the *Groupement*, and enjoying the continuity of direction provided by Lacour-Gayet from 1919 until his death in 1953, the Federation developed rapidly, integrating employers' organisations and unions in Paris and the provinces. In 1939 it boasted that it represented nearly 90 per cent of retail trade.[13] Active at the beginning of the Occupation in defending retail interests in the face of the hegemony of production, it survived the Second World War and was present at the time of the creation of the *Conseil national du patronat français* (CNPF).[14] The period rapidly surveyed here was a complex one, marked on the one hand by social anxieties amongst department store employers, and on the other by a commercial dynamism that followed the introduction of new management methods.

The world of department store employers is undeniably a conservative one. It is a conservatism which can be seen in both the political and the social spheres. A study of department store donations leaves in no doubt the support they gave to right-wing parties during the inter-war period. The *Fédération républicaine* of Louis Marin and the *Alliance démocratique* of Pierre-Etienne Flandin received donations in accordance with 'the evaluation of each establishment'. The interconnections between these parties and the business world is well known. The *Fédération républicaine* benefited notably from the support of François de Wendel, the influential director of Comité des Forges.[15] In 1933, 1934 and 1936 specific department stores funded the *Centre de propagande des républicains nationaux* led by Henri de Kérillis, political director of *L'Echo de Paris*. The centre was a technical organisation which from 1927 offered its services (public speaking school, publication of announcements) to right-wing parties and which, according to René Rémond, worked to unify the Right. The *Groupement*, on the other hand, made donations in its own right, in 1928, 1929, 1930 and 1933 to the *Jeunesses Patriotes*, donations which ranged from 5 000 francs to 12 000 francs. The *Jeunesses Patriotes* had been founded in 1924 as part of the *Ligue des Patriotes* and became autonomous in 1926 under the aegis of Pierre Taittinger, a Member of Parliament for Paris. This movement, with an appeal that was both paramilitary and anti-parliamentary, was none the less a republican one which sought to reform the regime through a strengthening of executive power. The attachment of department stores must be seen as an instinctive reaction on their part to the Cartel of the Left. But their attraction to antiparliamentary ideas is confirmed by their support in 1930 for the *Croix-de-Feu* movement of Lieutenant-Colonel de la Roque.

Furthermore, certain department store directors were involved in the debates of the early 1930s on state reform, which reached their climax with the establishment of Doumergue's government on 9 February 1934. The debate quickly narrowed to the question of the restoration of the right of dissolution. Doumergue's proposals attracted the support of the Right.[16] The Leagues (*Croix-de-Feu, Jeunesses Patriotes*) allied themselves very publicly with these changes, but the classic right wing supported the propositions with equal conviction.[17] *Le Temps* and *L'Echo de Paris* gave their approval to a project 'which would cauterise the rottenness of the regime'.[18] The hostility of the Left was aroused by these propositions, and this contributed to the fall of the Cabinet in November 1934. Nevertheless, the debate remained a lively one. Department store employers' organisations showed a new interest in the periodical *La Libre Opinion* founded in 1922 by the former Member of Parliament Henri Roux-Costadau.[19] While an initial request for financial support was refused in 1926, several establishments decided to give subsidies to the journal in 1935, at a time when it was publicly displaying its sympathies with pro-Mussolini forces and working for Marshal Pétain's accession to power.[20] The minutes of the meeting on 9 April 1936 reveal that Printemps and the Galeries Lafayette had paid respectively 1 800 francs and 300 francs to *La Libre Opinion*. Paul Bessand of the Belle Jardinière and Gabriel Cognacq of the Samaritaine had for their part participated in December 1934 in a banquet organised by the *Ligue des Révisionnistes*, whose publication was *La Libre Opinion*.[21]

This conservative political orientation went hand in hand with defending a system of labour management whose origins lay in the nineteenth century. The familial origins of department stores left a strong mark on the social policy of department store employers' organisations. Aristide and Marguerite Boucicaut, founders of the Bon Marché, or Ernest Cognacq and Louise Jay, founders of the Samaritaine, became cult-like couples for their employees, an atmosphere which survived in the enterprise long after their deaths.[22] Following the example of large industrial enterprises such as Wendel, Schneider, Michelin and Peugeot,[23] the founders of department stores established philanthropic and charitable works, of which the best known were the Cognacq-Jay foundations, which encompassed schools for embroidery, dressmaking, housekeeping and horticulture, as well as maternity homes, orphanages, nurseries, retirement homes and so on. It has been said that this paternalist system found its origins in both 'a monarchic conception of employer authority and a desire to relieve working class poverty.'[24] Recent analyses have sought to refine our understanding of the move from the concept of 'patronage' to that of 'paternalism'. Noiriel has shown how technological change and economic necessity in the late nineteenth-century metallurgical industry created conditions favourable to the emergence of a new type of social relations which sought a total control over the lives of employees.[25]

Miller's exemplary analysis of the social policy of the employers of the Bon Marché combines different approaches to underline the complexity of the paternalist system.[26] By situating his study in the economic context of the time, he reveals the significant changes taking place in the service sector, with its rapidly growing number of employees. Whereas towards the middle of the nineteenth century, the status of *employé* (white-collar employee) was an intermediary position, serving as a springboard to the acquisition of independent property ownership, a form of sclerosis towards the end of the century saw salaried positions in railways, banks and department stores become permanent, with working conditions remaining close to those of workers. The paternalism of a Boucicaut was a response to the frustrations bound up in this new source of social movement. Miller supports his position by using what Gueslin has called 'culturalist' arguments rather than by an economic analysis of the coming together of the dynamism of large commercial enterprise at its peak, and the new difficulties faced by its employees. The identification of the enterprise with the family, the mission to educate to which the Boucicauts felt committed, was an employers' attitude which represented less a return to employer authority and more the desire to create a working community which would suffuse all the relationships within the enterprise and which would allow a dialogue to begin between directors and employees.[27] The initiatives launched by the Boucicauts were aimed at integrating employees not only during their working day, but also 'before, during and after, at every step of the day, week or year of life' (Gueslin). The result was a provident fund set up in 1876, and a pension fund in 1886. Beyond this employers sought to maintain the sense that social mobility was possible – essentially within the enterprise – and to integrate the salaried staff into the bourgeoisie by conveying its values, above all those of saving and respectability. A moralising climate hung over the enterprise. The Bon Marché introduced music courses, fencing and lecture series for the employees with a view to spreading the bourgeois way of life. The department store for Miller was the site of an attempt at social reconciliation.[28] Miller does not however neglect more ideological criteria. He notes that the paternalism practised at the Bon Marché addressed itself only to white-collar employees with the distinction between them and the store's manual workers a strict one. The department store thus reproduced the hierarchy, even the segregation, of the French society of its day. Moreover he emphasises the way that paternalism served as a strategy destined to remove conflicts, one in which there was little scope for employee trade unionism. It was a system which had been used in industry to control the growth of the working-class movement.

In fact, employee trade unionism developed extremely slowly in the period before 1914. In that sense, retail employees at the beginning of the twentieth century occupied a distinctive and to a degree isolated place in the world of labour. Their lack of solidarity with the working class went hand in hand with an absence of *esprit de corps* amongst themselves. There were various reasons for this: competition amongst employees within the department store, fear of management, and anxiety to hold on to one's job. But there was also an identification with the interests of the establishment – the 'house spirit' demanded by the female sales assistants[29] – which encouraged a strong individualism amongst employees and delayed the appearance of trade union action, and according to our hypothesis retarded the appearance of employer organisations. The social conservatism of department store employers was well established before the war, an attitude which found it hard to accept a system of social relations different from that which it had itself created. The surprise, exasperation and fear felt during the strikes of 1919 and 1936 provide eloquent testimony to this. The reactions to the upheavals of the latter year are instructive. The strikes triggered off in department stores on 3 June 1936 were part of the second wave of strikes which unfolded in France after the Popular Front election victory a month earlier. The first large strikes by white-collar employees, and the first women's strikes, were spectacular in the sense that their scale was in inverse proportion to the level of trade unionism which preceded it. They are undeniably surprising, even if relations in some establishments had been hardening from the early years of the decade.

The events of 1919 had come as a major shock, but the traditional employers' discourse appeared just as attractive after the war as if the war itself had in no way changed the social order. 'Let these brave individuals return speedily to their posts, for in the thoughts they have expressed to us they have, in addition to a desire for revenge and reparation, voiced but one desire, but one solitary and simple ambition: to work,' one finds in the minutes of the Board of Directors of the Galeries Lafayette in November 1918, paying homage to the courage of their employees.[30] It is this vision which the Popular Front seemed to shatter. 'This was the only time in the history of this establishment that the relations between management and personnel have been so seriously disturbed', a special issue of *Printania*, the Printemps internal staff newsletter, acknowledged. Max Heilbronn, son-in-law of the founder of the Galeries Lafayette, testifies in his memoirs to the anxieties aroused by the rapid deterioration of the social situation in June 1936,[31] but it was Gabriel Cognacq, managing director of the Samaritaine, who offered the most vehement denunciation of the Popular Front. He attacked the 'Stalinist conception' and 'madness' of 'new destructive laws', and articulated his deep contempt for workers 'feasting on legal leisure-time'.[32]

The social crisis reinforced the hegemony of the *Groupement d'études des grands magasins* which gathered and disseminated information about each department store affected by the strikes, and which on 3 June 1936 decided for the first time in its history to hold meetings daily throughout the month.[33] Two days later it authorised Lacour-Gayet to make direct contact with the *Chambre syndicale des employés de la région parisienne*. It sent him as a delegate to Matignon during the night of 7–8 June 1936 which ended in a general agreement between the *Confédération générale de la production française* (CGPF) and the *Confédération générale du travail* (CGT). Finally, Lacour-Gayet represented the department stores during the branch negotiations begun on 8 June 1936, and which reached agreement on 21 June on the content of the collective agreement eventually signed on 9 December 1937. This is not the place to consider this agreement in detail. It is revealing to note, however, that the question of creating a disciplinary council was one of the most fiercely discussed, because it undermined the discretionary power of employer over employee. Department store employers participated in the large operations of 1938–39 which sought revenge for the measures of June 1936.[34] These movements were led by Jacques Lacour-Gayet. A high-ranking employers' official, he conceived of his public action as being restricted to the purely technical sphere. In addition, and in contrast to certain of his superiors, he appeared to wish to reserve his political polemic for the big occasion, insofar as we can find in his economic critique an indication of his personal preferences. On 7 November 1938 he appeared before the *Commission d'études du Conseil national économique* to denounce 'the electoral demagoguery which for fifty years has continually attacked large-scale retail enterprise,' as well as 'the rapid increases [of new social and fiscal charges], above all since 1936'. Even if a fiscal relaxation, real but only temporary, was obtained at the beginning of 1939, salary negotiations remained difficult right up until the war. The *Groupement d'études des grands magasins* (GEGM) found itself up against the inflexibility of the Ministry of Labour. Charles Pomaret, his position strengthened by the law of 11 July 1938 on the general organisation of the nation in time of war, did not hesitate to use the threat of increased intervention. In response to a letter of

27 October 1939 from the *Groupement* announcing the forthcoming 30 per cent reduction in the salaries of department store employees and the abolition of dismissal compensation, Pomaret retorted by return of post that he considered the letter to be 'invalid and of no consequence'. He added

> at a time when a sense of panic affects the lives of families, when many households of ordinary white-collar employees have been disrupted by the mobilisation of husbands and fathers, when material conditions are affected by so many difficulties as winter approaches, I personally implore you to abandon the employment system that you are planning to introduce.[35]

Whereas in the social sphere department store employers during the inter-war period show a refusal to contemplate new forms of social relations within their establishments, a degree of dynamism can be seen in commercial affairs.

Certain authors have sought to qualify the picture of commercial dynamism amongst French department stores during the inter-war period, identifying the Belle Epoque as the department store's finest hour. If their general costs had increased slightly with the development of advertising and customer services, their net profit remained constant at 5 per cent between 1880 and 1914, but this was no longer the case after the war when if fell to 2 per cent. The 1930s was the most difficult decade, seeing a substantial fall in department store turnover: in 1937–38 the Louvre registered a 44 per cent fall from its 1929–30 level and went into compulsory liquidation in 1939.[36] Philippe Verheyde has shown that in spite of some recovery after 1936, the Galeries Lafayette experienced a continual fall in turnover in real terms. Net margins saw a constant decline, a strong one until 1935, weaker but none the less real thereafter.[37] Department stores were nevertheless able to adapt to the new forms of competition represented by the expansion of chain stores into sectors other than food, the development of specialised clothing shops and the adoption of department store display and sales methods by specialised shops. They gave attention to improving their own sales methods and above all they gave key support to the development of *prix uniques* (single-price shops) in France.

If this particular method of chain store retailing was American in origin – the first five-and-ten-store was opened by F.W. Woolworth in Pennsylvania in 1879 – and might be seen as indicating a shift of retail innovation from Europe to the USA during the inter-war period,[38] it would be wrong to conclude from this that department store employers were inactive. Firstly, it must be noted that the single-price store was the ultimate expression of the great changes in the distribution sector over the nineteenth century, changes in which Europe took the lead. In addition, Europe had seen some previous attempts – at least as far as selling at 'a single-price' was concerned – through fares and bazaars. The Marks & Spencer stores in Britain launched one hundred or so penny bazaars before 1914. In reality, European thinking on retail distribution during the inter-war period did not need to feel second-best in relation to that in the USA, and the transatlantic exchange of experience needs to be addressed in terms other than those of the hegemony of one continent over another. Indeed, our own research points clearly to the quality of the collective reflection within the *Chambre de commerce internationale* (CCI) from 1931. In December 1932, the world of French department stores showed itself immediately receptive to the call from the *Comité de la Distribution* chaired by Francis Goodenough, the director of the Incorporated Sales Managers' Association of the United Kingdom, to establish an international bureau and national offices to research into retailing.

The CCI Washington Congress in 1931 marked the first recognition of the fundamental role of retailing in economic and social life. It was the first step in a process of reflection which was to continue through the succeeding congresses in Vienna (1933), Paris (1935) and Berlin (1937). A first report offering an overview of the state of retailing in Europe and the USA was presented by L. Urwick, director of the *Institut international d'organisation scientifique de travail* and by F.-P. Valentine, vice-president of the American Telephone and Telegraph Company. The general lack of knowledge about this sector of the economy became clear, as did the consequences of partly paralysing efforts to find adequate remedies. The report insisted that it was above all essential to reach 'a definition of the problem, a common terminology and an organised co-ordination of efforts to achieve these goals.'[39] It also stressed the deficiencies of available statistics, a theme which would return like a refrain through the CCI debates, and which stressed that 'an initial effort should be made in nearly all countries to establish essential statistical data.'[40] During the Paris Congress, held at the Château Vaux-le-Vicomte in June 1935, the participants assessed the overall effects of the crisis on the retail sector, and began the process of inter-pretation.[41] They were in agreement that the extensive modifications of the retail system resulting from the crisis had to be recognised, along with the paradoxical consequences of its prominence on the economic scene, notwithstanding the fact that the crisis was above all seen as a crisis of industrial overproduction. In the view of Edward A. Filene, the crisis showed the revolution produced by mass chain production of stand-ardised goods, something for which the current system of retail distribution was poorly adapted.[42] Mass distribution for the masses was the only kind of distribution which could thereafter succeed.[43] Emile Bernheim insisted in the course of the debate on the gap that existed between excessive production on the one hand, and consumption no longer capable of absorbing it, a gap which had led to the crisis and the responsibility for which, in his view, lay with a retail system whose modernisation had lagged behind progress in manufacturing production. At the same time, consumption was emerging as a new and important dimension of economic life. The early 1930s saw not only a challenge to outdated systems of distribution, but also the related first stages of thinking about consumption, in which the consumer had been defined by the time of the Washington Congress as 'the regulator and the purpose of economic activity'.[44] The remedies proposed to deal with the crisis were, for Emile Bernheim, firmly located within the logic of liberal economic principles: the issue was not to limit production to deal with insufficient market capacity, but instead to rely on the potential for increasing consumption. That required a more scientific understanding of demand, and consideration of the unavoidable modernisation of distribution.[45] It was therefore essential to lay stress on scientific knowledge in this economic sphere.

The method generally recommended by the CCI was the application to distribution of theories of scientific organisation. 'These diverse elements should be the subject of scientific studies as searching as those which have up to now been applied to production.'[46] The USA was the point of reference in this area. The lecture by the US industrialist Dennison to the New England section of the Taylor Society in 1921 came to be identified in retrospect as the key turning point: here, for the first time, was a call for the application to selling of the principles of scientific work organisation. The CCI recommended

> the diffusion amongst retail enterprises of new ideas and practises concerned with the methods of organising and the managing enterprises. Scientific organisation, embracing the control of budget, sales and stocks and the professional training of personnel, are amongst the modern methods and principles which the *Bureau international pour l'étude de la distribution* particularly recommend.[47]

This was to bring about modernisation in two major areas: the administration of the enterprise and the training of staff. The objective was 'to bring to the attention of business the clear opportunity that exists to use scientific methods of selling and to make use of the services of specially educated and trained personnel.'[48] The influence can be clearly seen of the ideas developing around organisations such as the *Bureau international du travail* (BIT) or, in France, the *Comité national de l'organisation scientifique* (CNOF) of Henri Fayol or the *Commission générale d'organisation scientifique* (CEGOS) of Auguste Detœuf. They recommended the rationalisation of methods of production, labour, management and selling within industrial and commercial enterprises, with a view to maximising returns for the lowest possible cost.[49]

If the CCI served as a catalyst for activity, the French department store world did not remain inert and passive. By the summer of 1928, on the initiative of Emile Bernheim, director of the Belgian department store Innovation, and of Pierre Laguionie, director of Printemps, the *Groupement d'études pour le perfectionnement de méthodes de travail dans les grands magasins* was set up, becoming in 1931 the *Association internationale des grands magasins* (AIGM). This grouped together the Swedish department store Nordiska Kompaniet, Tietz from Germany, De Bijenkorf from The Netherlands, the Danish Magasin du Nord, El Siglo from Barcelona, Rinascente from Milan, and the London Harrods and Shoolbreds stores, as well as Innovation and Printemps themselves. This initiative originated in the anxiety of European department store owners to control American competition. Following the example of large industrial employers, Bernheim and Lacour-Gayet had their gaze fixed on the USA during this period. They returned after 1945 to gather and report on new information about commercial practice there. By 1927 Emile Bernheim had been annoyed by the way Woolworth had set up in England and Germany and felt disturbed by the possibility that this competition could spell ruin for the chain stores just coming into existence in Europe. He proposed to his colleagues in the AIGM in 1932 that they set up an international holding company to control existing *prix uniques* chains and to serve as a commercial and financial defence against American incursions. To Ragnar Sachs, director of Nordiska Companiet, he wrote 'I believe that sooner or later, interest will be shown under one form or another between several countries and that, from the point of view of the future of our Association itself, this question must be worthy of serious consideration.' The arguments he used were clearly of an economic character: the strength that went with centralised purchasing; increased productivity as a result of combining for certain functions; easier finance, a reduction of the risks associated with national monetary policies, possibilities of tenfold expansion.[50] The initiative was premature, and it was rejected by his partners. The AIGM nevertheless did establish a framework for the sharing of experiences.

The *Groupement d'études des grands magasins* in France followed the proposition made by Pierre Laguionie in February 1933 that a *Bureau français d'études de la distribution* be formed in response to the CCI's call. The *Bureau* was to contain representatives of all types of distribution. The *Groupement* gave its agreement in May, and the *Bureau* was to be set up at the headquarters of the *Comité d'action économique et douanière*. Pierre Laguionie became President, Jacques

Lacour-Gayet one of the Vice-Presidents, and two leading members of the *Groupement d'études des grands magasins*, Roger Picard and Jacques Bondoux, took the positions of Director and Secretary-General respectively. The great majority of the members of the *Bureau français d'études de la distribution* were members of CAED. The interpenetration of these two organisations, with Lacour-Gayet pulling the strings, is striking.

How far were the new methods of management adopted in large-scale retail enterprise? We have too few monographic studies to give us any clear picture of the application of the principles of rationalisation to department stores. The success of certain pioneer enterprises cannot hide the slowness of adaptation amongst the majority. Modernisation of store management methods was nevertheless a reality for certain enterprises. The AIGM had since its creation encouraged its members to create research departments and budget control systems analogous to those established by Innovation since 1927. Thus Printemps created its own research department in 1928. The structural reforms introduced there between in 1926 and 1932 provided 'a model of organisation and rationalisation'.[51] In Meuleau's words, summarising his case study of Printemps, 'organisation was now given priority. A pioneer amongst department stores in France, it was also that in relation to large industrial enterprises. Pierre Laguionie, a disciple of Fayol, considered the structure as the instrument for entrenching his power.'[52] The rationalisation of Printemps took the form of a functional structure of management adopted in 1929, and which distinguished seven functions: buying, sales, publicity, accounting and finance, personnel, operations and research. It involved the separation of buying from sales, until then combined in the same person, thus allowing the establishment of a purchasing division, *Société anonyme parisienne d'achat en commun*. Another important reform was the introduction of budgetary control in 1930 which facilitated the management of the new organisation as well as the acquisition of new stores. 'Receiving the monthly calculation of margins produced by the research bureau as well as the predictions from these of the annual results, management was able continually to adapt its directives to conjunctural variations.'[53] Nevertheless, not all of the European enterprises in AIGM were affected by the rationalisation of their administration during the 1930s. A recent study by Amatori shows that the Milanese department store Rinascente did not really launch its managerial reforms until the middle of the 1950s with the introduction of management techniques of the kind just discussed. Rinascente experienced the dual influence of the USA, through the Harvard Business School and its centre devoted to the study of retailing, and France through CEGOS. It was not until 1956 that Rinascente created its own bureau of organisation and research, which would largely serve to train the enterprise's real directors, the managerial professionals, who until then had been lacking.[54]

The other area in which modernisation was relevant was the training of personnel, and here too we encounter a certain reticence. The CCI had given its unambiguous support to efforts directed at the professional training of staff. Amongst the resolutions approved at the Paris Congress was the concern 'to develop the teaching of selling both in professional and lower level schools, and the principles and methods of distribution in both universities and *écoles supérieures*, with a view to ensuring the professional training of sales employees and of those in personnel offices.'[55] In her chapter in this volume, Marie-Emmanuelle Chessel draws on her detailed research on the origins of specific sales training in the 1920s, which was primarily due to the impetus provided by the Chambers of Commerce, to show the limited role of department stores in this process, not least their 'general lack of co-operation' with the *Ecole technique de vente* founded in 1925 by Louli Sanua. Few of the students graduating from the *Ecole technique de vente* were recruited by department stores on leaving the *Ecole*, being hired instead by specialist shops. Chessel shows how department stores were reluctant to make use of this externally provided and formal training, preferring to develop their own in-house programmes which they saw as more relevant to their needs, and part of whose function was to enable new employees to embrace the stores' own house-spirit. This was the case at the Galeries Lafayette and the Louvre as well as at Printemps. Meuleau has acknowledged that 'human relations were a late arrival' at Printemps.[56] As Chessel concludes, 'The familial ethos of the department stores and their penchant for combining social paternalism with modern management methods may have discouraged the use of external sales schools and benefited in-house training instead.'[57] There is no doubt that a time-lag existed on the one hand between the display by large-scale French retailing of an interest in the general modernisation of its own economic sector, and on the other hand its daily practice, which tends to confirm the picture already offered of a world which was on social terms deeply conservative. Modernisation was primarily concerned with 'passive selling': the organisation of space, sales equipment, the formal aspects of retailing – accounting, commercial law and so on. The act of selling itself was quite distinct, concerning people, the sales assistants, their science, and the psychology of selling. It is therefore important not to extrapolate from the success of a handful of dynamic enterprises, and to imagine a widespread modernisation of retailing in the inter-war years.

The principal merit of the work done by the *Chambre de commerce internationale* had been to confirm the developing vision of distribution which was beginning to operate as a result of the crisis: from the old conception of 'retailing' as the step after production, to the modern conception of 'distribution' which proceeds from the study of consumption as a determinant of production. The *Chambre* encouraged the standardisation of statistical tools and methods of commercial management. It stressed the importance of education for the commercial world as a whole. The process of reflection about the modernisation of distribution which the *Chambre* initiated constituted a reference point for work carried out on this question in France both during the war and at Liberation. French large-scale retailing in the inter-war period was thus not some nebula from which emerged certain department stores in decline and the first popular but decried *prix-uniques* stores. It systematically organised itself under the leadership of active personalities, thus contributing to the establishment of new forms of distribution. In a larger perspective, it participated in a substantial international movement to analyse retailing, something which was required to increase both during the Second World War and more extensively in the years that followed.

Notes

1. See Henry Ehrmann, *La politique du patronat français (1936–1955)*, Paris: Armand Colin (1959); Bernard Brizay, *Le patronat: histoire, structure, stratégie du CNPF*, Paris: Seuil (1975); Georges Lefranc, *Les organisations patronales en France*, Paris: Payot (1976); Ingo Kolboom, *La revanche des patrons, Le patronat français face au Front Populaire*, Paris: Flammarion (1986); Richard Vinen, *The politics of French business*, Cambridge: Cambridge University Press (1991).
2. The present study rests in part on the systematic use of the unpublished archives of the *Groupement d'études des grands magasins* (GEGM) and the *Fédération nationale des entreprises à commerces multiples* (Fenacomult) during the research carried out for the author's thesis, *Un milieu libéral et européen: le grand commerce français (1925–1948)*, Paris: Editions du Comité pour l'histoire économique et financière de la France (1998).
3. This is not the place to explore the details of this struggle, but see Philip Nord, 'The small shopkeepers' movement and politics in France, 1888–1914', in Geoffrey Crossick and Heinz-Gerhard Haupt (eds), *Shopkeepers and Master Artisans in Nineteenth-Century Europe*, London: Methuen (1984), pp. 175–94.
4. See Stanley Hoffmann, *Essais sur la France*, Paris: Seuil (1974), p. 169.
5. François Faraut, *Histoire de la Belle Jardinière*, Paris: Belin (1993), p. 102.
6. GEGM, Procès-verbaux (PV) 1 July 1919.

7. GEGM, PV, 11 July 1919.
8. Ibid., 29 July 1919.
9. Ibid., 11 July 1919.
10. Ibid., 18 June 1925.
11. On the position of CAED during the debate on French tariff policy, see Laurence Badel, 'Trêve douanière, libéralisme et conjoncture (septembre 1929–mars 1930)', *Relations internationales*, n° 82, 1995, pp. 141–61.
12. Fenacomult, PV, 9 July 1937.
13. Fenacomult, Comptes Rendus Annuels, Assemblée Générale 23 June 1919, report of the Committee Director.
14. On the relations between large-scale retail trade and government during the Vichy regime, see Laurence Badel 'Grand commerce et pouvoirs publics (1938–1945)', in Jacques Marseille (ed.), *La révolution commerciale en France. Du 'Bon Marché' à l'hypermarché*, Paris: Le Monde éditions (1997), pp. 141–50.
15. Jean-Noël Jeanneney, *François de Wendel en République. L'argent et le pouvoir (1914–1940)*, Paris: Seuil (1976).
16. René Rémond, *Les droites en France*, Paris: Aubier Montaigne (1982 edition), pp. 186–7.
17. Jean Gicquel and Lucien Sfez, *Problèmes de la réforme de l'Etat en France depuis 1934*, Paris (1965), ch. 3, sect. 2, pp. 90–106.
18. Ibid., p. 98. Quotation from an article by Henri de Kérillis in *L'Echo de Paris*, 24 October 1934.
19. Elected Deputy of the Drôme in 1910, on the SFIO ticket, Henri Roux-Costadau repudiated Marxism after the war. In 1922 he founded *La Libre Opinion* which advocated revising the Constitution to strengthen the power of the executive. After the Second World War he joined the ranks of the PPF.
20. Guillaume Kérouredan, 'Un aspect de l'organisation patronale au XXᵉ siècle: l'Association nationale d'expansion économique (décembre 1915–mars 1951)', doctoral thesis, Université de Paris I, 1986, p. 725.
21. Ibid.
22. Michael B. Miller, *The Bon Marché: Bourgeois Culture and the Department Store, 1869–1920* Princeton: Princeton University Press (1981); Fernand Laudet, *La Samaritaine: le génie et la générosité de deux grands commerçants*, Paris: Dunod (1933).
23. Bernard Brizay, *Le patronat*, p.33.
24. Ibid., p. 33, citing Eugène Descamps (CFDT).
25. Gérard Noiriel, '"Du patronage" au "paternalisme": la restructuration des formes de domination de la main-d'œuvre ouvrière dans l'industrie métallurgique', *Le Mouvement social*, 144, 1988, pp. 17–35.
26. See André Gueslin's synthesis of approaches to this subject based on a survey of the recent historiography on industrial employers 'Le paternalisme revisité en Europe occidentale (seconde moitié du XIXᵉ, début XXᵉ siècle)', *Genèses*, 1992, pp. 201–11.
27. During the inter-war period this tradition was continued by Gabriel Cognacq, who studied at the *Ecole des hautes études commerciales*, and who offers according to Meuleau 'the best example of conformity with the traditional traditionalist spirit'. Meuleau quotes a 1934 discourse to the staff, 'an anthology of grandiose themes, such as the family enterprise, the employer as father and the founder-heroes': Marc Meuleau,

'Les HEC et l'évolution du management en France (1881 – années 1980)', doctoral thesis, Université de Paris X, 1992, vol. 1, pp. 746–7.

28. Michael Miller, *Bon Marché*, Introduction.
29. Monique Couteaux, *Les femmes et les grèves de 1936: l'exemple des grands magasins*, mémoire de maîtrise, Université de Paris VII, 1975.
30. Galeries Lafayette, Registre des délibérations du conseil d'administration, 8 November 1918.
31. Max Heilbronn, *Galeries Lafayette, Buchenwald, Galeries Lafayette*, Paris: Economica (1989).
32. Gabriel Cognacq, *Le Commerce intérieur*, special edition of CAED, Paris, July 1938.
33. GEGM, PV, 3 June 1936.
34. See Patrick Fridenson, 'Le patronat français', in René Rémond and Janine Bourdin (eds), *La France et les Français en 1938–1939 – La France sous le gouvernement de Daladier, d'avril 1938 à septembre 1939*, Actes du colloque de la Fondation nationale des sciences politiques, 4–6 December 1975, Paris (1978), pp. 139–58.
35. GEGM, *Notes*, 11 (1938–46), letter from Charles Pomaret, Minister of Labour to the President of GEGM, 28 October 1939.
36. Cf. Jacques du Closel, *Les grands magasins français, Cent ans après*, Paris: Chotard (1989), pp. 30–33.
37. Philippe Verheyde, 'Les Galeries Lafayette (1889–1955). Histoire économique d'un grand magasin', *Etudes et documents*, 5, 1993, pp. 201–53.
38. See Emmanuel Chadeau, editorial in *Entreprises et histoire*, 4, 1993.
39. Chambre de commerce internationale (CCI), Vienna Congress, 29 May–3 June 1933. *Distribution. Buts et travaux du Bureau international pour l'étude de la distribution*. Report of Jules Menken, Head of the Department of Business Administration at the London School of Economics, p. 5.
40. Ibid., p. 11.
41. Archives nationales (AN), F 60335, dossier C2L1, VIIIe Congress of the Chambre de commerce internationale. Report on the work of the CCI in 1934–35.
42. Chambre de commerce et d'industrie de Paris (CCIP), I – 7.60 (3), dossier of CCI, 24–29 June 1935. Meeting on the organisation of the distribution of consumer goods, pp. 29–31, speech by Edward Filene.
43. Edward A. Filene, *Vers l'organisation rationnelle du commerce de détail*, Paris: Dunod (1939), Preface by Roger Picard.
44. CCI, Vienna Congress, p. 7.
45. CCIP, I – 7.60 (3), speech by Emile Berheim
46. CCI, Paris Congress (1935). Theme 4: Organisation of distribution (consumer goods), sect. 1.
47. Ibid., sect. 3.
48. CCI, Vienna Congress, p. 7.
49. Gérard Brun, *Technocrates et technocratie en France (1914–1945)*, Paris: Editions de l'Albatros (1985); Aimée Moutet, *Les logiques de l'entreprise. La rationalisation de l'industrie française dans l'entre-deux-guerres*, Paris: EHESS (1997); Meuleau, 'Les HEC'.
50. Quoted by Jacques Lacrosse and Pierre de Bie, *Emile Bernheim, histoire d'un grand magasin*, Brussels: Labor, (1972), p. 93.

51. Meuleau, 'Les HEC', vol. 4, p. 1095.
52. Ibid., p.1150.
53. Ibid., p. 1113.
54. Franco Amatori, 'Managers and owners in an Italian department store: La Rinascente from 1920 to 1970', unpublished paper to Colloquium on the Department Store in European Society 1850–1939, Brussels, September 1995. See also Vera Zamagni, 'Le développement de formes modernes de commerce organisé en Italie aux XIXe et XXᵉ siècles', *Culture technique*, 27, 1993.
55. CCI, Paris Congress (1935). Theme 4: Organisation of distribution (consumer goods), sect. 3.
56. Meuleau, 'Les HEC', vol. 4, p. 1150.
57. See p. 288 of Chessel's chapter in this book.

Index